A Century of Pay

Also by E. H. Phelps Brown

THE FRAMEWORK OF THE PRICING SYSTEM
(Chapman and Hall, 1936)

A COURSE IN APPLIED ECONOMICS
(Pitman, 1951; 2nd edition with J. Wiseman, 1964)

THE GROWTH OF BRITISH INDUSTRIAL
RELATIONS
(Macmillan, 1959)

THE ECONOMICS OF LABOR
(Yale University Press, 1962)

A Century of Pay

THE COURSE OF PAY AND PRODUCTION
IN FRANCE, GERMANY, SWEDEN,
THE UNITED KINGDOM, AND THE UNITED STATES
OF AMERICA, 1860–1960

E. H. PHELPS BROWN
WITH MARGARET H. BROWNE

MACMILLAN London · Melbourne · Toronto
ST MARTIN'S PRESS New York
1 9 6 8

© E. H. Phelps Brown with Margaret H. Browne 1968

Published by
MACMILLAN AND CO LTD
Little Essex Street London W C 2
and also at Bombay Calcutta and Madras
Macmillan South Africa (Publishers) Pty Ltd Johannesburg
The Macmillan Company of Australia Pty Ltd Melbourne
The Macmillan Company of Canada Ltd Toronto
St Martin's Press Inc New York

Library of Congress catalog card no. 68–16620

Printed in Great Britain by
ROBERT MACLEHOSE AND CO LTD
The University Press, Glasgow

Contents

6   Contents

List of Figures

Tables in Text

Tables in Appendix 2

Preface

In 1950 one of the present authors with Sheila V. Hopkins published a paper on 'The Course of Wage-Rates in Five Countries, 1860–1939' in *Oxford Economic Papers* (N.S.) 2, 2. It was out of an endeavour to revise this study, and embody the results of subsequent inquiries by others, that the present work arose.

The initial survey of the published materials, and the first work on the French and U.S. estimates, were carried out by Elizabeth Durbin.

Dr A. V. Desai of Bombay allowed us to draw freely on his then unpublished thesis, and helped us by discussing the evidence. We owe to Dr C. H. Feinstein of Clare College, Cambridge, permission to make use of unpublished estimates of the U.K. capital stock, 1860–1913; but the reader is asked to bear in mind, in fairness to Dr Feinstein, that the figures we present as the end product of our own working are different from the original series he compiled. We are further indebted to Docent K.-O. Faxén and Professor J. W. Kendrick for the help they have given us by communicating unpublished materials. To Professor A. W. H. Phillips and the editor of *Economica* we owe permission to reproduce Fig. 7. Dr I. Aristidou has helped us by discussion of the estimates of investment in British manufacturing presented in his thesis, of which we have made liberal use.

Professor J. E. Meade has helped us by his discussion of growth models, and saved us from at least one error.

The findings now presented are the product of work that has occupied us through most of the last six years. It has been possible only through the support given by the London School of Economics, in money and by the resources of its library; and through the stimulus of its living tradition of inquiry.

Introduction

In the short span of time since the Fourth Ice Age, men have achieved two bursts of technical progress so concentrated and extensive that they deserve to be called Revolutions. One was the Neolithic Revolution, that came about ten thousand or more years ago. The other was the Industrial Revolution that took its rise quite recently, in the eighteenth century. It is the course of development that began then, and especially its effects on those who work for pay, that form the subject of this book. We shall study it in five countries. In three of them – France, the U.K. and the U.S.A. – its first stirrings came early, and the hundred years from 1860 to 1960 that we study form their second century of industrialisation. The other two – Germany and Sweden – came to it later, and 1860 lies near their starting point, but they were able to take over techniques developed by the first three countries, and complete within decades a development that had taken much longer where it originated.

The list of technical advances in the Neolithic Revolution is formidable – the cultivation of plants and the domestication of animals; spinning and weaving; pottery; housebuilding and the town; mining; the boat; the wheel; the axe and the axe-factory (Cole, 1963). Very likely the Industrial Revolution could match these, process for process and tool for tool, but it was distinguished by something more. This was the capacity to sustain itself, to make change that bred change. One upward spiral sprang from the raising of productivity by the use of more equipment. When an economy accumulated more equipment per worker it achieved a higher output per worker in the production, among other things, of equipment itself: this made equipment cheaper in terms of labour, and gave management correspondingly more inducement to substitute it for labour, and raise the amount of equipment per worker yet again. A second source of self-sustaining growth was the development of the technique of improving technique. If some discoveries continue to depend on accident and the flashes of insight in rare minds, others yield themselves to routine inquiry if it be sufficiently patient and extensive. A 'science-based industry' is one whose products and methods we expect to be often changing. R and D, research and development, is a process for producing new processes. The rise in

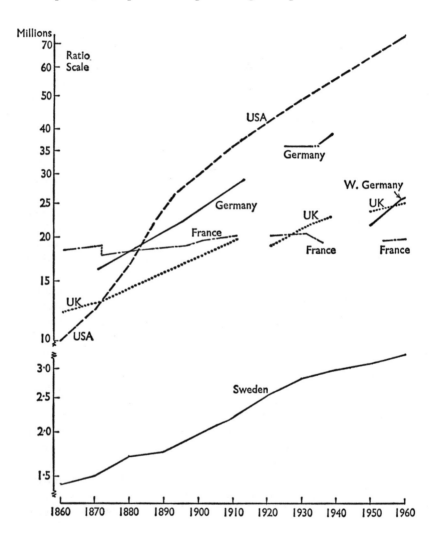

productivity it achieves makes more resources available to it, to achieve a further rise.

In these ways it has come about that the Industrial Revolution has kept on its course of progressively raising the amount and improving the forms of the worker's equipment. We do not know whether the vein of technology we are working now will be exhausted in the end, and if so how soon the end will come. But, so far at least, the western economies show no sign of a slower rate of growth: rather the contrary.

This rise of productivity is the more remarkable because it has been accomplished in the presence – some would say in the teeth – of a great growth of population. Fig. 1A shows how rapidly and persistently the occupied populations of all our countries save France have grown in the last hundred years. The rise set in about the middle of the eighteenth century. That it came in many countries at much the same time, in particular that it was no less rapid in Ireland than in Great Britain, suggests that it owed little to the industrialisation of the time, but was due, like the outbursts of population in some of the underdeveloped countries of our own time, to a fall in

---

Fig. 1A The Occupied Population in Five Countries, 1860–1960. Coverage: The economically active including unpaid family workers and the unemployed. Where the source is given as Appendix 2 E, references there to the removal of these groups should be ignored, but those to the adjustment of the number of unpaid family workers do apply here.

Sources and methods: The estimates of the occupied population which we have used for the study of Periods Two and Three differ from those given here in that they exclude unpaid family workers and the unemployed. References to this exclusion in the Sections E of Appendix 2 therefore do not apply to the present series, but the account in the same Sections of the estimation of the number of unpaid family workers does apply.

France :   Appendix 2 E.

Germany : 1871 to 1907 : P. Jostock, 'The long-term growth of national income in Germany' in *Income and Wealth V* (1955), ed. S. Kuznets, Table vi, col. 1. In 1907 the census figures show a marked rise apparently caused by a change in the definition of unpaid family workers, who are separately given for 1895 and 1907 at p. 90 of J. Müller, *Deutsche Bevölkerung-Statistik* (1926). We reduced the 1907 figure by assuming that unpaid family workers formed the same proportion of the total occupied then as in 1895. 1925 to 1960 : Appendix 2 E.

Sweden :   Appendix 2 E.

U.K. :   Appendix 2 E. Unpaid family workers are not included in 1946–1960, but their numbers will have been small.

U.S.A. :   Appendix 2 E.

morbidity. For England, 'informed opinion lays stress on two factors: the disappearance, after 1665, of the plague that had afflicted Christendom for centuries, and the lowered incidence of famine and the diseases resulting from insufficiency of food' (Ashton, 1955, ch. i). There is evidence that another such fall in morbidity had occurred in western Europe at the beginning of the sixteenth century; and that the mounting numbers then had brought mounting distress, and a drastic reduction in the real wage. So it was to be again in the nineteenth century in Ireland, where a mounting population, increasingly impoverished, lost its last remaining subsistence when the potato failed. In recent years the growth of Asian populations has brought underemployment and debilitation. But for the countries of the industrial revolution there was another possibility: the landless and masterless men, the overspill for whom there were no dead men's shoes in the countryside, could make their way to the new mines and manufactories. They did, and they found work there. Throughout the nineteenth century the populations of most western countries grew, commonly by more than ten per cent and sometimes by as much as fifteen per cent in each decade: but decade by decade the number of jobs grew at the same rate.

This brought with it, however, a radical change in the way of life, in the resources, security and status of the bulk of the population. Formerly most workers had been self-employed – small-holders on the land, or small masters selling their produce and not their labour, or workmen taking pieces of work from an employer without putting themselves under his orders as their master, entering into a contract for services, as the lawyers say, and not of service. Besides these there had always been some wage-earners, in town and country, men and women who worked under a master's orders, at his workplace or house and with his equipment; but they were a minority. Now the balance had to shift. In some countries, it is true, the sector of self-employment has remained wide up to a recent date. But it has been comparatively inexpensive: few of each year's extra hands have been able to find in it the livelihood with independence that it could provide; the rest have had to 'throw themselves upon the market'. In Gregory King's estimate of the population of England and Wales in 1695, only a third of the families had a wage-earner as their bread-winner, though there were also the domestic servants in the other households (Clark, 1937, ch. x). At the time of the census of 1911 in the U.K., six persons out of seven in the whole occupied population were employees working for salaries or wages, and the wage-earners alone made up three-quarters of the whole (Bowley, 1921, table ii). In Gregory King's day three-quarters of the population of England and Wales lived in rural districts, by 1921 only a fifth: three-fifths of the whole population was living by then in six industrial areas which between them covered only a fifth of the surface (Carr-Saunders and Caradog Jones, 1927, ch. iii).

So grew up the industrial society in which most people get their incomes under a contract of employment: in which, that is to say, the material welfare of most people depends on the level of pay and the conditions under which it is earned; and in which most people work under other men's orders. It is our object here to trace the growth of this society since 1860, measure the levels of income attained from time to time, and offer some account and explanation of the processes by which they were fixed and changed.

In the early days of the transition many observers saw little but misery ahead. As population rose, they argued, in countries whose land was limited, the output of foodstuffs could not possibly keep pace, and real wages must fall until penury raised death-rates and caused marriage to be deferred so as to offset the insistent tendencies of procreation. The effects of mechanisation were seen less as higher productivity than as the throwing on the labour markets of the handicraftsmen deprived of their livelihood by the competition of the machine. What in fact happened?

In one way, the change has remained for the worse. The transition from independence to the employee's position brought a loss of freedom and of satisfaction. Instead of autonomy in working life, there was a compulsion to work at set times and tasks, under the direction of others; instead of self-identification with the work, there was alienation. Even where the wage-earner's material standard of living today is high, these detriments remain. The standard of living is at its highest in the U.S.A.; but studies of the wage-earner's attitudes there in recent years have brought out 'a feeling among many working people that there is a basic, hard-to-define injustice in their lives which has not been erased by any of the benefits they have won, and, furthermore, that it must somehow be management's fault that this nameless wrong continues to exist' (Gellerman, 1963, p. 179). This wrong, this loss can of its nature not be measured by the yard-

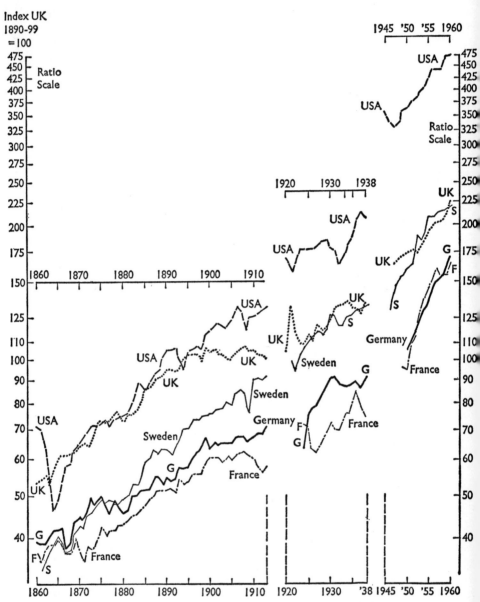

Fig. 1B Five countries, 1860–1960 : Indexes of wage-earnings in composite units of consumables, all as relatives to U.K. in 1890–1899 = 100.
Source : Appendix 3.

sticks we use here, but it must be borne in mind in any evaluation of the material progress that they do measure.

This progress has in fact been great. Fig. 1B provides a conspectus. Here wage-earnings are expressed in composite units combining in representative proportions the chief products on which money wages have been spent from time to time. A doubling of the wage expressed in such units – the real wage – means two basketfuls, on a given shopping list, instead of one. The actual factor by which the real wage has been multiplied over the hundred years of Fig. 1B is between 4 and $4\frac{1}{2}$ in France, Germany and the U.K., and about $6\frac{1}{2}$ in Sweden and the U.S.A. The extent of this rise is revolutionary in one way; but in another, since multiplication by $4\frac{1}{2}$ in a hundred years means an annually cumulated rise of only 1·5 per cent, and multiplication by $6\frac{1}{2}$ only 1·9 per cent, the improvement was slower than has come to be expected in recent years. None the less, it was achieved: the real wage per head was raised cumulatively, at a time when the number of heads rose persistently and, save in France, rose fast.

It has been a major task of our inquiry to find out how this came about. What appears from the record is, first, that the number of jobs increased at the same rate, decade by decade though not year by year, as the number of applicants; second, that the product per worker was, for the most part, progressively raised meanwhile; third, that the share of this product handed over to the worker himself as his wage, though by no means stable in the short run, did not rise or fall much in the long, so that wages, in terms of the product, rose in the same proportion as productivity. This rise in productivity can be attributed to improvements in the capacity, bodily and mental, of the worker himself, and to his working with a capital embodying an ever greater amount of current resources in equipment of progressively improved design. Had the increase in physical capital per worker been the sole change, it would not have been compatible with an unchanged share in the product for the worker, unless the rate of profit on the unit of capital had fallen; but in practice other changes at the same time raised his product in much the same proportion as the amount of capital with which he was equipped, and when this happens it is simply a matter of arithmetic that wages can continue to receive the same share of the product while capital continues to receive the same rate of profit. Such at least are the barest but essential outlines of the processes of growth and distribution in the records we study here.

So far this is an account only of the rise of wages in real terms; but it implies a certain relation between money wages and product prices. If productivity rose by 5 per cent over a certain span, and wages in terms of the product were to do likewise, then a rise of say 3 per cent in product prices would require money wages to rise by some 8 per cent; or constancy of money wages would require product prices to fall by some 5 per cent. Somehow, adjustments of these kinds do seem to have been worked out: but how? Which way did the adjustment run, or were the movements of money wages and product prices determined simultaneously? Making what inference we can from the record, we have tried to answer such questions as these by constructing a framework of explanation for the movement of the general level of money wages.

Such are the main themes of this work. The argument in which they are developed takes the form of 'reasoned history'. This is a partial kind of explanation, that does not confer the power to predict the course of events, but points out some linkages of cause and effect after the event. The military historian, for instance, may show that an army was defeated because when battle was joined its men were already exhausted by forced marches. Here he takes a causal sequence independently known – that exhaustion causes men to fight less strongly – and identifies an instance of it within the course of events. Thereby he helps us to see why the battle went the way it did. But in doing so he takes the marches simply as a fact of record. He lacks a general theory into which every factor has been fitted and which will enable him to predict the outcome of other campaigns. The economic historian, and in particular the analyst of the statistical record, is often in worse case than this. He cannot identify causal sequences here and there within the course of events, because he does not know those sequences independently: indeed he may have turned to the statistical record precisely in the hope of dispelling his uncertainty about them. Do money wages rise because there is an excess of vacancies over applicants in the labour market, or because profits have gone up, or because trade unions are pushing harder? One cannot appeal to everyday experience for a certain and an exclusive answer, and then use it to identify cause and effect when they make their appearance in the record. One has to start with the record, and ask whether any systematic association appears between money wage rises and the movements of some other variable, such as will suggest a link between them.

But here difficulties multiply. These systematic associations are all too plentiful: which of them mark links, and which are only the parallel movement of sticks floating down the same stream? The experimental scientist can do much to answer this question, because he can vary one factor at a time: if two situations are alike in all elements save one, and their outcomes differ, the probability is high that the one divergent element is the cause of the divergent outcome. The economist cannot experiment, only observe, but he still may be able to compare different situations. One way of doing this is to run regressions: a partial regression coefficient should tell us how far a difference in one factor, within two situations alike in all other respects, has been associated with a difference in the outcome. But this it can do only to the extent that one factor has in fact varied independently of the others, and economic series do that all too little for our convenience. Eliminating trends is still likely to leave us with concerted movements of the deviations: wages, employment, profits, investment, exports, trade union membership, the quit rate, all rise and fall together in the course of the trade cycle. To run regressions over a sequence of years, moreover, means treating the data from different situations as if they recorded the sole differences in situations otherwise alike: it means, that is to say, leaving out of account much that we know was actually important – a change of government, a big strike, a war. For these reasons we have run no regressions here.

Yet this has still left us with the possibility of using the comparative method if we will apply it less mechanically. If we compare a number of situations – trade cycles occurring successively in one country, for instance, or at the same time in several countries – and bring to bear all we know about them, their similarities and differences will sometimes help us to assess the probability that an association beween A and B appears because A causes B. If B appears in all these situations, then probably (though not necessarily) its cause is present in them all too, and an A which is present in some situations but not all is less likely to be the cause. Similarly, if an A is present in all the situations: a B that is present in some but absent in others is less likely to be its effect. What is expressed here simply in terms of 'present or absent' can be extended to cover 'present in different

B   B.B.C.P.

degree': thus if A and B are present in all situations, but in some a large A is associated with a large B and in others with a small B, then the probability of a causal link is reduced. What is expressed for only two elements can also be extended to cover the consideration of more elements together. The essential is only that the different situations be compared in detail but at the same time as a whole, and in the light of all our historical knowledge of them: and that we should regard such comparisons only as attaching greater or less probability to the identification of causal links.

It is in this way that we have tried in the following pages to work out explanations of the movements of pay in money and real terms, in the five economies we have compared.

But these explanations will be no more trustworthy than the record on which they are based. It has been our first, and in man-hours our main task, to establish this record in a consistent and significant form. In part we have been able to draw upon the major works of other scholars – of Hoffmann for Germany; Bagge, Lundberg and Svennilson for Sweden; Feinstein for the U.K.; Kendrick for the U.S.A. In some measure we have had to go back to the primary sources and compile our own estimates. Even, moreover, where the secondary sources were ready to hand we have often operated on them to make them comparable with one another. The great interest of the question to be answered has sometimes seemed to warrant the making of estimates in which the margin of error is inherently wide. We have had to judge whether that margin was so great as to lead to qualitatively mistaken conclusions, or small enough to enable us at least to reduce the area of nescience. The estimates in Fig. 24 of real capital per occupied person, in three countries but in a common unit, are a case in point.

The instance raises a general issue. We have confidence in the year to year movements that our series record; their absolute levels are much more affected by differences in coverage and roughness of estimate. Where we could ensure sufficient continuity of coverage, we have provided links that enable the reader to compare the levels of one series in two periods in one and the same country, but elsewhere such comparisons are hazardous. For comparisons between countries there is the additional hazard of the conversion of one currency into another: for some purposes we have been able to draw on special studies of the comparative cost of living, but where that is not appropriate we have only been able to use the par of exchange.

The ways in which we made our estimates are described in the Appendices. The detail into which we enter there is some indication of the detail in which we have worked. The nearer estimating gets to 'guesstimating', the more does it require a scrupulously close inspection of so much evidence as is available: the final figure is best arrived at by bringing a number of independently estimated elements together for aggregation or comparison, even though some of them are small. The numbers of occupied persons, though they might be thought readily available in the Censuses of Population, prove in practice among the most laborious to compile; but working through their detail inspires confidence in the end that nothing has gone wrong with the main proportions. In the course, for instance, of eliminating 'dealers' from the occupied population in industry in 1911, in the Irish county of Armagh we excluded five male and three female 'newsagents and newsroom keepers' from the labour force in printing; four 'makers and dealers' in musical instruments, and one in umbrellas, parasols and sticks, called for arbitrary decisions. But after marking out the boundary post by post in that way, we had more reason to trust our final figure for the area within it.

The purpose of the Appendices is to enable our workings to be appraised at all points, and checked by reworking. But only a few specialists will have occasion to do this. What assurance will other readers have that we are to be trusted? There are three ways in which we ourselves have assayed our findings.

The first is a check of statistical consistency. We have used or constructed time-series of money wages and of income per occupied person in each country. But in each country we also have observations of the levels of these variables at particular dates, one in each Period: and the time-series when linked ought to show the same change between those dates as appears on a direct comparison of the observed levels. More than this, at one date in each Period we have an international comparison of the cost of living that enables us to estimate the relative levels of real wages in different countries: if at one such date the level in A were say half that in B, and our indices of real wages showed that by the date of the next international comparison the level in A had doubled while that in B had risen by 50 per cent, then this second comparison ought to show that the level in A is now two-thirds of that in B. The outcome of these tests appears in Sections 2.A.6 and 3.A.4. Unfortunately this type of test has not been applicable to our estimates of capital.

A second if much less rigorous check has been by way of international comparisons. We hope it is a contribution of this work to have brought out the preponderant similarity and the significant differences between the courses of events in our five countries; together with some persistent differentials between the magnitudes prevailing in them. As those relations took shape and affirmed themselves, they provided criteria by which to judge the validity of new estimates. To have rejected a figure only because it was non-conformist would have been wholly prejudicial; but to ask whether there was bias or outright error in it, or it stood firm and imposed itself, was salutary.

There remains another structure within which our estimates have had to take their fitting and proportionate part – the system of the distribution of income within the economy. We have tried, in those countries and periods for which the data made it possible, to bring into an intelligible relation the growths of capital and of output per worker, the level and share of wages, and the rate of profit. The internal consistency of our estimates in this system has provided a third check on them.

It has been a discovery for us to find the proportions of that system emerging from the welter of events. Especially where the main subject is pay, as it is here, it is the power of groups, the force of personalities, even the chance turn of events, that on a realistic view might seem predominant. But what our inquiry has revealed as predominant has been the sway of economic forces, called impersonal because they aggregate the decisions of so many persons. In this we have only rediscovered what was described long ago by Alfred Marshall, in words that may stand as the motto of this book. Trade combinations, he said,[1] and

> 'alliances' and counter-alliances among employers and employed, as well as among traders and manufacturers . . . present a succession of picturesque incidents and romantic transformations, which arrest public attention and seem to indicate a coming change of our social arrangements now in one direction and now in another; and their importance is certainly great and grows rapidly. But it is

[1] *Principles* vi, viii, 10.

apt to be exaggerated; for indeed many of them are little more than eddies, such as have always fluttered over the surface of progress. And though they are on a larger and more imposing scale in this modern age than ever before; yet now, as ever, the main body of movement depends on the deep silent strong stream of the tendencies of normal distribution and exchange; which 'are not seen', but which control the course of those episodes which are seen.

Period One
1860–1913

1A Levels of wages and incomes, 1905 and 1909

1. Wages in money

It is in 1905 and 1909 that we shall compare the levels of wages country by country, for it was in those years that the Labour Department of the British Board of Trade carried out the inquiry into the costs of living of wage-earning households in England,[1] France, Germany, and the U.S.A., that gives us our sole opportunity within the period of comparing the levels of real wages in those countries. There was no inquiry into the relative cost of living in Sweden, but we shall include Sweden in our comparison of wages in money and of the wage/income ratio, and make shift also to estimate the comparative cost of living there by carrying back the results of an inquiry in 1931.

Our first step is to estimate the average wage in money in each country. At once the problem presents itself of what measure to use of the wage. There are two basic measures, the rate of payment per unit of work done, and the earnings obtained over a period of time. The interest of the first of these is that it may provide a measure of costs; but it does this only if we can also measure output. If it takes the form of a piece-rate, its movements mark those of unit labour cost only if the piece-rate does not vary with output, as it does in some systems widely used. If the payment per unit of work done takes the form of an hourly rate, its movements mark those of unit labour cost only if output per man-hour is constant: but differences in that output between two periods or two countries are likely to be both

---

[1] Great Britain comprises England, Wales and Scotland. The U.K. comprises these together with all Ireland in Period One, and Northern Ireland in Periods Two and Three. Generally our figures relate to the territory of the U.K. of their period. Some observations that relate to Great Britain or England alone are so described; but sometimes we accept data drawn from Great Britain as applicable approximately, or after adjustment, to the whole U.K.

large and unrecorded. If, moreover, our interest is in the standard of living of the wage-earner, or the share of labour in the national income, it is the second measure that we need, the earnings of the worker over a period of time. It also happens that in Germany and Sweden our best substantiated records of pay come from the wage-books of firms, and consist of the average annual earnings found by dividing the total wages earned by the average number of wage-earners employed in the course of the year.

These average earnings depend on many factors. The weekly rate, in the first place, consists of the hourly rate multiplied by the number of hours in the standard week. Agreements for reduction of these hours have usually provided that there shall be no 'loss of pay', and the hourly rates have been raised as necessary to provide the same weekly rate as before on a smaller number of hours: the unchanged rate for the standard week discloses neither the rise in unit labour costs that will have been imposed unless an offsetting rise in output per man-hour has come about, nor the increased leisure that enters into the standard of living of the wage-earner. The standard hours of any week or year, again, may include hours that are paid for though not worked – generally certain national holidays, and periods of vacation. The actual hours of work are always liable to differ from the standard: there may be short-time or overtime, and overtime is usually paid for at higher hourly rates. The hours actually worked by any one man also depend on himself, in that he may be absent for personal reasons, of which the chief is sickness. The average wage-earner further experiences some loss of hours through unemployment, and if our concern is with the standard of living of the wage-earners as a whole we must take account of this, together with any receipts from unemployment insurance; but for the study of the division of the national product between the factors that combine to create it, the relevant form of the average return to labour is the return to the worker in employment.

In the light of these considerations we decided to take as our measure of wages the average earnings in a year of employment that is normally continuous but subject to departures from standard hours through short time, overtime and absence for personal reasons.

In building up our estimates of annual earnings so defined, we have had to make some arbitrary assumptions. The detail of our working is set out in Appendix 1. To convert hourly rates of pay to weekly, we have drawn upon such evidence as was available for the standard hours prevailing from time to time. There was little evidence, however, to show how weekly rates should be converted to annual, and in particular what the average difference was between the standard hours and the number of hours actually paid for in the year. For men and boys in the U.K. in Period One, Bowley (1937, p. 52) reckoned 'the year less trade holidays' – at that time mostly without pay – as made up of 50·6 weeks, but considered 3·2 per cent as deductible for absence through sickness, and a further 3 per cent for the hours lost by the then high proportion of casual workers in the labour force. For the U.K. in Period Two, 'where it is necessary to use an arbitrary estimate of the number of working weeks representing full-time employment', Chapman (1953, pp. 9–10) followed the Ministry of Labour in taking 49·2 weeks – 'this allows for $3\frac{1}{2}$% time lost through sickness and other forms of unrecorded non-employment other than holidays, and for one week's holiday without pay'. We have adopted for all countries the assumptions of 49 weeks or 294 days in the working year in Periods One and Two; and in Period Three, to take some account of the increase in paid holidays, 50 weeks. That we applied these assumptions uniformly is a safeguard only if the required allowances were themselves in fact uniform, and this we do not know; we also do not know whether they were of the assumed size in the countries whose records provide annual earnings directly.

There is also the problem of which workers to include. In Periods One and Two we know very little about the salaried, and though for the wage-earners the coverage of our records is broad in all three Periods, it is far from complete. We have tried to get a similar coverage between different countries in each period, rather than between different periods in each country. Thus since most of our records of earnings comprise workers of all ages, but those for France in Periods One and Two relate only to adults, we have reduced the reported French average earnings in both periods by an estimated 9·4 per cent, on the basis of available evidence concerning the effect on the average of including juveniles – an instance of a correction based only on orders of magnitude being at least more accurate than no correction at all. In each country we found it advisable or unavoidable to use somewhat different coverages for our two purposes of tracing year-to-year movements throughout the Period, for which

Table 1 Five countries, 1860–1913: Coverage of (1) wage index; (2) average annual wage-earnings in 1905 or (U.S.A) 1909; (3) income generated per occupied person in industry (IGPOPI).

France

(1) Wage index   Wage-rates, mostly of men, in industry including mining and building.

(2) Av. annual   Based on daily rates of men in 20 industrial occupations,
wage-earnings   including coalminers and builders, (all provincial except Paris engineering), and of women in 7 occupations, with adjustment to comprise a due proportion of juveniles' earnings.

(3) IGPOPI   Not available.

Germany

(1) Wage index   Average annual earnings in:
    1860–1870: mining, metals, textiles, wood, printing, building.
    1871–1886: coal-mining, steel, machines, cotton textiles, printing, building.
    1887–1913: mining & quarrying, 18 manufacturing in-dustries, transport by land and water, warehouses, tramways.

(2) Av. annual   As for wage index 1887–1913 but excluding several series
wage-earnings   whose absolute values are not dependable.

(3) IGPOPI   Mining, manufacturing, and handicrafts (which are understood to include building).

Sweden

(1) Wage index   Annual earnings of men only, in mining, quarrying, iron & steel, metals & engineering, saw mills, pulp & paper, textiles, leather, rubber, chemicals, food products.

(2) Av. annual   As for the wage index but with the addition of women in
wage-earnings   textiles and food products.

(3) IGPOPI   Mining, manufacturing, and crafts including building.

U.K.

(1) Wage index   Wage-rates in agriculture (incl. Ireland), coal, puddling, engineering, shipbuilding, cotton, wool & worsted, furniture, printing, gas, building.

(2) Av. annual   Mining, manufacturing, transport, utilities, building, non-profit-
wage-earnings   making activities of local government.

(3) IGPOPI   G.B. only: net product of mining, manufacturing, gas, building and contracting.

U.S.A.

(1) Wage index   Average annual earnings in manufacturing
(2) Av. wage-   As in (1)
    earnings
(3) IGPOPI   Manufacturing.

an existing index number might serve best, and estimating average annual earnings in current money in 1905 or 1909. The main lines of the two coverages are set out in Table 1, together with those of the industrial sector for which, as will appear later, we have estimated the income generated per occupied person, for comparison with that part of it which goes to the wage-earner.

The detailed estimating, the adjustments and the assumptions that all these considerations call for have brought us in the end to the figures of average annual earnings that appear in row 1 of Table 2. For the U.K. the figure is firmly and widely based on the great census of wages in 1906, which Bowley (1937) used in preparing the figures we have drawn from him. In Germany, too, we have a firm and wide base in Dr A. V. Desai's recension of employers' returns of aggregate earnings and average numbers employed, under the scheme of workmen's insurance. The only source of major error here is that some employers reported not the average number at work over the year but the total number of names on their books, without deduction for turnover: to that extent the average earnings will be understated. For Sweden we have the similar records of employers' wages books, compiled in the work of Bagge, Lundberg and Svennilson. For the U.S.A. we could take the average annual earnings of a full-time worker in manufacturing estimated by Rees (1961). For France, however, where we have only the daily rates of pay of a limited variety of occupations, it has been a hazardous task to weight these rates according to the size of the groups they seem to represent.

The comparison of earnings in Table 2 therefore has its substantial margin of error. But this can hardly be so wide as to call in question the main findings. It appears that the average annual earnings of manual workers, in their own currencies converted at the par of exchange, were a good deal lower in the three European countries than in the U.K. The French earnings were about two-thirds the British, the German about three-quarters. Swedish earnings stood distinctly higher, but still perhaps no more than five-sixths of the British. But in the U.S.A. earnings stood nearly 80 per cent above the British, and were some $2\frac{3}{4}$ times as great as the French.

We can compare these relations with those which the Board of Trade calculated at the time from a small sample of weekly rates and earnings. They appear in row 3a, and they show money wages as

Table 2 I. Five countries, 1905 or 1909: Comparison of average annual wage-earnings, mainly in industry, in money and in composite units of certain consumables. II. Four countries, averages of 1905–1911: Comparison of income generated per occupied person in the whole economy and in industry, and of wage/income ratios in industry.

		France	Germany	Sweden	U.K.	U.S.A.
I. *1905 or 1909*						
Annual wage earnings						
1. in own currency	1905	919 frs	856 M.	851 Kr.	£56·1	
	1909				£59·0	$512
2. in £s at par of	1905	£36·5	£41·9	£46·9	£56·1	
exchange[1]	1909				£59·0	£105·6
3. as relatives to U.K.	1905	65	75	84	100	
	1909				100	179
3a. Relative money						
wages (Board of	1905	(75)	(83)		(100)	
Trade) for com-	1909				(100)	(230)
parison with (3)						
4. Relative cost of a	1905	105–114	111–119		100	
composite unit of	1909				100	145–152
consumables						
5. Relative annual	1905	57–62	63–67		100	
wage-earnings in					100	118–123
composite units of						
consumables,						
(3) ÷ (4)						

II. *Averages of 1905–1911*	France	Germany	Sweden	U.K.	U.S.A.
Whole economy, net					
domestic product per					
occupied person,					
6. in own currency		1349 M.	1178 Kr.	£96·4	$756
6a. in £s at par of exchange[1]		£66·0	£64·9	£96·4	£155·9
Industry (in U.S.A. manufacturing)					
only, income generated per					
occupied person,				G.B.	
7. in own currency		1522 M.	1675 Kr.	£90·0	$857
7a. in £s at par of exchange[1]		£74·4	£92·2	£90·0	£176·7
8. Annual wage-earnings		945 M.	964 Kr.	£59·4	$518
9. Wage/income ratio in industry					
(in U.S.A., in manufacturing),		0·62	0·58	0·66	0·60
(8) ÷ (7)					

[1] £1 = 25·15 frs = 20·45 M. = 18·16 kr. = $4·85.

standing higher relatively to the British than they do on our estimates of average annual earnings, by margins equivalent to a raising of the French wage by 15, the German by 10, and the American by more than 30 per cent. That all three differences are in the same direction suggests that the British wages taken by the Board as its basis of comparison were on the low side. This may be so, in that they were weekly rates, which may well have been somewhat lower than average earnings, whereas in France, for engineering and printing, in Germany, for engineering, and in the U.S.A., for all occupations, it was earnings that the Board took. But what is probably a much more effective cause of the divergences is that the Board's comparisons were based preponderantly on craftsmen's wages – seven crafts in building, four in engineering, and one in printing, with only two labourer's rates; whereas our own are based on the average earnings of all grades. For we know that unskilled rates bore a much lower ratio to the skilled in Germany and the U.S.A. than in the U.K. The ratio is given as follows for three German industries in 1905 (Bry, 1960, table A.14):

	%
Building (hourly rates)	35
Cotton spinning (annual earnings)	46
Dortmund miners (shift earnings)	29

In the United States in 1909 (Douglas, 1930, tables 18, 21, 39, 41, 58) the corresponding ratio in building seems to have been about 46 per cent, and this was also the ratio of average hourly earnings in what Douglas calls the 'payroll industries' to those in the 'union industries'; the median rate in the light unskilled occupations in 1907 was less than half the median skilled rate (Ober, 1948; see also Ozanne, 1962). In the U.K., on the other hand, the ratios of the time-rates of the unskilled to those of the skilled are recorded (Knowles & Robertson, 1951) as:

	1904 %	1907 %
Building	66	65
Shipbuilding	53	
Engineering	59	
Railways		51

But this cannot be the reason for the Board of Trade's estimate of relative earnings in France also being a good deal higher than ours: the daily rate for the unskilled that we used in our French average was very nearly two-thirds the craftsman's rate – the same ratio as in British building, and a much higher ratio than in British engineering. Nor can the reason be found in the wages of juveniles being relatively low in France. We took those wages to be 45 per cent of adult rates, for both sexes, whereas Bowley (1937, pp. 49–50) found that in 1911 in the U.K. the weekly earnings of lads and boys 'in ordinary industry' were only about 36 per cent of those of men over 20. To reach an average for wage-earners of all ages, we reduced our estimate for adults of both sexes in France by 9·4 per cent; Bowley's corresponding adjustment for males in the U.K. in 1906 is about 10 per cent. The French disparity remains unexplained except in so far as it was due to the Board's taking some French wages in the form of earnings but all the British as rates.

2. Measuring the comparative cost of living

We now come to the possibility of comparing the differences in money earnings with differences in the cost of living. There are difficulties in the way of using this comparison to measure relative standards of living. On the one hand, the money earnings we have estimated are not the same as household income, for they contain no allowance for unemployment, and they are an average of the earnings of wage-earners of both sexes and all ages: if, for instance, the relative number of gainfully employed women, or juveniles, is higher in one country than elsewhere, the average earnings will be to that extent lower, whereas the average monetary income of households will be higher, if the greater relative number marks (as it usually will) a higher participation rate. On the other hand, the familiar difficulty of comparing the cost of living in any two years is magnified when the comparison is between two societies with different customs and scales of values as well as different standards of living. This magnification comes about in two ways: the kinds of article concerned, and the relative amounts of a given article, are both likely to differ much more widely between two countries than between two years in the same country.

The difference between the kinds of article consumed appears partly in such salient differences of custom as that the French household drinks coffee and wine where the British drinks tea and beer; and, more widely, in differences of type and quality in articles nominally the same. One way out is simply to omit the articles that lack close counterparts. Thus the Board of Trade (1909, Cd 4512, p. xlii) in drawing up the English workman's budget to be priced in France as well as England omitted 'eggs, which it has been thought better to exclude owing to the variety of qualities, especially in this country (England); bacon and cheese, the qualities of which are very different in the two countries; (and) vegetables, the prices of which it is difficult to compare even in different districts of the same country, owing to the great range of qualities and the variety of units by which they are sold'. The expedient of omission is unavoidable when a commodity regularly consumed in one country is a rarity in another: the Board of Trade found no equivalent in France for the English workman's tea, and none in England for the French workman's vin ordinaire. Another way out is to devise an approximate counterpart. This the Board of Trade (1908) did when it came to price in Germany an English workman's budget that included 22 lbs of wheaten bread: 'as the Englishman could seldom purchase white household bread in Germany, we have credited him with the purchase of 22 lbs of flour, assuming, say, that he would bake at home. Actually 22 lbs of flour are not required for making 22 lbs of bread, but no allowance has been made for the cost of other materials nor of baking'. Similarly for clothing: the I.L.O. investigators whose inquiry we shall use in Period Two circulated a box of a Detroit family's clothes to the European cities and tried to get prices for them there. 'In some cases, however, no article similar to the sample could be found in the European shops ...; in others, recourse had to be had to prices relating to articles of clothing corresponding in use to the American samples; in all cases, considerable difficulty was met ... in obtaining prices based on the quality of the sample, without giving too much weight to the cut' (I.L.O. 1932, p. 21).

It is the inevitable consequence of these expedients that the remaining basis of comparison is narrow: there can be no question any longer of covering the whole range of outlay of the household, only of combining the prices of some leading objects of outlay. In Period One these objects comprise only food, fuel and housing.

Even where the same article is consumed in all countries, the relative amount of it consumed often varies widely – partly, no doubt, because customs differ, but also because the pattern of consumption varies with the standard of living, according to the Engel functions. Both sources of variation underlie the differences in the pattern of consumption of foodstuffs by working-class households in four countries in 1905 or 1909, shown in Table 3.

Table 3 Quantities of food taken as consumed by a working-class family in a normal week in the United Kingdom, France and Germany in 1905 and by an American-British working-class family in the northern United States in 1909.

		U.K.	France	Germany	U.S.A.
Tea	lbs	0·6	—	—	$\frac{1}{3}$
Coffee	lbs	—	0·6	$\frac{3}{4}$	1
Sugar	lbs	$5\frac{1}{3}$	$1\frac{3}{4}$	2	$5\frac{1}{4}$
Bacon	lbs	$1\frac{1}{2}$	—	$\frac{3}{4}$	$1\frac{3}{4}$
Eggs	no.	12	10	10	22
Cheese	lbs	$\frac{3}{4}$	—	$\frac{1}{2}$	$\frac{1}{2}$
Butter	lbs	2	$1\frac{1}{4}$	$1\frac{1}{4}$	2
Potatoes	lbs	17	16	26	21
Flour	lbs	10	—	2	$10\frac{1}{4}$
Bread	lbs	22	29	25	$8\frac{1}{4}$
Milk	quarts	5	4	$6\frac{1}{2}$	$5\frac{1}{3}$
Beef	lbs ⎫		3	2·2	$6\frac{3}{4}$
Mutton	lbs ⎪	$6\frac{1}{2}$	1	—	$1\frac{1}{4}$
Pork	lbs ⎬		$\frac{3}{4}$	1·6	$2\frac{1}{4}$
Veal	lbs ⎭		$1\frac{1}{4}$	—	$\frac{3}{4}$

Sources: U.K. Report of an Enquiry by the Board of Trade (Cd 3864 of 1908, p. xxviii).
France. Report of an Enquiry by the Board of Trade (Cd 4512 of 1909, p. xxiv).
Germany. Report of an Enquiry by the Board of Trade (Cd 4032 of 1908, p. xxvii).
U.S.A. Report of an Enquiry by the Board of Trade (Cd 5609 of 1911, p. xxxiii).

But it is in housing that the problem of the common unit makes itself felt most acutely. There are differences between the amenities provided as part of the typical dwelling of wage-earning households in different countries. Thus the I.L.O. investigators (I.L.O. 1932, pp. 17, 18) found themselves required to find what rents were being paid in the European cities they studied for the type of house in Detroit then occupied by employees of Ford on the lowest daily rate –

'a detached house occupied exclusively by the family, and equipped with electricity, gas, central heating and a bathroom'. But in most of the European cities, 'houses of such a type rarely exist': instead, the 2- and 3-roomed tenement predominates. If one seeks to find the rent payable simply for a certain number of rooms, ignoring the differences in the amenities that go with them, there are still the difficulties that the rooms in the European tenements were commonly bigger than those in the 4- or 5-roomed house in the U.K. or the U.S.A., and that in some European cities 4- or 5-roomed dwellings were found only in middle-class districts with higher site values. Similar differences, albeit less extended, embarrassed the comparison of the costs of housing in Period One. What the Board of Trade did, and we have not been able to improve on it, was simply to take the rent (exclusive of local taxes) of the same number of rooms in each country, without allowance for differences in size and amenities.

We saw that even where there are no such differences as these between the kinds of article consumed, there may still be big differences in the relative amounts of a given article in the typical budgets of different countries. How big these can be is illustrated by Table 3. Nor can they be disregarded on the ground that the relation of the home to the foreign price is much the same for different articles, so that the weighting is of little consequence: in fact that relation varies considerably. The German inquiry, for example, which we shall use in Period Three, found that the relation between the German and foreign prices of articles that enter mostly into the higher standards of living is commonly very different from that between the prices of the staples of consumption. Thus, with weights from budgets of 1953 the purchasing power parity between the German mark and the dollar in 1958 was found to lie between 2·50 and 3·49 RM to $1, but weights based on more recent budgets, at a markedly higher standard of living in Germany, set the limits for the same year at 2·97 and 3·66 RM.

No formula provides a solution to this problem of the differences in the weights. Where such differences appear between the budgets of the same group of households at two dates, it is usual to calculate the average change using first for both dates the weights appropriate to the earlier one (Laspeyre), and then those appropriate to the later (Paasch). The first calculation yields the *upper* limit to any rise in outlay needed to keep the consumers as well off at the later date as they were with given outlay at the earlier, and the second the corresponding upper limit on a move back from the later position to the earlier, that is, a *lower* limit for a move forward from the earlier. The change in total outlay that will keep the consumers who are free to vary their assortment as well off in the later position lies somewhere between those two limits, and it is convenient, if arbitrary, to take their geometric mean. But this reasoning implies that it is one and the same group of consumers that has adopted the two patterns of outlay, or, more precisely, that the two patterns are evaluated by consumers of the same tastes. In international comparisons, however, there is no such common evaluation. It is the British households alone that adopt the British pattern of outlay, whether they are thought of as implementing it at British prices or French, and similarly it is the French households alone that adopt the French pattern of outlay; and we cannot assume that these households have the same tastes. On a strict view, therefore, the relative costs of living reckoned in those two ways cannot be regarded as limits within which there lies a purchasing power parity between two positions in which the same consumers may find themselves. The two reckonings must rather appear as separate observations concerning different consumers, and standing in no known relation to one another – we do not know how either nationality would evaluate a given outlay on the other's pattern.

It may be that we really ought to stand on this ground, and say that, for all we know, the Indian wage-earner is more content with his ricebowl than the American with his steak, 'for East is East and West is West, and never the twain shall meet'. Evidently there is a sense in which this is true: we cannot measure contentment. But if our aim be only to measure the command of material resources, and we introduce evaluation only in order to be able to place basketfuls of different physical composition in a common scale, then the assumption may be permitted that consumers in different countries, though creatures of different habits, are potentially alike. At least this assumption may be permitted for consumers whose habits are not more different than those of the wage-earners of our five countries: the British wage-earner may be used to tea and have no liking for coffee, and he may prefer to have more house room but plainer food than the French wage-earner; but these are matters of habit, and habits may change. On this view there is – given time for getting used

to outlandish ways – enough of a common consumer in any two of
our countries for us to be able to treat the relative costs in the two
currencies of budgets drawn up according to each country's way of
life as marking, like Laspeyre and Paasch, the limits between which
there lies a purchasing power parity, the ratio between the sums in
the two currencies that will buy 'as much' as one another.

Only if we can do at least this have we any means of answering the
question whether real wages were higher or lower in one country
than another, for this question implies evaluation in a common scale.
The alternative is to say only that the money wages in two countries
can be expressed in common composite units of consumables – we can
express both French and British wages in basketfuls composed on the
pattern of the French way of life, or alternatively of the British. If the
outcomes are divergent, we do not regard them as conflicting, only as
alternative evaluations in alternative scales; nor do we regard them
as the basis for any deductions concerning evaluation in a common
scale. The wording of the rubrics in rows 4 and 5 of Table 2 does not
go beyond this limited view, it being left to the reader to supply a
further interpretation if he considers it warranted.

3. Relative real wages

Row 4 of Table 2 shows the relative costs of living reckoned by us
from the materials of the Board of Trade, by methods described in
Appendix 1. In effect, we first price the budget of a British wage-
earner's household both in sterling and francs, and then do the same
for a French household budget; but since in practice it is only
certain leading elements of the actual budgets that we can price in
this way, the rubric of row 4 speaks not of the cost of living but only
of the cost of a composite unit of consumables. This unit comprises
food, houseroom and (save for the U.S.A.) fuel. To obtain the
relatives in the form of row 4, we convert the outlays in all other
currencies into sterling at the current rate of exchange. The figures
105–114 given for France therefore mean that to buy as much food,
clothing and house room in France as 100s. would buy in Great
Britain would require 105s. or 114s., turned into francs at the current
rate of exchange, according as the list of articles is composed in a
pattern typical in the first case of French wage-earners' households,

in the second of British. We should expect that the higher of the relative costs reckoned in these ways would usually, though not necessarily, be found when using the British budget, because this will tend to give more weight to the articles that are cheaper in comparison with other articles in the U.K. than in the other country.

It will be seen that the cost of consumables, at least of so many as we have been able to include, ruled rather higher in both France and Germany than in the U.K., and to much the same extent. The level of prices in the U.S.A. is at a quite different remove – instead of 10 or 15 per cent above the U.K., more like 50 per cent. We lack a study for Sweden, but can base an estimate on the relative costs of consumables found for the U.K. and Sweden in 1931, carried back to 1905 by the index numbers of the cost of living in the two countries – we shall be seeing later how reliable this sort of linkage is in general. Used here, it suggests a relative cost for Sweden of 101–11.

That the cost of consumables was somewhat higher in France and Germany than the U.K. may be attributed to the difference between protection to agriculture on the one hand and the open ports of a food-importing country on the other. The much higher cost in the United States may mark the tendency of relative consumer prices to stand high in a country of high relative standard of living, attained by high relative physical productivity. A general advance in physical productivity in one country relatively to others with which it trades will enable it to raise its relative money incomes without raising its relative consumer prices. Usually, however, the advance will occur only in certain sectors: but if money incomes rise there, the rise is likely to spread into other sectors of employment, where it will entail higher prices. If these other sectors, as again is usual, are not predominantly export sectors, the higher prices will raise the cost of living relatively to other countries' without checking exports to them. The same kind of divergence may arise between regions of one country: in particular, it may be one factor making for the higher cost of living in large towns.

We can compare the levels of real wages in our five countries by dividing the relative costs of consumables into the relative money wages already estimated: that is, in Table 2, dividing row 3 by row 4. The outcome is set out in row 5. It appears that the German wage-earnings would buy only about two-thirds as much as the British, and the French less still – perhaps three-fifths. If we use our rough estimate of the relative cost of consumables in Sweden, we find the proportion there more nearly four-fifths: the standard of living of the Swedish wage-earner appears already to be higher than the German's. Real earnings in the U.S.A. did not stand nearly so high above the European as money earnings did, but they still stood some 20 per cent above the British, which implies that they were double or nearly double the French and the German.

4. Hours of work

When we compare real earnings we must take hours of work into account: the real income that a job provides will be greater or smaller, according as the basketful of goods that can be bought with the earnings is accompanied by more or less leisure. It often happens within one country that the jobs which provide the bigger basketfuls also allow of more leisure, and so it was between our five countries in Period One – the higher the real earnings, the shorter the prevailing hours of work. True, we can speak only of prevailing hours, for at this time, far more than later, there were wide differences between industries, and between the same industry in different regions. Thus the Board of Trade (1908) found that while in Germany '60 hours or 59–60 a week are markedly the most frequent for all trades except printing' (whose hours were 54), 'in England and Wales the distribution is, for the building trades at least, so irregular that it is almost impossible to give any rate narrower than 49–57 hours as at all predominant'. In Chicago, the week was of 48 hours in the breweries, but 70 on the trams, and 78 in the gasworks; in electricity supply the week was of 48–54 hours in New York, 54–60 in Cleveland, and 60–72 in Baltimore (Board of Trade, 1911). We can therefore only take the mode: but there was sufficient concentration about this for us to be able to speak of the prevailing or typical hours in any one country, and to compare these hours between one country and another.

In 1905 they were certainly shorter in the U.K. than in France, Germany and Sweden. The week of 53 or 54 hours prevailed over a wide range of industry in the U.K., even in gas and electricity, and only in transport do manual workers seem to have worked consistently longer hours. A number of industries in the U.K., moreover, had 'la semaine anglaise', which meant stopping at dinnertime on Saturday. Textile workers had got this in 1874; the building and engineering industries got a 12 o'clock stop in the 1890s. The continent for the most part could only admire this from a distance; and total weekly hours were also longer there. In France about 1905 the weekly hours were 63 or 64 in building in summer, in engineering 60¼, in printing 57½; a Factory Act of 1900 had provided for the reduction of the maximum for all classes of worker to 10 hours a day by 1904, but there was no legal requirement of any rest day. In Germany the weekly hours were substantially shorter in building, with a summer week of 59 hours, and rather shorter in engineering, with 59½ hours; but the 54 hours of printing stood out as exceptionally low. There had been a movement towards shorter hours since 1890, when an 11-hour day was common in factories; but in the collective agreements current in 1913 the average working day was still over 9½ hours. In Sweden it seems that the working week was longer still – six days each of 10 hours.

But if British hours were shorter than the continental, those of the U.S.A. were – at least by a majority – shorter still. In 1909 the summer week in building was much shorter – under 48 hours, against 52 in the U.K. Printers' hours too were shorter. In engineering it seems to have been the other way about – 56 hours or more in the U.S.A. against the British 53; but in manufacturing as a whole the American hours were not longer than the British, and in the railways and coalmines they were markedly shorter.

The differences between countries that appear in Table 2 when we measure the size of the basketful that the money wage will buy would thus be greater still if we took leisure into account, and attempted a measure of real income as a whole. In these comparisons of the general level between countries, as commonly in comparisons between particular occupations within any one country, the bigger the basketful the weekly wage will buy, the shorter the hours in which the wage was earned.

5. Income generated per occupied person

Part II of Table 2 gives estimates of the income generated per occupied person in the whole economy, and within the sector of industry. In Germany and Sweden this sector comprises mining, manufacturing and building; in G.B. it also contains public utilities; but in the U.S.A. it consists solely of manufacturing (Table 1).

The income generated includes all kinds of income – wages and salaries, incomes of the self-employed; profits; and rent. It thus fluctuated more in the course of the trade cycle than did the wage-earnings in the man-year of normally continuous employment in Part I of Table 2. To avoid the comparisons between countries in Part II being distorted by differences of cyclical phase, we have worked here with averages over 1905–1911, a span which generally covered a cycle, from one recovery to the next.

In the whole economy and in the industrial sector alike, a margin of uncertainty attaches not only to the figures of income generated, but also to the count of numbers occupied. There is no hard and clear division between the occupied and non-occupied, particularly in agriculture, where members of the family commonly do a good deal of farmwork without being paid employees. Part-time and occasional employees also form a shadowy border. Even in the same country different censuses have adopted different definitions, and the practice of enumerators may have varied in ways we cannot check. By comparison with these things, it is only a minor disparity that the age-limits, if any, within which the occupied population has been reckoned differ somewhat from country to country. Our aim has been to maintain comparability between our estimates for different years in each country; the comparison between different countries must rest on a less uniform basis.

The estimates of income generated per occupied person within industry raise difficulties of their own. The whole net national product can be estimated from records of personal incomes, or of production, or of consumption, but the firmest base lies in the first of these. For estimating the net product of industry it is not available. Instead, the estimator must rely on censuses of production, held only at intervals; or on records of physical output converted into value product by applying index-numbers of prices, or on attribution of average incomes to the numbers of wage- and salary-earners believed to be employed within the sector, together with an imputed part of the non-labour incomes of the economy. Equally there are difficulties when we come to estimate the occupied population within industry. We must rely mainly on censuses of population whose classification may be hard to align with the boundaries of the industrial sector as those were drawn in the estimates of income. This classification, moreover, may change from census to census, as may the practices of the enumerators.

It is a further though less serious difficulty that the boundaries of 'industry', being taken from the available estimates of net product, differ from country to country. They have been described in Table 1. What is by far the biggest element, however – manufacturing – is common ground; and the differences among the other components do not seem so great as to invalidate our comparison between countries unless it be in that our estimates for the U.S.A. cover manufacturing alone.

These comparisons, whether for the industrial sector or for the whole economy, are possible only after the incomes as originally estimated in each country's own currency have been converted into a common currency. For the comparison of wages we had estimates of the relative purchasing power of different currencies over the principal objects of expenditure by wage-earning households, but here we have simply used the par of exchange. The relative prices of given products stood in varying relation to this par. At one extreme were the products of highly insulated industries like building: we should be surprised if the amounts of houseroom that £100 or 2500 marks or 285 dollars would command, each in its own country, were nearly the same, even though these sums were equivalent at the par of exchange. At the other extreme were the products traded in international commodity markets: the amounts of raw cotton which the three sums would buy could seldom differ by much more than costs of transport would account for. How closely at any one time the relative purchasing powers of the different currencies over industrial products as a whole approached the pars of exchange is an open question. While divergencies over time were checked by expanding trade and improving communications, they were permitted by the raising of tariffs.

These misgivings particularly concern the U.S.A. Table 2 has shown that the number of dollars that would go as far as a given sum in pounds sterling in meeting wage-earners' needs was actually from 45 to 52 per cent greater than the par of exchange. Will not some disparity of that kind also have held for industrial products at large? Again, the comparisons made by applying the par of exchange imply that productivity in the U.S.A. was higher than in Europe to an extent that may seem improbable. Our estimates of income generated per occupied person can be regarded as broad measures of productivity in value terms, and if the pars of exchange are used to translate these measures into common terms, they show (row 7a of Table 2) that productivity in U.S. manufacturing was more than 70 per cent greater than that in British industry as a whole – to say nothing of its superiority over Swedish and German productivity.

Yet where comparisons of physical productivity can be made directly, without bringing prices into the reckoning at all, the American figures come out at a level which is far from suggesting that our use of the par of exchange gave the dollar too much purchasing power over industrial products – rather the contrary. That level is in fact about double the British. The comparisons are made possible by the British Census of Production of 1907 and the American of 1909. Work on them by Flux (1924), reported by him and by Taussig (1925), yielded the figures of Table 4. Flux further gave reason to believe that a ratio of as much as 2·5 : 1 held quite generally. He found, namely, that when he formed a cumulative frequency

Table 4 Physical product per person employed in certain industries in Great Britain, 1907, and the U.S.A., 1909.

| Industry | Annual product per person employed | | Unit |
	G.B.	U.S.A.	
Pig iron	39	84·5	tons
Steel	25	77	tons
Tinplate	25·6	100·4	tons
Cement	194	395	tons
Sugar refining	87	150–180	tons
Flour milling	212·5	325	tons
Ice	490	536[1]	tons
Butter	125	242	£[2]

[1] 600 tons of 2000 lbs converted to tons of 2240 lbs.
[2] Differences in price negligible.
Sources: A. W. Flux, 'The Census of Production', JRSS, 87, 3, May 1924; F. W. Taussig, 'Labor costs in the United States compared with costs elsewhere', QJE, 39, 1 Nov. 1924.

distribution in each country to show the proportion of the whole number of persons employed in manufacturing industries whose net output per head did not exceed a given figure, the two distributions virtually coincided when \$1200 was treated as the counterpart of £100 throughout: 1200 = approx. 100 × 4·85 × 2·5. 'All through the scale,' he said (p. 362), 'the United States figures for 1909 represent two and a half times the United Kingdom figures for 1907. In the main this does not appear to be the result of a higher price-level for the same commodities in the United States than in this country, but of a larger output per head.'

6. The wage/income ratio

We are concerned with annual wage-earnings not only as a main element in the standard of living of the wage-earner's household, but also as the return to a factor of production – that is, as a share in the joint product of labour, management and equipment. The broadest measure of this share is the division of the net product between pay and profits. Pay comprises the income of all employees, whether manual, white-collared or managerial; profit makes up all the remainder of value added in each branch of activity, and so comprises the return to any employers and self-employed therein engaged together with – usually by far its greatest part – the return on capital. We therefore wish to measure, and trace the movements of, the sum of wages and salaries, as a proportion of the whole net product.

But here we meet a statistical limitation at the outset: until later years, we frequently have no estimates of total wages, and never any of total salaries. We do have or can construct estimates of annual earnings for wage-earners, but we often lack the number of wage-earners with which to reckon the whole wages bill. The numbers we have are apt to be only those of the occupied population as a whole. Of the salaried, both their earnings a head and their numbers, our ignorance is likely to be complete. There is a way out, however, by a tolerable approximation. What we want to measure may be written as

$$\frac{W + S}{Y}$$

where W is the total wages bill, S the total salaries bill, and Y the whole net product or income generated. If we write $\overline{W}$ for average wage-earnings, and n_w for the number of wage-earners, so that $W = n_w \overline{W}$; with a corresponding notation for salaries: then the numerator in the above proportion becomes

$$n_w \overline{W} + n_s \overline{S}.$$

Let us now divide both numerator and denominator by n_t, the total number of occupied persons of all kinds. We then have, as the proportion we desire to evaluate,

$$\frac{\dfrac{n_w}{n_t} \overline{W} + \dfrac{n_s}{n_t} \overline{S}}{\dfrac{Y}{n_t}} \qquad (1)$$

What we can actually evaluate is often only the wage/income ratio, that is, the ratio of the average wage-earnings to the average income generated per occupied person,

$$\overline{W} \div \frac{Y}{n_t} \qquad (2)$$

where n_t is the total number of occupied persons, and is made up of n_w and n_s together with n_e, the number of employers and self-employed. If we write (2) as

$$\frac{n_t \overline{W}}{Y}$$

we see that the excess of (1) over (2) is

$$\frac{1}{Y} \left[n_w \overline{W} + n_s \overline{S} - n_t \overline{W} \right]$$

$$= \frac{1}{Y} \left[n_s (\overline{S} - \overline{W}) - n_e \overline{W} \right] \qquad (3)$$

If, as has sometimes been the case, n_s is not very different from n_e and $\overline{S}$ not very different from $2\overline{W}$, this excess will be small. For Great

Britain in 1913/14,[1] for instance, we can evaluate it at about $-1\frac{1}{2}$ percentage points: that is, the share of pay in the national product was then some $1\frac{1}{2}$ percentage points less than the wage/income ratio. But we know that in the course of time n_s has grown while n_e has contracted, and this opens a disturbing prospect of increasing divergence. There is a way out, however: since the employers and self-employed are most numerous in agriculture and the service trades, and relatively few in industry, we shall find a more stable relation between the wage/income ratio and the share of pay if we confine our reckoning to the industrial sector alone. In the industrial sector of the U.K. towards the end of Period One the share of pay seems to have been between 5 and 6 percentage points greater than the wage/income ratio,[2] and a difference of about this size will probably have obtained in earlier years.

But there is another, much stronger reason for our calculating the wage/income ratio as we do here only for the industrial sector of the economy. The share of pay in the product will commonly be very different in different sectors not because of any difference in the rates of return to the unit of labour or of capital, but simply because the ratio of capital to labour differs widely, and with it the output per

[1] From Routh (1965), table i, we have, for G.B. in 1911,

n_s (employees among managers and administrators; clerical
    workers; foremen, inspectors, supervisors):   1·70m.
n_e (employers and own account):   1·73m.

From op. cit., table 47, weighting by the relevant numbers in table 1, we have for 1913/14
$\overline{S}$ (average salary): £123 p.a.
$\overline{W}$ (average wage): £70 p.a.
Y, the net domestic product, can be put at about £1860m. for G.B. in 1913/14: from Feinstein (1961) we have £2032m. for the NDP of the whole U.K. on the average of 1913/14, and the deduction for Ireland may be put at about £172m. in 1913/14, on the basis of £110m. for Southern Ireland in 1911 (Bowley & Stamp, 1927, p. 47) raised to say £116m. in 1913/14, with some £56m. for Northern Ireland based on the proportion of its occupied population to that of Great Britain. We then have

$$\frac{1}{1860}\left[1\cdot70(123-70)-1\cdot73\times70\right]=\frac{-30}{1860}$$

[2] We can use the study of the Census of Production of 1907 in Bowley (1921). For the coverage of that Census he estimated $n_w = 6\cdot062$m., $n_s = 0\cdot460$m.; the number of employers and self-employed may be treated here as negligible, so n_t approx.$= n_w + n_s$, and n_s/n_t approx.$= 7$ per cent. We also derive $\overline{S} = £130$, $\overline{W} = £56\cdot7$, $Y/n_t = £92\cdot3$. The expression (3), now reduced to

$$\frac{n_s}{n_t}\left(\overline{S}-\overline{W}\right)\div\frac{Y}{n_t}$$

may thus be evaluated at about 5·6 per cent.

head. The wage/income ratio in the whole economy may therefore change progressively as different sectors expand and contract relatively to one another, even though there has been no change in the distribution of the product within any one of them. We can illustrate this by a shift out of agriculture into industry. In our Period One the output per head was higher in industry than in agriculture by a margin that ranged from 50 to over 100 per cent. For each man who moved out of agriculture into industry, there would therefore be a rise in the national product per occupied person; but there would be no necessary and associated change in average earnings per wage-earner. Our wage/income ratio in the whole economy would therefore fall, even though there had been no change in the wage-earner's share of the product within industry or agriculture by itself. The effect will be the same if no one actually moves out of agriculture into industry, but in a growing population the numbers occupied in industry rise relatively to those in agriculture. In practice, both processes were at work, and Table 5 shows how great a change they brought about. It follows that we cannot compare the wage/income

Table 5 Occupied population in agriculture (including unpaid family workers) as percentage of total occupied population at two census years within 1870–1911 in four countries.

Germany	1882 : 48	U.K.	1871 : 19
	1907 : 35		1911 : 12
Sweden	1870 : 83	U.S.A.	1880 : 49
	1910 : 50		1910 : 31

Sources: see under Appendix 2E Occupied Population.

ratios of different economies at a given time without regard to their structure. The contrasts implicit in Table 5 are brought out when we find that, in the early 1900s, for each 100 occupied in agriculture (including unpaid family workers) the numbers occupied in industry were,

in Sweden	(1900)	38
U.S.A.	(1900)	74
France	(1906)	79
Germany	(1907)	109
U.K.	(1901)	402

But if in each country we take the wage/income ratio within the industrial sector alone, we are more nearly comparing like with like.

A third reason for doing this is that with only minor exceptions our estimates of wage-earnings relate to occupations within the industrial sector alone.

We therefore shall not make any use here of wage/income ratios relating to the whole economy. The estimates of the net national product per occupied person in Table 2 will serve as a basis of comparison when we are concerned with social structure, and want to know the earnings of the wage-earner compared with the income available on the average of the whole community. We shall refer to them accordingly when we come to trace the rise of real wages. But in tracing changes in the share of wages in the product we shall confine ourselves to the sector of industry.

Though this limitation is necessary to give significance to the movements of our estimates of the wage/income ratio from year to year, it increases the margin of error in estimates of their level at any one time. We have seen that neither the income generated nor the occupied population can be estimated so closely for the industrial sector alone as for the whole economy. We therefore cannot attach great significance to the fact that in row 9 of Table 2 the industrial wage/income ratios of three countries lie within the range 0·58–0·62; nor can we be sure that the British ratio standing higher, at 0·66, shows that the wage-earner's share in the industrial product was in fact bigger in Great Britain than in the other three countries.

That the British ratio comes out so much higher must none the less give us pause. We are glad, therefore, to be able to compare our present workings with estimates by Bowley (1921): the comparison is made in Table 6. Rows 4 and 5 of this Table well illustrate the differences of coverage to which estimates of activity in industry, as distinct from the whole economy, are exposed. After this, we cannot regard the ultimate closeness of agreement of the wage/income ratios in row 8 as other than coincidental; yet since any big difference here would have been disturbing, we can at least say of its absence, 'so far, so good'.

One reason for pausing over the wage/income ratio in British industry was that in Great Britain alone, in our present workings, does the income generated per occupied person appear to have been lower in industry than in the whole economy. Comparison of rows

Table 6 U.K. or G.B.: Comparison of estimates of income generated per occupied person in the whole economy in 1911, and of the wage income ratio within industry in 1907, from Bowley and from present working.

I. Whole U.K., 1911		
	Bowley	*Present Working*
1. Home income generated	£m. 1896	£m. 1899
2. Total occupied population	20·150m	19·700m.
3. Income generated per occupied person (1)÷(2)	£94·1	£96·4

II. Industry only, 1907

Coverages: Both cover mining, manufacturing, utilities (at least in part), building and contracting. Bowley covers the whole U.K., but excludes government work and railway workshops. The present working covers G.B. only.

		Bowley	*Present Working*
4. Income generated	After deducting depreciation and excise duties	£m·587	£m·671
5. Occupied population	Wage-earners 6·062m. Salaried ·460m. Employers with incomes over £160 in 1911 ·135m.	6·657m.	7·045m.
6. Annual income generated per occupied person, (4)÷(5)		£88·2	£95·2
7. Av. annual wage-earnings	£m·344 divided by above no. of wage-earners	£56·7	£61·4
8. Wage/income ratio, (7)÷(6)		0·643	0·645

Sources: A. L. Bowley, *The Division of the Product of Industry* (1921), tables ii, iv, and ch. iv. Present working: as in Statistical Appendix, 2.

3 and 6 in Table 6 now shows that Bowley's workings too imply a lower figure for industry, and this by a wider margin. Moreover, there are reasons to expect such results. We have already seen that agriculture occupied a much smaller part of the labour force in the U.K. than in the other countries, and that income per head was

c   B.B.C.P.

generally a good deal lower in agriculture than in industry. The residual or tertiary sector, again, was bigger in the U.K. than in the other countries, and we shall see later (Fig. 16) that income per head in this sector was generally a good deal higher than in industry. We should therefore expect income a head in the non-industrial part of the economy to rule higher relatively to the industrial in the U.K. than in the other countries.

It remains for us to suggest a rough reckoning that may serve to bring out the significance of the level of the industrial wage/income ratios in row 9 of Table 2. We have estimated that in this Period these ratios were likely to understate the share of pay as a whole in the product by some 6 percentage points. A ratio of 0·64 would then indicate a share of capital of some 30 per cent. If the capital/output ratio were 2·5, this would imply a rate of return on capital of 12 per cent; if 2·0, of 15 per cent.

1B The course of wages, prices and productivity 1860–1913

1. The rise of money wages

The rise of money wage-earnings is shown in Fig. 2. Its most conspicuous feature is that in all five countries it was great. In fact, the cumulated rises from 1860 to 1913, with the corresponding annually compounded rates, were:

	%	% p.a.
U.K.	72	(1·03)
France	86	(1·18)
U.S.A.	113	(1·44)
Germany	160	(1·82)
Sweden	217	(2·20)

These rates of rise overall were reached through the cumulation of different rates in different periods. But the changes were not frequent or irregular. On the contrary, it is a striking feature of Fig. 2 that many segments of the curves lie along linear trends: that is, since this Figure has a ratio scale, they show a tendency of money wages to rise by much the same percentage year after year. If we examine the occasions of the changes from one segment to another we may learn something about the factors that bore on wage movements in general. But these changes are hard to locate by eye. Take, for example, the location of the hinge between the higher rate of rise prevailing in Germany, or Sweden, or the U.S.A. at least from 1900 onwards, and the lower rate that preceded it, at least before 1890: we shall place the turning-point differently accordingly as we carry the earlier trend forward to meet the later, or vice versa. Fitting an algebraic expression avoids this kind of arbitrariness, but only at the cost of introducing another, in the choice of expression, with the points of inflexion it allows, and its exclusion of abrupt changes and displace-

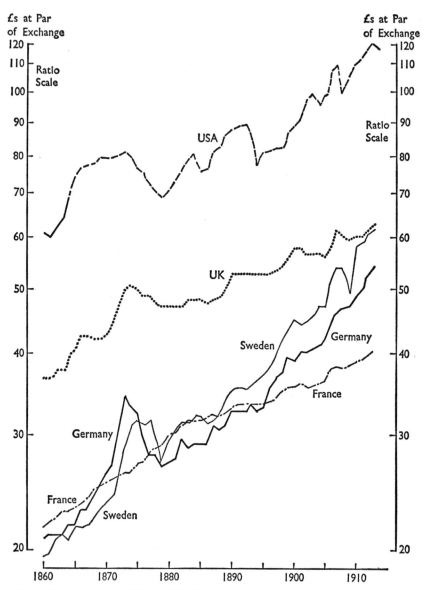

Fig. 2 Five countries, 1860–1913: Money wage-earnings, mainly industrial, in British £s at par of exchange.
Source: Appendix 3.

ments. We have therefore sought a measure of trend that would not impose any precast shape, but would keep close to the data year by year while excluding much of their fluctuation in the short term. The principal source of this fluctuation was the business cycle. In each cycle, let us consider those years in which activity was rising or on its crest as making up the positive phase, those in which it was falling or in its trough as making up the negative. Table 7 then shows that in Germany, the U.K. and the U.S.A. money wages generally rose in the positive phase and fell in the negative; and that in France and Sweden, though here the negative phases in the aggregate actually brought a rise, this was smaller – in Sweden very much smaller – than that brought by the positive phases. To see at what rate money wages were rising at any one time, cyclical fluctuation

Table 7 Average rate of change, in per cent per annum, of money wage-earnings per worker, over the cyclical phases in which activity was (a) rising or on its crest (positive phase), (b) falling or in its trough (negative phase); in five countries, 1860–1913.

	Total no. of years	No. of years	(a) *Positive* Av. change p. a. %	No. of years	(b) *Negative* Av. change p. a. %
France[1]	48	20	+1·33	28	+1·03
Germany[1]	51	30	+3·61	21	−0·66
Sweden	54	33	+2·97	21	+0·58
U.K.	52	29	+2·27	23	−0·48
U.S.A.[2]	42	24	+1·93	18	−1·54

[1] Years of Franco-Prussian War excluded.
[2] Years of the Civil War excluded.
Sources: Indexes of money wage-earnings from the tables in Appendix 3. Cyclical phases identified by present authors from W. L. Thorp's *Business Annals* (1926). The Swedish annals begin only in 1890, but from that time onward their phases resemble the German so closely that we felt able to assume that Swedish activity before 1890 was also in phase with the German.

apart, we therefore need to compare years occupying much the same position in successive cycles. We shall come near to doing this on the average if we compare years that are 8 years apart. This span is near the average spans of 7·6 years from crest to crest, and 7·7 years from trough to trough, in the British cycles identified by Beveridge (1944,

Appendix A) from 1860 to the First World War; and Hansen (1941, pp. 18–19) found an average duration of exactly 8 years for the major business cycle in the U.S.A., 1857–1937. In France, Germany, and Sweden the cycles we have identified from Thorp's annals (see note to Table 7) averaged 8·7, 7·8 and 8·2 years in duration respectively. The variations about these averages were considerable, and activity also showed fluctuations of a shorter period – thus in the U.S.A. Hansen distinguished a minor cycle with an average duration, between 1857 and 1937, of about $3\frac{1}{2}$ years, and Wesley Mitchell (Thorp, 1926, pp. 42–3) contrasted the average span of nearly 9 years between 'crises' with that of less than 4 years between 'recessions'. Nonetheless, we took it that the risk of measuring the rate of change between years of different prevailing levels of activity would be minimised if we compared each year with the eighth subsequent.

We therefore took the proportion by which, for instance, our index of money wages for 1868 exceeded that for 1860, and entered it, as an average annually cumulated rate of change, against 1864, as our approximation to the trend of money wages at that time; and so on. The outcome, displayed in Fig. 3, shows clear enough patterns.

It is apparent, first, that in all five countries there were even greater changes down to 1883 than afterwards. In the U.S.A. these changes coincided with the Civil War and the ensuing deflation; in Germany, Sweden and the U.K., with the extraordinary boom after the Franco-Prussian War of 1870, and the no less extraordinary depression that followed. But France strangely shows no mark of the War, nor does the course of its affairs find any counterpart in the other countries at this time: on the contrary, the rate at which its wages rose reached a crest when the other countries were in a trough, in the later 1870s, and then it came down as theirs went up.

About 1883 this time of upheavals came to an end. In the U.S.A., it is true, other wide fluctuations followed, in the deep depression of the 1890s, the swift rise of money wages that followed it, and the renewed depression after the crisis of 1907. In Germany and Sweden, however, money wages from about 1890 onwards rose without wide fluctuations about a trend of 2·0 per cent per annum or more. France and the U.K. present in common a contrasting pattern – no hinge in the 1890s, but money wages rising at much the same rate throughout from 1885 to 1909, a rate around 0·75 per cent a year in France and 1·0 per cent in the U.K., modest rates by comparison with the other

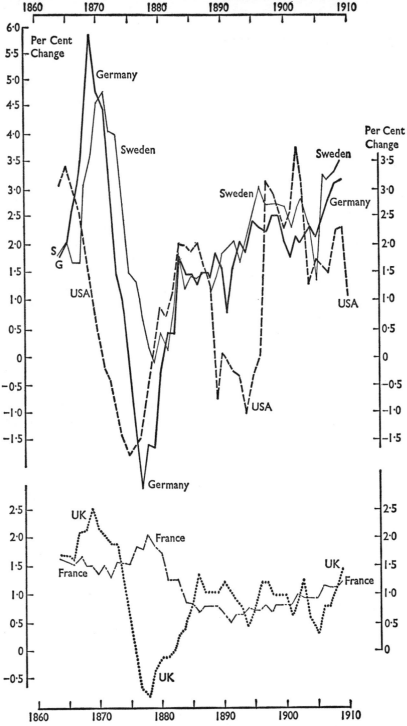

Fig. 3 Five countries, 1860–1913: Annually cumulated rate of rise of money wage-earnings over successive 8-year spans, entered against the fifth year in each span.
Source: Appendix 3.

three countries at this time. But either our very approximate index for France understates the rate of rise from the 1890s onwards, or there was a cleavage in the French wage structure then, with wages in some industries rising more rapidly, after the manner of the first three countries. From 1896 to 1911 our index for French wages as a whole rises by only 16 per cent, but in coalmining, engineering and building some representative earnings or rates rose by margins of from 18 to more than 25 per cent.

What account can we give of the trends of Fig. 2? Why were they all upwards? What made their rate of rise change from time to time within any one country, and why did different countries sometimes resemble and sometimes differ from one another in these changes? We have seen that most of the rise in wages – in three countries, more than all the net rise – came about in the positive phase of the trade cycle, and the most promising approach to the etiology of wage movements seems to be to explore the association between annual wage changes and the current stage of the cycle.

2. The relation between trends of money wages and the trade cycle

Table 7 has already made it clear that in all five countries money wages behaved differently in the positive and negative phases of the cycle: in the positive they rose substantially, in the negative they rose much less, or actually went down. Historical studies have filled this framework out, and related how the changes came about in response to the conjuncture year by year.

In the U.K., for instance, they[1] have shown how when business was profitable and expanding, trade unionists were more ready to risk a strike, and employers to concede a rise: the union rate went up, whether a craft union simply notified the employers in the district that its members would now work only for the higher rate, or a rise was negotiated. It might also be that a higher proportion of the workmen actually obtained the union rate. It was at this time that most strikes occurred, though usually they were short. But the rises were not confined to unionists, for the setting was one approaching full employment by recent standards. In the positive phases, the rate

[1] E.g. for the U.K., Clegg, Fox & Thompson (1964), especially 'The Boom Years, 1889–91' in ch. 4; W. Mosses (1922); K. D. Buckley (1955).

of unemployment among members of trade unions providing benefit (Beveridge, 1944, table 22) averaged 3·25 per cent over all years, including those in which activity first rose from a trough, and if we take the best year in each of the nine phases the average is under 2·2 per cent. Then as now, such rates can hardly have been reached in the national aggregate without shortages of labour appearing in some regions and trades, and we know that in fact such shortages were felt. The terms that the workman could get who made his personal bargain would improve as the value product of his labour rose and the ratio of applicants to vacancies fell. A contemporary observer, Alfred Marshall (1892, vi, v, 3) noted also 'the force of competition among the employers themselves, each desiring to extend his business, and to get for himself as much as possible of the rich harvest that is to be reaped when their trade is prosperous, (which) makes them consent to pay higher wages to their employees in order to obtain their services'. At times of brisk trade, moreover, unorganised workers formed a spontaneous combination and struck work together in support of a claim – craftsmen did this in Sweden in the 1870s and 1880s (Lindblom, 1938), as the unskilled did in the United Kingdom in 1889–1890 and again in 'the prairie fire in the Midlands' in 1913.

The same market forces as had pulled wages up when trade was good operated to pull them down when it fell off, save in so far as the investment of the preceding phase had raised productivity and so reduced unit labour costs relatively to the wage per man. But the downward pressure met both organised and individual resistances. It is to be expected that so far as trade unions were able to maintain themselves through the lean years they resisted cuts, and were able to reduce if not prevent them: the negative phase was in fact marked by relatively few strikes or lock-outs, but these were often protracted. But it is also to be expected that the feelings of the workman who made his own bargain would have been more strongly engaged to resist a cut than to press for a rise. The ratchet effect, by which the movement of money wage-rates is free in the upward direction but checked on the reverse, has long been recognised even where labour is unorganised.

Thus cyclical fluctuations tended to bring about a cumulative rise in money wages, because workers were able to seize the opportunity for rises afforded by the positive phases of the cycle, and offer effective resistance to downward pressure in the negative. The fluctuations in the demand for labour that came in with the industrial

C2   B.B.C.P.

revolution made for a progressive rise in money wages. Looking back from the third quarter of the eighteenth century, Adam Smith observed that 'in many places the money price of labour remains uniformly the same sometimes for half a century together,' and that wages did not change from year to year with variations in the price of provisions – great though these were at that time (*Wealth of Nations,* bk i, chs. viii, v). The change made by the cycle is illustrated by the wage-rates of English building craftsmen in Fig. 4. In some ways,

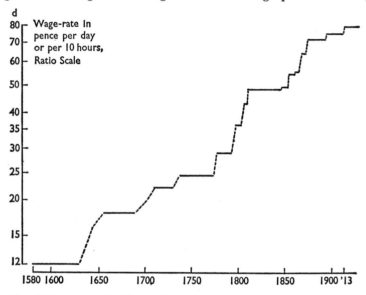

Fig. 4 Wage-rate of building craftsmen in Southern England, 1580–1913.
Source: E. H. Phelps Brown and Sheila V. Hopkins, 'Seven centuries of Building Wages, in *Economica* 22, 87, August 1955.

admittedly, this is a special case. Building was a sheltered industry, in which prices could be fixed to cover costs. It was different when products were sold for what they would fetch in a fluctuating market: here wages had always been more variable – in the eighteenth century days of stable wage-rates for the builders, the price rates of the worsted spinners of one district of Suffolk, for instance, ranged above and below an unchanged notional rate by a margin that varied with the state of the market from week to week (Burley, 1958). Again, when cyclical fluctuations in building become measurable they prove to have had a period longer than the eight years' average of the cycle in general activity. None the less, the wide perspective of Fig. 4 serves to contrast the frequency of change after 1848 with the years before, when the inertia of wage rates was rarely overborne save in time of war. In one way, indeed, the cycle acted like a war: it unclenched the dead hand of use and wont, overturned the judgment-seat of custom, and threw the wage question open. Thereby it gave men more opportunity to try to better their condition. Even, moreover, if the market had pressed down on wages as hard and long in the course of the cycle as it pulled them up, the ratchet effect would still have brought it about that the rises in wages were bigger than the cuts, and successive cycles would have raised wages cumulatively.

Our first answer to the question why money wages rose as they did in all five countries is therefore that these were all industrialised economies subject to the trade cycle, and each cycle operated on balance to raise money wages. But this can be only a first answer, for it explains the fact of rise only, and not the amount. We have still to show why the rise followed different trends in the same country at different times, or in different countries at the same time.

Since these trends grew out of the cumulation of the net changes cycle by cycle, a number of possible explanations offer themselves. One is that the pattern of the cycle varied, higher rates of rise of wages coming out of cycles whose positive phases were longer or more intense. Another is that the net rise of wages in each cycle was much the same, but the gradient of the trend of wages varied inversely with the length of the cycle. Yet a third possibility is that the cycles, though of much the same pattern and period, were of different amplitude: the rises of wages in the positive phase were generally large relatively to any falls in the negative, so that if the amount of the change in each phase varied with its intensity, a cycle of symmetrically greater amplitude would bring a greater net rise. These three possible explanations are not alternative: conceivably, all might hold together.

A first step in assessing them is to examine the movements of wages in the successive phases of each country's cycles. These movements, so far as they can be represented by the percentage change from first to last in each phase, are shown in Fig. 5. What differences appear between successive cycles or different countries, and does any absence of such differences rule out one or other line of explanation? In particular, what differences gave rise to the trends whose various

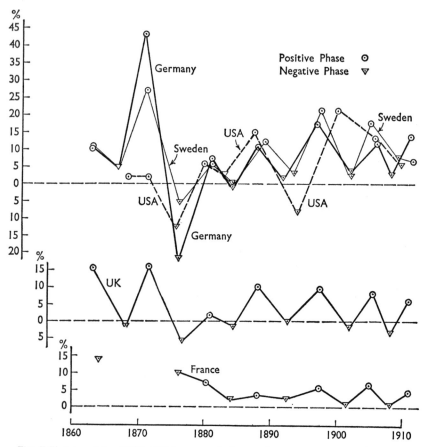

Fig. 5 Five countries, 1860–1913: per cent changes in money wage-earnings from end to end of successive cyclical phases, entered against mid-point of phase. Source: Appendix 3.

slopes appeared in Fig. 3? If we leave aside the mildly fluctuating course of French movements, we may say that two types of cyclical movement appear. There was first a wider swing of wages, both rise and fall, in Germany, Sweden and the U.K. in the 1870s and in the U.S.A. in the 1890s; there had also been a big fall in the U.S.A. in the 1870s, but this may be ascribed mainly to the return to gold after the greenback inflation. Second, there was a smaller swing, in which the negative phase brought only a small fall if any, and whose pattern was repetitive. Evidently the difference between these two types is associated with that between the periods of disturbed and of steady trends in Fig. 3.

But we must also ask of Fig. 5 whether any differences within the second, more stable type were associated with differences between the trends of their time. We can see some that were. That the German and Swedish trends were steeper from 1890 onwards is now seen to be due partly to the falls being somewhat smaller than before, partly to the rises being somewhat greater – that to the crest of 1897 much greater. That the U.K. and French trends were steady from 1885 onwards is associated in the U.K. with much steadiness of the pattern of cyclical movements, and in France with a symmetrical increase in rises and falls. In these two countries the trend rose less steeply than in Germany and Sweden from 1890 onwards, because the rises were smaller and the falls bigger. In no respect do differences in the period of the cycle, or in the relative impact of the positive and negative phases, seem to have been significant.

These observations converge upon two sorts of differences in the movements of wages within a cyclical pattern that is otherwise much the same throughout. The one sort is a difference of amplitude, a swinging of the pendulum more widely on both sides. The other is more like a tilting of the clock, by which the swing on one side goes farther while that on the other becomes shorter. Both sorts may have been due to differences either in the pressure that the trade cycle exerted upon wages, or in the reaction of wages to a given pressure. The second sort also suggests the intervention of some other force, that tended, for instance, to make rises bigger or falls smaller than in the given conjuncture they would have been otherwise. To throw light on these possibilities, we can begin by comparing the movements of wages with those of some indication of the cyclical pressure.

For the U.K. such an indication is provided, inversely, by the unemployment rate (Beveridge, 1944, appendix A). This is more narrowly based than the rates generally cited in more recent years, for it gives only the proportion of trade union members in receipt of unemployment benefit in those unions which provided such benefit; but it is none the less indicative of the course of industrial activity and of changes in the labour market at large. In Fig. 6 the movements of this unemployment rate are compared with the rates of change of money wages. To facilitate the comparison, we have taken the

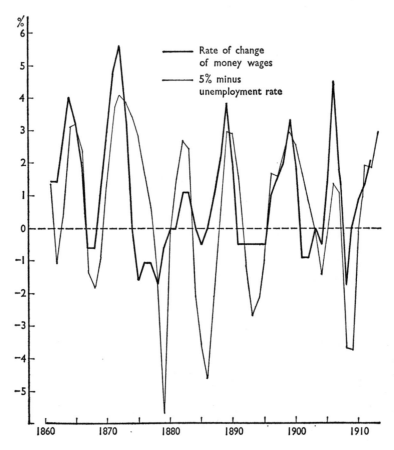

Fig. 6 U.K., 1861–1913: (1) Rate of change of money wage-earnings (first central difference for each year expressed as a percentage of earnings in that year).
(2) $(5 - U_n)$ where U_n is the percentage of trade union members in receipt of un-employment benefit in year n, entered against year n.
Sources: (1) Appendix 3: (2) W. H. Beveridge, *Full Employment in a Free Society*, pp. 312–13.

amount by which each year's unemployment rate falls short of 5 per cent – thus the 3 per cent of a good year is entered here as +2, and the 8 per cent of a slump appears as – 3. The rate of change of money wages has been obtained as half the change in our index of wage earnings from the year before to the year after each given year, expressed as a percentage of the index for that year. Fig. 6 shows the close agreement prevailing between the two series, alike in phase and, save in 1870–1885, in amplitude: evidently the movements of wages were closely associated with the conjuncture. But this association was by no means uniform. We notice, for instance, the rise in wages during 1871–1873 as altogether greater than we should expect from the behaviour of wages in other crests of activity, whereas the next rise in wages, in 1881–1883, was much smaller than we should expect. The troughs of activity bear a yet more variable relation to wage movements: in particular, the trough of 1908–1909 was much deeper than the preceding trough of 1904, yet it brought a fall of wages in only one year, whereas in that preceding trough there were falls in four successive years. Thus too many exceptions appear for us to be able to treat the change of money wages as predictable from the current level of activity alone.

The agreement that catches the eye in Fig. 6, moreover, is only in profile – in phase, and in the height of crests: the extent of agreement year by year remains to be examined. It has been studied by Phillips (1958), to whom we owe the diagram reproduced as our Fig. 7. The wage changes here have been reckoned from an index not altogether the same as our present wage series, but the differences are not great enough to affect the main finding. This is, that there was no clearcut relation between the level of activity and the change of money wages. When unemployment was low, very different rises in wages were associated with the same narrow range of unemployment; when it was high, a narrow range of wage changes was associated with very different rates of unemployment. Phillips has shown that part of this dispersion can be accounted for by bringing in the direction of change of unemployment: a given level of unemployment tended to be associated with a bigger rise in wages when it was reached in the upswing than on the run down. Even so, the differences between cycles remain too great for us to regard wage movements as governed by the conjuncture alone. Study of the relation between wage movements and what indications of the level of activity are available for other countries have equally brought out the clear association between them phase by phase, and the lack of any such association year by year. We might doubt, indeed, whether the relation between the level of activity and wage movements was continuous at all. There might have been only a 'traffic-light correlation'. When the light is green, the traffic moves, but the intensity of the light does not

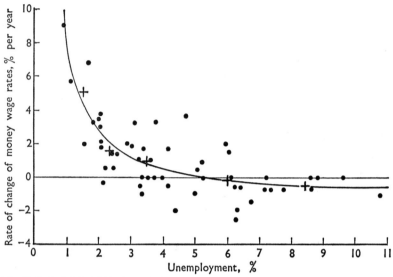

Fig. 7 U.K., 1861–1913: Rate of change of money wage-rates (first central difference for each year as a percentage of the index of that year) and percentage of trade union members in receipt of unemployment benefit in given year.
Source: A. W. Phillips, *Economica*, 25, 100, Nov. 1958.

affect the speed of the traffic; when the light is red, the traffic stands still. In the same way it might be said, so long as unemployment was below 5 per cent money wages rose, but by amounts which did not vary systematically with the actual rate of unemployment; and so long as it was over 5 per cent, whether it was so by much or little, wages would fall slightly or remain unchanged.

A correlation of annual data, however, in which each year is considered by itself, leaves out of account two factors that may well enter into the relation between levels of activity and wage movements in each cyclical phase as a whole. One is that of lags – some of the wage changes recorded in one year may be a response to the conjuncture of the year before: it is noteworthy, for instance, how often the first year of our negative phase – the year of the first drop in activity from the crest – brought a big rise in wages. The other factor is that of cumulation: high activity, or increasing activity, sustained through three successive years, for instance, may bring a rise in wages more than half as great again as in a span of two years. We can do something to take these factors into account if we reckon the average annual changes in wages and in the rate of unemployment over sequences of years of which the one sort is made up of our positive phase of the cycle together with the first subsequent year, and the other correspondingly consists of our negative phase less its first year. The outcome of this reckoning is shown in Fig. 8. It might be

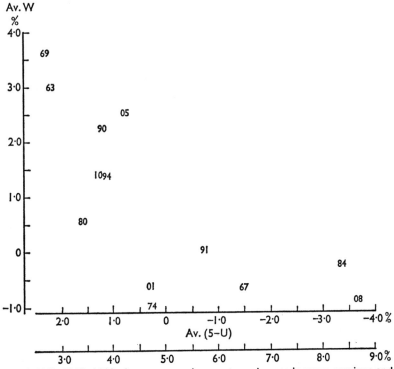

Fig. 8 U.K., 1863–1912: Average annual percentage changes in wage-earnings and average of annual percentages of trade union members in receipt of unemployment benefit (*U* in lower scale), in course of each cyclical phase, the positive phases including the first year after the lowest point of unemployment; the unemployment rate entered as (5–*U*) in upper scale.
Sources: Appendix 3 and W. H. Beveridge, *Full Employment*, pp. 312–13.

interpreted in the first place as revealing only a 'traffic-light correlation': when the average unemployment of a phase was under $4\frac{1}{2}$ per cent wages rose, but not at a rate that varied at all closely with the actual level of unemployment; when it was over $4\frac{1}{2}$ per cent wages fell, but only a little, and by an amount that was much the same

whether unemployment were 5 per cent or 10. But on the face of
Fig. 8 there is enough tendency for the change in wages to vary
inversely with unemployment to warrant a second interpretation: we
may see that tendency, namely, as a linear regression in which, over
the range up to 7 per cent unemployment, an increase of one
percentage point in unemployment is associated with a decrease of
about one percentage point in the average rate of rise of wages. But
the negative phases beginning in 1884 and 1908 lie outside this
relation: here average unemployment of over 8 per cent was
associated with a fall in average wages of less than 1 per cent,
whereas the regression would show a fall of around 3 per cent. There
were three phases, moreover, in which wages rose less, or fell more,
than the regression would show: the positive phase beginning in
1880, and the negative phases beginning in 1874 and 1901. The first
of these, we note, was unusually short; and the second, unusually
long. On the other hand, the wide movement of wages in the phases
beginning in 1863, 1867 and 1869 now fall into line, as corresponding
to the intensity of their cyclical setting.

So far, then, our findings for the U.K. are that the movements of
wages agreed with those of the trade cycle both in phasing, and in the
extent of movement, save in this latter respect that a ratchet seems to
have operated to prevent deeper depressions bringing greater wage
reductions, and that certain phases lie outside the prevailing relation.

How far does this compare with our other countries' experience?
For them we lack comparable measures of unemployment, but one
indicator of the cyclical swing that is available in nearly common
form for all five countries is pig iron output or, in Germany,
consumption. We have taken the annual deviations of this series from
trend (given by a 9-year average of the logarithms of the original),
and treated these deviations as we did unemployment in the U.K.,
finding the average relative for comparison with the average wage
change throughout each phase. But as it was rare for wages to rise
much in the year following the crest of pig iron output, we have not
now included that year in the positive phase; our phases therefore
remain as originally defined. For the most part they would have the
same dates whether we took the turning-points of the pig-iron
deviations or of activity at large as that is described in Thorp's
Annals, but where there was conflict or doubt it was the *Annals* that
we followed. The outcome is displayed in Fig. 9.

A first observation is simple but important: the same sawtooth pattern appears in wages as in pig iron – formally, the phases of positive deviation of pig iron output from trend coincided with phases of bigger wage rises; and the phases of negative deviation coincided with smaller wage rises or actual falls. In France, it is true, the changes from phase to phase in the rate of rise of wages were so small that the evidence is slight, but so far as it goes it is more in agreement than otherwise. Can we go farther, and trace an association with the sizes of the fluctuations of the two series? Some such association does appear in the heights of the peaks, but it is not general. In the U.K. and Germany it is fairly close throughout, save for 1882 in the U.K. In Sweden the five peaks in pig iron were of much the same height, those of wage rises differed more; the last three wage peaks lie on a rising trend, and it may be pointed out that so do the last three peaks in pig iron, but their differences are small. In the U.S.A. the rise of pig-iron output after the depression of the mid-90s was so sharp and sustained, that deviations from trend in these years lack their usual significance; but this apart, the rises of money wages seem to follow a course that may mark a trend, or a change of trend after the 1890s, but apparently owes nothing to the intensity of the contemporary booms as measured by our pig iron deviations. Here as in Sweden the peaks in wages differed more than those in pig iron. In sum, then, a tendency for wage rises to be bigger in the phases when pig iron output rose higher above trend was marked in the U.K. and Germany; in Sweden and the U.S.A. we have in one sense less to go by, because the peaks in pig iron differed less from one another, but in both countries there were differences in the wage peaks which must accordingly be ascribed to other influences.

The evidence of the troughs is largely negative. In Germany, it is true, there is an association between the depths of the troughs in the two series, save in 1868, but in the U.K. no such association appears, despite the big differences in the depths of the pig iron troughs. In each of Sweden and the U.S.A. the pig iron troughs are of much the same depth, save for 1886 in Sweden, but the wage troughs differ a good deal from one another. In general, a ratchet seems to have operated to prevent wages dropping more in response to greater falls in activity.

Our present inquiry thus reinforces the conclusion already reached, that in all our countries, though in France to a much smaller extent,

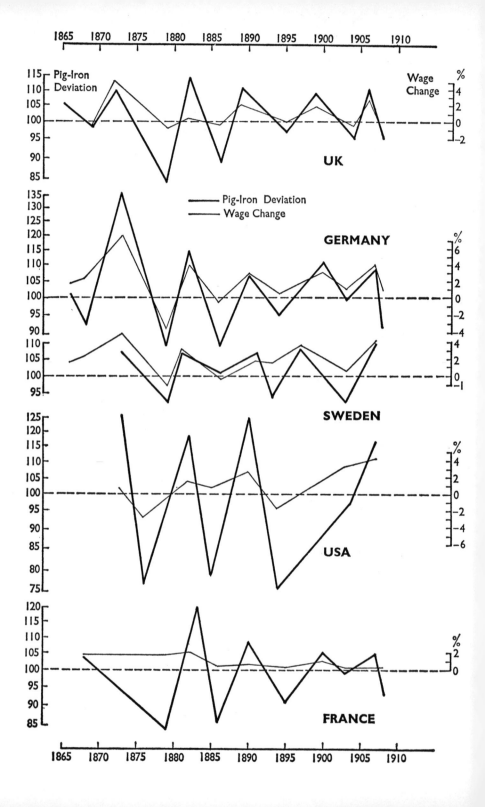

most of the rise of money wages took place in the positive phase of the trade cycle. It further shows that in the U.K. and Germany the extent of the rise varied with that of the upsurge of activity; but this was subject to exception in those two countries, and does not hold for the other three. In Germany alone does the severity of the check imposed by depressions on the rise of wages seem to have been much affected by the depth of the depression.

Only in part, therefore, can we attribute to changes in the intensity of the trade cycle the observed changes in the rate at which money wages rose from time to time. In so far as a given trend persisted through several cycles, and changes in trend were experienced by several countries together, we must seek these other factors in conditions which obtained persistently and widely. One of these might be the growth of population.

3. Population pressure and migration

In discussing the trade cycle we have already noticed that one of the ways in which it affected the movement of wages was by changing the balance of vacancies and applicants. It did this by changing the number of vacancies. But the number of applicants also changed from time to time, through the natural growth of population, the balance of international migration, and the movement of workers out of agriculture into the employment to which our figures of wages relate. In fact it grew at very different rates in different countries, and sometimes in different periods within the same country.

Now there seems to be no reason why a faster rate of growth in the number of applicants should be matched spontaneously by a faster increase of vacancies, and so we should expect it to keep wages down; and conversely for a slower rate. Writing in the United Kingdom in

---

Fig. 9 Five countries, 1860–1913: (1) Ratio of pig iron output in year of peak or trough output to trend output in that year.
(2) Change in money wage-earnings as an annually compounded rate in cyclical phase terminating at or near year of peak or trough in pig-iron output.

Sources: (1) S. Kuznets, *Secular Movements in Production and Prices: their nature and their bearing upon Cyclical Fluctuations.* France: table 43. Germany: table 35. U.K.: table 24. U.S.A.: table 8. Sweden: *Sweden, Historical and Statistical Handbook*, 2nd edn, English issue, part ii, ed. J. Guinchard (1914), p. 275. (2) Appendix 3.

the 1890s, Sidney and Beatrice Webb (1919: part iii, ch. ii, p. 660) observed that:

> it is, to say the least of it, unusual, in any trade in this country, for there to be no more workmen applying for situations than there are situations to be filled. When the unemployed are crowding round the factory gates every morning, it is plain to each man that, unless he can induce the foreman to select him rather than another, his chance of subsistence for weeks to come may be irretrievably lost. Under these circumstances bargaining, in the case of isolated individual workmen, becomes absolutely impossible.

It was noted again in the United Kingdom that the twenty years before the First World War, which saw a sustained check to the rise of real wages, felt the impact of a sharp increase in the rise of the number of men aged 20–64 (Layton, 1914, p. 39). Conversely, the fact that money wages rose more slowly in the 1950s in Western Germany and Switzerland than in most other European countries was attributed to the expansiveness of their labour supplies, with a confidence that was increased when from 1959 onwards the expansiveness ended and wages rose much faster.

In general, whether additional hands are or are not available for employment at the going rate of pay seems bound to be one of the factors affecting the movement of wages. In the short run this depends on the margin of unemployment in the committed labour force; in the longer, with which we are concerned here, on the rate of growth of that force.

But it is hard to measure the availability of labour in this sense. It is not an actual but a potential quantity. We can, it is true, enumerate the whole population of working age, but this is commonly half as big again as the number of gainfully occupied, and the activity rates that express the ratio of this number to the whole themselves depend on current opportunities for employment. This has been apparent in the differences between women's activity rates in districts in which different types of industry predominate, and in recent years it has shown itself also for men, in their lower activity rates in the districts of the United Kingdom with higher unemployment (*Ministry of Labour Gazette*, 1965). Our present concern, moreover, is primarily with non-agricultural employment, and this formed in some of our countries a modest, and in all of them a markedly changing, proportion of the whole. Emigration, again, kept down the number seeking employment at home, and though its fluctuations were due in part to the varying pull of the receiving economies, they also responded to the push of a faster rise in the number of young people at home.

The outstanding minor secular upswings in transatlantic emigration from Europe – for example from Ireland and Germany in the forties and fifties, from Sweden in the eighties, and from Italy from the turn of the century to the First World War, occurred at times when the proportion of young people in the population was exceptionally large as a consequence of the births cycle (Brinley Thomas, 1954, pp. 117–18).

To the extent that the emigrants looked for jobs at home before they left, the net growth of population after emigration will have masked the true growth of the potential labour supply. For all these reasons the changes in the rate of growth of the population of working age provide an uncertain indication of the pressure of supply from time to time in the labour market.

Nor can we escape these difficulties by going over to the committed labour force – those in jobs or unemployed, that is, seeking jobs. In the differences of activity rates and of rates of movement out of the agricultural sector we have already seen ways in which the committed labour force varies with the prospects of employment. It is hard to disentangle supply from demand in the labour market. A change in the rate of growth of the working population may mark a change in the availability of jobs rather than in an independently determined number of job-seekers.

We are in any case concerned not with supply alone but with the balance of supply and demand. Even if we could measure the independently given potential supply, we still could not use it to explain wage movements except in conjunction with a measure of the independently given demand. But this we lack: we cannot tell how many jobs employers would have filled if they could, at the going rate, from time to time. Indeed, the very notion of an independently determined demand is as elusive as that of supply. The intentions formed by potential job-takers and job-makers alike depend on the prospects of carrying those intentions out. We know that more people make themselves available for work when more jobs are offered. We may surmise that enterprise will create more jobs when and where it can expect to fill them. It is remarkable, in all developing countries, how changes in the rate of growth of population have been matched by corresponding changes in jobs without much, if any, associated change in the level of unemployment.

The apparently simple question, whether the movement of wages seems to have been affected by the availability of labour from time to time, therefore admits of no direct answer. But though the growth of population is an imperfect measure of the effective increase in the availability of labour, it is probably correlated with that increase. More exactly, the proportionate change in the number holding or seeking jobs within the non-agricultural sector will bear a steady relation to that in the whole population of working age, say 15–64, on the assumptions that:

(a) emigrants are mostly young, and go away without much previous participation in the home labour market; also they are intent on going, so that they are not potentially available to home employers at the going rate;

(b) the propensity of people in rural households to move into jobs in the non-agricultural sector is constant;

(c) activity rates – that is, the proportions of particular groups by age and status in the household who take jobs outside the household – are constant.

If changes in the population of working age are large between one decade and the next, they are likely to outweigh the effect of any departure from those assumptions meanwhile, except that changes in the relative prosperity of agriculture may bring a wide departure from (b). At least it seems worth while to trace the course of the growth of the population of working age in each country. We can also see how much depends on assumption (a), if we try the effect of inverting it, and assume that those who emigrated within a period did so only at its very end, and meanwhile all formed part of the population of working age – if we assume, that is to say, that the rate at which labour supply was growing is indicated by the sum of the change in the resident population of working age between the beginning and end of the period, and the total number of emigrants during the period. That some of the actual emigrants were children who would not have attained working age within the period makes the assumption the more extreme.

The rates of growth arrived at in these two ways, the one an actual rate, the other a hypothetical or potential, are set out in Table 8. For France we have been able to calculate only the actual rate, but emigration seems in any case to have been small. Levasseur (1889, iii, p. 357) gives figures for 1870–1889 which rise to 31,000 in the last year but over the whole span average less than 8,000 a year; net migration may well have been inward. In the U.S.A., where it was certainly inward, we also take only the actual rate of growth, which combines immigration with natural increase.

Table 8 France, Germany, Sweden, U.K., U.S.A. in Period I: Rate of growth of the supply of labour, in per cent per decade, reckoned from:
(a) increase in resident population of working age (15–64, except in Germany, where 15–60).
(b) the sum of (a) and total net emigration during the period (in Germany, emigration to the U.S.A. only).

Ten-year span (for France and U.K. one year later)	France (a)	Germany (a)	Germany (b)	Sweden (a)	Sweden (b)	U.K. (a)	U.K. (b)	U.S.A. (a)
1860–1870	− 0·4[1]			6·6	11·0	6·6		
1870–1880	0·3[2]	8·7[3]	10·7[3]	11·3	16·4	10·7	15·6	
1880–1890	0·2	9·8	15·4	0·6	14·2	10·6	18·2	28·9
1890–1900	0·1	14·6	16·7	7·6	16·9	14·6	17·2	23·2
1900–1910	0·2	16·4	17·4	8·7	17·0	10·4	14·6	25·3

[1] 1861–1872, expressed as rate per decade. Includes effect of loss of Alsace-Lorraine.
[2] 1872–1881, expressed as rate per decade.
[3] 1871–1880, expressed as rate per decade.

Sources:
France. *Annuaire Statistique Français Rétrospectif, 1961*, ch. ii, tableau viii.
Germany. Population: *Statistik des Deutschen Reichs,* Band 401, II, p. 555 (old frontiers). Emigration: Brinley Thomas, *Migration and Economic Growth* (1954), table 93, immigration to the United States from Germany from *Historical Statistics of the United States 1789–1945*, series B. 310.
Sweden. Population: *Historisk Statistik för Sverige* (Statistiska Centralbyran, Stockholm, 1955) vol. i, table A.16. Emigration: Brinley Thomas *op. cit.*, table 120.
U.K. Population: B. R. Mitchell & P. Deane, *Abstract of British Historical Statistics*, table 4. Emigration: *Statistical Abstract for the U.K.* (Cd 3991 of 1932), table 8, net loss by migration.
U.S.A. Population: *Historical Statistics of the United States, 1789–1945*, series A.74–83.

Table 8 shows that in Germany, Sweden and the U.K. the actual rates of growth were much less similar than the potential. Until the 1880s the potential rates rose, and thereafter they remained between 14 and 18 per cent per decade in all three countries, though the German and Swedish rates continued to rise whereas the U.K. rate fell. So far as the potential rate measures the impact of job-seekers on the labour market, its higher level from 1880 onwards suggests a check to the rise of money wages; but in none of the three countries did a check occur.

So far, however, as emigration took potential job-seekers off before they made their presence felt in the domestic labour market, the pressure of numbers is indicated not by the potential but by the actual growth of the population of working age. In Germany, Sweden and the U.K. the amount of emigration was in fact large in relation to natural growth. Taking the three countries together, and assuming that all emigrants would have been of working age on the terminal date, we find that the proportion of the potential increase in the population of working age that was removed by emigration was,

in the 1870s,   26·5%
in the 1880s,   31·1%
in the 1890s,   15·7%
in the 1900s,   16·8%

Changes in emigration could, therefore, take marked effect on the actual increase of the population of working age, and this did in fact vary a good deal. In Sweden the generally higher emigration made the rate of actual increase lower than in the other two countries; in the 1880s emigration was so high that it almost completely cancelled out the natural growth. By the test of actual increase it is the 1890s that take the most pressure in the U.K. The German experience was very much the same as the British until then, but whereas the British pressure eased off in the years before the war, the German rose again.

These variations are sufficiently prominent to make us look for their counterparts in the movement of wages, but these are far from clear. We might expect money wages to rise more rapidly in Sweden than in the other countries, including the U.S.A., through the last three decades: from end to end they did so, but from the mid-90s onwards money wages rose just as fast in Germany. We might expect the difference to be most marked in the 1880s, but it is not. We might expect the rise in British money wages to be checked in the 1890s and become faster again in the 1900s: there was a check in the 1890s, it is true, with the general level unchanged for six years, but perhaps what is remarkable here is that the general level did not actually fall in the recession at that time as it had done in some previous recessions, and was to do in the two that followed. We might expect money wages in Germany to rise more slowly after the 1890s, but in fact they rose faster.

In the U.S.A., however, we may have more to reckon with. In the years before the First World War immigration into the U.S.A. ruled much higher than ever before or since – through 1902–1913 arrivals averaged over 1·1 millions a year, against less than half a million on the average of the twelve years before; over 1900–1914 they made up 73 per cent of the increase in the labour force, against 60 per cent in the twenty years before (Lebergott, 1964, table 2–2 and p. 162). Contemporaries and later observers alike have believed that this high immigration took a marked effect on wages. True, Table 8 shows that its immediate effect was to increase the rate of growth of the population of working age only a little, and the high rate of growth in 1900–1910 was still not so high as that of the 1880s. But something had happened meanwhile to increase the pressure that a given rate of growth would concentrate upon the wages of hired labour – there was no longer much free land to be taken up. The report of the Census of 1890 noted that 'up to and including 1880 the country had a frontier of settlement, but at present the unsettled areas have been so broken into by isolated bodies of settlement that there can hardly be said to be a frontier line.'[1] After 1890 a given increase in the working population would mean a bigger increase than before in applicants for jobs. If we look for an effect on the movements of money wages, we find none evident, for they rose greatly – by over 40 per cent from 1890 to 1913, whereas over the twenty years before they had hardly risen at all; but when we come to the rise of productivity we shall find grounds for expecting them to have risen even more, and so for suspecting the operation of some depressive influence at the time.

This possible exception apart, what is remarkable is that the rate at which additional job-seekers entered the market from time to time does not seem to have been associated systematically with the

[1] 1890 Census, *Population*, vol. i, p. xxxiv. Quoted here from Lebergott (1964), p. 104.

movement of money wages. This is intelligible on one assumption: so far as the demand for labour is elastic, so far as enterprise and investment are expansive and responsive to opportunities of engaging labour, an increase in the supply of labour will do little to check the rise of money wages. The extent to which this assumption seems to have held is striking. All these economies were able to employ more job-seekers as they appeared, in numbers (save in France) always large but also fluctuating, without cumulative unemployment, and without apparent impact on their other trends of change.

We pass to other forces that may affect the course of money wages; and next, the extension of trade unionism.

4. The growth of trade unionism

Alfred Marshall (1892, vi, xiii, 5) noted the claim of the unions of his day 'to receive an earlier rise, a greater rise, and a more prolonged rise than they could get without combination.'

> When the time has come for the trade to reap the harvest for which it has been waiting, the employers will be very unwilling to let it slip; and even if an agreement to resist the demands of the men is made, it will not easily be maintained. . . . Unions further hold that the threat of a strike, though less powerful when the tide of prosperity is falling than when it is rising, may yet avail for the comparatively easy task of slackening the fall in the high wages they have gained.

The stress here is on greater gains in the positive phase. Later observers have held that trade unions made most difference in the negative. A workman bargaining singly found it hard to stand out against a cut in times of slack trade. He might do so on principle, not counting the cost; but the likely cost, in losing the job to someone else who would take it at the rate offered by the employer, was far higher than when it was not jobs but men that were scarce. The remedy was an agreement to maintain 'the rate for the job'. The historian of the rise of Swedish trade unions, discussing the strikes of 1880–1885 in which unions first played an effective part, observed that:

rises in wages won by unorganised strikes were easily taken away from the workers in times of depression, when the cost of living fell and unemployment rose, if the workers could not offer an organised resistance. The unorganised strike was a way of gaining momentary improvements in specially favourable circumstances. But only through organisation could these improvements be made lasting (Lindblom, 1938, p. 73).

In similar terms the historians of British unions from 1889 to 1910 have written: 'Unorganised or weakly organised workers frequently strike in years of good trade, but they lack the resources to sustain a defensive struggle during depression' (Clegg, Fox & Thompson, 1964, p. 362). H. Gregg Lewis (1963, p. 4), in his survey of the evidence for the effect of trade unions in the U.S.A. in raising the relative wages of their members in more recent years, has judged that 'the peak impact of the last forty years occurred ... about 1932–1933, near the bottom of the Great Depression. At the peak' (that is, the peak impact of unionism) 'the effect of unionism on the average wage of union workers relative to the average wage of non-union workers may have been above 25 per cent. In the ensuing inflation the relative wage effect declined sharply to a level between 10 and 20 per cent, I estimate, by the end of the 1930s' though this was after six or seven years of great trade union expansion and vigour in pressing claims.

These observations lead us to expect that a marked growth of trade unionism will bring a changed response of wages to the conjuncture. From 1890 onwards trade unionism did in fact grow markedly in all five countries. Some particulars of membership are given in Table 9. The reported membership, it is true, bears an uncertain relation to the effective, and this in turn to the resources and determination of the union. But when we combine these figures with what we know of the course of industrial affairs in each country, a conclusion emerges of no little generality and force: evidently it was at this time that trade unionism first extended from a few groups and places, with a total membership that can have been of small account anywhere save in the U.K., to cover a significant proportion of the manual workers, and make itself felt as a force to be reckoned with, in some at least of the industries of all five countries. Can we trace the expected effect?

A first relevant observation, already made, is that it was precisely in the 1890s that money wages began to rise along a steeper trend, to

Table 9 The extension of trade unionism between the 1890s and the First World War, in five countries.

	France	Germany	Sweden	U.K.	U.S.A.
In 1890s					
1. Occupied population in industry[1] (millions)	(1896) 6·4	(1895) 8·6	(1890) 0·4	(1891) 9·3[3]	(1890) 7·3
2. Estimated number of trade unionists (thousands)	(1890) 140	(1891) 344	(1886) 8–9	(1888) 750	(1890) 372
3. Approximate number of trade unionists per 10,000 occupied in industry	220	400	210	810	510
Approaching 1914					
4. Occupied population in industry[1]	(1911) 7·4	(1910) 12·0	(1910) 0·7	(1911) 11·9[3]	(1910) 14·7
5. Estimated number of trade unionists (thousands)	(1912) 1,064	(1913) 3,024	(1907) 231[2]	(1913) 3,205	(1914) 2,687
6. Approximate number of trade unionists per 10,000 occupied in industry	1,440	2,520	3,300	2,690	1,830

[1] Industry here comprises mining, manufacturing, building, utilities, transport and communications.

[2] 1907 was a high point, reached after a rapid rise from below 100,000 in 1904; through 1910–1912 membership averaged only about 188,000.

[3] G.B. only; not here excluding dealers.

Sources: *Occupied population:*
France: Études et Conjuncture, mai/juin 1953, pp. 246–47; the classification of 1911 differs from that of 1896.
Germany: W. G. Hoffmann, F. Grumbach & H. Hesse, *Das Wachstum der Deutschen Wirtschaft seit der Mitte des 19 Jahrhunderts*, part 2, table 20.
Sweden: G. Bagge, E. Lundberg & I. Svennilson, *Wages in Sweden 1860–1930*, part ii, p. 209, row (*b*), plus an estimate for transport workers based on 1930 Census, part vii, p. 59, giving change 1920–1930.
U.K.: B. R. Mitchell and P. Deane, *Abstract of British Historical Statistics*, ch. ii, table i.
U.S.A.: 1890, S. Lebergott, 'Labor force and employment 1800–1960', table i, in *Output, Employment and Productivity in the U.S. after 1800* (NBER, *Studies in Income & Wealth*, vol. 30, 1966). The number of transport workers was extrapolated from the numbers given for 1910, 1900 in S. Lebergott, *Manpower in Economic Growth: the American record since 1800* (1964), tables A–5, A–7. 1910, Lebergott (1964).

Estimated number of trade unionists:
France: L. Levine, *Syndicalism in France* (N.Y. 1914), pp. 70, 105, 194.

Germany: G. Bry, *Wages in Germany 1871–1945*, table 11.
Sweden: 1886, T. Lindblom, *Den Svenska Fackföreningsrörelsens Uppkomst,* p. 65;
1907, and later years, G. Bagge, E. Lundberg & I. Svennilson, *Wages in Sweden
1860–1930,* part II, table 188, p. 232.
U.K.: 1888, H. A. Clegg, A. Fox & A. F. Thompson, *A History of British Trade Unions
since 1889,* vol. i, table i; 1913, membership of registered trade unions reported by
the Chief Registrar of Friendly Societies, taken here from *Statistical Abstract for the
United Kingdom* (Cd 3991 of 1932), table 94.
U.S.A.: 1890, Lloyd Ulman, ch. 13, 'The Development of Trades and Labor Unions',
in *American Economic History,* ed. Seymour E. Harris; 1914, I. Bernstein, 'The Growth
of American Trade Unions', in *American Economic Review,* June 1954.

be sustained down to 1913, in Germany, Sweden and the U.S.A.
Yet they did not do this in France, nor in the U.K.: in those two
countries they rose at rates that varied little from 1885 onwards, and
were lower than in the first three.

It would in any case be hasty to look only at trends which, we have
seen, are the joint outcome of the varying intensities of successive
cyclical phases, and the varying response of wages to a phase of given
intensity. We can ask of Fig. 9 whether this response seems to have
changed with the rise of trade unionism. A change in the relation of
the two curves in Sweden and the U.S.A. suggests that there it did so:
in both these countries it shifted during the 1890s into the higher gear
in which, down to the war, rises in wages were greater in a given
phase and falls smaller than they had been before. But here again
there is no evidence of any such shift in France, Germany and the
U.K. In the U.K. especially it is noticeable that cycles of fairly
similar amplitude met with a fairly similar response.

We might infer that the extension of trade unionism from 1890
onwards took little effect on the trend of money wages, and that
where this trend grew steeper at the time the causes lay elsewhere.
Alternatively, it is the absence of apparent effect in France and the
U.K. that we might attribute to other causes. In France, we might
urge, what we have called trade unionism was really a quite different
movement, better known as syndicalism; strikes, though numerous
from 1904 onwards, were more like political demonstrations; only in
a narrow sector, in printing, the docks and the mines of the Pas de
Calais, was any semblance of collective bargaining achieved. In the
U.K., on the other hand, the very extent and solidity that collective
bargaining had already attained in 1890 may have prevented much
difference being made by an increase of membership which, though

large, was not of a kind to add much to the strength of those already bargaining effectively, or to extend bargaining procedures far into new fields. On this view, therefore, the extension of trade unionism would remain as a possible cause of the shift of gear apparent in Germany and the U.S.A. and, it may be, of the steeper trend of wages seen also at the time in Sweden.

So far, however, we have been concerned only with whole phases: we may be better able to assess the possible effects of trade unionism if we look for them year by year, and ask whether years which we know to have been times of special union activity or weakness also brought wage changes different from those we should expect from the conjuncture.

Hines (1964) has suggested that an indication of trade union activity, or pushfulness, will be provided by the current change in trade union membership as a proportion of the whole labour force. It may be objected that membership rises and falls according as market forces of themselves promote or inhibit advances in wages – that in the recovery, when wages are in any case likely to rise, workers will join the unions, and they will quit them in the recession when the union can offer little in return for its dues. Attendant changes work in the same way – men are less afraid of victimisation, or of leaving their job to strike, when employment is full. There is force in this objection, but the correlation it assumes is in fact imperfect. Davis (1941) in a survey of changes in union membership in France, Germany, the U.K. and the U.S.A. from 1890 to dates in the interwar years, found that in about two thirds of the phases classified by Thorp (1926) as 'prosperity' membership rose markedly, but in nearly a quarter it actually declined; and that the correlation with 'prosperity' is not so high as that with sharp changes in prices. He concluded that 'union growth proceeds by waves which are not closely synchronized with those of the business cycle. These waves indicate that there is considerable inertia in the movement of union membership. A major wave of growth, if not brought on by a war, will nearly always be found to have been preceded by an accumulation of wage-earners' grievances, as during a major depression, while the accumulation of employer resistances during a wave of growth is a factor in the ensuing period of absolute or relative decline.' Also 'the quality of the leadership in a particular critical situation may have a determining influence on the subsequent development of unionism'.

It is therefore possible that changes in union membership, at least in certain instances, will indicate the action of a distinct factor in wage changes. Fig. 10 shows that the direction of the year to year

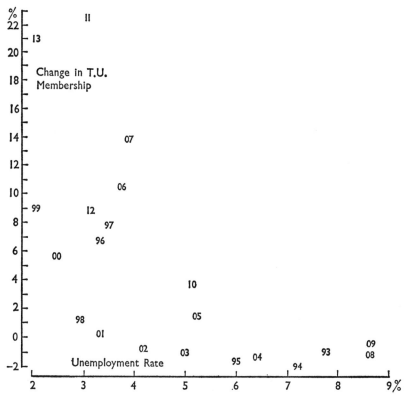

Fig. 10 U.K., 1893–1913: (1) Change from a year ago in total trade union membership at end of year.
(2) Percentage of trade union members in receipt of unemployment benefit in that year.
Sources: (1) B. C. Roberts, *Trade Union Government and Administration in Great Britain* (1956), appendix i, table 39; (2) W. H. Beveridge, *Full Employment*, pp. 312–13.

changes in membership in the U.K. from 1892 onwards did largely depend on the phase of the cycle: when unemployment was over 4 per cent, membership fell in seven years out of ten, when unemployment was under 4 per cent it rose in eight years out of nine. But within each phase the changes of membership are sufficiently

D   B.B.C.P.

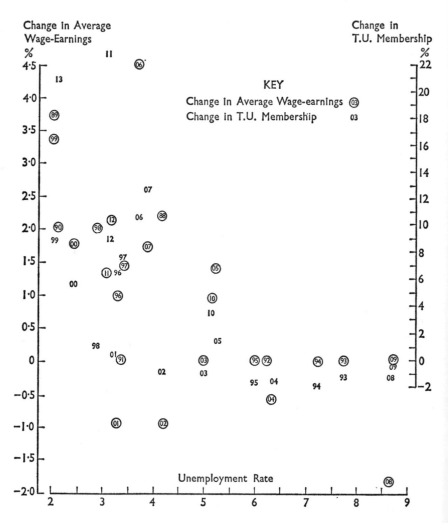

Fig. 11 U.K.: Regressions of (1) 1888–1912, annual rate of change in wage-earnings over two-year interval centred on given year (entered by ringed dates), and (2) 1893–1913, percentage change over preceding year of trade union membership at end of year (entered by unringed dates) on (3) 1888–1913, percentage of trade union members in receipt of unemployment benefit.

Sources: (1) Appendix 3; (2) B. C. Roberts, *Trade Union Government and Administration*, appendix i, table 39. (3) W. H. Beveridge, *Full Employment*, pp. 312–313.

independent of the level of unemployment year by year to reveal any direct connection between themselves and wage movements. If wages, for instance, changed in a given year otherwise than we should expect from that year's level of unemployment, we might find that the change in membership then was likewise something other than we should have expected from that level.

Fig. 11 enables us to investigate this possibility. Let us look first at the entries that take the form of ringed dates. These show the regression of each year's change in money wages on the current level of unemployment – the regression already illustrated (though with a somewhat different wage series) in Fig. 7. 'Each year's change in money wages' has been estimated by taking half the difference between the wage index of the year after and the year before, and expressing it as a percentage of the value of the index in the year itself. This is a reasonable way to arrive at the rate of change prevailing over the year from observations that must be regarded as centred on the mid-point of each year. It is liable, however, to impute to a given year changes that occurred entirely in the year before or after. We must remember this when we are looking for an association between the wage change, as we have estimated it, of a given year, and some other variable (such as the level of unemployment) that can be assigned to that year unambiguously: we shall need to take account at the same time of the wage changes in adjacent years. But for brevity we shall still speak of 'the rise in 1889' and the like. On this understanding, we can now single out certain years as exceptional. In the positive phases, the rises in 1889, 1899 and again in 1906 are bigger than the experience of most other prosperous years leads us to expect; in the negative, either 1901 and 1902 lay exceptionally low or 1909 stood exceptionally high, and 1908 in any case lay low.

Were these deviations associated with exceptional changes in trade union membership? To rank as exceptional, such changes must be large or small relatively not only to the average of all changes but to the changes generally associated with the current level of activity. In order to keep this in view, we have brought into Fig. 11 the regression of changes in trade union membership on unemployment already shown in Fig. 10. Each year's change in membership is entered by an unringed date, which will of course lie vertically above or below the entry for the wage change of that year. (We lack these entries for 1888–1892.) The two regressions have been entered on a common scale in that the standard deviations of the dependent variables have been given the same extension, and their means have been set at the same level on the ordinate. We have now to ask, in effect, whether each ringed date we have noted as exceptional has its unringed entry close to it or not: whether for instance, a wage rise greater than we should expect from the current level of unemployment is associated with a rise in union membership also greater than we should expect from that level.

We cannot compare the wage change of 1889 with the current change in membership, as we lack annual figures for total membership before 1892; but then it was over 1·5 million, whereas a single estimate for 1888 (Clegg, Fox & Thompson, 1964, table i) gives just half that figure, and all we know of the outburst of pushfulness signalised at the time as the New Unionism agrees with this estimated doubling of membership within four years, and suggests the attribution to that pushfulness of the outstanding rise in wages in 1889. That of 1899, however, does not seem to be associated with any exceptional rise in trade union membership: an evident alternative condition is the coming of the Boer War. But the association with membership reappears in the wage reductions of 1901 and 1902, which went with changes in membership clearly less favourable to the unions than would have been expected from current business activity alone; we know also that the unions lay at the time under the shadow of a legal decision, in the Taff Vale case, which exposed them all to the risk, and some of them to the experience, of actions for damages if they struck. The outstanding rise of wages in 1906 was associated with an increase of membership which itself was not much bigger than was to be expected from the level of activity during the year, but which should perhaps be considered in conjunction with the clearly exceptional increase of the year following, and with the Act of 1906 that removed the unions' disability in striking. There is no drop in membership of a size to account for the big fall in wages in 1908: what is remarkable is rather the extent to which membership held up then and in 1909, the two years of by far the worst unemployment in the whole span now under consideration. No doubt this inhibited the membership, however well its numbers were maintained. In such circumstances, numbers may be no guide to current pushfulness, even though their being kept up when in other such years they would have fallen off will make us look for a push as soon as trade improves.

So far we have been taking the exceptional changes in wages, and asking if they were linked with an exceptional change in trade union membership: we must now ask whether there were any entries of this second kind to be noticed. There is in fact one such, that of 1911, a year of high activity which brought a wage rise of no more than the size to be expected, and so in no way commensurate with the year's outstanding increase in union membership. But we should note that the next year, with no higher level of activity, brought a substantially greater rise in wages.

We conclude that some exceptional changes of wages occurred that were not associated with any difference in trade union pushfulness, in so far as that is indicated by the current change in union membership; and there was one big rise in membership that was not immediately associated with an exceptional rise in wages; but on three or four occasions an association did appear. This history of the times, moreover, gives us reason to believe that these associations mark causation, and reveal a differential effect of trade union pushfulness on wage movements. That this effect seems to have been confined to certain years may be ascribed either to changes in union membership providing only an intermittent indication of pushfulness, or to this pushfulness itself deflecting the course of wages only in certain circumstances.

To this study of some apparently exceptional years in the U.K. we can add one or two cases suggested by Fig. 9.

One is an earlier phase in the U.K. itself: the rise of wages in 1880–1883 was exceptionally small. It is tempting to connect this with the great weakening, indeed in some sectors the collapse, of trade unionism in the preceding depression, which had been unusually protracted and, in its last two years, extremely severe. The Webbs (1920, pp. 345–50) saw this as 'a general rout of the Trade Union forces'. 'The depression of 1879 swept . . . many hundreds of trade societies into oblivion. . . . Widespread national organisations shrank up practically into societies of least influence, concentrated upon the strongholds of their industries. . . . In some districts, such as South Wales, Trade Unionism practically ceased to exist.' Yet this was not a 'total collapse'. 'The backbone of the movement remained intact. In the engineering and building trades the great national societies, though they were denuded of their reserve funds, retained their membership. Nor was it only the trade friendly societies that weathered the storm. The essentially trade organisations of the cotton operatives, and of the Northumberland and Durham miners, maintained their position with only a temporary contraction of membership.' Such unions remained in a position to take traditional advantage of the improvement of trade that set in during 1880 and soon went far, while the membership that had fallen away was most of it a growth only of 1871–1874 and could not now lose a bargaining power it had not previously possessed. To these reasons for doubting whether the weakness of unionism by the end of 1879 was a sufficient reason for the failure of wages to rise much in the next recovery, we may add that the rise of wages was also exceptionally small at this time in France, where there could have been little change in the still negligible power of unionism. There is also in Sweden a later instance of an undoubted prostration of unionism being followed by what for the times was a big rise in wages. After the defeat of the unions in the general strike and the long drawn out struggle in the metal trades in 1909, membership declined until by the end of 1911 it was little more than half that of 1908, and the recovery in 1912 was small: yet by that year the average earnings of men in industry had also risen by $12\frac{1}{2}$ per cent over those of 1908 (Bagge, Lundberg, Svennilson 1933, part 2, table 188).

There were two negative phases in France when wages rose, those of 1874–1879 and 1909. The first came at a time when, at least until 1878, every sort of workers' organisation lay crushed, after the overthrow of the Commune, under a régime of surveillance and repression. The second, however, if it had stood alone, might well be connected with the growth of trade union membership by more than half over the six preceding years, and the increase in the number of strikes from an average of about 600 a year in 1898–1903 to nearly 1100 in 1904–1909.[1]

In the U.S.A. two phases seem exceptional. The negative phase of 1884–1885 brought an exceptionally small fall in wages. *Bradstreet* (Commons, 1921, vol. II, p. 361) said of the first year that 'among industrial wage-earners reductions in wages have been greatest where there have been no industrial organisations or weak ones. Where

[1] Levine, 1914, pp. 70, 105, 194; *Annuaire Statistique de le France, Rétrospectif*, 1961, ch. 6, table viii.

trade unionism is strongest contract rates and united resistance have combined to retard the downward tendency of wages.' In the next year resistance was even stronger, and it was signified by the success of two strikes, the first against a wage cut of 10 per cent, on Jay Gould's railroads – 'here a labour organisation for the first time dealt on an equal footing with the most powerful capitalist in the country' (Commons 1921, vol. II, p. 370). The organisation was the Knights of Labor, and this was its heyday, while at the same time the national unions devoted to 'pure and simple unionism' were gathering the strength that was to appear in the formation of the A.F. of L. in 1886. The second apparent exception was on the other side – that the rise in the positive phase of 1905–1908 was so small. This was a time when union membership, which may have increased fourfold between 1898 and 1904, suddenly ceased to grow, even fell back a little (Barnett, 1916). As both causes and complements of this there came the attack on unionism and the closed shop led by the National Association of Manufacturers, the purposeful opposition of the giant corporations, and the increasing use of the injunction by the courts.

The discussion here directed to the movement of wages should be extended to that of hours of work. In Section 11 below we note how emergent unions took the shortening of hours as a major aim, which they sometimes attained by strikes. There were waves of such action; and without it, what reductions there were in the hours of manual workers seem to have depended mainly on legislation, and the enlightenment of some advanced employers. It is therefore tempting to see in the shortening of hours an effect more clearly attributable to unionism than any in the course of wages. This is the more likely, because changes in the hours of work usually have to be applied to a number of workmen collectively, and cannot, so readily as changes in wages, be made in any one man's bargain: they are therefore naturally facilitated by the coming of collective bargaining. This does not mean, however, that they are impossible without it. The general tendency for shorter hours to go with higher rates of pay had established itself as a fact of the market before there was much trade unionism. That hours in a given industry were commonly shorter in the big cities may have been due not only to the greater strength of formal or informal combination there, but also to the general tendency of pay to rule higher there. The progressive rise in real wages in this period would have made men willing to give up some additional purchasing power to get more leisure, union or no union, and we cannot say that without the union they could not have given their wishes effect, though it might have been only later.

What is left in the mind by this survey of the association between trade union activity and wage movements may well depend on the presumptions with which one approached it. If one supposed that trade unions generally made the course of money wages very different from what it would have been in their absence, one will have been impressed by the lack of any clear and general association. Trends of membership and of wages do not invariably rise and fall together. The response of wages to the conjuncture has occurred in much the same way in differing states of unionism. The response is not invariable, but not all the exceptions can be attributed to some special strength or weakness of union at the time; and on the other side there have been exceptional changes in union membership without apparent disturbance of the response. Where an association between union activity and wage movements does appear, the activity may be effect as well as cause. But if, on the other hand, one had been inclined to think that collective bargaining mediated rather than deflected the market forces that bear on wage changes, one would have been given pause by a number of instances of wage changes that were not to be expected from the market forces of the time but were explicable by the current strength or weakness of the unions and the known course of events.

The upshot may well be, that trade unions exerted a pressure itself intermittent and varying in circumstances which sometimes did and sometimes did not allow it to take effect.

One of these circumstances will have been the current propensity of product prices to rise or fall. Evidently employers will have found it easier to concede a wage rise, for instance, at times when the prices of their products were already rising or when customers were unlikely to meet a raised price by buying less, than at times when if prices were changing at all they were coming down. Such variations of the market environment are suggested by the tides of commodity prices that rose and fell together in a number of countries. Let us see whether they can add anything to our understanding of wage movements.

5. The course of prices in world commodity markets

We know how long waves ran through many of these prices from 1815 to 1914, with an alternation of falling and rising trends each lasting for some 20 to 25 years, and largely in phase with one another (Kuznets, 1930). This tide of world commodity prices is charted from 1860 onwards in Fig. 12 by two indexes – Imlah's merchandise price index for the net retained imports of the U.K., and Rousseaux's overall index of the prices of the principal agricultural and industrial products in U.K. markets. Though both indexes thus relate to the U.K., we may take the prices in this, the principal internationally trading economy of those days, whose market moreover was almost completely open, as representative of the prices at which other countries generally would be dealing so far as they traded in primary products (Imlah) or also (Rousseaux) in manufactures. The indexes of the import prices of our other countries[1] in fact agree with Imlah so closely in their movements that we can take U.K. prices as a tide chart of commodity prices generally. The indexes of Imlah and Rousseaux also agree closely, save that Imlah's index bears more mark of the cotton famine of the 1860s, Rousseaux's of the boom of 1871–1873; and that Rousseaux's rises more than Imlah's from 1895 to 1913.

These indexes show a marked pattern in common. It has three phases. At the outset, prices ruled high – higher than they ever would again until the First World War, though not higher, we may add, than they had been in the preceding booms ever since the Napoleonic Wars. Then comes a long sustained fall. Imlah's index shows it as beginning with the recovery of American exports at the end of the Civil War, in Rousseaux's its onset is interrupted by the boom after the Franco-Prussian War. It went on until 1895, and it brought prices down by 40 per cent. But 1895 is a clearly marked turning point, and the third phase was one of a strongly rising trend, until the First World War.

We have reason to expect that these movements exerted some

---

[1] France: C. P. Kindleberger *et al.*, *The Terms of Trade: a European case study* (1956), table 2–4B, p. 24. Germany: *Vierteljahrshefte zur Konjunkturforschung* (1926), Ergänzungsheft 2. Sweden: *Statistisk Oversikt av det Svenska Näringslivets Utveckling, åren 1870–1915* (Kommers-kollegium, Stockholm, 1913); Kindleberger, op. cit., table 2–4B. U.S.A.: R. E. Lipsey, *Price and Quantity Trends in the Foreign Trade of the United States* (1963), table G.8, pp. 422–23, NBER index.

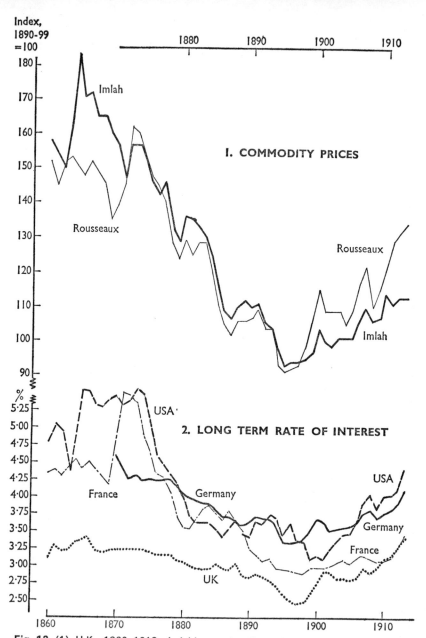

Fig. 12 (1) U.K., 1860–1913: Imlah's merchandise price index for net retained imports, and Rousseaux's overall index of the prices of the principal agricultural and industrial products, both 1890–1899=100.

(2) Four countries, 1860–1913: The long-term rate of interest.

Sources: (1) B. R. Mitchell & P. Deane, *Abstract of British Historical Statistics*, ch. xvi. (2) E. H. Phelps Brown with Sheila V. Hopkins, 'The Course of Wage-rates in five countries, 1860–1939', in *Oxford Economic Papers*, ii, 2.

influence, be it only permissive, on the course of money wages. Insofar as the prices of raw materials fall, it is true, money wages in manufacture can be raised without increase of unit costs; and conversely for rises in those prices. But other influences work the other way. A rise or fall in the prices of the raw materials and foodstuffs that enter into the wage-earner's consumption will strengthen or weaken the current propensity to claim a rise in wages. More generally, a sense of the direction in which the tide of prices has set will enter into the employer's judgement of the risk he is taking in raising his own selling prices, and therefore his ability to raise the money wages he pays without cutting into his profit margin. It could happen, conceivably, that a general rise in the prices of raw materials was attended by no more rise in product prices than was needed to offset the rise in costs on that account alone. In the short run, indeed, even less than this may follow, and the variations of raw material costs fall only on profit margins. Experience suggests, however, that in the longer run not only will profit margins be restored, but some sympathetic if not proportionate movement will occur in other elements of costs, and in prices. These other elements, especially pay, have their own inbuilt propensity to rise. The inbuilt resistance to this is the employer's sense of the risk he takes of damaging his business by the consequential raising of his prices. At a time when if prices are changing at all they are coming down he will rate that risk high. When their general tendency is upwards, even though that be due to causes quite other than wage rises, he will rate the risk lower, for in raising his own price now he will only be doing what others have been doing recently and others again are likely to be doing at the same time as he. Wage claims, in a word, will encounter less resistance when the market environment is soft than when it is hard (Phelps Brown & Hart, 1952). A general and sustained trend of prices in the world commodity markets must powerfully influence that environment.

That the rise and fall of the tide of world commodity prices was in fact accompanied by changes in the expectations and prevailing sentiment of the business community is borne out by the 'Gibson paradox' – the parallel courses of commodity prices and long-term interest rates. Fig. 12 illustrates this. It remains a paradox so long as we think in Quantity Equation terms, and suppose that, at a time when the quantities of goods sold were increasing, the price level would rise only in consequence of a sufficient expansion in the supply of money, for it is hard to see why the trend of interest rates should be upward when money was becoming ever more plentiful. The paradox disappears if we allow the possibility that the rise of the price level may come about without an antecedent increase in the stock of money, for such a rise implies (other things being equal) an extension of the demand for monetary balances, and higher rates of interest (Phelps Brown & Ozga, 1955). The general level of prices can rise in this way if particular price rises originating in the balance of supply and demand for particular products or factors of production are passed on, and compensated, by rises of other prices and money incomes. Recent years of full employment have shown how a tacit conspiracy to do this can be formed and perpetuate itself when once each man who takes part in it comes to believe that the others are in it too.

There are thus intelligible ways in which the tide of world commodity prices might exert a sympathetic influence on the course of wages. Does any such influence appear on a comparison of the indexes?

There is this in common at the outset, that in four of our five countries money wages were rising fast in the phase of high commodity prices in the 1860s. We cannot bring the U.S.A. into the comparison, because there the movements of wages were dominated by the Civil War and the sharp reaction that followed. But in all the other four countries the rate of rise of money wages was high, even before the boom of the early 70s gathered way. France, we have seen, went its own way, and the rise of 1·5 per cent a year there in the 1860s was to be surpassed in the 1870s, but was still a good deal higher than anything after 1885. In Germany and Sweden the 2 per cent or more a year of the 1860s exceeded the rates prevailing subsequently until the mid-90s. The U.K., also with 2 per cent, showed a much higher rate than ever after until the First World War.

In contrasting this first phase with what followed, we have already brought out another point of similarity – the generally lower rates of rise of money wages during part at least of the ensuing phase of falling commodity prices. But here, and in the transition to the phase of rising prices that followed, there was more variety in the course of money wages, and more divergence from that of prices. On the one hand, Germany, Sweden and the U.S.A. agree in a sharp lift of the rate of rise of money wages in the mid-90s, just when the tide of commodity prices turned so decidedly. The coincidence is suggestive; but before we read causality into it, we must explain why it does not appear in France and the U.K. In both these countries the great change in the rate of rise of money wages came about not in the mid-90s but ten years before, and in both countries thereafter the rate of rise kept on a level trend until the last few years before the War – a rate of not far from one per cent a year, rather less in France, rather more in the U.K. Neither in the inception of this phase, nor in its persistence through the 1890s, is there any sign of agreement with the phases of world commodity markets. That France was a relatively insulated economy is arguable, and certainly (as we shall see) the cost of living rose less in France from the 1890s than in the other countries. But the U.K. market was wide open at this time: if the argument about the effect of commodity prices on the market environment holds anywhere it should hold for the U.K. above all, especially in the presence of trade unions then at least as well able to press a claim as those of any other country. Admittedly, the rise in the price of imports was smaller in the U.K. than in the other countries except Sweden.[1] But we cannot put any weight on this without having to explain why the biggest increase in import prices, in France, went with a low rate of rise of money wages; and the smallest increase, in Sweden, with the highest rate.

We conclude that in three countries – Germany, Sweden and the U.S.A. – there was sufficient agreement in the phases of money wage and commodity price movements throughout, and especially in the sharp change of both at the mid-90s, to make us suspect some connection between them. But if this connection held also for France and the U.K. it was overlaid by other forces.

In our quest for these, we must next ask whether the wage-earner's cost of living moved differently from the prices we have been considering, and whether any such differences were associated with wage movements.

---

[1] According to Imlah's index and the indexes cited in fn. 1, p. 105, import prices in 1913 stood at the following percentages above the average of 1893–1897 (Sweden 1895 only):

France	29	U.K.	18
Germany	26	U.S.A.	21
Sweden	10		

The corresponding percentages for the components of Rousseaux's index are: agricultural products 28, principal industrial products 57.

6. The movements of the cost of living

For each of our countries we have an index of the cost of living, compiled to show the changes in the aggregate cost of a 'basketful' made up to represent the budgets of wage-earning households. We shall have more to say about the meaning of these indexes when we come to measure real wages (Section 11). For the present we are concerned with them only in so far as they suggest a pressure towards higher money wages in years when they were rising, and the suspension of that pressure when they were stationary or falling. They are shown in Fig. 13.

In part their movements only reflect those of world commodity prices. In all countries the cost of living was on a level or rising trend through the 1860s; stood lower in 1895 than it had done in the early 70s; and rose a good deal between 1900 and the war. But within similarities so broadly defined there is room for many differences, in extent of movement and the timing of turning-points. Such differences are to be expected. Many of the staples of world markets, it is true, were also staples of wage-earners' consumption, but their prices in the home market – food, for example, in Germany – might depend on tariffs; and a good deal else in the wage-earner's budget, especially housing, was not traded internationally. Hence differences amounting to contrasts between the patterns of the five countries in Fig. 13 – the fall from the 70s, for instance, reaching its lowest point in 1887 in Sweden but in France not until 1900; or Germany following a level trend through 1880–1899 while the U.K. and the U.S.A. both came down by a sixth or more; or the U.K. alone standing lower at the end of the whole period than at the outset.

Do such features, distinctive of the cost of living, promise to add anything to our account of the movements of money wages? A detailed comparison of Fig. 13 with the rates of rise of money wages in Fig. 3 compels us to answer, little or nothing.

That the fluctuations of the cost of living were contained within narrower limits in France than in any of the other countries might be connected with the relatively narrow movements of the rate of rise of French wages, were it not that there is so little agreement in the course of what change there is. It is true that a rate of rise sustained around 1·5 per cent a year was accompanied by a rising trend of the cost of living through the first two decades, but there was no change

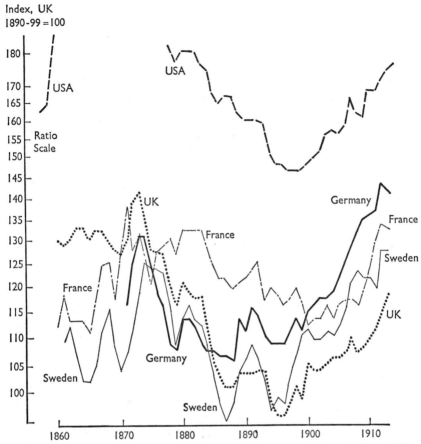

Index, UK
1890-99 = 100

Fig. 13 Five countries, 1860–1913: Indexes of cost of living, all as relative to U.K. 1890–1899 = 100.
Sources: Appendix 3 and Table 2, I. 4.

in this trend to account for the exceptional lift in the rate of rise of wages in the later 70s. It is true, again, that a lower rate of rise of wages, at less than 1 per cent, set in just as the cost of living began to fall in 1884, and was accompanied by a downward trend in that cost until its own termination about 1893; but while at that point the rate of rise of wages tended upwards, the cost of living continued to fall for some years – not until 1909 did it regain its level of 1893.

Among the greater fluctuations of the earlier years in the other four countries, the exceptional movements of money wages in the Civil

War in the U.S.A. and in the cycle of the early 70s in Europe were associated with equally exceptional movements of the cost of living. But after that the agreement was more qualified. In Germany, Sweden and the U.S.A., it is true, the rise of money wages proceeded at a lower rate until the mid-90s and thereafter at a higher rate down to the war, and in all three countries this agrees with the cost of living, which rose greatly from the later 90s onwards, whereas before it had been stationary or falling. It is also true that in the U.S.A., where the cost of living fell most in that earlier phase, the rate of rise of money wages was lower than in the other two countries. But only in the U.S.A. do the turning-points agree: the cost of living reached its lowest point in Sweden in 1887, in Germany in 1888, and the trends were upwards from those points onwards, whereas in both countries it was not until the mid-90s that the rate of rise of money wages increased. In the U.K., moreover, the biggest of all the falls in the cost of living, ending at the mid-90s in a sharp transition to a strong and sustained increase, went with a rise in money wages that for some thirty years followed the same steady trend of one per cent a year.

It will be seen that the movements of money wages agreed with those of the cost of living in so far as these in turn agreed with the course of world commodity prices; but not with those movements of the cost of living that are peculiar to itself. In an age familiar with cost of living escalation, this conclusion may be surprising. But before the First World War the cost of living was not generally measured. Nor was a rise in that cost accepted as the compelling argument for a wage rise that it has come to seem of late: the tradition was rather that of earlier years, when bad harvests brought a dear loaf from time to time but wages did not change on that account. Whatever the reason, the fact is definite. The agreement noted in Section 5 between the tidal movements of money wages and commodity prices cannot be explained by the varying pressure that those prices exerted upon money wages through their effects upon the cost of living.

It may be, however, that there was more connection between money wages and the prices of the wage-earners' own products. This connection will have run through productivity. With a given course of product prices, a greater rise in productivity will have allowed money wages to rise more; with a given course of money wages, it will have allowed product prices to rise less. We therefore go on to examine the evidence for productivity.

7. The rise of productivity

To find an indication of the changes in physical output per head of the occupied population, we shall draw on the estimates of national money income per occupied person that are described in Appendix 2, and reduce them to real terms with the aid of appropriate price indexes. For Germany we have been able to calculate the deflator implicit in the series given by Hoffmann (1965) for the net domestic product in current and in constant prices. Elsewhere we have had to put together our own indexes. The main components of final output are the sales of goods and services, and investment. The available price series do not match these components directly, and all that we have been able to do is to combine the cost of living, industrial wholesale prices and money wages, with weights 70, 15, 15. In Period Three the effect of applying this simple formula to deflate national income can be compared with the much more sophisticated contemporary estimates of the national product at constant prices, and in all five countries the two prove to run very close together indeed. It is arguable that at such a time as this, when prices of all kinds rose greatly, many indexes will give much the same result, and the test is not severe; but our index passes it as well for the U.S.A. as for any country, though the rise of prices there was smaller, and some of the changes from year to year were sharper, than elsewhere. In Period One we have at least no alternative, in four of our countries, to the use of some simple blend of the few available ingredients.

The course of final prices that our indexes suggest is shown in Fig. 14. There are three patterns. In the present instance, as in several others, Germany and Sweden follow a common course. They share with the U.K. and the U.S.A. the fall and rise that we have already seen in world commodity prices, but with this difference, that they reach their lowest point in the cyclical trough of 1885 or 1887, whereas the U.K. and the U.S.A. do not reach theirs until the trough of 1895–1896 or 1897–1898. In this, and in their general course between 1880 and 1913, the U.K. and the U.S.A. resemble one another and compose a second pattern. All four countries partake in the rise from the 1890s down to the First World War, but in none did it exceed an average annually compounded rate of 1·2 per cent. Our index of final prices in France shows a third pattern. This resembles the second in reaching its lowest point shortly after 1895, but differs from

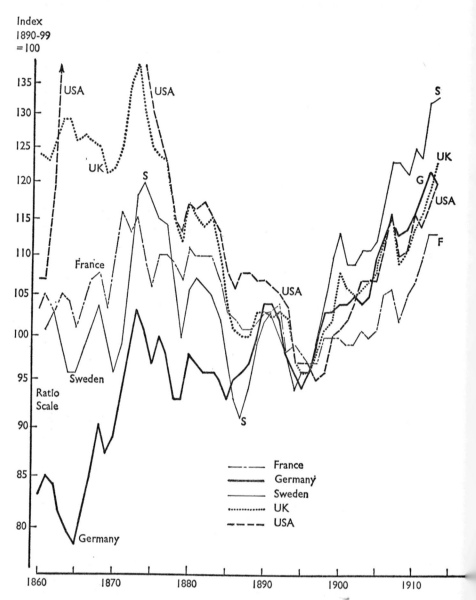

Fig. 14 Five countries, 1860–1913 : Indexes of G.N.P. deflator, based on 1890–1899 in each country.
Source : Appendix 3.

both first and second in sustaining its initially rising trend until after 1880, and in moving more gently, in both cycle and trend, at all times until 1905, when it begins to match the now rapid movements of the U.K.

The close similarity within each of the two pairs of countries, and the substantial elements of similarity between all five, suggest that here we have a factor which in each economy taken by itself was largely exogenous. Movements common to a number of countries arise, it is true, out of decisions taken in each of them, and these decisions are not explicitly co-ordinated. They are taken, however, in the light of circumstances of which some are common, notably the movements of international commodity markets. Divergences to which they may lead are checked by the balance of payments in international trade. Given experience of working in this setting, moreover, and knowledge of what others are doing, the decision-takers may find it prudent to fall into step with one another, they may develop and rely upon a consensus. The checks may then seldom be called into action; and this may be so, whatever (within limits) the pace, provided that they keep in step. In such a case, the movement of the level of final prices constitutes a largely exogenous factor in the determination of the course of money wages in each country: unless it be in a country which fills for the time the role of leader in the formation of the consensus.

This is a theme to which we shall return. In the meantime our object is to use the index of final prices in order to pull the veil of money aside and obtain an estimate of income per occupied person in real terms. When the index is used to deflate an index of national income (for Germany and the U.K., net domestic product) per occupied person, we get an index of real output of all kinds per person engaged in producing it: that is, on the broadest front, and with corresponding breadth of tolerance, an index of productivity.

The resultant series of real national income per occupied person appear in Fig. 15. It will be seen that we have made bold to express four of the series in a common unit, the £ sterling with purchasing power as in 1905: we expressed each series at the prices of 1905 in its own currency, and converted these series into £s at the par of exchange throughout. If the use of the par is justified – we discussed this in Section 1.A.5 – it enables us to compare not only the movements but also the levels of productivity in different countries.

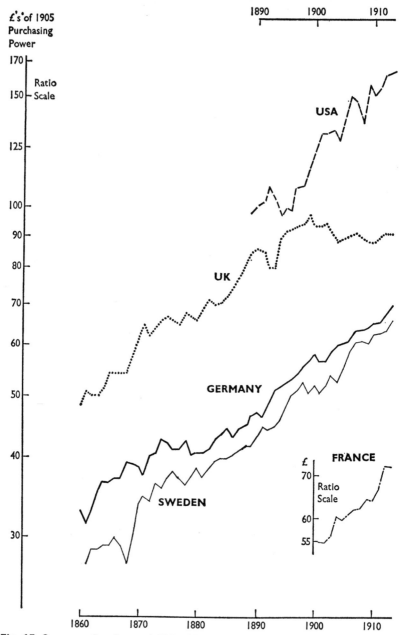

Fig. 15 Germany, Sweden and U.K., 1860–1913, and U.S.A. 1889–1913: Real income generated per occupied person in whole economy (national income per occupied person divided by G.N.P. deflator). France, 1901–1913: Gross product per occupied person in whole economy; all in £s of 1905 purchasing power.
Sources: Germany, Sweden, U.K. and U.S.A.: Appendix 3. France: G.N.P., A. Sauvy, in 'Rapport Général sur le Revenu National', *Journal officiel,* 7 April 1954, Conseil Economique, Avis et Rapports, 14; G.N.P. deflator, Appendix 3.
Series in other countries converted to £s at par of exchange.

But such comparisons are subject to two further qualifications. In each country, the estimated level of productivity in any year relatively to 1905 depends on the use of a deflator, and the deflators of the different countries are constituted variously. In all four countries, again, we have left the unpaid family workers in the occupied population, for lack of a sufficiently continuous enumeration within each country; but by the end of the Period, at least, it appears that they were proportionately more numerous in Germany and Sweden than in the U.K. and the U.S.A., and that their removal would raise the estimated product per head by as much as a fifth in the first two countries, against no more than a ninth in the second two.

We have hesitated to bring France into these comparisons. Our only annual estimates for France, those by Sauvy, are cast in 1938 francs, and though we can extend our composite index of final prices so as to reduce them to the prices of 1905, that means reducing them in the ratio of 1 to 9, and in so great a change the margin of error is wide. It happens also that Sauvy's estimates are of the gross national product, whereas in the other four countries we have taken the net. In Fig. 15 we have therefore shown the French series in a separate frame; but this still allows us to compare it with the four others in respect of its rate of rise.

What might strike the eye first in Fig. 15 is how high that rate was in all five countries: but in all of them save the U.S.A. it was in fact lower in this Period than it has been since 1950. The progress cumulated through forty or fifty years was great, but the average annual advance that built it up was still lower than that achieved, save in the U.S.A., since the Second World War.

When we turn to the relative movements of the different countries from time to time, we find a simple pattern: until the 1890s the movements are parallel; after that they diverge. From 1861 to about 1899 productivity as we measure it here rose at almost exactly the same rate from end to end – 1·65 per cent a year – in Germany, Sweden and the U.K. These countries agree, moreover, in three phases of variation about that trend – a more rapid rise in the 1860s, a slower rise from 1871 to 1886, and then ten years of more rapid rise again.

But the prevailing similarity ended with the century. Whether it included the U.S.A. we do not know; but the series that now becomes available shows a rise of productivity in the U.S.A. from 1895 to 1913 more rapid than we have found anywhere else – at as much as 2·81 per cent a year. For France our only available estimate shows a rise of nearly 2·4 per cent a year over 1901–1913. Swedish productivity maintained the higher annual rate of rise that it entered upon around 1886 – about 1·81 per cent. German productivity fell off a little from the rate of improvement it had kept up through the 1880s and 90s, and rose by no more than 0·94 per cent a year. But, most remarkable, in the U.K. productivity actually declined: it fell sharply from a peak in 1899, the fall was checked but there was no recovery, and productivity stood lower in 1913 than it had done twenty years before. This experience stands out in contrast with that of all four other countries at this time and, even more sharply, with that of the U.K. itself in earlier years: the abruptness of the change of course in 1900 is especially challenging. We shall come back to it in Section 12, and consider its possible causes.

The rate of rise in France seems high. We have derived it from estimates of the gross national product in 1938 francs by Sauvy (Appendix 2). There is one other source, Perroux's estimate (Appendix 2) of the national income in current francs in 1898 and 1909, that provides a basis of comparison. Deflating Perroux's figures by our own index of final prices, we derive an annual average rise between 1898 and 1909 in the real product per occupied person of only 1·3 per cent: our estimates based on Sauvy begin only in 1901, but over 1901–1909 they show an average annual rise of nearly 2·5 per cent. The difference is a warning: this is a field in which the materials for any close estimate are lacking. Yet that French productivity was in fact rising rapidly at this time is borne out by the estimates based on physical production in industry which we shall describe later in this Section.

Productivity in the economy as a whole can be raised in two ways – by raising output per head in any one sector, and by transferring labour from sectors of lower to those of higher output per head. We can make some estimate of the extent to which the rises of overall productivity that we have been considering came about in the second of these ways, in all our countries save France. The sources from which we have drawn our figures of the national product provide estimates of the income generated in different sectors, and we have ourselves assembled figures of the distribution of the occupied population between those sectors. This last task is hazardous by reason of disparities and uncertainties of classification, whether it be in matching the coverages of the production statistics and the census of population, or of one census and the next; estimates of the numbers effectively employed in agriculture give especial difficulty. But so far as we have succeeded, we can proceed to estimates of income generated per occupied person in each sector.

These estimates are shown in Fig. 16. It appears at once that in all four countries, save at 1871 in Great Britain, the income generated per occupied person was higher in industry than in agriculture, and usually much higher. The rise of numbers in industry relatively to agriculture which was going on in all four countries would therefore of itself raise income per occupied person in the economy as a whole. There was wide scope, moreover, for the relative growth of industrial employment: Table 10 shows how large the agricultural sector still was around 1890 in all countries save the U.K.

It follows that the rises of productivity in Fig. 15 owed a great deal to shifts between sectors. We have recalculated national income per

Table 10 Proportions of net national product contributed by agriculture and industry (as variously defined) at dates around 1890, in five countries.

| Country | Date | % of national product contributed by | |
		Agriculture	Industry
France	1892	37	32
Germany	av. 1886–1894	29	47
Sweden	1890	34	22
G.B.	1891	9	41
U.S.A.	av. 1889–1890	22	

Sources:
France: Income—F. Perroux, 'Prise de vues sur la croissance de l'économie française, 1780–1950', in International Association for Research in Income and Wealth, *Income & Wealth*, series v (1955), table ii.
Germany: W. G. Hoffmann, F. Grumbach and H. Hesse, *Das Wachstum der deutschen Wirtschaft seit der Mitte des 19 Jahrhunderts*, part 2, table 122.
Sweden: O. Lindahl, *Sveriges Nationalprodukt 1861–1951* (Konjunkturinstitutet, Stockholm, Meddelanden Serie B20), table 1.
G.B.: P. Deane & W. A. Cole, *British Economic Growth 1688–1959*, table 37.
U.S.A.: Income in agriculture—E. Budd, 'Factor Shares 1850–1910', in N.B.E.R. *Income & Wealth, no. 24. Trends in the American Economy in the Nineteenth Century*; see Appendix 2 of present work.

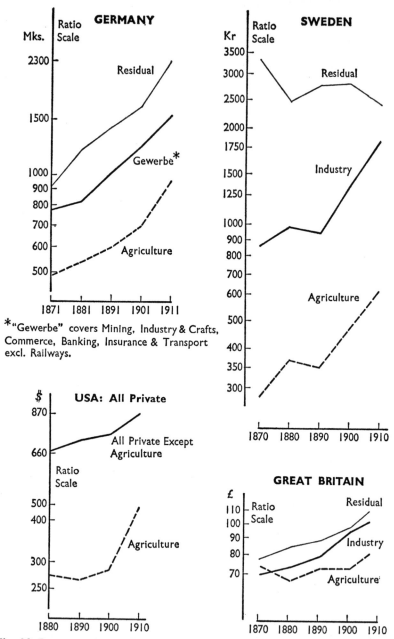

Fig. 16 Four countries, 1870–1911: Income generated per occupied person in agriculture and other sectors of the economy, at current prices in each country's own currency.

Sources: Germany: as in Appendix 2, D I (*b*) and Table 108. Sweden: Appendix 2, Tables 115 and 122. Great Britain: as in Appendix 2, U.K., D I (*b*) and Table 131. U.S.A.: as in Appendix 2, D I (*b*) and E I (*b*).

occupied person on the assumption that the deployment of the occupied population between sectors remained the same throughout as at first. In each country the income so calculated rose less than the actual: by the end of the period the actual income exceeded the hypothetical by some 2 per cent in G.B., 6 per cent in Germany, 11 per cent in the U.S.A., and more than 50 per cent in Sweden. This last figure may seem improbable, but it only shows the effect of an initially small industrial sector with a much higher productivity than its agrarian setting growing rapidly and taking much labour over from that setting.

The rise in productivity brought about in this way by inter-sectoral transfer, independently of improvements in any one sector, is not to be dismissed as a statistical artifact. No less than the rise in productivity brought about by technical advances, it provides a greater product out of which to remunerate the factors of production. The transfer of labour, moreover, will generally have been possible only because it was linked with investment. A sector of higher output per head will almost certainly be such because capital per head is greater there too, and very likely also because its labour force is more highly qualified. Labour therefore cannot be transferred to it without new investment, in equipment and probably also in training. This being so, the fact of transfer is in a sense irrelevant: what has raised overall productivity is a rise in the average amount of capital per worker and in the qualifications of the worker, and whether these changes are brought about on the worker's moving or where he is already is of minor consequence for our present purpose of tracing the rise in the product per head of the whole occupied population.

But for another purpose the difference between sectors is of major consequence. Productivity concerns us here especially as a factor in the determination of wage movements: with a given course of product prices, the greater the rise in productivity the greater can be the rise in money wages without a squeeze of profits. But the productivity here must be measured in the same sector as wages, and this means largely the sector called 'industry' in Table 1. For the purposes of Fig. 16 we have had to use classifications that divide up the whole economy, and these do not always draw the boundaries of 'industries' in the same way as Table 1; but it is the course of productivity within 'industry' as delimited in Table 1 that we now attempt to trace.

We can do this with the aid of existing estimates of the product of industry, which are described in Appendix 2. For France a League of Nations publication gave an index of production in manufacturing, 1894–1913, and the O.E.E.C. published an index of production in mining, manufacture and utilities, 1901–1913: the two agree in the rise from 1901 to 1913, end to end, but the League of Nations index runs higher through 1906–1912. Both indexes may overstate the rise in the aggregate, because the available figures of output come from industries which at this time were growing faster than the average. For Germany the work of Hoffmann provides annual estimates of total income generated by mining, industry and handicrafts at 1913 prices throughout. Similarly for manufacturing in the U.S.A., the work of Kendrick provides us with an index of the real output per occupied person. But for Sweden and G.B. only estimates at current prices were available, and these we have had to deflate with price indexes of our own making. We avoided wholesale prices in so far as they were prices of raw materials, and relied on such series as we could find of the prices of manufactures: here we could draw upon series for prices of manufactured exports (though these might well have a downward bias), and others for the retail prices of industrial products bought by households. In Sweden the materials did not allow us to go farther back than 1892. Our weights had to be adapted to what series were available, according to our impression of the relative size of each series' coverage, and they are rough at best. Of the resultant indexes neither is sufficiently comprehensive, and the movements of the prices that are comprised are likely if anything to have been wider than those of industrial products as a whole. The effect in Sweden and the U.K. would be to overstate the rise of productivity down to the turn of the tide of prices in the mid-90s, and understate it afterwards.

The resultant indexes of the physical product per occupied person in industry are shown in Fig. 17. Here the vertical distances between the curves for the four countries other than France express estimates of the relative size of the product per occupied person in the different countries, made in the same way as for the curves of Fig. 15, by applying the current par of exchange. When in this way we express in sterling the income generated per occupied person in each country's industry on the average of 1905, we find about £67 for Germany, £80 for Sweden, £86 for G.B., and £175 for the U.S.A., where our estimate is for manufacturing only. These figures provide

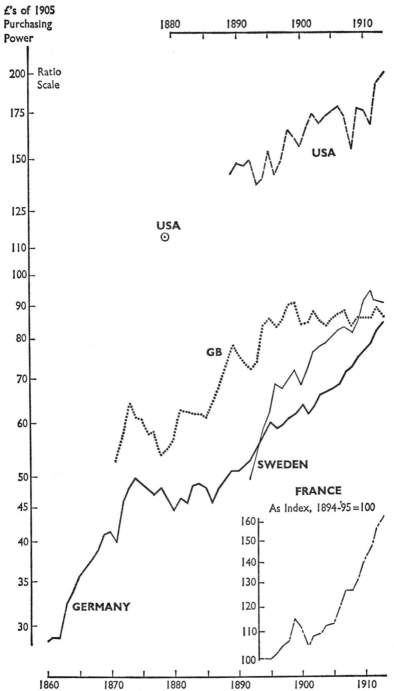

£'s of 1905 Purchasing Power

Ratio Scale

USA ⊙

USA

GB

SWEDEN

FRANCE
As Index, 1894-95 = 100

GERMANY

Fig. 17 Four countries, at dates from 1860, to 1913; Real output per occupied person in industry (in U.S.A., manufacturing only) all in £s of 1905 purchasing power. France, 1894–1913: Real output per occupied person in industry, as index 1894–95 = 100.

Sources: Germany, Sweden, Great Britain, U.S.A.: Appendix 3. France: as in Appendix 2, D I (c).

us with a peg for each country, on which to mount its own index. The
four curves in the main part of Fig. 17 therefore represent the
physical product per occupied person in the industry of each country,
expressed in £s sterling having throughout the purchasing power of
the £ over industrial products in 1905. But the French index appears
in a separate frame, because here we have no series for the value of
output that we can convert into sterling, only an index of year to
year movements.

Down to the turn of the century the relative movements of
productivity in industry shown for the different countries in Fig. 17
are much the same as those that Fig. 15 showed for productivity in
the whole economy. From 1900 onwards, again, the sudden and
sustained check to the rise of productivity in G.B. appears no less
markedly within industry alone than it did in the whole economy.
But in other respects what is most marked after 1900 is the difference
from overall productivity. Whereas this rose faster in Sweden than in
Germany, productivity within industry alone rose at about the same
rate in the two countries, with the Swedish rate of rise if anything the
lower: this is intelligible, in that overall productivity gained more in
Sweden than in Germany from the current transfer out of agriculture
into industry. In the U.S.A., again, though overall productivity rose
faster there than in any other country, the rise of productivity within
manufacturing alone seems not to have been outstanding – between
the mid-90s and 1912/13 it amounted to some 35 per cent in all,
against the 60 per cent by which productivity in the whole economy
rose over the same span.

We may ask whether our estimates for Sweden and G.B. show any
sign of the possible overflow of the amplitude of price movements,
noticed above. It is always possible that if we had had a broader-
based price index our estimates for Sweden would have shown a
smaller rise down to the mid-90s and a larger thereafter, but there is
nothing on the face of the movements in Fig. 17 to make us suspect
such a bias. The check to the rise of productivity in G.B. after 1900,
however, stands out, and if our price index did import a bias, it
would be to just that effect; but that the check is a fact and no statistical illusion is strongly supported by its undoubted presence in the
physical output of some British industries of this time – we shall
examine this in Section 12.

The extent of the estimated rise in productivity in French industry –

more than 60 per cent in less than twenty years – calls for confirmation. A recent estimate by Marczewski (Appendix 2) finds a
much smaller rise than we do between the averages of the decades
1896–1904 and 1905–1914 – 11 per cent, against our 27, and only a
small part of this difference can be due to his 'industry' including
building as ours does not. The rise of productivity as we estimate it
comes from a great rise in the index of total output, which almost
doubles. This is remarkable, but still not so remarkable as the rise at
the same time in the corresponding index (League of Nations and
O.E.E.C.) of German industrial output – from 1894 to 1913 the
French index rises by nearly 97 per cent, but the German by 154.
Both indexes probably show such great rises because their coverage is
limited to products whose output happened at this time to be growing
most rapidly, and Hoffmann's series for the output of German
industry, with its wider coverage, shows a rise over this span not of
154 but of 124 per cent. If we reduced the rise of the index of French
output in the same proportion, we should get about 78 per cent.

The course of our index of productivity in French industry also
depends on the figures we take for the industrial labour force. Here a
contrast with Germany appears – from 1896 to 1913, our figures for
this labour force in France (excluding building) rise by less than
17 per cent, in Germany (including building) by over 40; and when
total output is rising so fast, it is the higher rate that seems more
probable. Our estimates for France, moreover, are weakened by the
unreliability of the census of 1911. Yet a recent recension by a French
scholar, L. A. Vincent (Appendix 2) finds a rise in the French
industrial labour force from 1896 to 1913 even smaller than ours –
13·8 against our 16·9 per cent. The same source provides the following
estimates of output per occupied person in 1913 as a percentage of
1896: in coalmining (including lignite, coking and briquettes), 99·5;
in production of metals, 154; in metal manufactures, 156; in the
chemical industry, 154. While, therefore, the rise of productivity in
French industry at this time cannot be estimated except with more
than usual uncertainty, and the figure we ourselves give for it is
probably on the high side, there can be no doubt that it was rapid and
far-reaching, and that it stands in sharp contrast with the contemporary experience of the U.K.

Changes in productivity concern us particularly in so far as they
were a factor in wage determination. While on the side of the supply

of labour it is the wage per man that matters, on the side of demand what matters is the wage cost per unit of output. This unit wage cost is found by dividing productivity, that is, output per man, into earnings per man. Let us consider its movements.

8. Unit wage cost in industry

Our estimates of the movements of unit wage costs were made by dividing the productivity series of Fig. 17 into the corresponding series of wage-earnings in Fig. 2. The productivity series, it is true, give output per occupied person of every kind, whereas the wage-earnings were those only of manual workers; and if, other things being the same, the proportion of administrative, technical and clerical workers among all occupied persons rose, our measure of productivity would come to show too low an output per wage-earner, and too high a unit wage-cost. On the other hand, the increment of output obtained by the employment of more indirect workers will be at least partially absorbed by the payment of those workers: the movements of output per occupied person of every kind are therefore not so bad a guide to changes in the employer's ability to pay the manual worker alone. The relative numbers of indirect workers within industry were in any case much lower in our Period One than now, nor save perhaps in the last years of the Period are they likely to have been increasing very much. The proportion of white-collar workers among all occupied persons in German industry and handicrafts was 3·3 per cent in 1895, 5·8 per cent in 1907 (Hoffmann, 1965, part 2, table 24). In the whole occupied population of the U.S.A. in 1910, 'clerical and kindred' workers amounted to less than 14 per cent of the total number of manual workers outside agriculture; the corresponding proportion for Great Britain in 1911, but here combining the clerical workers with all foremen, supervisors and inspectors, and including farm workers among the manual, was under 8 per cent. Our indexes of unit wage costs are therefore unlikely to be much affected by changes in the relative numbers of indirect workers.

These indexes are shown in Fig. 18. A salient feature is the fall in British unit wage costs for some twenty years after 1877 – a fall, it seems, of exceptional persistence and extent. Perhaps, we might

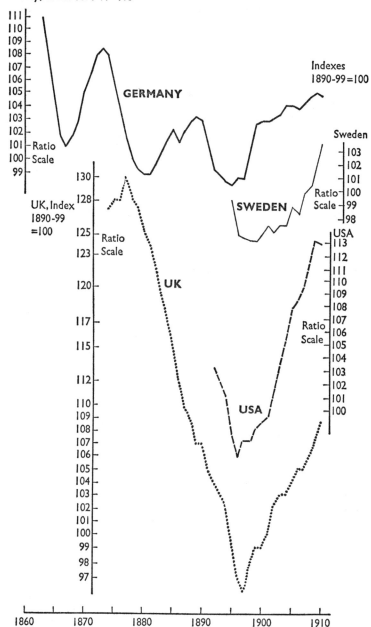

Germany, Index 1890-99 = 100

GERMANY

Indexes
1890-99 = 100

Sweden

SWEDEN

UK, Index
1890-99
= 100

UK

USA

USA

Fig. 18 Four countries, 1860–1913 : Indexes (1890–1899 = 100) of unit wage costs in industry (U.S.A. manufacturing), as 7-year moving averages.
Source : Appendix 3.

think, the movement as we see it is exaggerated, in that the curve begins at the top of an intense boom that brought with it more than the usual surge of inflation, so that the initial fall may well have done no more than bring the curve back to the level of the 1860s. But this does not seem to have happened. Between 1863 and 1873, it is true, money wage-earnings rose by more than 30 per cent, but the rise of the real product per occupied person in the whole economy (Fig. 15) was almost as great over the same span. We lack estimates before 1871 of the more closely relevant real product per occupied person in industry alone; but it would be surprising if this diverged so far, within the space of ten years, as to suggest a quite different conclusion. Most of the apparent fall in unit wage costs between 1877 and 1897 seems to have been no optical effect of cyclical fluctuation, but to have marked an effective displacement of levels prevailing in the longer term.

There remains another possibility of deception, however. Our index of industrial productivity is obtained by deflating estimates of the value added in current £s by an index of the prices of industrial products, and this index is unreliable. The available quotations are likely to contain too many semi-manufactures, responsive to the tidal movements of world commodity markets, and too few highly fabricated and therefore unstandardised products, with a greater labour content and less motile prices. In the twenty years between the mid-70s and the mid-90s, an index composed from these materials is likely to have fallen too much; and though we have sought to offset this bias by bringing in the prices of exported manufactures, if these had their own bias this too will have been downward. But if indeed our index of industrial product prices comes down too much, our estimated productivity will show too great a rise, and any fall in unit wage costs will have been correspondingly exaggerated. It is also possible that the motility of our price index contributed to the apparent sharpness of the rise in British unit wage costs after 1896.

That the German and British unit wage costs seem to have behaved so differently at this time may indeed provide a clue to the fall in the British. The industrialisation of Germany in the 1860s impinged upon a money wage-level about half the British. We have no comparative measure of the real output a head in the industries of the two countries then: but though we should expect the German to be lower, it is unlikely to have been lower by so much as a half – that is, unit wage costs in money at the current par of exchange are likely to have been lower in Germany than the U.K. in the mid-6os. Over the next forty years German money wages doubled, the British rose only by a third. Once again it is likely that there were divergences in productivity of a kind to offset the divergence in money to some extent but not altogether. It seems possible that the level of German costs was initially lower than the British, and that the extension of international competition in industrial products operated through the ensuing years not to let the German rise but to bring the British down.

It is thus possible that the fall of the British curve in Fig. 18 means what it says, and that this was an era when the British economy worked very differently from the way to which recent years have accustomed most economies. Productivity rose persistently, but money wages from end to end rose little, so unit wage costs fell progressively. But prices also fell, and – as we shall see in Section 11 below – real wages rose rapidly. It was the pressure on costs and profit margins, and not any failure of productivity and real wages to rise, that gave the era its cognomen of the Great Depression. Alfred Marshall, in his evidence to the Gold and Silver Commission in 1888, said:

> I was very much struck by observing that in some of the evidence given to show that the fall of prices was doing great harm, it was argued that we were suffering from general over-production, a malady which I contend we cannot suffer from, and that that was partly due to the fact that improvements were going on now much faster than at any other time; and the reason given for this was that when prices are falling, manufacturers are put on their mettle and exert themselves to the utmost to invent improved methods and to avail themselves of the improvements made by others, and I know, from my own observation, that this is true. But when prices are rising manufacturers are well content to let things go on as they are (Q.9816; Keynes, 1926, pp. 91–92).

We have been concerned with the distinctive movement of British unit wage costs down to the 1890s. But from then onwards, the movements in different countries do at least resemble each other much more than did those of wage-earnings in Fig. 2: divergences in wage-earnings were offset by divergences in the rise of productivity in industry. In particular, the relatively slow rise of British wages went with an even slower rise of productivity – indeed, virtually no rise at all – so that unit wage costs in industry rose substantially more in G.B. than in Germany and Sweden, though hardly more than in the U.S.A. where wages rose so fast at this time. We should expect international competition to work in this way, except where the competitors set out from different levels of costs. The divergent movements of money wage-earnings and the similar movements of unit wage costs from the mid-90s onwards may alike be attributed to the employers' resistance to wage claims having varied with the current ability of their foreign competitors to undersell them.

But while this may account for different countries moving together, it leaves unexplained the direction in which they moved. That this changed from time to time may have been due to factors operating on the competitors in common. It is significant that Fig. 18 shows much the same pattern of movements as we have already seen in world commodity prices (Fig. 12), the cost of living (Fig. 13), and final prices, or G.N.P. deflator (Fig. 14) – a high point in the early 1870s; a descent to a low point in the mid-90s; and then a rise until the War. Two common factors whose movements fit this pattern are the course of prices of primary commodities in world markets, and the rate of expansion of the supply of gold. A case for giving priority to the first of these has been argued by Phelps Brown and Ozga (1955). But whatever the ultimate cause, it is apparent from the annals and from contemporary discussion that the business communities of the day entertained different expectations from time to time about the trends of prices, and felt themselves to be working in market environments that were now more and now less repressive towards the raising of prices. However this appreciation of the situation was formed, once established it would tend to realise and perpetuate itself. A consensus of expectations that product prices would tend downwards would make any one manufacturer exceedingly apprehensive of the effects of a rise in his own costs, and disposed accordingly to bear the loss and odium of a stoppage rather than concede a wage rise that outran any rise there had been in productivity. When the consensus of opinion was rather that rises in prices were only to be expected, he would evaluate the relative cost of stoppage and concession differently.

Our observation of the degree of similarity in the movement of unit wage costs therefore suggests a hypothesis concerning the determination of wage movements. We may suppose, namely, that a recurrent if not continuous pressure to raise wages was exerted by labour, whether or not organised in trade unions. The resistance that this pressure encountered depended on the contemporary rise in productivity and on that consensus of expectations among employers which constituted for each of them his market environment. In so far as productivity rose, wages could be raised without a rise in unit wage costs. In so far as a rise in wages would raise unit wage costs, the resistance it would meet depended on employers' expectations of the consequences of covering the higher costs by higher prices. At times when prices generally, if they altered at all, were being reduced, be it only because prices of raw materials were falling, employers would feel that to raise their prices was to deviate from accepted practice, affront their customers, and risk loss of business; and where the downward trend of prices was associated with increased competition through the entry of new producers to the international market, they may even have felt themselves under pressure to get their prices down. In such a hard market environment the pressure to raise wages would be strongly resisted. At other times the general tendency of prices was upwards. Rises themselves only the consequence of higher prices of raw materials might provide a precedent for other rises that made increases possible in unit wage costs or in profit margins. Employers fearful at first of the consequences of raising their own prices would find by experience that their businesses had not suffered, because in fact they had only been taking part in a general movement. So long as each did not go farther than the others, he could accept rises in his own costs, and maintain his profit margin by raising his selling prices, without loss of business. A consensus might form from time to time, as it has done in more recent years of full employment, about the currently viable rate of rise. In such a soft market environment the pressure to raise wages would meet relatively weak resistance so long as the implied rise in unit wage costs did not go beyond the rate currently accepted as viable.

The hypothesis concerning wage determination then is, in sum, that an international trend of unit wage costs was set up that at any given time acted as an externally imposed constraint upon any given wage negotiation, such that, so long as profit margins remained unchanged, money wage-earnings could rise above the international trend of unit wage costs only to the extent that productivity rose.

But the reference here to profit margins is important. If these were squeezed, wage-earnings could rise more. There is nothing in the hypothesis, moreover, to ensure that wage-earnings will in fact be pushed up as far as the constraint will allow: if they are not, the profit margin can be widened. How in fact did the profit margin behave? We can throw some light on this from the course of the wage/income ratio in industry.

9. The wage/income ratio in industry

The significance of the ratio that average earnings per wage-earner bear to the value added per occupied person within industry was discussed in Section 1.A.6. We saw there that the movements of this ratio through time should indicate fairly closely the course of change in the division of the product of industry between pay and profits. We therefore turn to it now, to see whether times of falling unit labour costs were times of rising profit margins, and conversely.

To calculate it, we have needed estimates of the numbers occupied in the industrial sector of each country, and of the income generated in that sector annually. The estimates of numbers occupied have to be formed from the census of population, and there are familiar difficulties both in matching the classification of any one census with the boundaries of 'industry' as those are drawn in the statistics of income, and in maintaining consistency between one census and the next. The estimates of income generated are needed in current monetary terms, to match those of wage-earnings, and they are so stated in our sources for Sweden and the U.K.; but the sources for Germany and the U.S.A. give the product only in real terms, and we have had to reflate these series by applying index-numbers of prices that we have constructed ourselves. There are evident hazards here.

In these ways, however, we did obtain the series for income generated per occupied person in industry that are shown in Fig. 19: though here what is entered, as shown in the vertical scales, is only 60 per cent of the actual income throughout. This proportion has been chosen as bringing these curves conveniently near to those of wage-earnings that appear country by country in the same Figure: if the curve of wage-earnings lies above that of income, the wage-

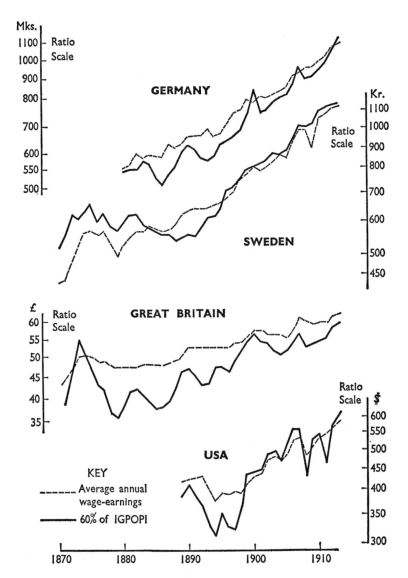

Fig. 19 Four countries, at dates from 1870, to 1913: Income generated per occupied person in industry (I.G.P.O.P.I.) reduced to 60 per cent of actual amount, compared with average annual wage-earnings, both at current prices in each country's own currency.
Source: Appendix 3.

income ratio will be above 60 per cent, and conversely. What strikes the eye first in Fig. 19 is the extent to which the two series coincide or run parallel – so far as they do this, the wage/income ratio will have remained much the same over the years. But there are substantial exceptions. In G.B. from 1880 to 1900 the income generated in industry rose faster than money wage-earnings, so that the wage/income ratio in industry will have fallen progressively. In Sweden, on the other hand, the opposite relations obtained from the outset until 1890.

The movements of the wage/income ratio are shown explicitly in Fig. 20. Because the original series are much agitated by the ups and downs of income in the trade cycle, the ratio rising sharply in the slump and falling in the boom, we present its course here in the smoothed form of a 7-year moving average. We have already noted the uncertainties of the estimated level of the ratio at any one time (1.A.6). These uncertainties do not affect its estimated changes from one time to another, but these in turn depend on the index-numbers of prices which we have used to arrive at our estimates of income in Germany and the U.S.A. We have seen that such index-numbers are apt to give much weight to the prices of primary and semi-manufactured products, and so to swing too widely for our present purpose. If they have done so here, our wage/income ratios will rise too much down to the turning point of the tide of prices in the 1890s, and fall too much afterwards. Our estimates for the U.S.A. barely begin before that turning point, and their big fall from 1895 to 1902 marks a cyclical swing rather than a trend. The movements of the German ratio are small; and though the rise down to 1895 and the fall thereafter might both have been smaller still had it not been for the swing of the price index, comparison with the much greater rise and fall of the Swedish ratio, which we could calculate without having to apply a price index, gives no reason to believe that the swing of the price index has affected the German estimates.

The movements of such curves as appear in Fig. 20 before 1890 are more extensive and diverse than we find later. The great rise in the Swedish ratio is specially striking, but receives some confirmation from Jungenfelt (1966, figs. II 5, II 6). It comes about through a rapid and sustained rise in money wage-earnings outrunning the income generated per head as we have estimated that here. The implied fall in the share of profit was not necessarily incompatible

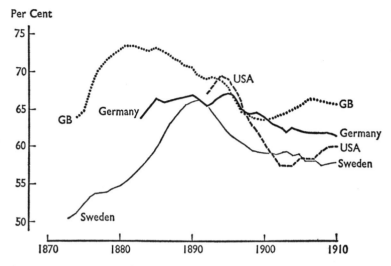

Fig. 20 Four countries at dates from 1873, to 1910: 7-year moving averages of the wage/income ratio in industry (U.S.A. manufacturing only). Source: Appendix 3.

with the maintenance of the rate of return on capital, at a time of rapid technical advance, when the capital/output ratio may well have been falling. It would have to have fallen by a third, say from 3 to 2: this is not inconceivable, but we lack evidence. An alternative explanation, suggested by the difference already noted in the showing of Fig. 20 on either side of 1890, is simply that our estimates are less reliable the farther they go back.

This may also account for the outstandingly high level of the British ratio in 1877–1886, and its subsequent progressive fall, such as we should not expect at a time when the continued fall in world commodity prices made for a hard market environment and a squeezing instead of a widening of the profit margin. Yet both these findings can be upheld as intelligible. The high level was reached initially, like the 1894 peak in the U.S.A. ratio, in a depression of exceptional severity: what we have to explain is why the British ratio did not decline in the subsequent recovery of activity, as the U.S.A. ratio did after 1895. The explanation may be that the British recovery of 1880–1882 was neither vigorous nor extensive. The return and persistence of unprofitable trading led by 1886 to the appointment of a Royal Commission on 'the depression of trade and industry', and the evidence before it revealed, as Marshall observed later, 'a depression of prices, a depression of interest, and a depression of profits. . . . I cannot see any reason for believing that there is any considerable depression in any other respect. . . . I believe that a chief cause of the depression of profits is that the employer gets less and the employé more' (Royal Commission, 1888, Qs 9824, 26). There is thus good reason to believe that the share of profits in the product of British industry at this time was exceptionally low. Equally, the pressure to restore it might well have taken effect through the ensuing years: Fig. 18 showed a fall of unit wage costs in British industry of over 13 per cent in the ten years after 1886, and this would have made it possible to combine a further reduction of product prices with a gradual widening of the profit margin. In Fig. 22 we shall see an estimate of the rate of profit on capital in the British economy outside agriculture that shows a rise setting in after 1883 and largely persisting, though checked in 1890–1893, up to a peak in 1897 corresponding to the low point in that year of the wage/income ratio.

From the early 1890s onward the movements of the wage/income ratios in Fig. 20 resemble each other more than before. There is first a phase of substantial fall. The Swedish ratio, that had been rising so long and steeply, reached a peak in 1891, and began to come down no less steeply than it had risen. In the mid-90s the British ratio accelerated its decline. After 1895 the German ratio also fell. The ratio in U.S.A. industry came down most of all, though this, as we have seen, marked the recovery from the depression of the mid-90s.

This common movement might be found surprising, because it occurred just when unit wage costs in all four countries turned upwards (Fig. 18): we might expect this to have made profit margins harder, not easier, to widen. Certainly it would have worked in that way if the market environment had remained the same; but if this changed meanwhile from hard to soft, unit wage costs and profit margins might rise together. That the market environment did so change about this time, is suggested by the turning of the tide of world commodity prices.

The new set of that tide, however, persisted down to the First World War, whereas in G.B. and the U.S.A. the fall of the wage/income ratio in industry was checked and reversed soon after 1900.

In the U.S.A. money wages rose at this time at much the same rapid rate as in Germany and Sweden, but productivity in industry seems not to have risen so fast, so unit wage costs in the U.S.A. rose more. In G.B. the rise in money wages was smaller than in any of the other countries, but productivity stood in even greater contrast – we have seen that it hardly rose at all: so that unit wage costs in the U.K. rose much like those in the U.S.A., and more than in Germany and Sweden. This relative rise in unit wage costs pressed against a price ceiling which was certainly rising now, but which any one country could still hardly raise for its own part ahead of the others. The rise of industrial product prices between the 1890s and 1912/13 was in fact very uniform: according to our index numbers it amounted to some 16 per cent in Germany, 15 in Sweden, 17 in the U.K. and 23 in the U.S.A. Even in the soft-market environment, therefore, where unit wage costs could rise in all countries, the profit margin could still be squeezed in some.

In the course of this commentary on Fig. 20 we have treated the movements of the wage/income ratio as indicating inversely those of the share of profits in the product of industry. What happened to this share, however, did not in itself tell us what was happening to the *rate* of profit on capital: we noticed, for instance, how the apparently large fall in the share of profit in the product of Swedish industry between 1870 and 1890 would have been consistent with a stable rate of profit if the capital/output ratio had declined by a third over the same span. We may remind ourselves of the identity

$$\text{share of pay} \equiv 1 - (\text{share of profit})$$
$$\equiv 1 - rk,$$

where r is the rate of profit per unit of capital, and k is the capital/output ratio, the number of units of capital per unit of output. When the share of pay was rising, rk must have been falling: but this could have come about consistently with r being constant or even rising, if k were falling. Can we make any observations of the movements of r and k at this time?

Fig. 21 displays some estimates of k. The difference between the levels of k in the three countries – with the British ratio near 2·3 in 1910, for example, the U.S.A. ratio near 2·6, and the German 3·3 – may arise in part from the sheer inadequacy of the ultimate sources of information; from divergences in any one country between the

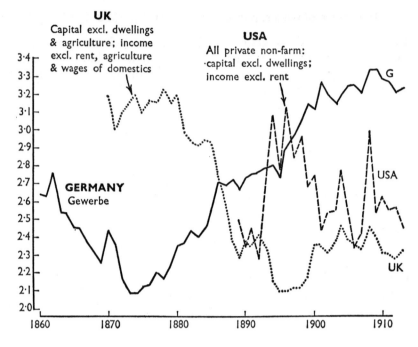

Fig. 21 Germany, U.K., U.S.A., at dates from 1860, to 1913 : Capital/output ratio in : Germany, 'Gewerbe'; U.K., whole economy excluding dwellings and agriculture; U.S.A., excluding dwellings, agriculture and government.
Sources : Appendix 3.

coverages of the estimates of capital and output; and from differences between countries in the coverage of the estimates of capital, and in the way the capital is valued. A note at the end of this Section gives some account of this last source of difference, and describes our endeavour to place our estimates for the three countries on a tolerably common footing.

But for the present it is in any case sufficient for us to compare only the year-to-year movements. The German ratio shows a remarkable and largely sustained rise, from 2·1 to over 3·2, through the nearly 40 years after 1874: in conjunction with the stability of the wage-income ratio in the 1880s and 1890s, shown in Fig. 20, this implies a progressive reduction of the rate of profit. The U.S.A. ratio, after its cyclical convulsion in the 1890s, shows no clear trend down to the War: in this it resembles the U.S.A. wage/income ratio in Fig. 20, and here the parallel movement carries a multiplicative, not a compensating implication – it leads us to expect a steep rise in the rate of profit from 1895 to 1901, with little change thereafter. The British ratio almost exactly inverts the movement of the German, but does so in 15 years instead of 40: between 1880 and 1895 it falls from near 3·2 to 2·1. A sharp reaction follows, between 1898 and 1904, but thereafter the fall is if anything resumed. Here, as in the U.S.A., we find capital/output and wage/income ratios on parallel courses, with the same implication of an opposite and even wider swing of the rate of profit.

With these expectations about the movements of the rate of profit in mind, we turn to what observations we can make of that rate directly. For this we need independent estimates of profits, but these are available as an annual series only for the U.K., with three snapshots at ten-year intervals for the U.S.A., and a single snapshot for Germany. For the rest, we can only quantify the inferences the preceding discussion has drawn qualitatively from the relative movements of the wage/income ratio and the capital/output ratio.

The independent estimate of profits for the U.K. is found in the non-farm profits at current prices, given by Feinstein (1961, Table IV). When this is related to the stock of capital, also at current prices, which we used to estimate the capital/output ratio, we get the annual rates of profit that appear in the thick line at the bottom of Fig. 22. This Figure gives the wage/income ratio within the coverage of the capital/output ratio shown in Fig. 21; the rate of profit inferred from these is shown by the lighter of the two lines below.

This inferred rate has been calculated on the assumptions of Section 1.A.6. Like the rate directly calculated from an independent estimate of profits, the inferred rate depends on our figures for the capital stock within industry. Any movement of these figures will affect both rates in the same way: the striking fall in both from the late 1890s onward, for example, is due in great part to an upsurge of the figures for the capital stock at this time. But the other elements in the two calculations are distinct. On the side of the directly calculated rate there is only one such element, the estimated profits in industry. The inferred rate, given the formula by which we calculate it, depends ultimately on three elements – the average annual earnings per wage-earner, the number of persons occupied in industry, and the income generated in industry. The last of these, if not yielded directly by censuses of production, will have been built up from elements that include the estimated profits in industry: otherwise the sources of the elements on the two sides are independent. Save in so far, therefore, as the courses of both the directly calculated and the inferred rate are dominated by the movement of the estimates of capital stock, their agreement adds to their credibility. In fact the

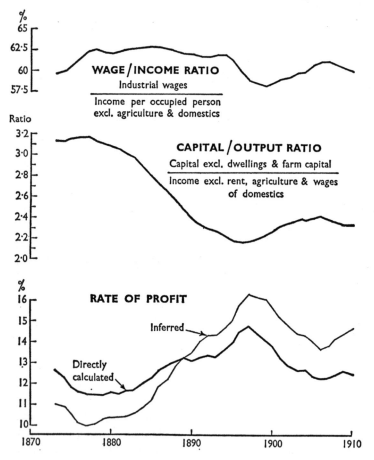

Fig. 22 U.K., excluding agriculture, 1870–1913: (1) Wage/income ratio. (2) Capital/output ratio. (3) Directly calculated rate of profit. (4) Rate of profit inferred from (1) and (2). All as 7-year moving averages.
Sources: (1), (3) and (4), Appendix 2, F1 and Table 137; (2) Appendix 3. (4) has been calculated on the assumptions of Section I A 6.

two curves at the bottom of Fig. 22 follow courses that would be very closely the same were their linear trends changed, that of the directly calculated rate rising more, or that of the inferred rate rising less, or something of both. The directly calculated rate would rise more if the estimates of capital stock rose less, but then the capital/output ratio would trend downwards from end to end more than in Fig. 22, and the inferred rate would trend upwards even more than it does now. The trend of the estimates of profits is unlikely to be far out, for these have had to fit into estimates of the whole national income. We can therefore look for adjustments only to those other elements, named above, on which the inferred rate depends – the average annual earnings per wage-earner, the income generated in industry and the number of persons occupied in industry. It is in the last two of these that a false trend is most likely to have crept in: our inferred rate will lie about a trend that rises too much if the wage/income ratio rises too little, and this will be the case if our estimates of the income generated in industry rise too slowly relatively to our estimates of the numbers occupied within the same bounds. This may well be so: the estimates of income are even more hazardous than those of numbers.

These problems of divergent trend apart, we are interested in the course of movement phase by phase. The light line at the foot of Fig. 22 spells out the inference we have already drawn in general terms from the courses of the wage/income and capital/output ratios – a fall in the rate of profit in the 1870s; a recovery setting in after 1882 and persisting to 1897; and then a fall until at least 1907. The last phase is particularly unexpected, in the light of our general impression of the times, and the upward trend of prices after the mid-90s. What is significant for us now is to find that the directly calculated rate of profit moves in the same way as the inferred, not least closely in this last phase.

The three snapshots for the U.S.A. come from estimates of profits in the whole private non-farm sector by Budd (1960); they are for 1889/90, 1899/1900, and 1909/10. We have related them to estimates of capital within industry, in current dollars, which we made by reflating the figures for this capital in 1929 dollars given by Kendrick (1961) with an index-number of the wholesale prices of metals and metal products, and building materials, which we constructed ourselves. The resultant rates of profit for the three dates are 10·4, 10·0 and 11·3 per cent respectively. The corresponding rates inferred from the wage/income and capital/output ratios in manufacturing alone are 12·7, 13·3 and 13·7. The course of these inferred rates, smoothed by a seven-year moving average, is shown in Fig. 23. Even this smoothing fails to remove the impact of so great a depression as that of the mid-90s. But if we take the peaks in the annual series, we find 13·7 per cent in 1890; 14·1 in 1901; 15·8 in 1906; with 14·8 as the last entry, in 1913. There is no clear evidence here of any trend.

For Germany, we are told by Hoffmann (1965, p. 502) that there is only one reliable source in this period, a study of the income and capital in Prussia in 1902 of some 44,000 persons whose income was derived mainly from industry. This gave a prevailing rate of return of 6·58 per cent. Hoffmann makes certain adjustments that raise the rate to 6·68 per cent, and applies the adjusted rate as a constant to the whole of 1850–1913. Dawson (1919, p. 87) observed that 'the German manufacturer is helped in his endeavour to produce cheaply by the fact that the national standard of life is still far less pretentious than in England and this holds good in every class of society. . . . The consequence is that the German manufacturer is contented with less profit than is expected in England.' A rate of less than 7 per cent is still, on an international comparison, strikingly low. The rates which we have inferred from the wage/income and capital/ output ratios, and which are shown in Fig. 23, come out higher,

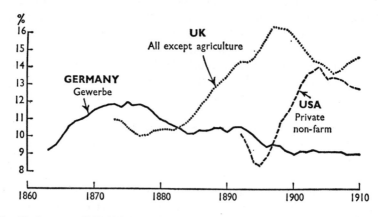

Fig. 23 Germany, U.K., U.S.A. at dates from 1863, to 1910: 7-year moving averages of the rates of profit inferred from the wage/income and capital/output ratios. Sources: Appendix 2, F1 and Tables 113, 137, 149. Inferred rates calculated on the assumptions of Section I.A.6.

between 9 and 12 per cent; but they are still low by comparison with the U.K. and the U.S.A. Their progressive decline through the 1880s and 1890s, moreover, inferred by us above from the wage/income and capital/output ratios, appears now as a movement from the upper to the lower of those limits. It is also remarkable that in Germany, just as in the U.K. and the U.S.A., the rate of profit does not appear to have risen in the years of rising prices after the mid-90s.

Fig. 23, for what it is worth, suggests that there were large changes in the prevailing rate of return on capital from time to time in all three countries. These changes need to be considered over against those in the amount of capital per occupied person in industry that are displayed in Fig. 24. The underlying estimates of the stock of capital at constant prices are from the sources cited on p. 150; they have been divided by estimates of the occupied population within the same sectors. The resultant series, expressed in 1913 prices in each country, have been converted into £s at the par of exchange. The room for bias here, both in the price indexes for capital goods within each country, and in the conversion, needs no pointing out. The sharp contrast between the level trend of the British series – with even a downward course between 1881 and 1895 – and the sustained rise of the German, from 40 per cent of the British level of equipment to equality with it just before the War, agrees with some familiar features of the economic history of those years. In the U.S.A. the level of equipment now appears as having been some three times as great in 1910 as in Germany and the U.K.: this ratio seems high, and will owe something to our use of the par of exchange if this overvalued the purchasing power of the dollar over industrial buildings and equipment. But in the 1950s the corresponding ratio for capital per worker in manufacturing in the U.S.A. and the U.K. has been put at $2\frac{1}{2}$ (Paige & Bombach, 1959, p. 69). Levels apart, the rate of rise is as remarkable in two countries as is its absence in the third: in the U.S.A. the rise was near 40 per cent even in the short span from 1889; and in Germany there was a near doubling in that same span, and a trebling in 1860–1913.

Thus baldly stated, this rise in the amount of capital per occupied person might be thought to have made for diminishing returns to capital: the capital/output ratio would have risen progressively. But we know that it did not do so. This makes us look for other factors that offset the tendency to diminishing returns. We may find them in technical progress and the improving quality of the worker. Both factors imply a change within our nominal physical units. Our unit of capital is an assortment of products aggregated at constant prices for the materials of which they are constructed: but the form these products took changed radically as technique advanced. Our unit of labour is 'the occupied person': but the capability of the average person increased as education extended and higher standards of living brought more health and strength. In one way, therefore, the

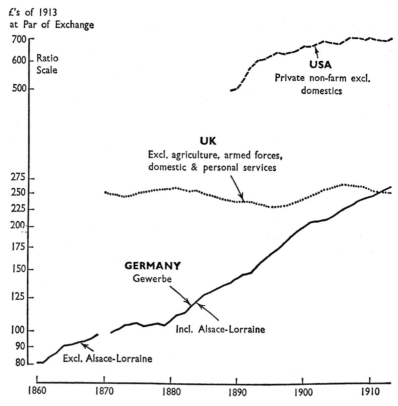

Fig. 24 Germany, U.K., U.S.A., at dates from 1860, to 1913: Real capital (excluding dwellings) per occupied person in: Germany, 'Gewerbe'; U.K., whole economy excluding agriculture, armed forces, domestic and personal services; U.S.A., private non-farm economy excluding domestic services; all in £s of 1913 purchasing power— other currencies converted at pars of exchange.
Source: Appendix 3.

comparative stability of the capital/output coefficient only marks its own artificiality.

Yet it does pose a further question: why, within its own convention, should it have followed the course it did? On the account we have given so far, anything might have happened. If £1000 currently invested will now buy an electric motor instead of a steam engine, why should the return on it not be twice as great? or ten times? Or alternatively, if the average worker now has £1000 worth of equipment at his elbow instead of £500, why should the return on it not have fallen greatly despite all the improvements in the form it takes?

One possible answer rests upon the manager's decision to invest. With a given and unchanging technique, additional investment runs into diminishing returns, and will be carried so far only as it promises a required rate of return. Improvements in technique and the capacity of labour make greater investment possible at not less than that rate. Let us suppose that this rate which provides the threshold for investment decisions remains constant through time. The amount of investment will then vary with circumstances, but so as always to obtain, at least in the aggregate, a given rate of return. In formal terms, the amount of capital will be adjusted, in the presence of changes affecting the production function, so as to hold the marginal productivity of capital constant. The builders of models of economic growth have analysed the conditions on which such an adjustment of a progressive increase in the amount of capital per worker will result in constancy also of the capital/output ratio and of the share of wages in the product (e.g. Meade, 1961, chs. 4 and 5).

It remains for us to allow that with any given level or course of the capital/output ratio it was always possible for the shares of pay and profit to rise or fall at one another's expense. Whether a general rise in wages, the outcome it may be of a wave of trade union militancy, would raise the share of pay, seems to have depended on the market environment of the time. If that environment was soft, firms generally would be able to edge prices up so as to maintain the same profit margin as before over the now higher unit wage cost. Only in the hard market environment, when there was no escape route through higher prices, were trade unions when they bargained about wages also bargaining about their share in the product. But though in the soft market environment product prices rose in a number of countries together, the viable rate of rise for any one of them might still appear as externally imposed. If there were special pressures towards higher pay in any one country, therefore, or if a no more than average pressure was associated with a less than average rise in productivity, so that unit wage costs rose exceptionally, then profit margins might be narrowed even in a soft market environment.

NOTE ON ESTIMATES OF THE CAPITAL STOCK

(1) Estimates of the capital stock, like those of other economic aggregates, are vexed by changes in price levels and in the type of product. If we leave these vexations aside, there remain some ambiguities peculiar to estimates of capital. There are a number of different ways in which the magnitude of a capital stock can be defined in principle, and the estimates to which these lead may lie far apart.[1]

(2) Suppose a shipping line today has a fleet of 20 similar ships: each ship lasts 20 years until it is scrapped, and through the past 20 years one ship has been built and taken into service annually. The Perpetual Inventory method of arriving at the present magnitude of the fleet takes the past 20 years, within which every ship was built that is in use today, and cumulates the investment of those years. The outcome depends on how we take account of the ships' wearing out. This we may do on two principles.

(3) On the first principle, we regard some part of each ship as being used up and worn away in the course of each year of the ship's working life. There are various ways of reckoning this annual depreciation. One way, that of linear depreciation, is to spread the using up of the whole ship evenly over its 20 years of life, and write off one-twentieth of its value each year. The reckoning of net investment will then proceed as follows. In the first of the past 20 years gross investment was one ship, and there was no depreciation of any part of the present fleet to be set off against it. In the second year, gross investment was again one ship, but one-twentieth of the ship taken into service the year before will now have been written off, and net investment will have been 19/20ths of one ship. In the third year it will have been 18/20ths; and so on. In cumulating the net investment we are thus summing an arithmetic progression of 20 terms, 1·0, 0·95,

[1] The issues are helpfully discussed in Feinstein (1965, chs. 1, 2), Goldsmith (1951), and R. and N. Ruggles (1961).

0·90 ... 0·05: the sum is 10·5. The terms of this series can also be seen as an inventory of the fleet at any one time – one ship newly built, one ship a year old and 5 per cent worn away, and so on, down to the ship that has only a year of life left. Thus 20 ships afloat and at work are evaluated at little more than half as many new ships. But on another and familiar way of reckoning annual depreciation, the proportion will be smaller than this. By the 'reducing balance' method, each year's depreciation is reckoned at a fixed proportion of the depreciated value of the asset brought in at the beginning of the year: thus if the proportion were two-thirds, a ship at the end of its second year would be valued at $\frac{2}{3}$ of $\frac{2}{3}$, or $\frac{4}{9}$, of its initial value, and so on. We now have a series in geometric progression, leaving less than 5 parts in 10,000 of the initial value at the end of 20 years. Its sum is a little less than 3. On the other hand, each ship may be depreciated down only to a scrap or secondhand value: in that case the aggregate value of the fleet, on any method of depreciation, will come out higher than if the terminal value is zero.

(4) All the methods of depreciation we have considered so far have in common some annual reduction in the valuation of equipment while it remains in service, and they yield a Depreciated Value. But on the second principle we reckon depreciation only terminally, when equipment is scrapped. Each ship is regarded as retaining its initial value so long as it remains in service, and each year's depreciation of the fleet consists only of the scrapping of that year. Once the fleet of 20 ships has been accumulated, this method gives the same annual depreciation as that of linear depreciation – namely the equivalent of one ship, whether this is seen as one whole ship scrapped, or one-twentieth of each of twenty ships depreciated. But on the way up, in the course of cumulation, the outcomes of the two methods differ radically: on the second principle there is no depreciation to be set against the annual gross investment until we reach the twentieth year, and by Perpetual Inventory we reach a total not of 10·5 ships but of 20. We might regard this as a valuation of the ships now in service at the cost of replacing them with ships of the same capacity. It is called the First Cost Value.

(5) The ratio of the Depreciated Value, reckoned as in the above examples, to the First Cost Value, depends on the length of life of the equipment. If this were only three years, the ratio would be two-thirds. With 10 years of life, it becomes 55 per cent; with 20 years, we

have seen that it is 52·5 per cent; with 40 years it is 51·25 per cent. In two actual instances, at least, it has come out close to the 52·5 per cent of our example. Goldsmith (1951, pp. 53–54) noted that the Bureau of Internal Revenue's valuation of the net capital assets of U.S. railroads at years within 1930–1946 were about double his estimate of the Depreciated Value: the difference, he said, 'seems to be due mainly to the fact that the railroads in their tax reports, as in other accounting statements, make little use of depreciation, but generally rely on replacement accounting,' whereas his estimates were 'based on regular depreciation of cumulated capital expenditures at the rates applied to all business . . .' Feinstein (1965, table 3·50) presents estimates of U.K. fixed assets at both Depreciated Value and First Cost Value, at five dates within 1920–1938, which show the former as from 52·5 to 55·4 per cent of the latter.

(6) The different procedures we have been considering have in common the cumulation of investment over a run of years up to the date of the evaluation. There is an alternative family of methods that have no regard to the past but set a value on the stock by reference only to present or expected future circumstances. They are mainly four. One takes the value at which the equipment of a firm is currently carried in its balance sheet – say, at original cost less the accumulated depreciation fund. Another asks how much a willing buyer would give for the equipment. If this test is applied to a piece of equipment that is detachable and can be sold off by itself – a car, for example – then the reference is to the secondhand market, and for such equipment the firm's method of depreciation is likely to be chosen so as to conform with the general course of that market, so that the second method will give much the same result as the first. But most equipment has to remain in situ, and can be sold (unless for scrap) only as a whole and as a going concern, and here the second method merges in a third. In this, the value set on the capital stock is found by capitalising the expected income to be derived from operating it. The capitalisation will be carried out by using the rate of return commonly obtained in the industry concerned: if this is 12$\frac{1}{2}$ per cent, then the capital stock will be valued at 8 times the expected income. To the extent that entry is free, and used in practice without much lag, but only to that extent, this third method of valuation will lead to results not very different from those of the first and second methods.

(7) The sources from which estimates of present value may be constructed include valuations for fire insurance and for property taxes. These in turn may have been made by one or more of the above methods. But there is one basis of valuation that constitutes a fourth method. This proceeds on the assumption that a piece of equipment will not generally be worth less to its present owner, and cannot be worth more, than the cost of replacing it by a product that will give the same current service. The notion of 'the same current service' is difficult: the actual replacement is likely to be newer, and to give the same physical service at a lower running cost; in practice also it is likely to be of an improved design. There is a further difficulty in its cost: allowance may be made for such changes in this as are part of the movement of the general level of prices, but hardly for such as come from improvements in the processes by which it itself is made, or from shifts in the relative prices of its component materials. None the less, the concept of replacement cost does provide guidance in practice. We have met a variant of it already, in the Perpetual Inventory method that uses retirements instead of annual depreciation.

(8) The methods of instantaneous valuation have in common an affinity to the ways in which firms generally will reckon the capital on which their profits are the return. If this reckoning yields a different total from that reached by a cumulative method, the realised *rate* of return will also be assessed differently. The possible causes of such differences have been discussed by Goldsmith (1951, pp. 52–57). They lie mainly in differences between the rates of depreciation applied; the writing up of book capital; and the omission from the figures of annual investment of development costs charged as current expenses. The probable net effect is that totals built up from balance sheets will tend to be somewhat bigger than those reached by Perpetual Inventory with annual depreciation.

(9) Estimates of capital may be confined to fixed assets or include stock-in-trade and work in progress. The proportion that stocks bear to fixed assets will vary according to the fluctuations of their prices and physical size in the course of the trade cycle. There may also be differences in the way the line is drawn in different studies between fixed assets and inventories. But the proportion will always be substantial. A number of studies have assumed that stocks in the aggregate amount to 40 per cent or more of the net product: if for

fixed assets alone the capital/output ratio is about 2, stocks will then amount to some 20 per cent of fixed assets. For industry, trade and transport in the U.K. in the 1920s and 1930s Feinstein (1965, tables 3·50, 3·60) gives a book value of stock in trade and work in progress that is from 14 to 19 per cent of the Depreciated Value of the stock of fixed assets. Whether estimates of capital do or do not include stocks therefore makes an important difference.

(10) Our endeavour here has been to use estimates for countries and periods that would as far as possible be the same in method and coverage. The sources are described in Appendix 2. We have been able to include only Germany, the U.K., and the U.S.A. In all three our estimates are mainly of the Depreciated Value of fixed assets in the non-farm private sector of the economy, together with stocks as currently valued.

(11) In Germany the valuation of industrial buildings may form an exception. It rests on the assessments for the Prussian building tax: 'in principle the assessment follows the use-value that is set equal to the capitalised rent,' but as few industrial buildings are leased, 'one can assume that in the great majority of cases the use-value is arrived at by taking the building cost', and this appears to be the First Cost (Hoffmann, 1965, p. 224). But the other components of the German total are installations and stocks. In Period One 'the installations are valued at original cost less depreciation, and the stocks at current prices, or, it may well be, at the average price of the best two or even three years' (op. cit., p. 240). In Periods Two and Three the estimates are made by cumulating net investment on a valuation of the capital stock in an initial year – 1923, 1948: at least in Period Three the outcome is said to be 'the annual stock at First Cost' (op. cit., p. 248).

(12) For the U.K. we have used the estimates by Feinstein (1965, and unpublished materials) of the depreciated value of fixed assets on the Perpetual Inventory method; and of stocks as currently valued.

(13) For the U.S.A. our figures are taken from Kendrick (1961), who in turn used the estimates made by Goldsmith (1956). 'Goldsmith's basic method,' says Kendrick (p. 51), 'was to estimate annual gross outlays for plant and equipment by major types, deflate to 1929 prices, depreciate the real outlays by the straight-line method over average lengths of life as prescribed by Bulletin 'F' of the

Treasury Department, and then cumulate the net additions to stock.'
That is, it was the Perpetual Inventory method with linear depreciation, as described in para (2) above.

(14) It is a matter of judgment whether our estimates are sufficiently alike in method and coverage to warrant the international
comparison of levels, as distinct from that of year-to-year movements.
The comparison of levels also requires conversion of currencies: in
the absence of particular studies of the comparative prices of the
relevant assets, we can only use the current rates of foreign exchange.
In the end we have decided to present the estimates in a way that
does invite the international comparison of levels; but this discussion
will have warned the reader, should that be necessary, of the wide
discrepancies by which such comparisons may be vitiated.

10. Factors affecting the course of money wages: a framework

The discussion of the preceding section has suggested how a number
of factors bore upon the course of money wages. We can now bring
these suggestions together in a framework.

(i) Money wages lay under the persistent influence of the wage-
earner's desire for a higher wage, which he claimed indivi-
dually or through a union; and the same influence resisted
wage cuts.

(ii) Custom inhibited change, but was broken up by the trade
cycle, which gave openings to those who sought to change
money wages.

(iii) But though the phases of the cycle provided the occasion and
permissive setting for changes in money wages, they did not
determine the amount of those changes, unless the intensity
of a phase rose over a certain threshold, when the demand
for labour acted directly to raise or lower money wages, as
in Germany, Sweden and the U.K. in the intense boom and
slump of the 1870s.

(iv) Changes in the supply of labour did not take any evident
effect on the course of money wages, but we should allow for
the possibility that they acted to intensify or mitigate the
influence of shifts in the demand for labour in the course of

the trade cycle, and fix the threshold beyond which this took effect.

(v)   The contemporary change in productivity decides what change in unit wage costs will accompany a given change in money wages. In so far as there were forces inhibiting the rise of unit wage costs, an improvement of productivity therefore increased the possibility of a rise in money wages. But it did not directly cause such a rise, and it could equally be associated with a change in unit wage costs alone.

(vi) One condition on which money wages could rise relatively to productivity was that the resultant rise in unit wage cost should be absorbed without any rise of selling price, through a reduction of the profit margin. This in turn could come about if the capital/output ratio fell, so that a lower profit margin could yield the same rate of return for unit capital; or if a lower rate of return was accepted. There were considerable variations in both respects from time to time, but the tendency in the longer run was for the capital/output ratio to change little, and for the rate of profit not to fall below a certain level. Rises of unit wage costs beyond a certain point were therefore dependent on the possibility of raising prices.

(vii) Prices could be raised to cover higher unit wage costs if the market environment, constituted by the expectations of management as these were moulded by the trend of world commodity prices and the degree of competition in world markets, was soft. If it was hard it would stop unit wage costs from rising, or even force them down, and money wages would then be able to rise only in so far as the improvement of productivity allowed.

(viii) Within the tolerances allowed by the demand for labour (iii), the supply of labour (iv), productivity (v), the capital/output ratio and the rate of return on capital (vi), and the market environment (vii), the rate of rise of money wages depended on the vigour with which claims were pressed.

The record has thus led us to treat the factors that bear on the course of money wages, other than (i), the drive for improvement, as predominantly blanket conditions. So long as they do not pass a certain threshold of intensity, they permit movements of money wages, or reduce or inhibit them, but they do not initiate movements, and variations of their intensity do not affect the amount of the rise. When they pass that threshold, however, they do initiate movements. Thus the positive phase of the trade cycle was permissive of rises in money wages as the negative was not, but its own intensity does not seem to have determined the amount of those rises save when it was exceptionally great. The market environment likewise seems to have operated only as a blanket condition, to permit or repress rises in unit wage costs, save in one instance of great intensity.

We may note that the presence of a similar threshold has been found more recently in another part of the labour market – in the relation between changes in the relative earnings of different industries and the reallocation of the labour force. In their study of earnings and employment in the U.K. in 1948–1959, Phelps Brown and Browne (1962) found that when the rises in men's hourly earnings over that span in some 130 industries were plotted against the associated change in the male labour force, no correlation appeared within a range that extended from a decline of 5 per cent to an increase of 30 per cent in that force.

> Within these boundaries, it seems, a more than average rise in earnings was no more likely to come about in an industry that was expanding steadily at $2\frac{1}{2}$ per cent a year than in one that was actually contracting. . . . Outside the central range the picture is different: there is an absence of low rises at the one extreme and of high at the other. In all the industries that expanded by more than 30 per cent the rise of earnings was below average in only 5; in all that contracted by more than 5 per cent it was above average in only 2.

Similarly when the rises in earnings industry by industry were plotted against associated unemployment rates, and against concentration ratios (the proportion of all employment in an industry that was given by the three largest firms in it): in both these regressions, as with that on changes in employment, 'within certain boundaries no association appears, but at the boundary a displacement of the scatter does suggest some association'. The threshold in the effect of changes in employment appears also in some measure in the postwar U.S.A. (Ulman, 1965).

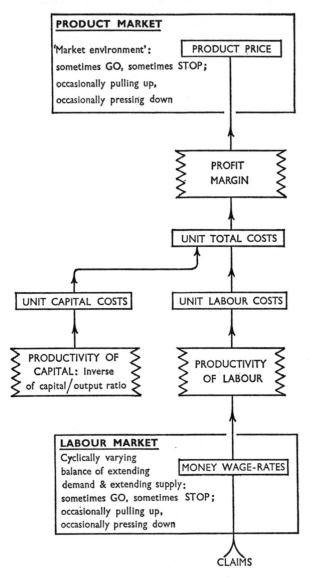

PRODUCT MARKET

'Market environment':
sometimes GO, sometimes STOP;
occasionally pulling up,
occasionally pressing down

PRODUCT PRICE

PROFIT MARGIN

UNIT TOTAL COSTS

UNIT CAPITAL COSTS

UNIT LABOUR COSTS

PRODUCTIVITY OF CAPITAL: Inverse of capital/output ratio

PRODUCTIVITY OF LABOUR

LABOUR MARKET
Cyclically varying
balance of extending
demand & extending supply:
sometimes GO, sometimes STOP;
occasionally pulling up,
occasionally pressing down

MONEY WAGE-RATES

CLAIMS

Fig. 25 Framework of factors affecting the course of money wages.

We are accustomed to think of the interplay of economic forces as of a system in mechanics, which combines the forces in functional relations that are continuous, so that any change in any force takes a determinate effect upon the outcome. The blanket conditions and thresholds we have been discussing do not act in that way, and cannot be so represented. It is useful none the less to bring them together in a schema, that will serve at least to fix them in the mind's eye, and suggest some possibilities of their interplay.

This schema appears in Fig. 25. The general tendency of the worker to press for a rise and resist cuts is represented by the arrowhead marked 'Claims' at the bottom of the Figure. This upward thrust is exerted in the Labour Market. Here the cyclically varying balance of the extension of the demand for labour and the extension of the supply provides a setting that will stop wage rises when the excess of supply over demand lies within a certain range (represented, say, in the U.K. by an unemployment rate of over 4 per cent); and permit wage rises when the excess is less than this. On particular occasions when the excess is very great, there can be an active pressure downwards on money wage-rates; and on other occasions when the excess is very small overall – which means that in particular sectors it is demand that exceeds supply – the competition of employers for labour will be an active force pulling money wage-rates up. We must remember, however, that much more enters into the calculations of the parties to the wage-bargain on these occasions than the size of the excess, which may indeed itself serve only as a thermometer indicating the current state of expectations.

In the connection between a change in the money wage-rate and a change in the price of the product there are three possibilities of variation, represented in Fig. 25 by the three boxes whose concertina'd sides indicate their possible shortening or lengthening. A rise in the productivity of labour, for example, will reduce the rise in unit labour costs otherwise imposed by a rise in money wage-rates. Such a rise in productivity has usually owed something to an increase in the amount of capital per worker: if the output per worker increases equally, that is if the capital/output ratio remains the same, there is no change in the cost of capital per unit of output; but if the capital/output ratio rises, an increase in the capital cost per unit of output must be brought into the total change in cost per unit of output, and conversely if the capital/output ratio falls. Whatever the change in unit total costs taking labour and capital costs together, the amount of change in the final selling price of the product depends on what happens meanwhile to the profit margin; and this is represented by the third of our concertinas.

All the relations thus represented are, in a sense, only arithmetic – given a rise of a quarter in the productivity of labour, unit labour costs fall by a fifth, and so on; but when we reach the price of the product we enter a market again where the possibilities are various. The awareness of the pressure of price competition and the expectations concerning the behaviour of other sellers that are comprised under 'the market environment' may at one time be permissive of any rises in product prices for which the factors already considered are making; and at another time forbid them. But its phases do not act only in this way as a traffic light: occasionally, in their greatest intensity, they may exert an active force, pulling prices up or pushing them down, and imparting a motion backwards through the linkages, to raise or lower money wage-rates.

It will be seen that this account of the movements of the price level does not regard them as locked into a monetary system, in the sense that they are under a rigid constraint from the side of an independently regulated monetary supply, or occur only as the outcome of changes in the balance between that supply and the volume of transactions. Of course the Quantity Equation – more properly, Identity – always holds, but it cannot tell us how far the price level will in practice adjust itself to the supply of money, or the supply of money to the price level. Phelps Brown and Ozga (1955) have given reason to believe that it was largely in the latter way that the causal sequence ran, down at least to 1913. The monetary supply did not respond without reactions, notably through interest rates, which in turn will have affected money incomes and prices; but it seems possible to regard these as capable of movement on their own and without a preliminary permissive or causal movement on the side of money.

For the rest, our account of how the course of money wages appears to have been determined uses only elements familiar in recent discussion of the labour market – wage claims; the state of the demand for and the supply of labour; the unit wage costs that a given wage per man entails after taking productivity into account; and the readiness of employers to cover a rise in unit wage costs by higher prices, in the current state of price trends, competition, government policy and expectations. If there is anything new in the account, it lies rather in the scope assigned, in the operation of these elements, to the blanket condition and the threshold; and in the application of an analysis developed for full employment to times when employment was full only in some sectors and phases.

11. The course of real wages (wages in composite units of consumables)

The money wages we have been considering were spent in ways recorded in household budgets collected at the time. These budgets provide the weights with which to combine the movements of prices, always in principle and usually in practice retail prices, so as to form index-numbers of the cost of living. When such an index-number is divided into the corresponding index of money wages, the quotient measures the changes from time to time in the size of a basketful of goods, of representative and stable composition, that the wage would command. We cannot go nearly so far as to say that it measures the changes in the material welfare of the wage-earner. It leaves too much out of account for that – the hours of work, the physical and social conditions of the work place, the quality of housing, the means of meeting misfortunes such as sickness and unemployment, the prevailing level of health, the squalor and the amenities of the towns; as well as the number of dependents in the household. For this reason even to speak of real wages will suggest too much, unless we take 'real' in its proper sense of 'in terms of things'. For we can best regard our indexes of real wages – and for brevity we must call them that – as tracing changes in wage-earnings when these are expressed in terms of a composite unit of consumables. But at the same time, when we find that between 1860 and 1913 the real wage so conceived nearly doubled in three of our countries and much more than doubled in a fourth, we know ourselves confronted with a greater change in the wage-earner's life than can be expressed simply as twice as much bread or meat, twice as much coal, or cloth, or mileage by train or tram.

This greater change would show itself in part through a change, according to the Engel functions, in the proportions of the household budget (Allen & Bowley, 1935). It is therefore a weakness of our present study that in Germany, Sweden and the U.K. our indexes have fixed weights. In France and the U.S.A. the expected effect of higher real wages is shown by a decline in the proportion of household expenditure that went on food – from 71 per cent in the 1860s in France to 64 per cent after 1900, and in the U.S.A. from 57 per cent to 44 – as also by the proportion being lower in the U.S.A. than in France throughout. Our fixed weights for Germany and the U.K. are derived from household budgets towards the end of the period, and our indexes probably give too little weight to food in the earlier years. Though the weight of food derived from the British budgets of as late as 1904 was still as much as 60 per cent, Bowley (1937, p. 33) thought it a not unreasonable assumption that the corresponding proportion in 1880 had been 75 per cent, and that, within this, meat, bacon, tea and sugar had only half as much weight in comparison with bread, flour, potatoes and butter as they had in 1904. In Sweden it is from the pattern of outlay in the middle of the period

Table 11 1860–1913, five countries: Weights used for index-numbers of cost of living.
[Fixed weights throughout the Period in Sweden and the U.K. In France, Germany and the U.S.A. the weights differ somewhat in different sub-periods; those cited here are for the later years].

Date of budgets for weights cited here	France 1900–1919	Germany 1907–1908	Sweden 1881–1890	U.K. 1904	U.S.A. 1890–1914
Object of outlay	%	%	%	%	%
Food	63·65	60·5	55	60	44·1
Clothing	10·52	9·2	12	12	17·9
Fuel		5·9	3	8}	7·2}
Light		2·2	1·5		
Rent		22·2	10	16	22·3
Rent & housing supplies[1]	17·15				
Home furnishings					4·5
Miscellaneous	8·68		18·5	4	
Liquor & tobacco					4·0
	100·00	100·00	100·00	100	100·0

[1] including heat, light, kitchen equipment, furnishings, cleaning materials.

Sources: As in Appendix 2.

that the fixed weights are taken, though this pattern is not that of the wage-earner's budget, but of national consumption as a whole. A comparison of the weights used in the five countries is afforded by Table 11.

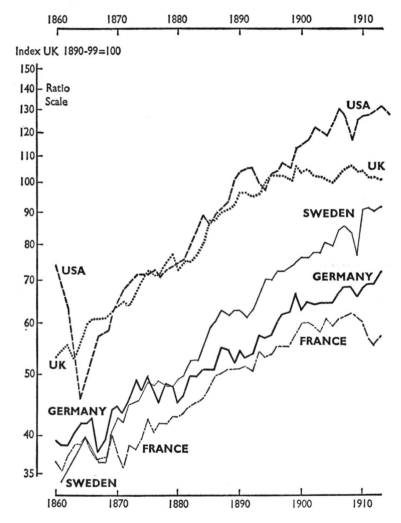

Fig. 26 Five countries, 1860–1913: Average wage-earnings expressed in composite units of consumables, all as indexes relative to U.K. 1890–1899 = 100.
Sources: Appendix 3 and Table 2.

When these indexes of the cost of living are divided into those of money wage-earnings, we get the indexes of real wages that are shown in Fig. 26. The curves here are spaced according to the estimates of comparative real earnings for 1905 or 1909 set out in Table 2.

The first finding in Fig. 26, and at the last still the most important, is that there was a great rise in real wages in all five countries. Over 1860–1895 – that is, until the rate of rise fell off in France, Germany and the U.K. – the annual improvement was by 0·95 per cent in the U.S.A., 1·09 in Germany, 1·10 in France, 1·92 in the U.K., and 2·18 in Sweden. These are modest rates by comparison with the 1950s, but their cumulative effect was still great enough to bring a transformation about. From end to end, between 1860 and 1913, the size of the basketful that the average wage-earnings would buy was raised by

Table 12 U.K., 1880 : Estimated weekly budget of a wage-earning family, husband earning 26s. 6d. a week, with wife, and three schoolchildren.

	Quantity			Outlay in
	lbs	Kgs	Calories	pence
Bread	44	20	55,000	55
Meat	4	1·8	4,800	28
Bacon	1	0·45	2,685	11·5
Suet etc.	1	0·45	3,540	6
Butter	1	0·45	3,605	15
Cheese	0·5	0·23	1,030	4·5
Milk, fresh	(10 pints)	(5·7 litres)	4,060	20
Potatoes	28	12·7	8,680	22
Rice	2	0·9	3,260	4
Tea	0·375	0·17		12·75
Sugar	4	1·8	7,440	14
Total Food			94,100	192·75
Rent				42
Fuel & light				18
Clothing				24
Sundries				41·25
Total, all items				318

Source: Mackenzie (1921).

57 per cent in France, 78 in the U.S.A., 84 in Germany, 91 in the U.K., and no less than 172 per cent in Sweden.

The significance of such changes appears more clearly when we consider what the levels were through which they passed. The U.K. in 1880 lies near the middle of the whole range, from Sweden in 1861 to the U.S.A. in 1913. The weekly budget of a British wage-earning household in 1880 has been estimated as in Table 12 by Mackenzie (1921; see also Bowley, 1937, pp. 35–6). The household has one breadwinner, with wife and three children; its income is the wage of the average semi-skilled wage-earner of the time. When we said 'breadwinner', the term was not archaic – much more than half the family's total of calories came from bread: though Bowley thinks the price taken for bread too low, and the quantity reckoned as bought correspondingly too high. By the test of calories alone, the dietary was adequate. According to the recommended dietary allowances of the U.S. National Research Council, 1945 (1947, Ministry of Food) the household required not more than 12,000 calories a day: it was getting over 13,400. In 1860 the corresponding intake had been rather more than 12,500 calories; by 1914 it had risen above 15,000. But a diet can provide enough calories and still be inadequate, even unhealthy, if it does not provide a balance of nutrients – proteins, fats, carbohydrates, minerals and vitamins. By this test the present dietary appears pinched, not least in the deficiency of such protective foods as fresh milk, vegetables and fruit.

But the most stringent limitation of the budget appears in the narrowness of the margin left for all a household's needs beyond food and houseroom. To clothe five bodies, for instance, the budget leaves 2s. 0d. a week – less than the cost of five 4 lb loaves; and little more than the cost of eight loaves is all that is left for furnishings, kitchen equipment, cleaning materials, the journey to work, books and newspapers, writing materials, postage, trade union dues, and medical expenses or subscriptions to a friendly society – to say nothing of drink and tobacco.

It is true that this household is far from the average, not in the number of dependents, but in having only one wage-earner – the average household drew the equivalent of about one and a half weekly wage-packets of a man. On the other hand, it does illustrate one of the phases of stringency through which any family was liable to pass. Its single wage-earner, moreover, was credited with a good

F

deal more than men's average earnings, which were put at no more than 24s. in 1886 (Bowley, 1937, Table x). In any case, the dispersion about that average was wide. In particular, the unskilled workers then were relatively both more numerous and worse off than in later years. Seebohm Rowntree (1902), defining poverty as falling short of 'the minimum of food, clothing, and shelter needful for the maintenance of merely physical health', found that more than 40 per cent of the wage-earning households of York in 1899 were below that line: 28 per cent because they were not making the best use of an income that would have kept them above the line if husbanded carefully enough, and 15 per cent because with the best of husbandry their incomes would still have been too small. Other surveys indicated that this dispersion was typical of British towns at the time. The rise in real wages through the fifty years before the First World War was most significant of all in its lifting of households over the poverty line (Phelps Brown, 1959, ch. i).

This is made explicit in other terms in the study by Mackenzie (1921): 'In 1860, one-quarter of the population appear to have been insufficiently nourished, even when the lower standard of 3000 calories per man per diem is accepted, while about the same proportion managed to attain to the higher standard' (of 3,500 calories per man-day). 'During the next twenty years, the general standard of living increased, so that all were above the lower standard, and even the lowest decile and lowest quartile were not much below the higher.' If we can suppose that the dispersion of the incomes of wage-earning households was not sensibly greater in other countries than in the U.K., then we can draw across Fig. 26 a belt whose boundaries are the levels reached by the U.K. curve in 1860 and 1880, and regard the years of any country's passage through this belt as the period in which outright hunger was banished from wage-earning households, so long as their earnings were not cut off by sickness or unemployment.

Another way of assessing the budget of 1880 is to set it in a longer perspective of history. Phelps Brown and Hopkins (1956) compiled an index of the prices of some of the main materials of consumption over the seven centuries through which they had traced the course of builders' wage-rates in Southern England. The prices are mostly at wholesale, so they will have fluctuated more than retail prices in the short run, and the relation of the two may have had its trends in the long. But the prices taken do cover (though with gaps at times) the staples of consumption – the bread grains; mutton, beef, and herrings; butter and cheese; malt; charcoal and candles; canvas and woollen cloth. These price series were combined with fixed weights chosen as representative of budgets whose main proportions seemingly changed little over the centuries. When the index thus obtained is compared with the movements of the wage-rate of the carpenter, the mason, or the bricklayer, and the wage comes to be expressed in composite units of the raw materials of consumption, it is found to have traversed a plateau of prosperity through most of the fifteenth century. It was a high plateau, by comparison with what went before and, no less, what came after. Between the Black Death in 1350 and the 1420s the wage-rate in physical units about doubled. Between 1510 and 1590 it halved again. It fell even lower before the Civil War; in the worst days of the Napoleonic Wars it was no better. Only after those wars did it take off on the path of climb that was to take it by the end of the nineteenth century to levels never reached before. In the course of that climb, it regained for the first time the level of the fifteenth century plateau – as it happens, precisely in 1880.

We have considered in various ways the significance of the middle of the range of Fig. 26. When we come to compare the places of different countries in that range, what surely is most remarkable is the place of the U.S.A.: not until after 1900, it appears, did the real wage in the U.S.A. draw ahead of the British.

There are certainly grounds to believe that, at least along the eastern seaboard, the American real wage had stood well above the British in earlier times. Adam Smith said in his *Wealth of Nations* (bk. I, ch. viii) that 'in the province of New York, common labourers earn (1773) three shillings and sixpence currency, equal to two shillings sterling, a day', and 'house carpenters and bricklayers, eight shillings currency, equal to four shillings and sixpence sterling'; 'wages are said to be as high in the other colonies as in New York'. In southern England in 1773 a builder's labourer would generally be getting 16 pence a day, and a carpenter or bricklayer 2s. (Phelps Brown & Hopkins, 1955). So on this reckoning the American labourer was getting half as much again in money, the American craftsman more than double – the wider differential for skill in America appears here as in 1909 (1.A.1 above). Nor, according to Adam Smith, were these higher money wages offset by higher prices: on the contrary, 'the price of provisions is everywhere in North America much lower than in England. A dearth has never been known there. In the worst seasons, they have always had a sufficiency for themselves, though less for exportation. If the money price of labour, therefore, be higher than it is anywhere in the mother country, its real price, the real command of the necessaries and conveniences of life which it conveys to the labourer, must be higher in a still greater proportion.' William Cobbett, in his *Year's Residence in America* (1818, para. 313), said that a good day-labourer had 'upon an average, a dollar a day' – this likewise would be in the eastern states. If we take that as 4s. sterling, it is half as much again as the building labourer's 32 pence a day in Southern England at this time – the same ratio as in Adam Smith's report for 1773. And Cobbett adds his testimony that American prices were lower.

> Groceries, as they are called, are upon an average, at far less than *half* the English price . . . Sweet oil, raisins, currants; all the things from the Levant, are at a *fourth* or *fifth* of the English price . . . Candles and soap (quality for quality) are half the English price . . . Apples, pears, cherries, peaches at a *tenth* part of the English price . . . All the materials for making people drunk, or muddle headed, are much cheaper here than in England . . . Wearing apparel comes chiefly from England, and all the *materials* of dress are as cheap as they are there; for, though there is a duty laid on the importation, the absence of taxes, and the cheap food and drink, enable the retailer to sell as low here as there . . . *Household Furniture*, all cheaper than in England (paras. 331–7).

Certainly this is laid on very thick, and Cobbett was contrasting the benefits of free institutions with 'the hellish oppression' of taxation that the English people were living under; nor in any case do we know that the prices he specified were more favourable than those of which Adam Smith had said only that they were 'much lower' than the English. But he can take a great deal of deflation and still leave us reason to believe that the superiority of the real wage of the American labourer was no less in 1818 than it had been nearly half a century before.

Eleven years later the wage-rates given by Zachariah Allen in his *Science of Mechanics* (1829) indicate that the U.S.A. rates were higher than the British, not by the 50 per cent suggested by Adam Smith and Cobbett, but by only about 25 per cent, both for the skilled and, if we omit maidservants, the unskilled (Rosenberg, 1967). Unless American prices now stood higher relatively to the British than before, this would still leave the American real wage substantially the higher.

There is thus reason to doubt whether we are right in putting the American real wage, from the end of the Civil War down to the 1890s, at figures that are generally little higher than the British. In part this is the outcome of our making our indexes of real wages pass through pegs fixed in 1905 or 1909 according to the available estimates of average money earnings and the Board of Trade's estimate of the comparative cost of living in those years. The estimates of earnings are firmly based in the studies of Bowley (1937) and Rees (1961). It is very relevant here that these are the average earnings of wage-earners of all grades and regions within their industrial coverage. In the U.S.A. of those years, with its wide differentials by skill and region, such an average comes out much lower than the earnings of craftsmen in a high wage region such as the eastern seaboard, which figured largely in the comparisons we have drawn from Adam Smith. On top of this effect comes the wide disparity in the cost of living as measured in 1909: 'the food of the average English family,' the Board of Trade found (1911, p. xxv), 'would cost about 38 per cent more in the United States, and . . . the rent would be as 207 : 100.' The relative positions of the two indexes in 1909 therefore appears intelligible.

But that they are close together in earlier years is also in part the outcome of the American index rising so much more from the 1890s to 1909 – that is, of its setting the earlier years so much lower relatively to 1909. This in turn is the outcome of our adopting the index of the cost of living in Rees (1961, table 43), which stands at just the same level in 1909 as in 1890, whereas Douglas's index (1930, table 9), which was generally relied upon previously, showed a rise of about one-sixth. Had it been Douglas's index that we divided into our money earnings, we should therefore have obtained an index of real earnings in 1890 that stood higher by a sixth, relatively to 1909, than our present index. Since this present index already stands above the British in 1890 by some 8½ per cent, the American index based on Douglas's cost of living would have stood 26 per cent or more above the British in 1890; and throughout the preceding years, ever since the recovery from the Civil War, the American real wage would have appeared to be about that much higher than the British.

That our present estimates show the levels of real wages in the U.S.A. and the U.K. as much the same in the mid-90s, stands in contrast with our estimates of productivity in industry (Fig. 17), which put the American level at that time at as much as 60 per cent above the British. Most of this disparity is explained by our having in effect reduced the American money wage-earnings, for purposes of comparison, by the excess of the comparative cost of living over the par of exchange, and in the mid-90s this was near 50 per cent; whereas it is the par of exchange alone that we have used to convert the net dollar product of industry into sterling (1.B.7).

Whatever the true relative level of real wages in the U.S.A., at least until 1895 they do not seem to have been distinguished from others by a higher rate of rise. After 1895, however, though the U.S.A. shared in the general slowing down of the advance, it slowed down less than the other countries and its rate of rise now stood relatively high. The annual rates of rise from 1895 to 1913 were: the U.K., a slight fall; France, 0·38 per cent; Germany, 1·27 per cent; U.S.A., 1·33 per cent; and Sweden, 1·48 per cent.

It is noteworthy, and perhaps contrary to expectation, that the rise of real wages from first to last was not greater in Germany. Its money wages rose in step with those of Sweden – or perhaps we should put the linkage the other way about; but in any case there was no such common course of real wages. These rose in Germany until the last few years no faster than in France. The German showing appears to more advantage after 1895, though this is admittedly due mainly to one great bound forward, from 1895 to 1899, after which real wages returned to the trend of preceding years.

Through the various movements we have been discussing there runs in all countries a common theme – the barter terms between the products of factory and farm. Our wage-earners, mostly industrial, realised much of their wage – nearly 45 per cent in the U.S.A., 55–60 per cent in Europe – in the form of food: how much food could they get in exchange for the unit of their own produce? The answers, country by country, are indicated by Fig. 27. Where imports were not obstructed, the curves of this Figure move inversely with the tide of world commodity prices, with those secondary secular fluctuations (Kuznets, 1930) that brought the relative prices of foodstuffs down through 1875–1895, and raised them thereafter down to the war: we see this in France and the U.K. down to the 1890s and in all five countries from then onwards. But protection to home agriculture denied the benefits of the first phase to the German wage-earner.

The quantity of food obtainable in exchange for the unit of manufactures was a main component of the wage-earner's barter terms comprehensively defined as the number of composite units of the objects of his consumption obtainable in exchange for the composite unit of his own products. This is one of the three factors which together make up the real wages of industrial workers. There is first the productivity of labour, the output per worker in each industry expressed in units of that industry's product. Second, there is the share of that industry's product which goes to the wage-earner: applying this to the first factor gives the steelworker's wage in tons of steel, the bootmaker's in pairs of boots, and so on. Third, there are the barter terms just noticed, on which these units of the wage-earner's own product can be exchanged from time to time for composite units of the objects of his own consumption. Formally, we have the following identity:

$$\underset{\text{wage}}{\text{Real}} \equiv \text{Productivity} \times \underset{\substack{\text{wage earner} \\ \text{in product}}}{\text{Share of}} \times \underset{\substack{\text{consumables} \\ \text{obtained per unit} \\ \text{of product}}}{\text{No. of units of}}$$

If we consider a span of time, and express the value of each variable in the last year as a relative to its initial value, we might find, for example, that a rise of 50 per cent in the real wage was made up of a 60 per cent rise in productivity, a fall of 10 per cent in the wage-earner's share in the product, and an improvement of 4 per cent in the quantity of consumables obtainable by the wage-earner in exchange for the unit of his own product –

$$1 \cdot 5 \text{ approx.} = 1 \cdot 6 \times 0 \cdot 9 \times 1 \cdot 04.$$

If we express these end to end movements as average annual percentage rates of change, and these rates are small, then we can approximate the multiplication of the three factors against one another by adding the percentage changes together. Thus if the span of years in the above example were 25, we should have, in annual percentage rates of change,

$$1 \cdot 64 = 1 \cdot 90 - 0 \cdot 42 + 0 \cdot 16.$$

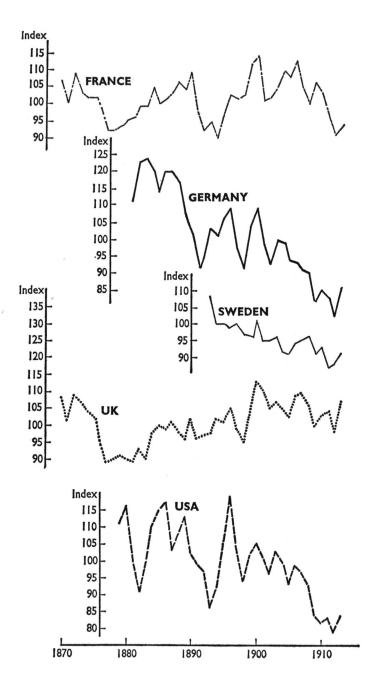

That is, a rise in the real wage at the average rate of 1·64 per cent a year was made up of a rise of productivity of 1·90 per cent a year and a reduction in the share of the product going to the worker at the rate of 0·42 per cent a year, partially offset by an improvement at the rate of 0·16 per cent a year in the quantity of consumables the wage-earner could obtain in exchange for a unit of his own product.

In Table 13 we fill out this identity with the actual rates of change that we can calculate for the movements from end to end of certain periods in four of our countries. Each end is fixed in a single year, and this brings an arbitrary element into the calculations for the wage/income ratio and industrial productivity, whose annual values fluctuated with the trade cycle. Our spans are long enough, however, to bring any marked trend out nonetheless. It is clear that such a trend was present only in productivity, and that it was by this rise in productivity that the greatest part of the rise in real wages was brought about. As a rough demonstration of this we may aggregate the figures for all countries and periods save the one case – the U.K. from 1895 to 1913 – in which real wages fell from end to end, and in which the rise in productivity was negligible. We then find an aggregate rise of real wages amounting to 7·65 percentage points, made up approximately of a rise in industrial productivity of 9·65 points, less 1·92 points for the combined adverse effects of changes in the wage/income ratio and the barter terms for industry. We notice that in the period of increasing union membership and pressure,

---

Fig. 27 Five countries, at dates from 1870 to 1913: Quantity of food obtainable in exchange for a unit of industrial products; indexes, bse 1890–1899 except Sweden 1893–1899.
Sources, (1) Food. (2) Industrial products. *France.* (1) *Annuaire Statistique Rétrospectif* (1961), ch. xxxii, 'produits alimentaires' in 'indices de prix de gros de 45 articles'; (2) C. P. Kindleberger, *The Terms of Trade, A European Case Study* (1956), table 2–4A, merchandise export unit values.
Germany. (1) *Statistisches Jahrbuch 1939/40,* viii, table 6: (2) Kindleberger as for France.
Sweden. (1) G. Myrdal with S. Bouvin, *The Cost of Living in Sweden 1830–1930* (1933), table A, col. 18; (2) Kindleberger, as for France, but here corrected for cumulative error suggested in the same author's 'Industrial Europe's terms of trade on current account' in *Economic Journal,* 65, 257, March 1955.
U.K. (1) B. R. Mitchell & P. Deane, *Abstract of British Historical Statistics,* ch. xvi, table 4 (Sauerbeck); (2) Mitchell & Deane, as in (1), ch. xi, table 15 (Imlah, merchandise exports).
U.S.A. (1) *Historical Statistics of the U.S.* (1960), E.16; (2) *Historical Statistics,* as in (1) U.32, unit value of exports of finished manufactures.

Table 13 Four countries, periods between 1871 and 1913: Average annually cumulated percentage rise in real wages as made up of average annual rates of change in; industrial productivity, the wage/income ratio in industry, and the barter terms between industrial products and the articles of wage-earners' consumption.
[Col. (1) does not always exactly equal the sum of cols. (2), (3) and (4), by reason of the rounding off of the original indexes whose rates of change are calculated here].

	Average annually cumulated percentage change in			
	real wages	industrial productivity	wage/income ratio in industry	barter terms for industry[1]
	(1) %	(2) %	(3) %	(4) %
Germany				
1880–1895	1·62	2·04	0·32	−0·74
1895–1913	1·27	1·93	−0·45	−0·20
Sweden				
1895–1913	1·48	2·13	−0·24	−0·40
U.K.				
1871–1895	1·94	2·06	−0·15	0·05
1895–1913	−0·11	0·03	−0·32	0·16
U.S.A.				
1895–1913	1·33	1·49	−0·77	0·61

[1] Number of composite units of wage-earner's consumables obtainable in exchange for a composite unit of industrial products, i.e. index of industrial product prices divided by index of wage-earner's cost of living.

Sources: Cols. (1)–(3) Appendix 3; col. (4) industrial product prices, as under G.N.P. deflator and Table 106 in Appendix 2, and wage-earner's cost of living, Appendix 3.

between 1895 and 1913, the distributive shift was negative, at least as between those terminal years, in all four countries. But we cannot treat the rise of real wages as effectively dependent upon productivity alone. In Germany over 1880–1895 it was substantially reduced by an adverse movement of the barter terms. In the U.S.A. over 1895–1913 the changes in both the wage/income ratio and the barter terms for industry were of the order of half the rate of rise of productivity, though they largely offset one another. Particularly when distributive changes and changes in the barter terms worked in the same direction, as in Germany and Sweden from 1895 to 1913, their effect was substantial.

The wage/income ratio we have just been considering is that within industry alone, and we gave our reasons for not calculating a corresponding ratio for the whole economy. But we said at the same time that the relative movements of wage earnings and income generated per occupied person in the whole economy would be of interest when we were tracing the rise of real wages, and we now display them in Fig. 28. In Germany, Sweden and the U.K. the cyclical fluctuation of national income per occupied person is greater than that of wage earnings, which it will be remembered are estimated for a year of normally continuous employment; but in the U.S.A. the fluctuations of earnings are also marked. In the longer run, however, it is the absence of divergence that stands out in Sweden and the U.K.: here from end to end of half a century, if not in every intermediate phase, the average wage maintained a very steady relation to the income generated per head of those engaged in all the activities of the economy in all its sectors. Because the generated income differed from one sector to another, and the relative sizes of sectors were changing, such steadiness implies an internal compensation that we can regard only as coincidental. It is to the absence of such complete compensation that we must attribute the progressive if slow fall of wage-earnings relatively to the average income generated in Germany. In the U.S.A., so far as our records run, the divergence in the same direction was conspicuously great. It was the joint outcome of two processes: the fall in the wage/income ratio within manufacturing recorded in Table 13 above, and a rise in the income generated per occupied person outside manufacturing, notably in agriculture (Fig. 16).

It remains for us in this discussion of the rise of real wages to take account of one non-monetary benefit. We have noted that our measure of real wages takes no account of many things that enter into the wage-earner's welfare; but of one of these, his hours of work, we can at least record that in all of our countries there was some reduction, to add increased leisure to the bigger basketful that the wage came to buy. Hours remained generally very long by more recent standards; vacations for the manual worker were only beginning to be heard of; changes were scattered and sporadic, and the record is correspondingly scrappy. That in all countries there were some reductions and no extensions, however, there is no doubt.

The improvement was least marked in France. Down to 1870, if

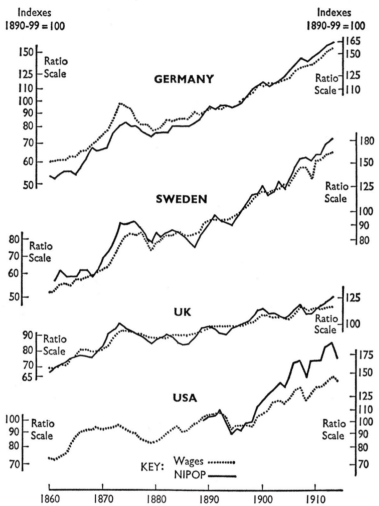

Fig. 28 Four countries, 1860–1913 : Indexes (1890–1899 = 100) of national income (or net domestic product) per occupied person (NIPOP), and average money wage-earnings, both at current prices.
Source : Appendix 3.

not even later, a 12-hour day and 72-hour week was usual, though 10 hours seem to have prevailed in Paris (Rist, 1897, p. 391; Duveau, 1946, pp. 310–13). This was the maximum for men set by an Act of 1892; but an Act of 1900, if observed, would have reduced the maximum for all workers to 10 by 1904 (Sée, 1951, pp. 346–47). The hours of work given for 1905 by the U.K. Board of Trade inquiry that we drew upon in 1.A.5 above, though still long, were at least generally well below the 72-hour week of 1870 – in engineering, we saw, the weekly hours were now cited as 60¼ (Board of Trade 1909).

In Germany as in France the 12-hour day prevailed around 1870, though some craftsmen in the cities had a 10-hour maximum. But as trade unions grew up they aimed at shorter hours, and conducted some successful strikes to get them. By 1890, the 11-hour day had come to predominate in factories. An official enquiry in 1897 put the average working day at between 9 and 11 hours. It probably remained at 10 hours, with a 60-hour week, in 1913, but for workers organised in unions it was not much more than 9½ hours. (Bry, 1960, pp. 45–6; Clapham, 1928, p. 405.)

In Sweden equally the shortening of hours was an object of successful pressure by the unions. In the sawmills, for instance, there was a general reduction from 11 hours to 10 between 1895 and 1902; in metals and engineering the 70-hour week of 1860 had come down to near 60 by 1900 and 55 by 1913. In industry as a whole the average workday was reckoned to have been 11·1 hours in 1885 and 10·0 hours in 1905–1906 (Bagge, 1933, pp. 59, 119, 151–3, and 277, fn. 4).

In the U.K., building generally adopted the 54-hour week in the 1870s, engineering in the 1880s. In the 1890s came a wave of 8-hour days, adopted in more than 500 establishments, including government dockyards and workshops, nearly all municipal gasworks, and most London engineering (Webb, 1919, fn. 1 to p. 352). Hours were often shorter in the big cities. The achievement of the week not exceeding 54 hours and providing the Saturday half-holiday was unique in its time and celebrated as 'la semaine anglaise'. But factories generally retained the 60-hour week in 1901, while much longer hours were still common on the railways. Then came a further modest but widespread reduction: by 1913, Clapham (1938, p. 479) estimated, the working week had been shortened by 10 per cent at the most, and by an average of between 2½ and 5 per cent.

In the U.S.A. the differences between regions, industries, and even firms in the same industry, were extraordinarily wide. But the workday calculated on the weighted average of 13 industries in the Aldrich Report came down, though only from 10·9 to 10·1 hours, between 1860 and 1890: we should multiply by six to get weekly hours. Between 1890 and 1913 the average workday in all manufacturing was further reduced to under 9·4 hours (Long, 1960, p. 37; Rees, 1961, p. 33).

In all countries the actual hours worked will have varied around the normal day and week according as firms worked short-time and overtime. These varied with the trade cycle. So far as hours changed in the longer run, it will have been partly through legislation and still more through trade unions limiting overtime, particularly where, as on the British railways, overtime had formerly been worked systematically, often without extra payment even at the normal hourly rate. Since a change in hours usually requires a collective decision, it is not so amenable as wages to individual bargaining, and much more than wages it provides a field in which we might expect to distinguish the impact of trade unionism. Certainly some of the conspicuous reductions of hours were obtained by trade unionists after a struggle. But other reductions had been obtained before the general extension of unionism from 1890 onwards; and in any case hours were generally shorter for the white collared workers who as yet had few unions or none.

The hours worked in the year depend also on the number of public holidays and days of vacation; but there is no evidence as yet of any extension of these, save by a few advanced employers.

When hours of work were so long, many workers found relief through absenteeism, often on 'blue Monday' or 'St Lundi' or the 'trois jours de libation', and not then alone. In some times and places at least absenteeism prevailed on a scale of which we have little conception today. In so far as it represented a reduction of annual hours to a tolerable total, it may well have fallen when daily hours were reduced, and in this case annual hours will have changed less than daily. Experience with munition workers in wartime makes this seem probable, but we have no records.

12. The springs of productivity: a comparative study of the U.K. 1890–1913

When we followed the movements of productivity, in Section 1.B.7, we contrasted the similarity of the rise in different countries down to the 1890s with the divergence thereafter. One exceptional part of this divergence stood out in Fig. 17: the rise of productivity in British industry was halted abruptly in 1900, and the check persisted down to the War. Our object now is to throw light on the origins of this check by asking why it should have been experienced at this time and by the U.K. alone of our five countries.

We may begin by looking behind the aggregate of British industry to some of the particular industries that composed it. At the top of Fig. 29 we see indexes of productivity in four industries for which we have estimates from 1871 onwards both of output and of numbers occupied or employed. Among the estimates of output, those for iron ore and coalmining measure output in tons, without distinction of quality. That for shipbuilding covers only so much of the output of the yards, whether mercantile or naval vessels, or repairs to either type, as was paid for in the U.K.: it does not include exports, which are recorded only from 1899. This is unfortunate, for exports made up a substantial part of all output – in the aggregate of 1899–1913 nearly a sixth. This share, moreover, fluctuated cyclically, being over a quarter in the peak years and little more than a tenth in the trough. Within 1899–1913 there is no apparent trend in this share; but supposing there were one through the earlier years, it would take a considerable effect on our estimates of productivity. If, for example, exports had been half as big relatively to the output for the home market in the 1870s as in 1899–1913, actual productivity would have risen between those periods by some 60 per cent instead of the 50 per cent we estimate here. The output of shipbuilding is recorded by value, and this has evident advantages over a reckoning by tonnage, but not a little will depend on the suitability of the index of construction costs that we have drawn on to obtain an index of output in physical terms. For the railways, however, we measure output by receipts in current pounds sterling. This is for lack of any index of the myriad fares and freights of the British railways; but actually these changed little – from 1892 to 1913, indeed, they were effectively frozen by Act of Parliament (Clapham, 1938, pp. 360–61). The numbers of persons occupied, which we use to obtain output per head, is in coalmining the number actually employed, as reported year by year at the time, but in the other three industries it is based on the numbers reported in certain occupations by the decennial censuses of population, and we have obtained numbers for the intervening years simply by interpolating, with adjustment for unemployment only in shipbuilding. The cyclical fluctuation of the

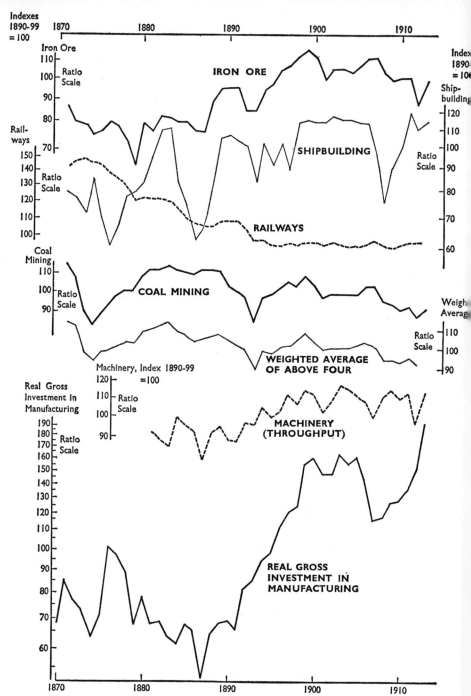

Fig. 29 U.K., 1870–1913: Indexes (1890–1899 = 100) of (1) productivity in iron ore mining, shipbuilding, railways and coal mining; (2) weighted average of the above four indexes; (3) productivity (where production is estimated from throughput) in manufacture of machinery; (4) real gross investment in manufacturing.
Sources: Appendix 2, U.K. G (a).

estimates of productivity that we derive from these three series will therefore be wider than that of the product per person actually employed. The numbers in all series are of persons, without distinction of age, sex or skill, or adjustment for hours worked.

These first four industries selected themselves because they alone would yield estimates of productivity as far back as 1871, but the selection proves useful in showing four different courses of change. In both iron ore and shipbuilding productivity was lifted by something like 50 per cent between the 1870s and 1900, but thereafter it declined in iron ore, and remained at the same level (save for one sharp depression) in shipbuilding. In coalmining, after a wide cyclical movement in the 1870s, with the low point of productivity in the boom, productivity declines through the thirty years after 1883, irregularly but progressively. Railways show a progressive decline too, but all in the first thirty years: by 1900 productivity had come down by a third, but after that it hardly changed at all.

That the courses of change in four industries should be so different suggests at once that the movements of productivity as we estimate them for industry as a whole may have come about at least in part by the summation of the effects of factors that were specific to particular industries and affected them variously. The early decline in productivity on the railways, for instance, may be attributed largely to the extension of lines and services that attracted less traffic per unit of equipment and labour than the arterial services provided earlier: the number employed grew steadily, and grew faster than receipts. The downturn in the mid-80s of tonnage per man-year in coalmining, again, has been ascribed in great part to the exhaustion of the most easily worked seams, no longer offset by sufficient technical improvements (Taylor, 1961–1962). On the other hand, iron ore and shipbuilding do show a check to the rise of productivity at or near 1900. This does not show itself in the curve of Fig. 29 that traces the progress of the four industries in the aggregate, for this is dominated by coalmining – in 1891 the numbers occupied or employed were, in thousands, in iron ore 21, shipbuilding 94, railways 213, coalmining 668. But these numbers remind us that the four industries together contained little more than a tenth of the whole number occupied in industry in 1891. It is therefore quite possible that, outside these four, some major force was operating on a wide front, to turn the tide of productivity about 1900.

When we turn to the next series in Fig. 29 we seem to see that force at work. This series shows the throughput of steel per occupied person (excluding the unemployed) in engineering. It covers a wide sector of the occupied population – more than half a million, against coalmining's two-thirds, in 1891. It should, moreover, be sympto-matic. We have treated it separately from the first four partly because difficulty in identifying the numbers occupied in the censuses before 1881 obliges us to begin only with that year, but also and especially because it is based not on output but on the estimates compiled by Cairncross (1953, tables 36, 37) of the ingot tons of iron and steel used annually by the engineering industry. It therefore takes no account of those changes in the man-hours spent on the ingot ton that were due to changes in design, as distinct from changes in equipment and the skill and effort of the worker. In practice it will have been next to impossible to disentangle the two factors: if design began to call for greater precision, that may well have been because improved equipment made this attainable in the same time as before, or even less. But in principle one can ask how long it would take to carry out today's design with yesterday's equipment and labour, and if the actual time today is less, ascribe the difference to improvements in equipment and labour, that is, to higher productivity. On this hypothetical way of reckoning, we might well find that productivity had risen when the throughput of steel per man-hour had fallen. But here we can only take that throughput to indicate productivity as it stands. If the trend of design was towards requirements which with unchanged equipment and labour would have reduced throughput, the course of throughput understates the actual rise in productivity.

With that qualification in mind, we are still bound to attach significance to so sharp a change of trend as appears at 1900. Through the 1880s there had been little change save for the deep trough of 1886; but in the 1890s came a lift, that raised the throughput per man by a sixth between 1893 and 1899; and then comes if anything a downward trend. We note that this repeats the pattern of iron ore, except that there the lift began earlier, in 1887. In the clear marking of the change of course this pattern resembles that which first caught our notice in 'all industry'; but here the trend after the change is downward, whereas in 'all industry' it was level.

These five series are all we have for particular industries with a run of years before 1900. We can, it is true, deduct them from the total for 'all industry', in order to follow the course of change in the residual sector – mostly manufacturing other than engineering; transport; utilities; and building. But since this residual sector contained so great a part of the labour force in 'all industry' – in 1891 nearly 84 per cent – we shall expect productivity within it to behave not very differently from that already estimated for 'all industry'. So in fact it did; we therefore do not show it in Fig. 29. It is a pity that we cannot separate the part played by building here. We know that the number of new houses built went through a great cycle between 1895 and 1910, with the peak in 1899 but a high output sustained as far as 1906 (Cairncross, 1953, table 35), and we should expect productivity to rise and fall with output. But a great part of the output of the building industries consists of repairs, and we lack any index of output at this time that includes these.

In Fig. 29 we have still one series to notice, that of real investment in manufacturing; but before we bring it into the argument we should consider some further evidence concerning productivity in particular industries, though it begins only with 1900. It comes from the indexes of production by Lomax (1959), which we have combined with our own estimates, based on the Censuses of Population in 1901 and 1911, of the number occupied in each industry, to form indexes of productivity; the detail of our working is described in Appendix 2. For the intercensal years we have had to rely on linear interpolation: we have no means of knowing what actual changes there were from year to year in the numbers who, whether employed or unemployed, would be classified as occupied in the industry. In only five series have we been able to adjust the interpolations for unemployment. In their year to year movements, therefore, though not their trend, our indexes of productivity largely mirror the indexes of production.

Both sorts of index are shown in Fig. 30. A first finding here is again that different industries fared differently. In paper and printing, textiles, clothing and utilities, productivity followed a rising trend. But in the six other industries that are now shown separately there was little or no rise, or an actual fall. There was no rise in productivity in chemicals, and little in food, drink and tobacco. The sharp drop and recovery in leather is exceptional, but leaves us with a fall from end to end. The trend in mining, metal manufacture and mechanical engineering seems to be downward. Where indexes of production and productivity are shown together as they are here, we expect to find

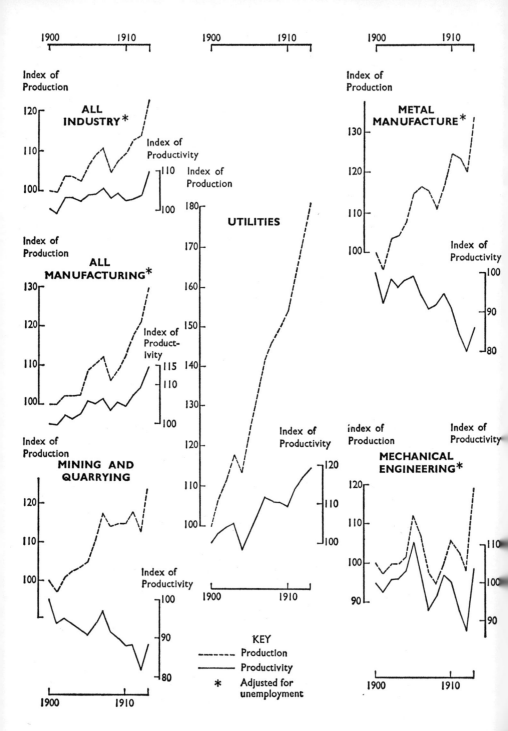

Fig. 30 U.K. 1900–1913: Indexes (1900=100) of produc

Source: Appendix 2, U.K. G (b).

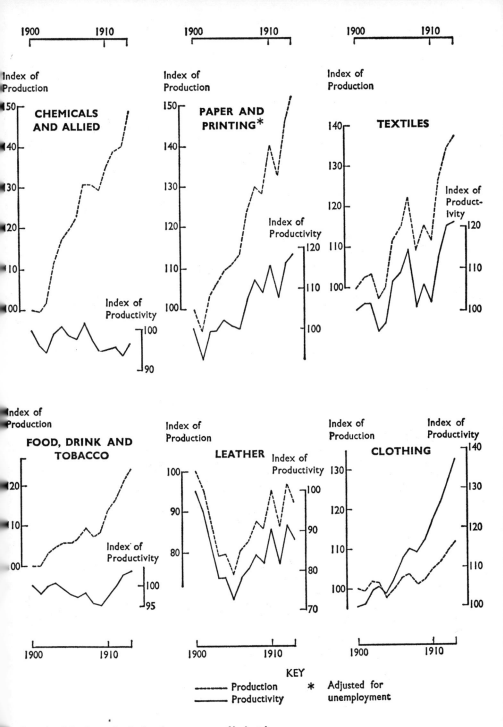

KEY
------- Production   * Adjusted for
——— Productivity   unemployment

of productivity in twelve industries or groups of industries.

some association between their movements: at least in recent experience of movements in the short run, rises in production have generally gone with rises in productivity, and conversely. Here we certainly do find this in the four industries in which productivity rose too, and the inclusion of such a technically stable industry as textiles is significant. Yet production also rose in other industries in which productivity rose little or not at all – food, drink and tobacco; and chemicals – or actually fell – mining; and metal manufacture.

Out of this variety of experience, industry by industry, what came in the aggregate? The indexes of productivity in manufacturing and in 'all industry' both move differently before and after 1910. In manufacturing productivity rises until 1905, and changes little from 1905 to 1910; but in the next three years it goes up by 10 per cent. In 'all industry' the same two phases appear, though with less lift overall, down to 1910; here too a steep rise follows, though only in 1912–1913. The years after 1910 were a time of cyclical revival and, by 1913, near boom, but we are confronted here with a movement on more than the cyclical scale. It may well be, then, that the change of course in 1900 brought in no more than a pause in a process of development that resumed its progress after ten years. In Part Two we shall see that it continued after the First World War. History records other such pauses. Fig. 17 shows that not until 1886 did productivity in British industry regain its level of 1873; nor did German industrial productivity regain its level of 1874 until 1889. A break that was not merely a pause but an actual setback has been recorded by Butlin (1962, table 13; 1964, table 2) in the rapid development of Australia. Here the real gross domestic product had increased fourfold between 1861 and 1891, but after that year it did not rise again until 1903/1904: instead it fell back nearly a fifth. As the workforce continued to grow fast meanwhile, productivity fell sharply – in 1900 it was actually lower by nearly a sixth than ten years before. But when in 1903/1904 the advance was resumed, it was rapid.

Yet if what the U.K. experienced in 1900–1910 was only a temporary interruption to the course of growth, such as any economy is liable to experience occasionally, we still want to know how this particular interruption came about. What made the difference, about 1900, firm by firm, up and down the country? Our survey of those all too few industries in which we can estimate the course of productivity separately has revealed much diversity: in two industries at least

productivity was declining before the 1890s, in others it continued to
rise until 1913. Yet it still seems probable that many industries were
affected in much the same way at much the same time. The four
industries of Fig. 30 in which productivity rose contained between
them in 1901 a little less than a third of the labour force covered by
the curve for 'all industry'. Evidently there is room among the
remaining two-thirds for other industries in which productivity
likewise rose. But if the room so occupied were wide, the actual
course of productivity in 'industry' would imply that in the other
particular industries productivity fell, and fell substantially. It seems
more probable, since a pause in the rise of production is easier to
account for than an actual fall, that the pause shown by our indexes
for 'industry' in the aggregate was experienced in common by a
substantial number of the particular industries making that aggregate
up.

We have therefore to look for some common influences. Of any
that suggest themselves we must ask, did they impinge with especial
force upon the U.K. in the 1890s? and can they be seen to act on the
U.K. at this time, singly or in combination, as they did not on the
other four countries?

One such influence might be looked for in the fluctuations of
investment. Sometimes surges of investment arise from the expansion
of new industries or processes in which productivity is above the
average of the time. Whether in new industries or old, investment
may be the carrier of technical innovation which raises productivity.
Even without technical change, net investment was required year by
year in the U.K. of these times simply to maintain the level of
equipment per worker in the presence of a remorselessly rising
number of workers – the number of persons in manufacturing rose by
14 or 15 per cent in each of the three decades between 1881 and 1911.
For all these reasons, variations in the rate of investment might be
associated with nearly contemporary changes in productivity. We
come back, therefore, to the curve at the foot of Fig. 29 which shows
real gross investment in buildings and equipment in manufacturing
industry, and which we have taken from Aristidou (1965). What
catches the eye here is the upsurge during the 1890s. Might not this
help to explain the abruptness of the check that ensued? Might not
this upsurge have offset for a time a slowing down of productivity
that had set in already and would reassert itself sharply when the

upsurge ended? But this suggestion does not fit the facts. It is true that the upsurge of investment through 1892–1900 overlaps a rise of productivity through 1893–1898; but this rise was largely a cyclical recovery which did little more than bring productivity back on to the trend along which it had been mounting since 1871. The peak, moreover, came in 1898, and productivity then dropped back to a lower level, whereas investment remained high for no less than eight years more. Earlier, through the eleven years 1881–1891, investment had ruled very low, but Fig. 17 indicates that this brought no check to productivity, which rose over those eleven years at the rate of more than one per cent a year, whereas over 1894–1906, when investment was more than twice as big, it did not rise at all. This one per cent of the 1880s, moreover, was as rapid a rise as had been achieved during the preceding investment boom of the 1870s. It thus appears that, in this time and place at least, there was no dependable relation between aggregate gross investment in manufacturing and the rate of rise of productivity in the aggregate of industry. We cannot seek the explanation of the changed course of productivity in the fluctuations of investment.

But it will be said that those fluctuations have to be very large to make much immediate difference to the amount of capital per worker, and it is this that is the dominant influence on productivity. The estimates that we presented in Fig. 24 of the movements of real capital per occupied person in the non-farm sector of the British economy suggested two reflections, one for the long run and one for the short. It will be remembered, first, that the level of equipment so defined seems actually to have declined somewhat through 1882–1895: the contrast with the rapid and sustained rise of the corresponding German series at this time prompts the thought that British productivity was checked about 1900 because too little had been invested through the years before. But through these thirty years, it seems, a steady or even declining level of equipment had in fact been consistent with rising productivity: if it was indeed the failure of that level to rise that checked productivity about 1900, at a time when the level had been rising for some years, why was the effect so long delayed? Our attention is directed not to the physical quantity of the capital but to the extent of technical innovation that it embodied. But, second, as to the short run: we have just noted that when the check to productivity came the level of equipment was rising –

Fig. 24 shows it as rising through 1898–1906. This implies a fall in the output per unit of capital, that is, a rise in the capital/output ratio. Fig. 21 in fact indicated that the capital/output ratio rose from 2·1 in 1895–1898 to a level of from 2·3 to 2·4 or more from 1900 onwards.

A shift of this kind can come about as the result of one or both of two sorts of change. First, the effective input of the human factor may decline. Capital of given type and amount, operated by a given labour force, may yield a smaller product than before because labour works fewer hours in the year, or is less willing and energetic while at work; or because operations are less efficiently directed by management. Second, with unchanged efficiency of the human factor, the product per unit of capital may still fall because the aggregate of capital now contains a higher proportion than before of types of equipment that, with given labour input, yield a product smaller than the average product of all types. It is of course unlikely that investment will be made in equipment technically inferior to what has already been installed. But it can well happen that investment continues, so as to raise the amount of capital per worker, after recent opportunities for obtaining a high yield have been used up, while for the time being technology fails to create new opportunities of the kind. In such a case investment can only add to the amount of equipment of existing types. If none the less it continues, so as to raise the amount of capital per worker, it will run into diminishing returns: the marginal product of capital will fall, and with it the average.

There is reason to believe that both these kinds of change were taking place in the U.K. from the 1890s onwards.

We know, for one thing, that the weekly hours of labour were reduced then. The major reduction, it is true, had been brought about already – it was in the 1870s that the 54-hour week with the Saturday half-holiday had been widely adopted. This, moreover, remained the predominant arrangement down to 1914. But it was subject to much variation, often by informal local agreement. In 1892, for instance, there was a general reduction of hours in the London building trades, to a week, averaged over the seasons of the year, of under 49 hours. 'We have the adoption, between 1889 and 1897, of the Eight Hours' Day in over five hundred establishments, including the Government dockyards and workshops, nearly all municipal gasworks, and a majority of the London engineering and bookbinding establishments, together with isolated firms all over the country' (S. & B. Webb, 1919, fn. 1 to p. 352). In coalmining down to 1908 hours were reduced by local agreements, and then throughout the industry by Act of Parliament – 'in that year a decline of 7½ per cent in the hours of work of those employed at the face was matched by a 6½ per cent decline in general net productivity' (Taylor, 1961–1962, p. 56), though this was a year that also saw many stoppages. On the railways there had been no 54-hour week gained by the 1870s, or anything like it – in 1886 the week of 72 hours was still common; and an Act of 1893 that provided a procedure for complaints against excessive hours took little effect. But what did take effect was trade union pressure, through which the extraordinarily long hours that some crews had been required to work were precluded, and the week of six 10-hour days was obtained by 1905 'on some railways for many grades'. The Board of Trade's inquiry into earnings and hours in 1906–1907 found an average week of 58·3 hours on the railways, against 54·4 hours in all the industries covered; but that still marked a reduction of near 20 per cent from the hours prevailing twenty years before (Halverson, 1952). In printing, the week was reduced during the 1890s from 54 to 52 hours, and by 1914 in the large towns it had become 50–51 hours. An Act of 1901 effectively reduced weekly hours in textiles by one hour. In his survey of 1887–1914, Clapham (1938, p. 479) reached the conclusion 'that the working week in British industry had been shortened by a maximum of about 10 per cent in the most favoured trades, and by an average which probably lay somewhere between 2½ and 5 per cent'.

There are unmistakable instances of the reduction of hours bringing a fall in output per man-year – the coal industry in 1908, already mentioned, or the change from 12-hour to 8-hour shifts in Cleveland pig iron (G. T. Jones, 1933, p. 127). But even if every reduction brought productivity down in strict proportion, the annual effect of a total of 5 per cent – to take Clapham's upper limit for the average of all industry – spread over twenty years or more, would have been small. Nor, as we have seen, was this a course of change that set in for the first time in the 1890s, and the trend of productivity had not been broken off by the earlier reductions. But in any case we can by no means assume that productivity tended to fall in proportion to weekly hours. On the contrary, it was part of the case for shorter hours, accepted by many an employer because endorsed by experience, that they would not lower the output per man-year: with less accumulated fatigue, the hourly output would rule higher, while a reduction of the commonly high rate of absenteeism would help maintain the number of hours actually worked in the course of the year.

The reduction in hours, moreover, was not peculiar to the U.K. One particular instance is in coalmining. We have given shorter hours as one cause of the fall of British productivity here: but in French and German coalmining likewise productivity fell at this time, and at least in the Silesian field the shortening of the shift was alone enough to account for it (Kuczynski, 1945, pp. 151–2; 1946, p. 179). Hours were not reduced in coalmining alone: in Section 1.A.4 we have cited evidence for reductions in all four countries other than the U.K. Though hours were generally shorter in 1900–1913 in the U.K. than in the other countries, it is by no means clear that in the U.K. they were now being shortened more rapidly. In these countries, however, there was no check to the rise of productivity. There remain two possibilities: either shorter hours exerted little adverse influence on productivity in any country; or they did exert such an influence, but in the other countries it was more than offset by factors not operative in the U.K.

It may be urged, however, that any reduction in effort brought about in the U.K. by shorter hours would in any case have been small in comparison with that due to the changed attitude of the worker, which to many contemporary observers was unmistakable. The pressure for shorter hours had itself been both permitted and instigated by the rise in real rates of pay, and the same effect was seen in a reduction of effort by pieceworkers who did not need to produce so much as before in order to obtain a given real weekly wage. But much more than this, there was a withholding of co-operation formerly given, an increased resistance to management, a resentment and denial of its authority. Hobsbawm (1960) has characterised this change as a watershed in the nineteenth century history of the employment of industrial labour. The old principle of 'a fair day's wage for a fair day's work' had meant 'the relative wage which custom assigns to a worker of given status, in return for work done at a customary level of performance'. But now, instead of asking whether his relative wage was commensurate with his status, the wage-earner asked whether it was as high as it should or could be, for a member of society in which wealth was conspicuous; and whether the employer had been made to pay as much as he could really afford in the present state of the market. Increasingly now the wage-earner was literate, and his reading widened his horizons, and made his narrow means seem narrower.

If then the wage was perceived as low, the evident response was to do little for it. If employers for their part turned away from custom and appealed to the law of the market, they must expect to get no more than they paid for. The Seamen's circular of 1896 that gave currency to the term Ca' Canny put the point:

> Employers of labour declare that labour and skill are 'mere marketable commodities', the same as hats, shirts or beef. . . . Then the possessors of such commodities are justified in selling their labour and skill in like manner as the hatter sells a hat or the butcher sells his beef. They give value for value. Pay a low price and you get an inferior article or a lesser quantity (Phelps Brown, 1959, p. 290).

If wages, moreover, are to be fixed in the market, then the wage-earner can get a better price if he can keep his kind of skill scarce, by limiting entry, and enforcing lines of demarcation that no other man may cross to do his job. If these restrictions did not suggest themselves to the wage-earner as a means to higher wages in a good year, they would force themselves on him as a defence against unemployment in a bad one.

If, as the record of the times suggests, these considerations came to be much more widely and actively entertained during the 1890s, we must expect some general reduction of industrial effort. The author of the Oxford history of England in this period, himself sympathetic to socialism as a young man at that time, had no doubt that there was one. Discussing the 'check to the national productivity and prosperity' after 1890, he attributes it, among other causes, to trade unionism. 'In itself it was a healthy growth. But it early became associated in Great Britain (as in no other European country to the same extent) with a piece of mistaken economics (sometimes called "ca' canny" and sometimes the "loomp o' labour" theory) – the doctrine that there is only a fixed amount of employment to be had, and that, therefore, the less any worker does, the more there will be for others to do.' Employers contended 'that from about 1900 onwards the tightening of trade-union control had resulted in a definite lowering of British productivity. Some of the complaints were doubtless exaggerated; but it seems significant in retrospect, that the stop in the progress of British productivity did in fact occur at that time' (Ensor, 1936, pp. 501–2).

But here again the comparison with other countries gives us pause. The change of attitudes in the U.K. was signalised by the rise of the New Unionism, which connoted both the extension of organisation to the unskilled and the infusion of a more militant spirit into the established unions. In Section 1.B.4, however, we have seen how unionism was also extending rapidly between 1890 and 1914 in all four other countries; and that there too its spirit was militant was shown by many and often bitter conflicts. For all the famed docility and discipline of the German worker, the number of man-days recorded as lost through industrial disputes in the course of 1899–1913 was greater in Germany than the U.K. (Bry, 1960, table A.1; Mitchell & Deane, 1962, ch. 2, table 9).

That in these other countries none the less there was no check to the rise of productivity may mean that the resistances were not so strong there as in the U.K. We cannot measure militancy, it is true, but we do know that in 1890 trade unionism covered a greater part of industry in the U.K. than in any of the other countries. Even more important, in the U.K. it was old-established in the industries which in other countries were now growing the most rapidly, steel and engineering; here it had conserved working practices over which the craft unions now fought management, and lines of demarcation over which they fought one another. But in the other countries these industries in their more recent growth had recruited newcomers to industry, who if they now became unionised joined unions which generally conserved no craft traditions. Burn (1940, pp. 146–48) tells how the German steel industry was growing so fast that it had to recruit labour from East Prussia and from Italy. Two characteristics he notes of the labour force of the British steel industry enforce the contrast we have indicated. One, the high rate of absenteeism, was partly due to drunkenness, and exhaustion by the 12-hour shift; but also, 'probably the workers had not lost the tradition of spasmodic activity associated with handicraft industry; it was a tradition that puddling might nurture and which rolling might tolerate if the plant were primitive'. Secondly, there was a propensity to go slow. In steel this was associated with the introduction of new equipment and with rate-fixing. 'In the declining malleable iron industry it was, and had been, chronic'. American observers thought it was due to strong unionism.

But not only does it seem probable that labour was more militant or obstructive in the U.K.: it also seems to have met with less effective opposition from the employers there. Among the factors that Lloyd Ulman (1961, p. 389) has recorded as reacting against unionism in the U.S.A. at this time were 'the rejection and decisive defeat of the Iron and Steel Workers' Union in 1901 by the newly formed United States Steel Corporation', and the 'opposition of the National Association of Manufacturers . . . representing independent businessmen and conservative elements in the small towns and the Middle West'; 'opposition to unionism frequently took the form of community-wide crusades by local "open shop associations" and "citizens' alliances" '. Union action was also increasingly inhibited by injunctions granted by the courts. French employers replied to the doctrine of direct action proclaimed by the C.G.T. in the Charter of Amiens in 1906 by forming associations for mutual insurance against the losses imposed by strikes; but it was the government, with Clemenceau as Minister of the Interior, that reacted most strongly against strikes, arresting trade union leaders, and sending in troops who opened fire. When the railwaymen struck in 1910 they were called to the colours and their strike committee was arrested. In Sweden after a political general strike in 1902 the employers formed a cohesive national confederation: in 1909 it met some local strikes by locking out most of three industries, and in the general strike that followed it beat the unions, whose membership in the next two or three years fell by a third. A strike of textile workers in Saxony in 1903 led to the formation of two nationwide associations of German employers whose purpose was to fight the unions: in 1909–1911 lockouts affected nearly twice as many workers as did strikes (Dawson, 1912, pp. 205–206). In any case the cartels gave great power to the relatively small number of industrialists or bankers who dominated them; some, it is true, shared their monopoly gains with their workers, but the director of the great Westphalian coal and iron cartel refused to negotiate with any union whatsoever (Dawson, 1919, pp. 195–203).

In the United Kingdom, by contrast, there was no effective national association of employers. It is true that the engineering employers quickly built up a strong national organisation in 1897, to meet what they felt to be a challenge by the unions to their authority in their own workshops; and many other associations were formed, most of them local, but with some national federations. But in the open market of a free trade country the cartel was impracticable, and the British employer typically remained competitive with other employers and suspicious of them. Nor, save for the shipowners and the railway directors, were British employers generally inclined to attack the unions; if they associated it was more often to negotiate with unions whose leaders they respected (Phelps Brown, 1959, ch. v, p. 8). The historians of British trade unions since 1889 record counter-attacks on the New Unionism in the 1890s, whose object was to enable employers to put through changes in their workshops despite traditional craft controls; but the outcome at the most was 'to convert unilateral regulation of working conditions by the craft societies into joint regulation by collective bargaining'. When the Taff Vale judgment, moreover, gave the employers an opportunity to break the unions, those who tried to take advantage of it were few. 'The experience of the first five years of the twentieth century suggests that, despite Taff Vale, the majority of organized employers preferred to make a serious attempt to work with the unions' (Clegg, Fox & Thompson, 1964, chs. 2 & 4, esp. pp. 168–178; ch. 9, esp. pp. 362–63). But working with the unions meant willingness not to push changes in working practices through too fast, and to give some up altogether.

In sum, there is reason to believe that in the changed attitude of the workers, and the employers' response to it, there was a factor inimical to productivity that impinged with differential force on the U.K. from the 1890s onwards. So far as it meant only a reduction of the input of effort per man-year, its impact on any one workshop would have been once for all. If such impacts were concentrated on the boom of 1898–1900, they might have offset other changes tending to raise productivity meanwhile, and account for the immediate check to productivity in 1900; but the continuance of the check through the ensuing decade would be accounted for only if the impacts were spread out in time, so that their once for all effect was felt by a number of workshops in each year. There may have been something of this, but it seems likely that the continuance of the check owed more to another facet of changed attitudes, the resistance to changes in methods and the use to the full of labour-saving equipment. This resistance once set up would have continued to inhibit those minor but cumulative changes that contribute some part of the annual rise of productivity. Yet it can hardly have acted on a bigger scale than that. It might have held productivity back by offsetting minor innovations, but if major innovations had continued to come forward, it might hardly have been noticed. What G. T. Jones (1933, p. 97) found for the London building industry may stand as an epitome of the composition of forces in industry at large. Between 1850 and 1910, he concluded, the efficiency of the industry, as measured by the real input per unit of output, was raised only by some 17 per cent, and this was 'almost entirely due to the introduction of machinery to the joiners' shop': the other trades – brickwork, plastering, masonry, roofing, plumbing and painting – contributed little or nothing.

This conclusion does not imply that other developments such as the use of electric derricks and cranes to haul materials into position, or of motor transport on the road, have not effected considerable economies per se. The evidence is simply that economies arising from the progress of industrial techniques and from inventions have been neutralised by diseconomies associated with growing discontent among the workmen leading to increased cost of supervision, to a shorter working day even in fine weather, and to the direction of the masters' energies to meet trade union requirements.

We conclude that though the changed attitude of labour took effect to offset or preclude some part of the normal course of productivity-raising change, we have to look beyond it to a shortfall of major innovations if we are to reach a sufficient explanation of a halt in the rise of productivity so complete and so long. We come back, that is to say, to the second of the two kinds of change that we noted as possible causes of a rise in the capital/output ratio – a drop in the rate at which new techniques are being embodied in current investment.

We have no means of measuring that rate, but there are indications that it was slower in the U.K. at this time than before, and than in other countries at the same time. By 1900 the application of steam to power and transport, and of steel to equipment, had been largely worked through. New techniques, in electricity, chemicals, the man-made fibres, and the internal combustion engine with its applications to transport, were being developed, but mostly as yet were only at the stage of the pilot plant: their impact would not be massive until after the First World War (Phelps Brown & Handfield-Jones, 1952, para 10). The technical development of engineering and the steel it used could still be rapid. But in the aggregate it may well be that the technical advances at the stage of widespread application were fewer at this time than they had been before and were to be again. On this view, a pause in the rise of productivity impended over all western economies at this time. They could escape it, however, in so far as, like Sweden, they still had part of an earlier stage of development to work through; or, like the United States, had great natural resources to exploit; or, like Germany, expanded vigorously the industries of engineering and steel in which most of the current harvest of innovation was to be reaped (Richardson, 1965). The last course lay open to the U.K. Why did it fail to take it?

Much has been held due to the inertia of British management. In 1886 the Royal Commission on the Depression of Trade had noted 'some falling off among the trading classes of this country from the more energetic practice of former periods' (Final report, paras. 74–6, 106). Marshall (1903) observed how a combination of causes had 'made many of the sons of manufacturers content to follow mechanically the lead given by their fathers. They worked shorter hours, and they exerted themselves less to obtain new practical ideas than their fathers had done'. It has been pointed out how a traditional system of values, in which the greatest esteem attached to the pursuits of a landed aristocracy on their estates and in public life, drew off businessmen as they made their fortune, and absorbed their descendants. It has also been remarked how the whole cast of British education, by its emphasis on the arts of leisure and the culture of the learned professions, turned young men's minds away from business, while an extraordinary lack of schools of technology deprived those who did enter business of a training that to many of them should now have been indispensable.

But this decline in the energy and adaptability of management as the generations turned over was only one of the ways in which British enterprise was handicapped by the very length of its history. Growth had already gone so far that towns were congested, and further expansion was stopped by the physical limits of present sites. Urbanisation brought external economies, but the principal English conurbations, which had grown by 15 per cent in each of the two decades before 1901, were able to grow by less than 10 per cent in the next. (Mitchell & Deane, 1962, ch. i, table 6). Particular plants, sidings, docks, were cramped within boundaries fixed years before (Landers, 1963, p. 562). Some firms did make a fresh start in the country; but the easier path of growth was by adding to an existing plant, and that might be blocked. Even where it could be followed, moreover, it might not lead to an efficient layout: the Departmental Committee of the Board of Trade (1918), sitting during the First World War to examine the prospects of the engineering industries, contrasted the British works in which old plant had been extended piecemeal with the numerous German plants laid out from the first on an orderly plan. In the nature of things these German plants also had more modern equipment. It can be argued that the inheritance of so much equipment from the past should, like any other gift of resources, have increased the ability of British firms to buy new equipment; but it decreased the pressure on them to do so; and where space was limited its very physical presence was an obstacle. That most British managers in 1900 were working with equipment and processes inherited from an earlier generation also inhibited growth by fixing traditional ideas in men's minds and making them inhospitable to new ones.

There is force in all this. Since moreover contemporary observers drove it home by contrast with the qualities of enterprise in Germany and the U.S.A., we can accept it as a factor peculiar to the U.K. But it does not pass the further test of having impinged with special force on the 1890s. Its influence had been apparent before, but until 1900 it had been compatible with a continuing rise in productivity. It was in any case of a kind to effect only a gradual deceleration.

If the check at 1900 is to be explained in great part by a sharp reduction in the rate of innovation, we must therefore look beyond the gradually changing qualities of managers to some marked change in the factors bearing on their investment decisions. We may find it in the course of international trade. Because technical advance in any one industry is commonly spasmodic, the rate of growth of an economy can be maintained only if the energies of enterprise are from time to time diverted into those industries, whether old or new, that currently offer fresh scope for that advance. We have already noted that in the state of technology about 1900 this principle required British enterprise to develop the steel and engineering industries. But such a development depended in turn on the expansion of the exports of these industries, because only so could the volume of output be obtained that would warrant investment in plants of a size to combine new processes with the economies of scale; and, in the short run even more, because the prospect of expanding sales that only export markets could provide was needed to stimulate enterprise sufficiently – so at least we may infer from the inquiries into the differential growth of economies in recent years that have brought out the association between expanding exports and higher rates of growth (Beckerman, 1966). But it was precisely in the 1890s that the competition of other countries in the international market for steel and machinery held British exports back increasingly. The competition came especially from Germany. Fig. 31 shows how in 1894 German exports of steel and of machinery alike began a rise, to be sustained until 1914, far more rapid than the British – a rise which was to bring German exports of machinery up from a third of the British to 40 per cent above them. Denied the stimulus to investment in innovation that prospects of expansion would have afforded, the British economy might have been so troubled by its balance of payments that the Government would have been forced to enter the field of redeployment then as it has been since. But that goad was withheld: Kindleberger (1964) following Coppock (1956) has shown how exports in the aggregate were raised, and the need for change put off, by the selling to sheltered markets of increasing quantities of traditional exports, made by traditional processes – cotton textiles, railway material, galvanised iron sheets and tinplate.

The change in international competition in the 1890s that the curves of Fig. 31 illustrate is thus the second of the two impacts on that decade about which we may build our explanation of the halting of the rise of productivity in 1900. The first was that change in the will and power of organised labour to resist management which was signalised by the New Unionism. We held that this did tend to reduce productivity at the time of its impact, and to decrease the rate at which productivity rose over time, but that its power to hold productivity down was still small in comparison with that of technical innovation to raise it. Very widely, however, the 1890s had brought a slackening in the rate of innovation, a gap between the general application of steam and steel, and the development of new techniques to the stage of widespread application. In the meantime the industries

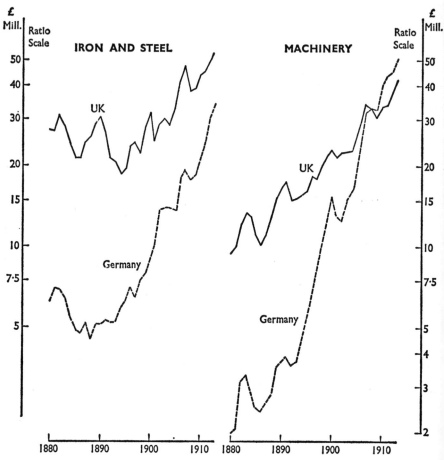

Fig. 31 Germany and U.K., 1880–1913: Exports of iron and steel and of machinery (including electrical), in £m. at current prices, figures in marks being converted at par of exchange.
Sources: Germany: W. G. Hoffmann and others, *Das Wachstum der deutschen Wirtschaft seit der Mitte des 19 Jahrhunderts* (1965), part 2, table 165. U.K.: B. R. Mitchell and P. Deane, *Abstract of British Historical Statistics*, ch. xi, table 8.

whose growth offered the best prospect of continued innovation were steel and engineering. Despite the traditionalism and the slackened energies of British management, that growth might have been achieved under the stimulus of a sufficient prospective expansion of exports; but now foreign competition removed that prospect. By

1900, therefore, the rate at which technical innovation was being realised in new equipment and processes ceased for a while to be more than enough, in the aggregate of industry, to offset the tendency to diminishing returns to investment under unchanged techniques, together with some continuing decrease in the effective contribution of labour.

Period Two
1920–1938

2A Levels of wages and incomes, 1930–1931

When in Section 1A we introduced the international comparisons of wages and incomes at 1905 and 1909, we discussed some of the problems of principle and method that any such comparisons will raise. This discussion will have served also to introduce the figures now to be presented for 1930–1931: the bases of comparison and the methods of estimating are much the same here as there.

1. Wages in money

The figures in row 1 of Table 15 are for the average of 1930 and 1931, because January 1931 is the date of the only available estimates of the comparative cost of consumables. It is a date we should have avoided were we concerned with money wages alone, for it falls in a time of rapid recession and mounting unemployment. But our measure of wages, it will be remembered, is 'the average earnings in a year of employment that is normally continuous but subject to departures from standard hours through short time, overtime and absence for personal reasons' (p. 42). Though this measure varies relatively to the hourly rate as the actual hours worked rise and fall in the course of the trade cycle, it is independent of the proportion of the labour force employed. We must remember, however, that it always exceeds the average earnings of the labour force taking employed and unemployed together, and in 1931 exceeded it greatly.

The coverage of our estimates is summarised in Table 14, and an account of the sources and our use of them is given in Appendix 1. The hazard most likely to distort comparisons is in the striking of an average that gives due weight to men, women and juveniles, when the relative earnings of those three groups, and the relative numbers in them, differed widely from one country to another.

Table 14 Five countries, 1920–1938: Coverage of (1) wage index, (2) average annual wage-earnings at 1930/1931; (3) income generated per occupied person in industry (IGPOPI).

France
(1) Wage index   Weekly earnings of men in 10 crafts including building, of weavers and of unskilled labourers, and of women in 7 occupations, all in provincial towns; of coal miners; and of Paris metal workers.

(2) Av. annual   As above, with the addition of the same 10 crafts in the Paris
wage-earnings   region, and adjusted for the earnings of juveniles.

(3) IGPOPI   Not available

Germany
(1) Wage index   Average annual earnings of all manual workers in mining, manufacturing, building, transport, gas and water.

(2) Av. annual   Manufacturing and building.
wage-earnings

(3) IGPOPI   Manufacturing, handicrafts and mining.

Sweden
(1) Wage index   Average annual earnings of all manual workers in mining; manufacturing and handicrafts; building; some transport; and a few services.

(2) Av. annual   As in (1)
wage-earnings

(3) IGPOPI   Mining: manufacturing and handicrafts; building.

U.K.
(1) Wage index[1]   Average earnings per full-time man-year in mining, manufacturing, building, transport and communications, utilities, local government and a few other services.

(2) Av. annual   Actual average wage-earnings within coverage of (1)
wage-earnings

(3) IGPOPI   Manufacturing.

U.S.A.
(1) Wage index[1]   Weekly earnings in manufacturing, bituminous coal mining, and class I steam railroads.

(2) Av. annual   As in (1)
wage-earnings

(3) IGPOPI   Manufacturing.

---

[1] In the calculation of the wage/income ratio in manufacturing we used only the manufacturing component of the wage index.

Table 15 I. Five countries, mean 1930/1931 or Jan. 1931 : Comparison of average annual wage-earnings, excluding agriculture and personal service, in money and in composite units of consumables.
II. Five countries, averages of 1924–1930 : Comparison of income per occupied person in the whole economy and in industry, and (excluding France) the wage/income ratio in industry.

I. *Mean 1930/31 or Jan. 1931* *Average annual wage- earnings,*	*France*	*Germany*	*Sweden*	*U.K.*	*U.S.A.*
1. in own currency	8347 frs	1870 M.	2517 Kr.	£118·8	$1121
2. in £s at par of exchange[1]	£67·2	£91·4	£138·6	£118·8	£230·2
3. as relatives to U.K	57	77	117	100	194
3a. (for comparison with row 3) : the correspond- ing relatives in 1905, 1909	(65)	(75)	(84)	(100)	(179)
4. Relative cost of a composite unit of consumables	96–106	102–112	113–125	100	134–148
5. Relative annual wage- earnings in composite units of consumables. (3) ÷ (4)	53–59	69–75	94–104	100	131–145
5a. (for comparison with Row 5) – the corre- sponding relatives in 1905, 1909	(57–62)	(63–67)		(100)	(118–123)

II. *Average of 1924–1930* *Whole economy, net domestic product per occupied person,*					
6. in own currency		2274 M.	3251 Kr.	£192·4	$1872
6a. in £s at par of exchange		£111·2	£179·0	£192·4	£384·4
Industry or manufacturing only, income generated per occupied person,					
7. in own currency, industry		2842 M.	4010 Kr.		
manufacturing				£170·2	$1856
7a. in £s at par of exchange,[1] industry		£139·0	£220·8		
manufacturing				£170·2	£381·1
8. Average annual wage- earnings, industry		1743 M.	2437 Kr.		
manufacturing				£119·0	$1270

Table 15 *(continued)*

Industry or manufacturing only, income generated per occupied person,	France	Germany	Sweden	U.K.	U.S.A.
9. Wage/income ratio, (8)÷(7),					
industry		0·61	0·61		
manufacturing				0·70	0·68
9a. (for comparison with row 9) : wage/income ratios, average of 1905–1911 :					
industry		(0·62)	(0·58)	(0·66)²	
manufacturing					(0·60)

¹ £1 = 124·2 frs = 20·45 RM = 18·16 Kr. = $4·87.   ² G.B. only.

In row 2 of Table 15 we have converted these earnings into sterling at the pars of exchange of January 1931. These were the rates that had been adopted as order was restored in the foreign exchanges from 1924 onwards, and that had not yet been swept away by the depression that set in during 1929. The relative money earnings that they yield, in row 3 of the Table, may be compared with the corresponding relatives at 1905 and 1909 in row 3a. The chief change is the rise in the position of Sweden and the U.S.A. relatively to the other three countries. Sweden had been neutral in the First World War; the manpower and industry of the U.S.A. had been involved for a shorter time and less deeply than those of France, Germany and the U.K. We shall therefore not be surprised to find later that the advance of productivity since 1913 had been greater in Sweden and the U.S.A., and we may anticipate this finding to suggest here a condition permissive of a relative rise of money wage-earnings in those countries.

2. Measuring the comparative cost of living

The inquiry carried out by the I.L.O. for the Ford Motor Co. in 1931 provides particulars of consumer prices collected on the spot in great detail and with great care. But it did not take the usual form of an inquiry into the comparative costs of living of the wage-earners of different countries. It was intended rather to find how much must be spent in each of six European cities to maintain the standard of living and way of life of a Detroit household whose head was earning about $7 a day on the Ford plant. This way of putting the question raises three difficulties for us. First, some of the articles of consumption in Detroit had no equivalent in Europe. We have already met this difficulty, in Period One, in the lack of an equivalent in France for the British workman's tea, and an equivalent in Great Britain for the French workman's vin ordinaire. The solution, to omit such articles altogether, is acceptable when they are only some of many articles within a category of consumables, and we could accordingly omit children's garments from the inventory of clothing in the present inquiry without great loss. But the loss was great when, for the same reason, we had to omit all housing, and work with food and clothing alone. Second, the inquiry provides us with a budget, and therefore with weights, only for Detroit, whereas we want to see the results of reckoning the comparative cost of living in Detroit and e.g. Paris, first with Detroit and then with Paris weights. We have tried to fill this gap from budgetary materials available in other sources for the European countries. Third, the prices were collected only in certain cities – Paris and Marseilles; Berlin and Frankfurt; Stockholm; Manchester; and Detroit itself – and we have reason to believe that prices in these cities differed from those prevailing in the country concerned as a whole; but it is these that we want to compare. Were the difference in the same proportion in all countries there would be no problem; but again we have reason to believe that it was not. All that we have been able to do is to try the effect of assuming that, for example, the ratio of prices in Paris to those prevailing over France as a whole was the same for food and clothing in 1931 as it was for food alone in 1905, on the evidence of the Board of Trade inquiry that we followed for that year; and similarly for the other cities, except that we lack even this basis for adjusting Stockholm prices to Swedish. That the adjustment is in any case hazardous appears when the level of prices derived for France from Marseilles comes out more than 20 per cent lower than that derived from Paris.

For all these reasons we could not regard the comparisons we based on the materials of the Ford inquiry as firm enough in themselves. But we were able to compare them with estimates made by carrying down to 1931 comparisons made on a broader and more usual basis at another date. We found, for example, that in 1905 the cost of a composite unit of consumables in France stood, at the current rate of about 25 francs to the £, at from 5 to 14 per cent above the corresponding cost in the U.K. Continuous indexes of the cost of food, clothing and fuel show it raised between 1905 and 1930–1931 by a factor of 7·22 in France and 1·66 in the U.K. So far, then, we should infer that in 1930–1931 the costs of consumables in France and the U.K. stood in the ratio of (from 105 to 114) × 7·22 i.e. to 100 × 1·66, of from 457 to 496 relatively to 100. But meanwhile nearly five times as many francs as before had come to exchange against the £. The above ratios must therefore be divided by nearly 5 (more exactly, by 122·4 ÷ 25·15), and we get a French cost of consumables in 1930–1931 of from 94 to 102 per cent of the British. This we compare with a bracket of from 88 to 114 per cent derived by us from the Ford inquiry: the midpoints of the two ranges, at 98 and 101, prove sufficiently close to give us some encouragement.

In fact we have carried this procedure out for all countries, with three different inquiries as starting-points: that for 1905 or 1909 already instanced, that for 1950 by Milton Gilbert in his *Comparative National Products and Price Levels* (O.E.E.C., 1958), and that for 1953 by the Statistical Office of the Federal Republic of Germany. With the last two starting-points we had of course to follow the cost of living index-number within each country backwards through time, but there is no difference of principle. We have worked here with relatives not to the U.K. but to the average of all countries, to preclude the possibility that an error in the figure for any one country or city chosen as base would express itself in opposite errors in the relatives calculated from it for all the others; the method of working is described in Appendix 1. The results are set out in Table 16, which thus confronts us with an array of two estimates for Sweden (rows 1 and 5) and four for each of the other countries (rows 2–5). We surveyed these with the aim of adhering as closely to the findings of the inquiry based directly on 1931 as the weight of the other evidence would allow. In fact there is a fair amount of agreement: only for the U.S.A. did we have to differ greatly from the 1931 inquiry. Having selected a central value, we allowed a range of about 5 per cent on either side of it, and the resultant brackets appear in row 6. In row 7 they are expressed as relatives to the U.K., and in this form they are entered in Table 15 at row 4.

Table 16 Various estimates of the cost of food and clothing bought by wage-earning households in each of seven cities of five countries, relative to the average cost in all, in January 1931 (rows 1, 2) or on the average of 1930/1931 (all other rows)

	Manchester U.K.	Paris France	Marseilles France	Berlin Germany	Frankfurt Germany	Stockholm Sweden	Detroit U.S.A.
1. From ILO inquiry	86	103–105	96–97	91–92	101	103–105	113–114
2. (1) adjusted to national average[1]	88	100	77–78	92–95	95		124–125
3. (1) carried forward from 1905 or 1909[2]	83–88	83–86		96–98			133
4. (1) carried back from 1950[3]	107–113	77–89		96–112			92–114
5. (1) carried back from 1953[4]	89–90	82–86		89–103		105–110	111–135
6. Relatives chosen	84–92	85–93		89–99		100–110	118–130
7. Row 6 relative to U.K.=100	100	96–106		102–112		113–125	134–148

[1] On the assumption that the costs of food and clothing in the cities concerned bore the same ratio in Jan. 1931 to the average cost for the whole country as was found for food alone, in France and Germany in 1905 and in the U.S.A. in 1909, by the Board of Trade inquiry described in Appendix 1, I. B.

[2] The relative costs of food, fuel and housing derived from the Board of Trade inquiry in 1905, 1909, as described in Appendix 1, I. B., carried forward to average 1930/1931 by use of the index numbers of cost of living described in Appendix 2 and set out in Appendix 3.

[3] The relative costs of food, alcohol, tobacco, clothing, and fuel calculated by us from tables 19, 26, and 27 of Milton Gilbert & associates' *Comparative National Products and Price Levels* (O.E.E.C., 1958) and carried back to average 1930/1931 by use of the index-numbers of cost of living described in Appendix 2 and set out in Appendix 3.

[4] Relative costs of a household budget, average 1930/1931, calculated by the West German Statistisches Bundesamt, with their findings for 1953 as starting point (Preise, Löhne, Wirtschaftsrechnungen, Reihe 10, *Internationaler Vergleich der Preise für die Lebenshaltung. Stand Januar 1960*: Statistisches Bundesamt, Wiesbaden).

The effect is that the costs of food and clothing purchased by wage-earning households in 1930–1931 seem to have been much the same, at the rates of exchange prevailing until September 1931, in France, Germany and the U.K., unless it was that they were somewhat higher in Germany; in Sweden they seem to have been higher by some 20 per cent; and in the U.S.A. higher still, almost certainly by more than a third, and probably by as much as 40 per cent.

3. Relative real wages

Combining the relative annual wage-earnings of row 3 of Table 15 with the relative costs of consumables in row 4, we arrive at the relative real wage-earnings of row 5. The differences in the costs of consumables were mostly small in comparison with those of money wages, so that the rank order of the relatives is the same for real as for money wages, save for Sweden: the excess of the Swedish money wage over the British seems to have been offset by higher costs of consumables, so that Swedish real wages were probably no higher than the British.

Row 5a repeats the relatives of 1905, 1909, for comparison. We see that in 1930/1931 the rank order of the four countries was unchanged, but Germany and the United States had both risen relatively to the U.K. Probably Sweden had risen relatively too. There is no entry for Sweden in row 5a, because we lacked a study of the comparative cost of living in Sweden in Period One; but it will be remembered that our own rough estimate of that comparative cost implied a real wage at that time about four-fifths that of the U.K. The equality of 1931 is therefore likely to mark a greater rise in Sweden, and this is probable on general grounds.

4. Hours of work

Our account of real wages needs to be supplemented by particulars of the prevailing hours of work. At the end of the First World War these underwent a revolutionary change. We have seen how before the War weekly hours were shortest in the U.S.A. and the U.K., but even here the modes can hardly be put lower than 52 and 53 hours; and in France, Germany and Sweden the predominant week was of a full 60 hours. At the end of the War all five countries came down to 48 hours or near it. In Germany, it is true, the decrees that within a month of the Armistice enjoined the 48-hour week failed of effect during the ensuing upheavals; but when activity was running high in 1928–1929 the average daily hours in industry were only about 7½. In France equally the 8-hour day and 48-hour week were given the sanction of law soon after the War, and equally here the law was at first ineffective; yet by the later 1920s an actual 8-hour day was prevalent in French industry. In Sweden by this time it was standard. In these three countries, however, it meant 8 hours a day for six days in the week: the Saturday half-holiday had yet to be gained. But in the U.K. the 8-hour day meant a week of only 44 hours. Here a great wave of reductions in 1919, when nearly 6½ million workers had their working week reduced by some 6½ hours without loss of pay, had brought average weekly hours into the range of 44–48. Only in the U.S.A. was the movement partial. In the later 1920s only half the workers in manufacturing had a 48-hour week, a number of leading industries were working 50 hours or more, and the average of all manufacturing was over 47. But these hours were still a good deal shorter than those prevailing before the War.

It was natural that a reduction of hours should be desired at the end of a war in which many wage-earners had maintained long hours under cumulated fatigue. What is more, they had earned more money than ever before at a time when there was little that money could buy: the marginal hour of work was more burdensome, the return to it was less significant as an increment of money income, and still less significant when it came to be spent. The end of the fighting, moreover, released an impulse of reform and betterment born of the solidarity of the war, and of a political regard to the returning servicemen: the shortening of hours was part of a programme of welfare and resettlement. But this was so in part because the prevailing hours had long been attacked as harmful. The Eight Hour Day had given its name to a movement. Once it had been visionary; since the 1890s it had become practical. The trade unionism that extended so widely through those pre-war years adopted shorter hours as a chief aim.

It could do so ultimately because the wage-earner could increasingly afford to give up purchasing power for leisure. In any one negotiation and settlement a given cost to the employer might be made up either of an increase in weekly earnings for the same hours as before, or of a decrease in hours worked for the same weekly earnings as before. For the wage-earner the choice depended on how much he needed the extra goods that increased earnings could buy, in comparison with the value he set upon reduced fatigue and increased leisure. As his real wage rose his need for extra goods diminished, while his valuation of leisure must if anything have increased, for greater command of amenities calls for more free time to enjoy them in. In a frictionless world such a changing equivalence might conceivably take effect in some small reduction of hours as part of each settlement. In the actual world the pressure towards shorter hours has built up through years in which most settlements have changed earnings alone, to break through in a wave of substantial reductions of hours that spread across a wide field of employment and spent itself within two or three years. It was such a wave that broke in all our countries in 1919–1920.

None the less, the cumulated changes of a span of years that includes such a wave may be regarded as expressing a collective judgment on how the available gain in real income should be divided between greater command of goods and greater leisure. Clark Kerr (1958, pp. 172–73) says 'it is fairly common to assume that the division is about half and half. This was the apparent rate of sharing in the United States over the past century'. But from 1920 to 1950, he adds, it was in the proportion of 3 parts greater command of goods to 2 parts greater leisure; and for Great Britain, Sweden and Australia, also from 1920 to 1950, he put the proportions at more like 8 to 2. What were they here?

We must first estimate the total available gain. To do this we may convert that part which has actually been taken out in the form of shorter hours into an equivalent increase in money earnings. If at the end of a span of years the wage-earners offered to restore the weekly hours that ruled at the outset, what increase in weekly earnings per man could they expect in return? ('Per man', because we need not raise the question of how many would be employed.) It seems likely that the employers could raise weekly earnings in at least the same proportion as hours without raising unit costs: because of fatigue the extra hours might add to output at less than the average rate of the previous hours, but overheads of all kinds, including time lost at starting and stopping, would now be spread over a bigger output.

Then if over a certain span real weekly earnings had risen by 20 per cent, and hours had been reduced from 54 to 48, we might put the total gain available in the end at $20 + (\frac{6}{48} \times 120)$ or 35 per cent of the initial earnings; and this will have been divided between greater command of goods and greater leisure in the proportions to 20 to 15.

We can draw here upon the estimated increases in real earnings between 1905 and 1930/1931 that will be shown in Table 17. The reduction of weekly hours meanwhile was from near 60 hours to about 48 in France, Germany and Sweden; from rather less than 54 hours to rather less than 48 in the U.K.; and, even more roughly, from a mode of around 52 hours to one around 49, in the U.S.A. Putting these magnitudes together as suggested above, we get (in round figures) for France an available gain of 54 per cent, divided between greater command of goods and greater leisure in the proportions 4, 6; for Germany, 74 per cent, divided as 5, 5; for Sweden 105 per cent, divided as 6, 4; for the U.K. 45 per cent, divided as 6, 4; and for the U.S.A. 38 per cent, divided as 8, 2. These proportions are arbitrary in themselves, because they depend on the dates we take for our span: if we had started it ten or twenty years earlier, for instance, we should have seen the command of goods increase much more than that of leisure. But they are at least taken over the same span, in which the major reduction in hours comes at much the same point for all, and so they are comparable with one another.

It is remarkable that in the first four countries, despite the differences in the available gain, the proportions in which it was divided between increased command of goods and increased leisure differed so little. These proportions also lay around the proportion of half and half which Clark Kerr found for a much longer span in the U.S.A. But in our own reckonings the U.S.A. stands out by the comparative smallness of its reduction in hours. That the initial hours were shorter in the U.S.A. than in the other countries might seem to account for this. But they had been nearly as short in the U.K.; perhaps what is most remarkable is that the U.K., with not only these comparatively short initial hours but a comparatively small gain to divide, took out so large a part of the gain in the form of shorter hours.

We began by noticing that the rises of real wages in different countries must not be compared without regard to the reductions in hours that came about over the same span. Fig. 32 now shows that when these reductions are brought into account the improvements in the economic welfare of the wage-earner in France, Germany and Sweden stand higher relatively to the U.K. and, still more, the U.S.A., then when real wages are considered alone.

The reductions in weekly hours are no sufficient guide to the change in the number of man-hours worked per year. It is likely, for

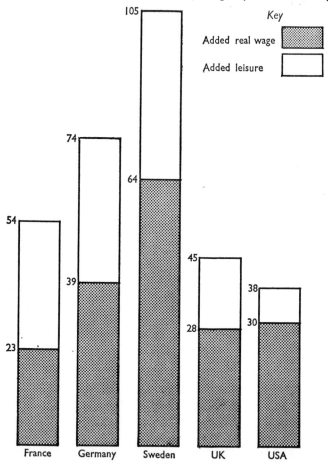

Fig. 32 Five countries: Total gain available to wage-earners from 1905 or (U.S.) 1909 to 1930/1931, expressed as percentage of the average real wage in each country at the initial date, as realised in the forms of (*a*) added real wage, (*b*) added leisure. Source: See the text at Section 2.A.4.

one thing, that they were offset by more regular attendance. We lack measures, but absenteeism in the U.K. at least was by general consent on a scale before the First World War to which there has been no counterpart since. It was due to fatigue (Vernon, 1943) and drunkenness, which in turn may have been in part an escape from fatigue. Shorter hours must have abated both causes. In 1890 the firm of Brunner Mond changed from 12-hour to 8-hour shifts, without loss of pay, in their chemical works at Northwich in England: 'the doctor had to attend only half as many men in the year 1893 as in the year 1889, and ... drunkenness, very common four years ago, has largely disappeared' (Rae, 1894, p. 76). Drunkenness in the U.K. was also reduced by the rise in the taxes on drink during the War. Wherever the material standard of living rose, moreover, the rise will have opened up more alternative activities and enjoyments. There will also have been some addition to the number of man-hours actually worked during the year through shorter weekly hours making it more practicable for a wife to take a job: not only because she would now not be so long away from home, or so tired on her return, but also because her husband would have more time and energy for a share of household tasks. Long (1958, p. 141) found that 'in the United States there was, apparently, a close association between the reduction in the average full-time work-week of all major industry groups and the increase in female labor force participation.' In what similar comparisons were possible in Canada, Germany and Great Britain, 'the association ... was close – though less so than in the United States – and it was still closer when the workweek in manufacturing was the measure of hours rather than the less well documented average for "all industries".' A third factor will have acted in the opposite direction on the total man-hours worked in the year: there was an increase in holidays with pay. In the U.S.A. these were extended to most white-collar workers after the First World War; during the 1930s they were also to be gained by many manual workers' unions, as they were in France in 1936. In the U.K. by 1938 more than 40 per cent of the manual and lower-paid white-collar workers had annual holidays with pay. Here again there will have been some offset through lower absenteeism.

So far as man-hours per annum were kept up, annual output would have been kept up too. But what happened to output depends also on the effect of shorter hours on productivity, as measured by output per man-hour. There is little doubt that shorter weekly hours, at least down to 40, will generally have brought at least some compensating increase in output per hour. Chapman (1909), surveying the experience of his day, found no instance at all of shorter hours bringing a fully proportional fall in weekly output; in the Lancashire cotton industry each successive reduction of hours in the course of the preceding three-quarters of a century had brought some increase in hourly output, if in varying degree. It is highly probable that the shortening of hours after the First World War likewise brought with it some compensating increase in hourly output. But whether this was big enough to maintain weekly output is doubtful. That it would have been when the initial hours were as long as 60 is implied by the experienced effect of extending the hours of munition workers to that region and beyond, in two World Wars: output rose at first, but then fell back to its original level, or even lower (Northrup & Brinberg, 1950, pp. 21–23). One widely experienced observer (Florence, 1924) judged that by the 1920s the 48-hour week had come to provide 'probably the optimum length of hours for ordinary business efficiency'. But observations of different industries and occupations give differing results (Viteles, 1933, ch. xxii); and we cannot appeal to the observed movements of aggregates, for these will also have been affected by the current changes in machines and methods, even though some of these may have been precipitated by the shortening of hours.

One other effect of shorter hours may be suggested. Because they left more time for travel to and from work, they will have widened the range of jobs to which a worker had access from his present house. Thereby they will have reduced employers' monopsony, and made it more likely that rises in wages would come about at much the same time throughout the local labour market.

Here we have been concerned with the hours of work that had come to prevail in the 1920s. The changes that followed under the impact of the great depression that began in 1929 we shall discuss as we follow the course of money wages through those years.

5. The wage/income ratio in industry

In 1.A.5 we gave our reasons for estimating the wage/income ratio within the sector of industry alone, and for comparing the ratios of different countries only through the averages of a number of years.

In two countries, the U.K. and the U.S.A., we have now gone farther than that, and confined our estimates to manufacturing, for which alone we could get adequate estimates of the income generated. Row 7 of Table 15 gives our estimates of income generated per occupied person, on the average of the seven years 1924–1930; we found no adequate basis of estimate for France. Row 8 presents the averages over the same seven years of our estimates of annual wage-earnings; where our estimates of the wage/income ratio are confined to manufacturing, we have taken wages likewise within manufacturing alone, so that for the U.K. and the U.S.A. the wages cited in row 8 are drawn from part only of the main and wider wage series cited in row 1.

The implied wage/income ratios appear in row 9. That for Germany is close to the level of 1905, but those for Sweden, the U.K. and the U.S.A. now stand higher. Such rises are not unexpected, for it has long been recognised that in more than one country the distribution of the national product shifted towards employment income between 1913 and the mid-1920s. Thus, to cite some recent estimates, in the U.K. income from employment was about 54 per cent of the net domestic product over 1905–1911, but more than 66 per cent over 1924–1930 (Feinstein, 1964); and in the U.S.A. it rose from 55 per cent of national income over 1905–1914 to more than 60 per cent over 1920–1929 (Kravis, 1962). In Swedish industry, however, Jungenfelt (1966, tabell 9) finds a fall in the share of wages in value added from 54 per cent in 1905–1911 to 49 per cent in 1924–1930. Rises have been reported in the share of earned income in all personal income in France (Lecaillon, 1968), and of labour income in all taxable income in four provinces of Germany (Jeck, 1968). But our present estimates show no rise in the wage/income ratio in German industry, and there are several ways in which the share of pay in the whole national product can be raised, and probably was raised at this time, without there being necessarily any rise in the wage/income ratio within industry or manufacturing alone. It will generally have been raised by the relative contraction of agriculture, in which the share is low, and the expansion of the public service, in which it is high – in some parts of which, indeed, pay appears not as a part of the product but as the whole. The share of pay will also have been raised by the general expansion of salaried occupations and the contraction of self-employment. To these intersectoral shifts happened to be added at this time an inflation which, together with controls, lowered the share of rent. But though in this way we can account for an increase in the share of pay in the national product without having to invoke any rise in the wage/ income ratio within industry or manufacturing, such a rise, in a sector that contributes so great a part of the national product, would clearly help to explain the increase. The rises in the wage/income ratios in manufacturing that our present estimates suggest for the U.K. and the U.S.A. gain in credibility accordingly. That there seems to have been no such rise within German industry may perhaps be explained by money wages having been initially set low relatively to prices in the fresh start that both made in the new currency of 1924.

We have to note, however, that solely within the business sector of the U.S.A. Grant (1963) has found no upward or downward trend in the share of employee compensation in the gross product over 1899–1929. This compensation includes salaries, the share of which will have been rising at this time. The gross product, on the other hand, includes supplies and services bought in, and depreciation, and the wage/income ratio could rise consistently with the stability of Grant's share if these latter components were relatively declining; and in the U.S.A. in the 1920s raw material prices at least stood only about 50 per cent above their pre-war level (Fig. 35), whereas money wages were more than doubled.

6. The relative levels at 1905, 1909 and 1930/1931, compared with the movements of our indexes between those dates

In his study of British wages, Bowley (1937, p. 5) was able to compare the difference between the average wages calculated from the wage censuses of 1886 and 1906 with the movement of his wage-index over the twenty years' span between those dates. We can make a similar check here. Our own estimate of average annual wage-earnings in the U.K. in 1905, for instance, was £56·1; linking our index-numbers of wages in Periods One and Two, we find a rise of 111 per cent between 1905 and 1930/1931, which would put the average in 1930/1931 at £118·4: the average independently estimated for 1930/1931 is £118·8. It is true that if the earnings at the two dates were both taken from a series that was continuous and of the same coverage in the two periods, and this also provided the index-numbers, then the only check we could make in this way would be of our arithmetic. But in no country is this wholly so. In Sweden, it is true, our average earnings in 1930/1931 are taken from the same series as yields our index-number of wages in that Period, and in the U.S.A. there is a similar coincidence in both Periods. But even here the series that yield the index are of different coverage in the two Periods; and elsewhere the averages at the two dates and the indexes in the two Periods generally make up four distinct estimates. Divergences may arise from differences in coverage and weighting between these four. There is also a hazardous link to be made between the indexes in the two Periods – we have in fact always attempted it by forming an estimate for the one year 1913 or 1914 on the same basis as for our index in Period Two.

A similar check is possible of the change in the comparative cost of consumables, though here we cannot work simply within one country at a time, and have to take account not only of the change in the prices confronting wage-earning households in each country but of the changes that took place meanwhile in the pars of exchange between the different countries' currencies. We have already given an example of the calculation (p. 204). In general, the indexes of the cost of living that we use for Periods One and Two in each country are based on substantially different inventories of purchases; we have linked them at 1913 or 1914 by carrying back the inventory of Period Two. Generally again these inventories have been more comprehensive than those used for the international comparisons. Since there were substantial divergences between the movement of the prices of different articles in the inventories we cannot expect to find the check more than roughly satisfied. It is in any case a check not of two figures but of two brackets: it will be remembered that both in 1905 and 1909 and in 1930–1931 we were able to express the 'relative cost of a composite unit of consumables' only as lying within a certain range.

In Table 17 we have set out the checks of these two kinds, for money wage-earnings and for the comparative cost of consumables, in all our countries, except that lacking materials for the cost of consumables in Sweden in 1905, we cannot make the second check there. Table 17 also shows corresponding calculations for real wage-earnings: as checks these calculations of course add nothing to those of the first two kinds, in which they are implicit, but they are set out here for the convenience of those who wish to compare the rises in

Table 17 1905 (U.S.A. 1909) and 1930/1931 : Wage-earnings in money, comparative costs of consumables, and comparative real wage-earnings, as calculated for 1930/1931 by carrying forward from 1905, 1909 by means of time series, and as estimated directly at 1930/1931.

	France	Germany	Sweden	U.K.	U.S.A.
Wage-earnings in money					
1. In 1905 or (U.S.A.) 1909	919 frs	856 M.	851 Kr.	£56·1	$512
2. 1930/31 as per cent of 1905 or 1909, according to linked time series	888	223	309	211	224
3. *Implied levels at 1930/31,* (1) × (2)	*8161 frs*	*1909 M.*	*2630 Kr.*	*£118·4*	*$1147*
4. As estimated directly for 1930/31	8347 frs	1870 M.	2517 Kr.	£118·8	$1121
5. (3) – (4) as per cent of (4)	–2·2	+2·1	+4·5	–0·3	+2·3
Comparative cost of consumables					
6. At 1905 or (U.S.A.) 1909	105–114	111–119		100	145–152
7. Cost in each country at 1930/31 as per cent of that at 1905 or 1909, according to linked indexes,					
base 1905	725	161		166	
base 1909				163	175
8. Comparative costs at 1930/31 implied by (6) × (7)					
base 1905	761–826	179–192		166	
base 1909				163	254–266
9. Ratio of no. of units of own currency per £ at par of 1930/31 to no. at par of 1905 or 1909[1]	4·938	1·0			1·0
10. (8) adjusted for changes in par of exchange, i.e. ÷ (9),					
base 1905	154–167	179–192		166	
base 1909				163	254–266
11. (10) rel. to U.K. = 100, i.e. *implied comparative costs at 1930/31*	*93–100*	*108–116*		*100*	*153–160*
12. Comparative costs from inquiry at Jan. 1931	96–106	102–112		100	134–148
Comparative real wage-earnings					
13. In 1905 or (U.S.A.) 1909, rel. to U.K. = 100	57–62	63–67		100	118–123

Table 17 *(continued)*

Comparative real wage-earnings	France	Germany	Sweden	U.K.	U.S.A.
14. Level 1930/31 as per cent of that of 1905 or 1909 in each country, according to linked indexes,					
base 1905	123	139		128	
base 1909				123	130
15. Comparative real wage-earnings at 1930/31 as implied by (13) × (14),					
base 1905	70–76	88–93		128	
base 1909				123	153–160
16. (15) rel. to U.K. = 100, i.e. *implied relative real wage-earnings at 1930/31*	*55–59*	*69–73*		*100*	*124–130*
17. As estimated directly for 1930/31	53–59	69–75		100	131–145

[1] The only change of substance in the pars of exchange was that the number of francs per £ rose from 25·15 to 124·2.

real wages in the different countries over the span of Table 17, and see what effect they had on relative standards of living.

For the most part, the checks reveal no great divergence in our estimates. In money wage-earnings the divergence is less than $2\frac{1}{2}$ per cent in all countries save Sweden, where it is $4\frac{1}{2}$ per cent. The brackets for the comparative cost of consumables overlap in France and Germany; but not in the U.S.A., where the lower limit of the bracket found for 1930/1931 by carrying forward from the bracket of 1909 lies at 153, well above the upper limit of that directly obtained for 1930/1931 from the I.L.O. inquiry. Since the international comparisons of the costs of consumables in any one year are more hazardous than the estimates of the movements of those costs from year to year in any one country, this disparity is probably due to the cost of consumables in the U.S.A. being reckoned too high relatively to the U.K. in 1909, or too low in 1931, or something of both. On the whole, however, the outcome is satisfactory. Those who have worked on the original evidence, now in its paucity and now in its diversity, know how far their findings are not solely determined by it but depend on their own acts of judgment. They may well be relieved to discover no more divergence in the outcome than appears in Table 17.

2B The course of wages, income and productivity

1. Phases in the course of money wages

If one pattern is to be found in these movements as they appear in Fig. 33, it will be that of the trade cycle whose peaks came in 1920, 1929 and 1937. At least in the second of the two spans between these peaks the imprint of the familiar sequence of recession, trough, and recovery is unmistakable, and if this cycle differs from earlier ones it is only by the very depth of the impression it made on wages.

In the first span, however, the pattern was subject to more irruptions and variations. It is true that many features are familiar. Thus in all our countries save Germany a high boom breaks in 1921, and activity drops far and fast to a trough in 1922 or 1923. The rising activity that followed in 1923–1929 contained investment booms, in both housing and manufacturing in the U.S.A., and in the public sector in Germany. There were also a number of speculative manifestations, not in Wall Street alone. But much more entered into the story of the times than cyclical movements of the kind familiar before the war. The early 1920s were dominated by the consequences of the war. The boom that reached its peak in early 1921 rose in an unprecedented surge as the liquidity inherited from the war years and increased by subsequent budgetary deficits poured over the physical scarcities that the war had imposed. When the boom broke, the fall in prices was generally of no less unprecedented rapidity and extent: in world markets the prices of basic commodities in 1922 were commonly half what they had been two years before; in the U.K. the cost of living was precisely halved in only fifteen months. But in Germany until the end of 1923, and in France from 1923 to 1926, the course of prices was dominated by inflation, which in Germany ended only when the currency had lost its value entirely.

Though these consequences of the war had been mostly worked through by 1925, it is only in part that the four following years

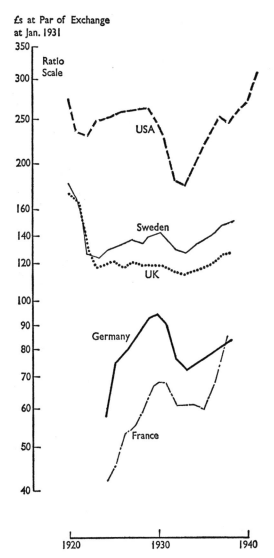

Fig. 33 Five countries, 1920s and 1930s: Money wage-earnings in £s sterling at par of exchange of January 1931.
Source: Appendix 3 and Table 15.

present the familiar picture of the rising phase of the trade cycle. Two of their features are unfamiliar. First, in the U.S.A. the general level of prices did not rise, and in Sweden and the U.K. it continued to fall. Second, Table 18 shows that though in the U.S.A. unemployment ruled much lower through the years of rising activity in the 1920s than it had done in the years before the First World War, in Germany, Sweden and the U.K. the opposite held – instead of rates of 5 per cent or less, as here reckoned, it was 11 per cent or more that now prevailed in all three countries.

Table 18 Estimated unemployment in four countries on the average of (i) a number of years ending with 1913, (ii) the years of rising activity ending with 1929.

1. Germany		
(i) % of all TU members unemployed,	av. 1904–1913	2·1
(ii) % of all TU members unemployed,	av. 1924–1929	11·4
2. Sweden		
(i) % of organised workers unemployed,	av. 1911–1913	5·0
(ii) % of organised workers unemployed,	av. 1923–1929	11·3
3. U.K.		
(i) % of members of certain TUs unemployed,	av. 1904–1913	5·0
(ii) % of unemployed among those insured against unemployment,	av. 1923–1929	11·0
4. U.S.A.		
(i) % of non-farm employees unemployed,	av. 1904–1913	10·0
(ii) % of non-farm employees unemployed,	av. 1923–1929	5·5

Sources: 1 (i), *Statistisches Jahrbuch 1914,* xviii, 12c. 1 (ii), *Statistisches Jahrbuch 1928,* ix. B, 10, and corresponding tables in later vols. (2 (i), *Statistisk Årsbok 1914,* table 119. 2 (ii), I. Svennilson, *Growth & Stagnation in the European Economy* (U.N., E.C.E., 1954) table 3. 3 (i) and (ii), W. H. Beveridge, *Full Employment in a Free Society,* tables 22 and 1. 4 (i) and (ii), S. Lebergott, *Manpower in Economic Growth,* table A–3.

We have said that the course of events from 1929 onwards bears the stamp of the trade cycle much more clearly than the years before. But it also has distinctive features of its own, be these only the effects of the very violence of the cyclical downswing. The disturbances of currencies were renewed, and relative labour costs were displaced by fluctuations of the rates of foreign exchange. In three countries, Germany, the U.S.A. and France, the political reaction to the depression brought radical changes in the way wages were regulated, and in the last two an unprecedented rise of wages amid persistent underemployment of resources.

It therefore seems best to divide the Period into two at the onset of the great depression in the fall of 1929, and study the years before and after separately.

2. The movements of money wages through 1929

It is from 1924 that we can follow these movements in all of our countries. The next five years brought rising output generally, but we have seen that in some other respects these years did not follow the usual course of the rising phase of the trade cycle. We may well suspect a connection between the two ways in which they diverge – that the trend of prices continued mostly downwards, and that unemployment remained generally high. In particular we may ask whether the trend of prices was not downwards because the usual tendency of money wages to rise was inhibited by the high levels of unemployment that now prevailed. Certainly wages rose less now in three of our countries than they had been doing before the war. In Sweden they rose at the rate of 2·0 per cent a year over 1923–1930, as compared with 2·8 per cent in 1908–1913, the last rising phase before the war, and 2·9 per cent over 1896–1913 as a whole. In the U.K. average money wages were virtually the same in 1930 as they had been in 1923, whereas they had at least risen by 0·9 per cent a year in 1908–1913, and at the rate of nearly 1·1 per cent over 1896–1913. In the U.S.A. they had gone up by as much as 4 per cent a year in 1908–1913, and by 2·4 per cent over 1896–1913, but through the rising activity of 1923–1929 their annual rate of rise averaged less than one per cent. France and Germany show a very different picture. In both countries money wages rose rapidly, and this after the end of their inflations – in France at the annual rate of 6·6 per cent over 1926–1930, in Germany over 1925–1929 at nearly 6·1 per cent. Are these differences associated with differences in the level or course of unemployment?

To answer this question we need to put our measures of un-employment in the different countries on a common basis. We have attempted this by expressing the estimated absolute number of unemployed as a percentage of the whole occupied population

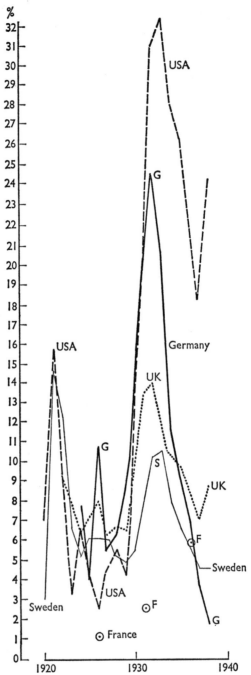

Fig. 34 Five countries, 1920s and 30s: Unemployment as a percentage of the non-agricultural labour force.
Sources: Labour force — censuses, with some minor adjustments. Unemployment — France: censuses; Germany, Sweden: Appendix 2, E.II (*a*) (ii); U.K.: E.II (*a*) (iii); U.S.A.: S. Lebergott, *Manpower in Economic Growth* (1964), table A.3.

outside agriculture in each country: the results are shown in Fig. 34. It now appears that neither the prevailing levels nor the year to year changes of unemployment offer a sufficient explanation of the divergent course of money wages in the later 1920s. In Sweden and the U.K., it is true, modestly rising or stationary money wages were associated with a sustained high level of unemployment; and the rapidly rising French wages went with what seems, on fragmentary evidence, to have been a very low prevailing level of unemployment. But the other two countries stand out: the prevailing level of unemployment was lowest of all in the U.S.A. where money wages rose little, and highest in Germany where they rose fast. Evidently there are two chief possibilities: either the level of unemployment took little influence on the course of wages in any country, and where high unemployment went with small wage rises the association was fortuitous; or it tended to be negatively correlated with the rise of wages in all countries, but other and stronger influences were at work to bring about the positive correlation in the U.S.A. and Germany.

One such influence might be looked for in any tension left within the system by the upheavals of the war, the post-war inflation, and the sharp deflation that followed. Table 19 is designed to bring any such tension to light. It has been calculated from estimates some of which differ from our main series because we have adjusted either the pre-war or the post-war estimates to give both the same coverage. Some of the figures of Table 19 therefore differ from those which would be obtained from a comparison of the values for 1913 and 1924 or 1925 in the series we give for the two Periods. In the U.K., for instance, Table 19 shows the wage/income ratio in industry (mining, manufacturing, utilities and building) as the same in 1924 as it had been in 1913, namely 63 per cent; our series for Period One agrees in the ratio of 1913, but that for Period Two covers manufacturing only, is compiled from different sources, and comes out in 1924 at 70 per cent.

In Table 19, two divergences of present significance stand out. In Germany, with the introduction of the new currency, the general level of wages and industrial prices stood lower, relatively to 1913, than in the other countries, save for industrial prices in the U.S.A.: so that though German industrial productivity seems to have been lower if anything in 1925 than in 1913, unit wage costs in 1924 or 1925 stood considerably lower, relative to 1913, in Germany than in the other three countries. There was therefore at least elbowroom for

H   B.B.C.P.

Table 19 Four countries: Germany, Sweden and U.K., industry; U.S.A., manufacturing only: Changes between 1913 and 1924 (Germany 1925) in income generated per occupied person in industry; productivity; money wage-earnings; and unit wage costs. Wage/income ratios.

	Germany	Sweden	U.K.	U.S.A.
	—Post-war year as % of pre-war—			
1. Value product per occupied person	139	209	195	171
2. Money wage-earnings	139	207	193	213
3. Index of industrial product prices	146	160	170	142
4. Productivity (1) ÷ (3)	95	130	115	120
5. Unit wage costs (2) ÷ (4)	146	159	168	178
6. Wage/income ratio 1913	59	60	63	58
1924 or 1925	59	59	63	72

Sources: *Row 1.* 1913, all countries; Appendix 2. D. I (*c*) and E. I (*c*); 1924 or 1925, Germany, Sweden and U.S.A.; Appendix 2, D II (*b*) and E II (*b*) except that in Germany we have retained unpaid family workers as in Period One, and in Sweden we estimated the occupied population by extrapolation from 1910–1920 and adjustment by the index of employment in G. Bagge et al, *Wages in Sweden 1860–1930* vol. ii, part two, table 187. U.K.: coverage as in Appendix 2 D I (*c*). Gross product from P. Deane and W. A. Cole, *British Economic Growth 1688–1959*, table 41, less depreciation, C. H. Feinstein, *Domestic Capital Formation in the U.K., 1920–1938*, 3 B (*d*) in relevant tables. Occupied population; Censuses of 1921, England and Wales, *General Report* p. 139; Scotland, vol. iii, table 12; Censuses of 1931, England and Wales, *General Report*, table xlix; Scotland, vol. iii, table 15, both including the unemployed. 1924 was interpolated in 1921–1931 and an estimate for Northern Ireland was added, based on the 1926 Census. The unemployed (U.K.) were deducted. (*Statistical Abstract of the U.K.* 1936, tables 126 and 127).
Row 2. All countries, Appendix 2, A I & II.
Row 3. Germany, Appendix 2, D. I *c* (ii) & D. II *b*. Sweden, Appendix 2. D I *c* (ii) D. II *b* (ii). U.K., *The British Economy, Key Statistics* (London & Cambridge Econ. Service, 1965), table C, indexes of wholesale prices of raw materials and manufactured products, and of prices of capital goods, combined by us with weights, 3, 1. U.S.A., *Historical Statistics of the U.S.* (1960), E. 14.
Row 6. Quotient of original series in Row 2 divided by original series in Row 1.

a substantial rise of money wages in Germany – one of 15 per cent, with unchanged productivity, would have left German unit wage costs no higher than the British relatively to 1913. The second significant divergence is in the U.S.A.: whereas the wage/income ratio in industry seems to have been virtually the same in each of the other three countries in 1924 or 1925 as in 1913, in the U.S.A. it seems to have been sharply displaced, from 58 to 72 per cent. The movement seems too big to be credible, but some shift of this kind has been found by other analysts of the period. 'Despite the drastic fall in prices 1920–1921, the general level remained about 50 per cent above the pre-war level for nearly a decade; yet hourly wage rates, outside of agriculture, were sustained at more than twice that level. . . . Since the output per man had not risen in proportion, this meant an increase in labour costs per unit of product and this was an appreciable factor in the maladjustment of the period' (Wright, 1949, p. 771). Schuller (1953, Table 10) found that the share of all employee compensation in the income generated in the private non-farm economy was 54·6 per cent in 1913, and 59·9 per cent in 1924; though in so broad a sector as this, the share of employees may rise simply by reason of a decline in the relative number of the self-employed, such as was in fact going on at this time. Levinson (1951) shows that the net change in wages between 1914 and 1923 differed according as workers were unionised or not. In the deflation of 1920–1921 the wages of the non-unionised fell much more, and though they also rose somewhat more in the subsequent recovery, the extent to which wages in 1923 stood above their level of 1914 was greater for the unionised workers, in all four of the classes into which Levinson divided the workers according to the levels of their wages in 1914. The extent of the net rise, and the difference between the unionised and the non-unionised were both greater where the initial wage was lower: thus in the highest class of initial wages, the wages of the unionised in 1923 stood 99 per cent above their level in 1914 and those of the non-unionised 81 per cent, whereas in the lowest class the corresponding figures were 157 and 128 per cent.

    In the widening or narrowing of profit margins as these emerged from the post-war upheavals, we thus have a possible reason for money wages rising so much in Germany despite high unemployment, and so little in the U.S.A. where unemployment was low – or at least, for their so doing initially: but how long can we expect the effect to have persisted? In the U.S.A. the displacement of the wage/income ratio in manufacturing seems to have been so great that firms may well have used the current rise in productivity to restore profit margins rather than raise wages throughout 1924–1929. German unit wage costs, however, would have been brought up to the same level as

Index 1910-14 = 100 (Sweden, 1913=100)

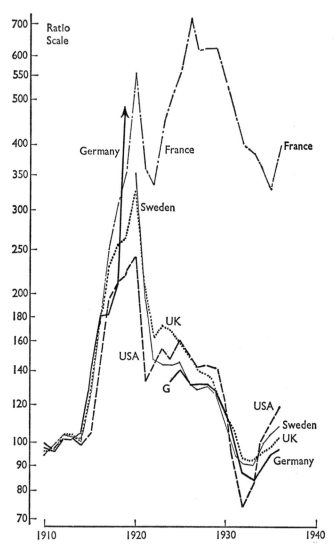

Fig. 35 Five countries, 1910 to 1936 (Sweden, 1913, 1920–1936): Index numbers of the prices of 40 basic commodities in each country, in its own currency.
Source: G. F. Warren & F. A. Pearson, *World Prices and the Building Industry* (1937), ch. ii.

British relatively to 1913, if – with unchanged productivity – German money wages had risen by 15 per cent, and the actual rise from 1925 to 1929 was by more than 25 per cent. Some other factor is to be looked for here. We have in any case to bring into our field of view those elements of the framework of factors affecting the course of money wages (Fig. 25) that we have not yet considered.

One of these elements is the market environment as that permits or represses rises in product prices. There is no doubt that the market environment from 1921 onwards was the reverse of permissive in all countries whose currencies did not depreciate relatively to the dollar at this time. Fig. 35 traces the course of the prices of forty basic commodities in the markets of each of our five countries and in that country's currency. Most of these commodities were traded internationally on a sufficient scale for their price movements in different countries to be kept in step with one another, subject to changes in tariffs and, of course, in the rates of foreign exchange of those countries' currencies. Fig. 35 shows how, when trade was opened up again after the war, these prices in Sweden, the U.K. and the U.S.A. rose in 1920 to a peak which in the U.S.A. was nearly $2\frac{1}{2}$ times, and in the other two more than $3\frac{1}{4}$ times, their pre-war level; but then they came down, violently at first when they were virtually halved within two years, and through minor fluctuations more again after that, so that in all three countries they stood lower in 1929 than ever before since the war began. The experiences of France and Germany were different. France experienced the drop in these prices after 1920, but depreciation of the franc then allowed them to rise again, and when the franc was stabilised it was at a rate of exchange that allowed them to stand in 1929 at more than six times their pre-war level, whereas across the Channel in the U.K. they were then only one third higher. In Germany a far more violent inflation carried prices up and out of sight into the stratosphere where the purchasing power of money is diffused into nothingness; but in the new currency with which a fresh start was made, these prices came out lower in 1924 relatively to pre-war than in any other of our countries, and on balance by 1929 they stood a little lower still. Thus save for France, and Germany until 1924, the course of world commodity prices exerted a downward pressure on the domestic structure of prices and costs.

Since any one country formed only a minor part of the world market in these commodities, the movements of their prices within that country, save in so far as it varied them through its foreign exchange policy, were imposed on it by a largely external force. Because this force was impersonal, moreover, it might well seem to have the inevitability of the forces of nature. Certainly there is evidence that the post-war level of costs and prices was felt to be artificial, and the pre-war was seen as the norm to which the economy must return. Thus Lord Inchcape, chairman of a great British shipping company, spoke in August 1918[1] of 'difficulties in front of us when the adjustment' (from war to peace) 'comes to be made, when the inflated currency disappears and when prices come back more or less to normal. It will then be no easy matter to get people to realise that money . . . is only a measure of value and that it is the real wage that counts.' Again in 1919 the same speaker said,[2] 'In the future, as in the past, prices will go down when the bank rate goes up, and nothing short of this will enable us to get rid of the inflated currency necessitated by the war. The whole financial structure today is artificial; we must get back to a sound policy.' It is noteworthy also that in the subsequent British discussion of whether to return to the gold standard, that return was widely assumed to be not merely to a fixed price for gold but to the pre-war price – the question was, in effect, should we fix the par of exchange at \$4·86 to the £, not should we return to the principle of the par while specifying this at a rate now appropriate, say \$4·40. In the U.S.A., again, the promise of a 'return to normalcy' was part of the appeal of the successful candidate in the presidential elections of 1920. Of Sweden we are told (Montgomery, 1939, p. 240) that 'right down to 1929 the year 1913 was more or less recognised as a "normal" year, to the standards of which economic life had once more to readjust itself.'

The picture thus suggests itself of a general sense that the height to which costs and prices had risen by 1919 was as abnormal and transitory as other consequences of the war; and of this sense being reinforced and co-ordinated by the conspicuous fall of world commodity prices that set in when trade re-opened. This state of the market environment provides an explanation, alternative or additional to the high prevailing unemployment, for the absence of much or any rise in money wages in Sweden and the U.K. It also provides an explanation, alternative or additional to the initial squeezing of

[1] Hansard, House of Lords, 1918, vol. 31, 5 Aug., p. 475.
[2] Hansard, House of Lords, 1919, vol. 35, 16 July, pp. 652–653.

profit margins, for the small rise in money wages in the U.S.A. where unemployment was low. But how can it be reconciled with the big rises in money wages in France and Germany?

Some light may be thrown on this by another element in our framework, the course of productivity and its effect on unit wage costs. Our estimates of productivity in industry appear in Fig. 36. For France we have only an index-number, but for the other four countries we have estimates in each country's own currency of the income generated per occupied person in industry, or manufacturing, at the prices of 1925–1929; we have converted the estimates for Germany, Sweden and the U.S.A. into £s sterling, at the pars of exchange that obtained through the years of restored order in the exchanges from 1925 to 1931. The rise of productivity in the later 1920s is now seen to have been marked in four countries, in two of them really rapid. In the U.K. it was at the rate of little more than 1½ per cent a year. But in Germany and the U.S.A. it averaged over 3 per cent; in Sweden 4 per cent; and in France more than 4½ per cent.

Since in Sweden and the U.S.A. the contemporary rises in money wages were modest and in the U.K. there was no rise at all, we expect to find falling unit wage costs in these countries, and Fig. 37 confirms this. In France and Germany, on the contrary, money wages rose so much as to raise unit wage costs. How can we explain this divergence, consistently with the general tendency of unit wage costs in internationally trading countries to follow parallel courses?

Evidently one factor still to be brought into the discussion is the variation of rates of exchange. The French franc, for instance, was not stabilised until 1926, and then was under-valued, so that French costs could have risen as they did without making French products dearer in terms of other currencies. In Fig. 38 the indexes of Fig. 37 have been brought together on a single scale after adjustment for the changes year by year in the rate of exchange between each country's currency and the £ sterling. Between 1925 and 1929, for example, the index of French unit wage cost in Fig. 37 rose by some 22 per cent; but meanwhile the French franc had depreciated relatively to the £ sterling by some 18 per cent; so on balance French unit wage costs were virtually unchanged in terms of sterling ($1.22 \times 0.82 =$ approx. 1.0). When each index is in this way made to run in terms of the same currency, we get an indication of the change in the comparative position of these countries in international trade,

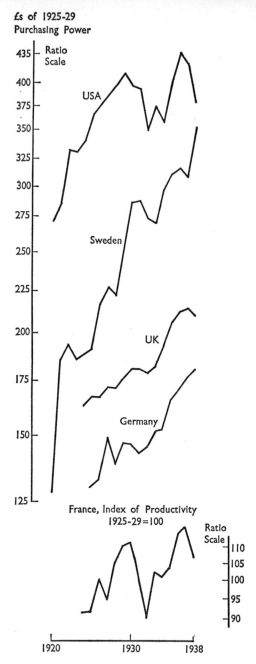

£s of 1925-29
Purchasing Power

Fig. 36 Four countries, 1920s and 30s: Productivity in industry or (U.K. & U.S.A.) in manufacturing only, in £s of 1925–29 purchasing power. France: Productivity in industry as index 1925–29 =100.

Sources: Four countries: Appendix 3. France: Production – O.E.E.C. *Industrial Statistics 1900*–(1955), table 2, index of production in mining, manufacturing and utilities; Labour force – L.-A. Vincent, 'Population, production et productivité dans 21 branches de l'économie française (1896–1962)', table 1, *Études et Conjoncture*, Feb. 1965, adjusted by estimated unemployment.

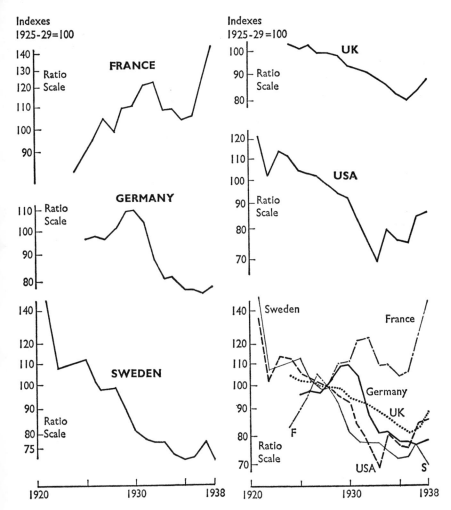

Fig. 37 Five countries, 1920s and 30s: Unit wage costs in industry or (U.K. &
U.S.A.) manufacturing only, as indexes, 1925–29 = 100.
Sources: Four countries: Appendix 3. France: Productivity – as for Fig. 36; Wages –
Appendix 3.

save in so far as this position was being changed at the same time by
changes in tariffs. The parallel decline in Fig. 37 of the indexes for
Sweden, the U.S.A. and the U.K. reappears in Fig. 38. The French
curve now diverges less; the undervaluation of 1926 brought French
costs in terms of sterling down so far that though they rose rapidly

again, in 1930 they still stood lower than in 1924. Only the German curve still rises over this span as a whole.

How can we account for this? Two factors suggest themselves. One is the heavy German borrowing from abroad which, so long as it lasted, sustained the rentenmark in the foreign exchanges even though the rise of German relatively to other costs might by itself have taken adverse effect on the balance of payments. The inflow of capital financed a programme of investment, especially in the public sector, and this would have provided a permissive setting for wage claims. But something more than this seems to have been at work. In Fig. 40 we shall see the course of the wage/income ratio in industry. In the later 1920s this ratio changed little in the U.K. In Sweden and the U.S.A. it fell, as is usual in times of rising activity. In Germany, no less, activity was rising, with a credit expansion that made a rise in profits relatively to wages additionally probable. But Fig. 40 shows that the wage/income ratio in German industry actually rose greatly. We must infer some push to raise wages from below, and this is the second factor. The big rises necessitated in 1924 and 1925 by money wages in the new currency having been set initially far too low may have raised expectations. The social philosophy of the Weimar Republic, and the sympathy of the arbitrators to whom wage claims went in the last resort, may have reinforced the unions. Some such factors, at least, must be invoked to explain why wages rose relatively to profits in German industry in a cyclical phase in which they would normally have fallen, and did fall in Sweden and the U.S.A.

The effect on the German position in the international market, once the flow of capital stopped and was even reversed, appears from the extent to which the German curve of unit costs in Fig. 38 had diverged from all save France by 1930. The divergence is a measure of the readjustment that was to be required of the German economy domestically, given that devaluation was unthinkable. It is thus a measure also of the stresses that brought Hitler to power.

From this survey of a number of elements in the situation, some conclusions emerge concerning the determination of the course of money wages in the 1920s. Because high unemployment was consistent with a big rise of money wages in Germany, and low unemployment was not accompanied by much rise of money wages in the U.S.A., we cannot attribute to unemployment any exclusive or dominating influence. We might still think that high unemployment was the

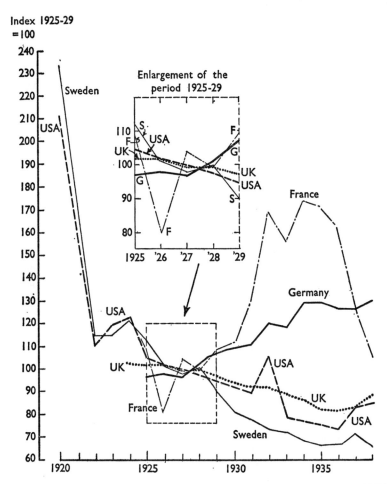

Fig. 38 Five countries, 1920s and 30s: Index numbers of unit wage costs, 1925–29 = 100, expressed in £s sterling at the current rates of exchange.
Sources: Appendix 3 and data from I. Svennilson, *Growth and Stagnation in the European Economy* (U.N., E.C.E., 1954), pp. 318–19.

effective brake on money wages in Sweden and the U.K. in the absence of such special factors as acted on Germany, but then it would have to be to other such factors rather than to low unemployment that we should have to attribute the big rise of money wages in France. It therefore seems more probable that it was the hard market environment that offered the major resistance to the rise of money wages in Sweden and the U.K., and added its influence to the initial squeezing of profit margins to prevent the rise of productivity being used to raise wages much in the U.S.A.; while France and Germany were sheltered from the downward pressure of the market environment, the one by the external undervaluation of its currency, the other by its borrowing from abroad.

3. The movements of money wages 1930–1939

The Great Depression that set in with the collapse of the bull market in Wall Street in October 1929 impinged on all of our countries forthwith, but with very unequal severity. Table 20 shows, by the

Table 20 Five countries: The level in 1932, as a percentage of the level through 1925–1929, of (1) Final prices; (2) Non-agricultural employment; (3) Real product per occupied person in the whole economy and; (4) Money wage-earnings.

	France %	Germany %	Sweden %	U.K. %	U.S.A. %
1. Final prices	97	68	89	83	77
2. Non-agricultural employment (no. of occupied persons in jobs)	(104)[1]	83	104	97	79
3. Real product per occupied person in whole economy		97	99	116	83
4. Money wage-earnings	110	91	96	95	71

[1] 1931 as percentage of 1926.
Sources: (1), (3) and (4) as in Appendix 2; (2) as in Fig. 34.

measures of the general price level and employment how much further the contraction had gone by 1932 in Germany and the U.S.A. than in the other three countries. It shows also that it was likewise in Germany and the U.S.A. that money wage-earnings had fallen most from their average of 1925–1929. Are the differential movements of money wage-earnings explained by the differential pressure of unemployment?

The way this question is put implies that a certain rate of unemployment was imposed on each economy by 1932, irrespective of how money wage-earnings there had behaved meanwhile. But this assumption is arbitrary, indeed untenable. For a given economy, it is true, the first drop in employment may have been imposed from without, through a fall in exports, and the impact on expectations and investment decisions of the news of depression elsewhere. Further falls in exports may also have been determined almost wholly externally. But how domestic activity moves meanwhile depends also on the other locus of the first impact – on the course of expectations. This will not be uniquely determined by events abroad: it will depend also on the prospective changes in domestic demand for both investment and consumption goods. These in turn depend on many factors – what line the government is expected to take; whether some current investment (as in electrification) will continue to follow a long-term programme, or (as in housing, or the wide application of a technical breakthrough) has its own momentum; how far expendable incomes, whether of the employed or unemployed, will be maintained in the home market. One factor here is the prospective movement of money wage-earnings. If these are expected to fall, without equal reductions in product prices, sales in the home market will be expected to fall too, and the actions that firms take in this expectation will tend to realise it. At the same time, if not altogether consistently, wage cuts will be seen as increasing the threat of price competition, as making it riskier to hold stocks, as multiplying the hazards of all outlay not immediately indispensable. It may therefore be as true to say that employment fell more in Germany and the U.S.A. because money wage-earnings were cut more there, as the other way about.

But in that case we have to find an alternative explanation of why the fall in money wage-earnings differed so much between economies. One explanation that immediately suggests itself is that trade unionism covered a far greater part of the labour force in Sweden and the U.K. than in the U.S.A. Within the U.S.A. itself, moreover, just as money wages had risen more in the unionised sector than outside it during the 1920s (Levinson, 1951) so now in the depression they fell much less in that sector, and the difference between wages in the two sectors was never wider than when wages generally were at their lowest (Gregg Lewis, 1963). On the other hand, the narrow coverage of trade unionism did not prevent U.S. industry from coming out of the upheavals of money wages and prices after the First World War with a higher level of money wages relatively to product prices, and correspondingly smaller profit margins, than seem to have been arrived at in the other countries. The reduction of money wage-earnings, moreover, was great not only in the U.S.A. but in Germany, and it cannot be the narrow coverage of unionism to which we appeal here: in 1929 the German trade unions had more than a third of all manual workers in membership – a higher proportion than in the U.K. at that time – and three out of four manual workers were covered by collective agreements (Bry, 1960, pp. 35, 42).

It seems not impossible to reconcile this conflict of evidence. As to the U.S.A., it is arguable that the downward pressures of 1921–1922 were less powerful, as certainly they were less protracted, than those of 1930–1932: the resistance of unorganised workers could have been more effective in 1921–1922 because the drop in output was smaller then, and unemployment at its worst was only half what it was to be in 1932. As to Germany, the success of the trade unions in raising wages in 1925–1929 had depended in no small degree on the ultimate resort to state arbitration, and the influence on this of the Social Democratic government. In March 1930, however, the Social Democratic Party left the government, and though arbitration was now used increasingly it was made to work to very different effect. Then in December 1931 'Reich Chancellor Brüning, in his Fourth Emergency Decree, ordered an across-the-board reduction in wage rates to the level of January 10, 1927, regardless of existing collective agreements. This was the beginning of wage determination by fiat' (Bry, 1960, p. 43).

In France the fall of money wage-earnings from 1930 to 1932 was intermediate between Sweden and the U.K. on the one hand, Germany and the U.S.A. on the other. We have no measure of the change in employment meanwhile: what count we have of the unemployment comes from the Census of Population in 1931 and suggests a very low level, but even if it were accurate it would not show how far employment had fallen, for many of those who lost their jobs in industry at this time returned to their families in the countryside or to the foreign lands from which they had recently immigrated. It may have been the absence in France of the un-employed who were so sadly conspicuous in the streets of other countries at this time that gave rise to the belief that the impact of the world depression on France was long delayed. That is not borne out by the fall in money wage-earnings after 1930, nor by the index of productivity in Fig. 36: the fall of this, due almost entirely to the fall in the underlying index of physical production, and greater than in any other of our countries save the U.S.A., makes it appear surprising that, in the presence of a fragmentary and ineffective trade unionism, wage earnings were not cut even more.

Our findings on the fall of money wages from 1929 to 1932 can therefore be summarised as follows. We cannot treat the ultimate severity of the depression in any one country as independent of that country's reactions to its onset. These reactions will include the reduction of money wages, and we have argued that the farther this went, the deeper we should expect the downward spiral of activity to descend. There were other and distinct elements, however, making for a greater or less severity of depression country by country – the initial bursting of the bubble of widespread speculation in the U.S.A.; the violent overturn of the German balance of payments when international capital movements were reversed; the comparative buoyancy of the markets for Swedish exports; the maintenance of domestic investment in electrification and housing in the U.K. The consequent differences in the severity of depression are associated with corresponding differences in the reduction of money wage-earnings, and we may regard the association as significant. But we may also find some place for differences in the strength of trade unionism. Sweden and the U.K. were the only two of our countries at this time in which the unions both had a wide coverage and maintained their independence. To this their members may have owed it that the reduction of wages was not greater under a given severity of depression; and the whole economy may have owed it that the depression did not become more severe.

We have been discussing the divergence of the fall of money wages in the recession, but this was as nothing in comparison with the divergence of the rise in the recovery. Nor was this the kind of disparity of one element that is offset by the opposite disparity of another: Fig. 38 shows that when we bring the movements of productivity and the foreign exchanges into account, the unit wage costs of different countries in terms of sterling fan out, from the Swedish that fell to more than 30 per cent below their level in 1925–1929, to the French that at their highest stood more than 70 per cent above it. These differences sprang from political even more than from economic upheavals. It is true that though the changes of government brought by the depression in Sweden and the U.K. were in politically opposite directions, the recovery policies that followed ran parallel. Certain variables were manipulated, but within the existing framework of institutions and ideas: in particular, the ways in which changes in money wages were brought about were essentially the same in both countries in 1938 as they had been ten years before. But in the other three countries it was very different. Germany, with the seizure of power by the Nazis in 1933, the destruction of the trade unions and the freezing of wage-rates; the U.S.A., with President Roosevelt entering on office in 1933, the inauguration of the New Deal, and the backing by government of a campaign to raise wages and prices; and, three years later, the victory of the Popular Front in France, and the raising of hourly wage-earnings by 60 per cent within nine months – in these countries what happened to wages was determined politically. Let us consider the two types of experience in turn.

Sweden and the U.K. resembled each other not only in policy but in the course of events. Unemployment, it is true, was never so bad in Sweden as in the U.K., but its rise and fall followed the same pattern (Fig. 34): in the U.K. it reached its worst in 1932, in Sweden in 1932–1933, and recovery then brought it down by 1937 to a level in Sweden a little lower, in the U.K. a little higher, than that of 1929. The movements of money wage-earnings were closely the same (Fig. 33) – a very modest fall to 1933, and a recovery which by 1937 had risen above the 1929 level. In both countries, moreover, industrial productivity continued to rise: by 1938 it stood above its 1930 level by 15 per cent in the U.K., 25 per cent in Sweden (Fig. 36). The outcome in both countries was a sustained decline in unit wage costs, with the Swedish the greater in the earlier years (Fig. 37), when it had been the Swedish money wages that were the more reduced.

It is noteworthy that the general tendency of money wages to rise was able to assert itself here in the presence of still heavy unemployment – in 1935 the proportion of the whole labour force outside agriculture that was unemployed was about $6\frac{1}{2}$ per cent in Sweden and 10 per cent in the U.K. The rise in wages was possible because the contemporary rise in productivity made it compatible with a continuing reduction in unit wage costs. Indeed we may ask why money wages did not rise more in these two countries when, as Fig. 38 now shows, unit wage costs in terms of sterling stood much higher relatively to 1925–1929 in France and Germany. One reason might be that U.S.A. unit wage costs in terms of sterling were also kept down. But something might also be due to a directly inhibiting effect of the depression on wage claims, or to firms' endeavour to widen profit margins that the depression had squeezed. The striking fall in the wage/income ratio from 1933 to 1937 in both Sweden and the U.K. to a level much below that of 1929 (Fig. 40) suggests that the second of these two factors was not the only one at work. It seems likely that money wages would have risen more than they did, had not the readiness of trade unions to present wage claims, and of employers to resist them, both been still affected by the experience of 1931–1932.

There were also wage rises in the face of unemployment in the U.S.A. – much bigger rises, and much heavier unemployment. In Sweden and the U.K. the rises were brought about by established procedures. In the U.S.A. they were due to a revolution: a new unionism, recruiting new members, armed with new statutory powers and encouraged by a new purpose of government, obtained recognition and agreement from employers who had never dealt with unions before. But this is not to be seen only as a political tornado, proving nothing about how wages change in normal weather. No doubt firms felt they had no alternative to some concession, but in deciding how much, they would have had regard to the facts that the pressure was on employers generally, and that public policy was permissive of higher product prices – the New Deal had provided a soft market environment. They could also take into account the current recovery in productivity, by which big rises in money wages were transmuted into much smaller rises of unit wage costs (Fig. 37), and were made compatible with a rebound of the wage/income ratio from its peak of 1932–1933. The effect on competition in manufactures of what rise there was in unit wage costs was reduced again by the fall in the external value of the dollar, so that in 1938 unit wage costs in U.S. industry in terms of sterling seem still to have been lower than in 1929 (Fig. 38). The inferences are twofold. First, the other factors bearing on wage movements can raise wages even in the presence of heavy unemployment. Second, the proclaimed policy of government can do much to align expectations, and determine the market environment. This is an inference to which we shall return when we come to the movement of wages under full employment, in Period Three.

What happened in France in 1936–1937 (Kalecki, 1938; Marjolin, 1938) may be regarded as a concentrated version of the New Deal with its new unionism. In both, a new militancy, unity and expectancy ran through the wage-earners, and was accompanied and intensified by a reversal of the philosophy of government: wages were raised both by bargaining and by law. In France the rise of money wages was more concentrated, and far too rapid to be offset by the contemporary rise in productivity. Yet there seems to have been little squeezing of the profit margin: already by 1938 the rise since 1935 in the general level of final prices was of the same order as that in annual wage-earnings – both had risen by about a half. The experience was seen as a justification of Keynes's intuition in taking the wage-unit as an exogenous variable and the numéraire of his system. But it was possible only because of the associated fall in the external value of the franc: Fig. 38 shows that by 1938 this had brought unit wage costs in French industry, in terms of sterling, back to and even below the level of 1930. They remained higher, however, than in 1925–1929, whereas in the U.S.A. and the U.K. unit wage costs in the same terms were now lower than then, and in Sweden much lower. Evidently there were adjustments still to be worked out when war supervened.

The German experience from 1933 to 1939 was a powerful demonstration of recovery by increased investment, albeit much of this was in armaments. At the outset, nearly one person in every four of the whole occupied population outside agriculture was unemployed; but, alone among our five countries, Germany reached full employment before the war. Rates of pay were stabilised, but our measure of annual wage-earnings rose because longer hours were worked, and payment by results – the use of which was extended – yielded more; latterly also there was probably some covert raising of effective rates of pay by employers competing for labour. None the less, the rise in wage-earnings was less than that in the income generated per occupied person in industry, and Fig. 40 shows that the wage/income ratio fell from its peak of 68 per cent in 1931 to near 59 per cent in 1937. Moreover, the rise in wage-earnings was less than that in industrial productivity, which was sustained (Fig. 36); so unit wage costs in industry declined (Fig. 37). True, they did not do so sufficiently to offset the appreciation of the German mark relatively to other currencies, at the official rate of exchange (Fig. 38), but this was a calculation of little consequence when foreign trade was brought under control, and subjected to bilateral agreements and discriminatory exchange rates. Thus there could hardly have been any pressure from the international market to keep unit wage costs down.

That they did not rise more is naturally attributable to the Nazis having destroyed the trade unions and established a rigorous control of wage-rates. But A can be historically the cause of B without our knowing that in A's absence there would have been no B. We have seen that the wage/income ratio in industry fell at this time in Sweden and the U.K. even more than in Germany. In two countries, that is to say, where the trade unions remained intact, money wage-earnings lagged farther behind the rise in the value product per head in industry, than in a country with no effective unions at all.

4. The trends of productivity

Convulsive though this period was, its recorded span of fourteen or fifteen years should be long enough to let us see what trends were running through it. In three countries, at least, the trends of productivity in industry rose very steadily. Fig. 36, which presents estimates of the output per person actually at work, indicates that the drop in total output after 1929 reduced industrial productivity in Germany and Sweden only briefly, and in the U.K. less than the general strike had done in 1926.

Since in the milder recessions of more recent years employment has generally fallen less than output, we might expect a sharper drop in productivity here. Perhaps dismissals cut deeper in the interwar years; but there may also be simply a statistical deception, through our indexes of the prices of industrial products being biassed towards materials and semi-manufactures and falling too much in the recession, so that when they are used as deflators they yield too high a real product. Whether or not the cyclical setbacks were greater than appears, however, there is no doubt about the trend. Table 21 shows that the rise in productivity from end to end was substantial, save only in the U.S.A.; and here the rise had in fact been rapid in the 1920s – at the rate of over 5 per cent a year from 1922 to 1929 – but the depth of the depression thereafter, and the slow and partial recovery, left productivity in 1938 still lower than in 1930. The other countries also suffered a great depression, but the setback it brought went deep only in France, and in all four countries was followed by a recovery that lifted productivity to new heights (Fig. 36).

Table 21 Five countries: Average annually compounded rate of rise of real product per occupied person in industry, 1898–1913 and in Period Two; the unemployed deducted from the number of occupied persons in Period Two.

	France %	Germany %	Sweden %	U.K. %	U.S.A. %
1898–1913	2·9	2·2	1·75	(fall)	1·3
Period Two:					
1923–1938				4·4	2·2¹	1·1
1924–1937	1·8				
1925–1938		2·6			

¹ G.B. only.

Source: Appendix 3.

Table 21 also shows that in Germany, Sweden and the U.K. the rise of productivity in the course of this Period was greater than it had been over the last 15 years before the First World War. The most striking instance is the U.K. In an era to which many people looked back, amid the troubles of the inter-war years, as one of growing prosperity, productivity in industry does not in fact seem to have grown at all; but through the troubles it did. We find a rise of 2·2 per cent per annum in the product per occupied person over 1923–1938; Rostas (1948) arrived at 2·4 per cent for the product per wage-earner over 1924–1937. 'The springs of technical progress in Britain, 1914–1939' have been traced by Sayers (1950). His observations will have their application to the other countries too.

Fig. 36 enables us to make a rough comparison of the levels of productivity in the different countries. It does so by converting the original series for Germany, Sweden and the U.S.A., expressed in each country's own currency at the prices of 1925–1929, into £s sterling at the pars of exchange prevailing in that period: the assumption that these pars were not far from purchasing power parity over industrial products is vulnerable – they have been believed, for instance, to over-value the £ – but no basis of closer approximation is available. Our findings may be compared with those obtainable from the estimates of net output per head of factory operatives by Rostas (1948, Table 2). He took the value of net output at current prices, for Germany in 1936, the U.K. in 1935, and the U.S.A. in 1937, and used for conversion 17·08 RM = $4·94 = £1, rates 'chosen to correspond to relative purchasing power in terms of commodities in general'. On that basis he found that net output per factory operative was higher in both the other countries than in the U.K. – in Germany by 11 per cent, in the U.S.A. by 125 per cent. Our own estimates for the same years put the German output per occupied person actually lower than the British by as much as 17 per cent, and the U.S.A. higher than the British by no more than 107 per cent. The difference in our comparative findings for Germany may be due in part to our German estimates covering all industry, whereas our estimates for the U.K. and the U.S.A., like Rostas's estimate for Germany, cover only manufacturing. The difference in our comparative findings for both countries might conceivably be due in part to our having followed a different method – namely, expressing the value added at 1925–1929 prices, and converting these amounts at the then pars of exchange, 20·45 RM = $4·87 = £1; but applying this method to Rostas's original data leads to much the same results as his – the German superiority now appears as 8 per cent instead of 11, that of the U.S.A. as 123 per cent instead of 125. It thus appears that for some reason our figure for the U.K. stands higher than Rostas's relatively to the other two by a wide margin.

We can look beyond productivity in manufacturing or industry to productivity in its widest sense, the real income generated per occupied person actually at work in the whole economy. Our estimates are shown in Fig. 39. In this period, unlike the first, the records of unemployment are generally sufficient to enable us to estimate the numbers actually at work from year to year, and the series of Fig. 39 have been obtained by dividing the real net domestic product by the number of occupied persons in jobs. We expect slower progress in the whole economy than in industry to the extent that measurable productivity rises more slowly in the service sectors than elsewhere. On the other hand, in the Great Depression the income of those sectors will have dropped less. For an economy such as the U.K., moreover, which imported a large part of its food and raw materials, the fall in their prices relatively to those of the manufactures

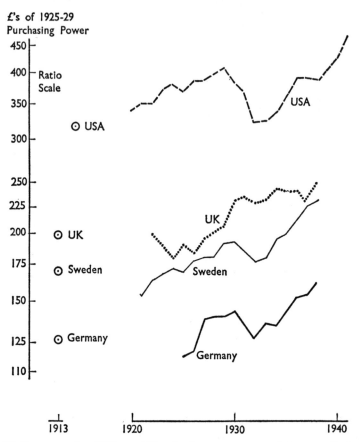

£'s of 1925-29
Purchasing Power

Fig. 39 Four countries, 1920s and 30s: Real output per occupied person (index of national income or net domestic product per occupied person divided by G.N.P. deflator), all in £s of 1925–29 purchasing power.
Source: Appendix 3.

against which they were exchanged amounted to a sharp rise in the productivity of manufacturing in terms of consumables. On balance, these factors yield rates of rise that are lower in the whole economy than in industry in all our countries. Thus over 1923–1938 the annually compounded rate of rise in the whole economy was 2·2 per cent in Sweden and 1·8 per cent in the U.K., against 4·4 and 2·2 respectively in their industrial sectors, in the U.S.A. the corresponding rates were 0·2 and 1·1 per cent, in Germany 2·5 and 2·6 per cent. That the rate of rise so reckoned for the whole economy is highest for Germany arises from the German span beginning at a low point, the check to activity on the introduction of the new currency in 1924.

The dots at the left of Fig. 39 show for each country the real output per occupied person in 1913 (or 1914 for the U.S.A.) when this is reckoned in the same way as in Period Two. The pre-war relations thus indicated are not quite the same as those reached by the series of the same kind at the end of Period One (Fig. 15): in the present Figure the U.S.A. does not stand so high relatively to the European countries, and among these Sweden now appears to have risen, with a productivity substantially higher than the German instead of somewhat lower. One reason will be that the numbers of occupied persons used for the present series all exclude unpaid family workers, whereas in Period One they were included, and in discussing Fig. 15 we saw that their removal would lower the number taken as occupied in greater proportion in Germany and Sweden than in the other two countries. The way prices are handled, moreover, is different in the two periods. Though the rates of exchange used to convert the other currencies to sterling were virtually the same (save for the franc) in 1925–1929 as in 1905, we do not know that their relations to purchasing power parity were the same; and the deflators used to take out the year to year movement of prices in each country were constituted differently.

The entries for 1913 or 1914 in Fig. 39, however, are as nearly as possible comparable with those for the same countries in the 1920s. So considered, they make clear the setback brought by the war to the three European countries: Sweden did not regain the pre-war level until 1924, Germany and the U.K. not until 1927 or 1928. Since in the U.K. overall productivity had actually stood a little lower in 1913 than in 1899 (Section 1.B.7), our estimates show no rise in the U.K. from end to end of thirty years, from 1899 through to 1928.

In the U.S.A. alone of the four countries of Fig. 39 was productivity in the 1920s always higher than before the war; but the depression that followed was so much more severe in the U.S.A. that, as we have seen, the annual rate of rise reckoned from end to end of 1923–1938 was very small. Fig. 39, however, also includes the recovery of 1939–1941, during which the U.S.A. raised its overall productivity so steeply as to regain the trend that we might project from the thriving

1920s: over the whole span 1920–1941 the annually compounded rate of rise was as much as 1·6 per cent.

It is remarkable also that in Germany, Sweden and the U.K. the trend of overall productivity rose considerably more steeply in this period than it had done in the years before the war. Table 22 compares the average annual rates of rise reported above for 1923–1938 with those reported for earlier periods in Section 1.B.7. We may see the rates of the interwar years as the net effect, on the one hand, of initial dislocation, persisting structural unemployment and a great depression, and on the other of that widespread application of a new surge of technical progress which we have noted as described for the U.K. by Sayers (1950). It was the technical progress that was the more powerful, save in the U.S.A., where the greater depth and persistence of the depression biases 1938 downwards as a terminal date. Even over the span 1920–1941, however, the rise was much slower than the exceptionally rapid rise of 1895–1913.

Table 22 Four countries, the inter-war years compared with two pre-war spans: Average annually compounded rates of rise of real national income per occupied person.

	Germany %	Sweden %	U.K. %	U.S.A. %
1923–1938	2·5	2·2	1·8	0·2
1920–1941				1·6
1899–1913	0·9	1·8	neg.	
1895–1913				2·8
1861–1899	1·6	1·6	1·6	

Source: Appendix 3.

5. Fluctuations of distribution

This Period opened with industrial structures wrenched, and inflation, sometimes wild, followed by severe deflation. Later it saw a depression of exceptional severity that brought political upheavals in its train. Unemployment ruled higher throughout most of the Period in Germany, Sweden and the U.K., and through the latter half of it in the U.S.A., than ever for so long before. Trade unionism, battered by post-war struggles in the U.K. and effectively opposed by employers in the U.S.A., was suppressed altogether in Germany in 1933, and gained new support, enthusiasm and power, in the U.S.A. under the New Deal, and in France under the Popular Front. What effect did all this take on the distribution of the product of industry?

The answer is in one sense hard to find, because the record shows us fluctuations so much more clearly than trends. Within these fifteen or so years the trade cycle set up waves in the course of distribution so big that we can hardly trace what movement there may have been of the tide. Unfortunately, too, here as before, we lack an adequate record of income generated in French industry. But with the other countries, though we cannot fit a trend, nor even compare an initial with a terminal year at the same cyclical stage, we can at least ask whether or not there are indications of any major change.

In Fig. 40 we first indicate the course of the wage/income ratio in industry by graphing on the same scale the average annual wage-earnings, and 60 per cent of the income generated per occupied person in industry – so that if the two curves lie close together, as they do in the 1920s in Sweden, we know that the wage/income ratio in industry is itself not far from 60 per cent. The curves of income generated follow a common pattern. Save in the U.K., they rise from an initial trough in 1922 or 1923 to a peak in 1929 or 1930; but in British industry the years 1924–1930 brought remarkably little change. There follows in all countries a descent, steepest in the U.S.A. and least marked in the U.K., to a trough in 1932–1933. In the ensuing recovery, however, there is a marked difference between Sweden and the U.K. on the one hand, with an upsurge that by 1938 carries income per occupied person 20 per cent above the level of 1929, and Germany and the U.S.A. on the other, where the recovery though steep still leaves the income of 1938 below that of 1929. In Germany this was largely due to wages and prices having been allowed to rise so little from 1933 onwards: Fig. 39 showed that in real terms the recovery took productivity far above 1929. In the U.S.A., however, the check was not in value terms alone, but real.

We expect wage-earnings to move in sympathy with the cyclical pattern of the income generated per occupied person, but to a less extent, so that the wage/income ratio falls when activity is mounting, and rises as activity drops back. The left-hand side of Fig. 40 shows that this was so in all four countries after 1929, but what happened

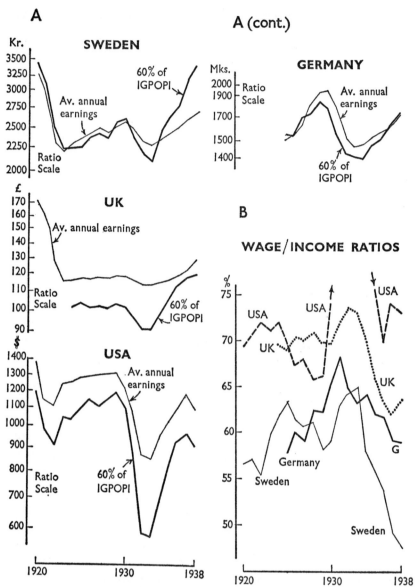

Fig. 40 Four countries, 1920s and 30s: A. Income generated per occupied person in industry (IGPOPI), reduced to 60 per cent of actual amount, compared with average annual wage-earnings, both at current prices in each country's own currency. B. Wage/income ratios.
Source: Appendix 3.

before then is less clear or uniform, and we need to look at the right-hand side, where the movements of the wage/income ratio implicit in the curves of income and wage-earnings are shown explicitly.

Here we see that the wage/income ratio in industry in the later 1920s was much higher in the U.K. and the U.S.A., where it lay around 70 per cent, than in Germany and Sweden where, though changing more, in 1926–1928 at least it was not far from 60 per cent. Equally in the years before the war (Fig. 20) it was the British wage/income ratio in industry that was the highest. We have already seen (Section 2.B.2) how the U.S.A. ratio had come to rise since then. The German ratio started low in 1925, because when the new currency was established money wages were set at what proved to be a low level relatively to prices; their subsequent rise carried the wage/income ratio up through its pre-war level to the region of the U.S.A. and U.K. ratios. The Swedish ratio, however, was still below 60 per cent in 1929.

Evidently it is not easy to generalise about the course of distribution of the product of industry as that is indicated by the wage/income ratio in the 1920s. In the U.K. there was exceptionally little change. We have suggested that there was initial pressure to restore the profit margin in the U.S.A., and it may have been this that kept the wage/income ratios there moving downward from 1924 to 1929. Whatever the reason, the course of events in Swedish industry from 1925 to 1929 was like that in the U.S.A.: as activity mounted to its peak, wage-earnings rose less than the income generated per occupied person. The special factors bearing on German wage-earnings have already been noted.

There is more similarity in the effects of the depression of the 1930s. But these include what seems to have been an exceptional movement in Sweden and the U.K. The recovery from the trough of 1932 or 1933 brought the wage/income ratio down in all four countries, as was usual in cyclical recoveries, when profits that had just fallen more than wage-earnings now in turn rose more. In Germany, where the trade unions were suppressed, and in the U.S.A. where they impinged on wages widely and vigorously, the fall in the wage/income ratio did no more than bring it back to the level prevailing before the depression. But in Sweden and the U.K. the fall went much farther. We have seen that the wage/income ratio had lain around 70 per cent in the U.K. in the later 1920s, but in 1937 it touched 62. The movement in Sweden actually seems to have been from 60 to 61 per cent to as little as 48. Jungenfelt (1966, fig. II 5) agrees in finding a marked fall at this time in the share of wages in the value added by industry, but to a level only a little lower than that of the mid-1920s. One possible explanation is that our estimates of income generated per occupied person in industry rise too steeply in both countries. Alternatively, we may suppose that the solid trade unions of both countries had been so inhibited by the mounting of the unemployment of a deep depression on that persisting through the better years before, that they did not react to the rising activity of the 1930s as promptly as they would normally have done in that phase of the cycle. We have already seen (Sections 1.B.2 and 1.B.4) that wages in the U.K. did not rise as much in 1880–1883 as we should expect in such a time of rising activity, and that this might have been due to the inhibition of trade union activity by the exceptional severity of the preceding depression.

Because of this uncertainty about Sweden and the U.K., we can arrive at no firm and general conclusion when we compare the first and last of these stormy years, and ask whether they seem to have shifted the prevailing level of the wage/income ratio in industry. For Germany and the U.S.A. we can at least answer that there is no indication of any such shift. For Sweden and the U.K. we shall never know whether the lowness of their ratios in 1938 did mark such a shift or was only temporary.

The course of the ratio is only a partial indication of what is happening meanwhile to the rate of profit: we have seen how this depends also on the movements of capital per occupied person and the capital/output ratio.

The first of these movements is shown in Fig. 41 for the three countries which alone provide estimates. What is striking here is the absence of the rises of capital per occupied person that marked the pre-war years in Germany and the U.S.A. (Fig. 24). Even in the prosperity of the U.S.A. in the 1920s, investment seems to have been high enough to raise the capital stock only a little faster than the occupied population; and then came so sharp a cutting back of investment in the depression that the capital stock ceased to grow as fast as the occupied population – this includes all those classified as occupied, including the unemployed – and the per capita figure seems

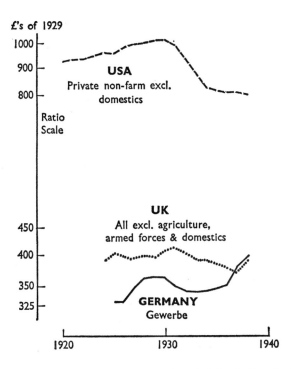

£'s of 1929

Fig. 41 Three countries, 1920s and 30s: Real capital (excluding dwellings) per occupied person in: Germany, 'Gewerbe'; U.K., whole economy excluding agriculture, armed forces and domestic service; U.S.A., private non-farm economy excluding domestics, all in £s of 1929 purchasing power.
Source: Appendix 3.

to have fallen by as much as 20 per cent. In Germany there was more accumulation (thanks to overseas loans) in the 1920s, a smaller fall in depression, and a sharp recovery in the later years of the Nazis. The U.K. series is remarkable for its stability, though here too there was some decline in the depression. It will be noticed that the amount of capital per occupied person in the non-farm sector appears now to have been from 2 to 2½ times as great in the U.S.A. as in the U.K.; our estimates for the twenty years before the war (Fig. 24) indicated a ratio of 2·7 to 1.

Though the physical amount of the equipment per occupied person seems to have been actually lower in the U.K. and the U.S.A. at the end of this Period than at the outset, our knowledge of the widespread application of technical advances at this time makes us expect that a given amount of equipment would have taken an improved form, and that the capital/output ratio would have fallen. Fig. 42 shows how this ratio, on our estimates, did in fact behave.

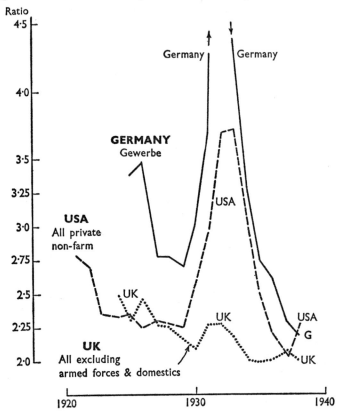

Fig. 42 Three countries, 1920s and 30s: Capital/output ratio in: Germany, 'Gewerbe'; U.K., whole economy excluding dwellings, agriculture and the pay of domestics and of armed forces; U.S.A., private non-farm economy excluding dwellings. Source: Appendix 3.

The movements of the German and U.S.A. curves here are dominated by the catastrophic fall of output, and consequent peak of the capital/output ratio, in the depression. But this for our present purpose is an incident of transitory effect: what is significant is rather the downward trend of the ratio in all three countries, clearly marked in the U.K. curve whose fluctuations are much smaller, but shown also in Germany and the U.S.A. by the level, much lower than in the opening years, to which the ratio came down when output had recovered to no more than its level of 1937–1938.

We have set out (Section 1.A.6) an approximation by which a rate of profit can be inferred from the wage/income ratio and the capital/ output ratio. We have used a similar approximation, somewhat differently quantified,[1] for the present period, and the results appear in Fig. 43, where they may be compared with estimates of the rate of profit calculated directly by relating independent estimates of total profits in the industrial sector to our figures of the capital stock there. The sources of these independent estimates are described in Appendix 2.

Most interest attaches to the directly calculated rates, though they cannot be compared without regard to the uncertainty, statistical or definitional, of the materials out of which they are built. The extent of this uncertainty in all estimates of capital we have noticed already; but it enters also into the estimates of net profit, by way of the deduction for depreciation. In the U.K., for instance, we have deducted from gross profits the annual estimates of depreciation made by Feinstein (1965) by applying a write-off over a length of life for each type of equipment, according to current accounting practice. This should provide a fair approximation to the actual wearing out and

---

[1] In Section 1.A.6 we used, for the excess of the share of pay over the wage/income ratio, the approximation

$$\frac{n_s(\bar{S} - \bar{W})}{\varUpsilon}$$

where n_s is the number of salary-earners, $\bar{S}$ and $\bar{W}$ are the average salary and wage-earnings, and $\varUpsilon$ is the total income generated in the relevant sector. From A. Chapman, *Wages and Salaries in the U.K. 1920–38*, tables 1, 4, we have for coalmining, manufacturing, building and contracting in 1930, $n_s = 0.8066$m., $\bar{S} = £221$, $\bar{W} = £125$. We note that A. L. Bowley, *Studies in the National Income, 1924–1938*, p. 155, gives particulars from the Census of Production, 1930, which yield a $\bar{W}$, within the same coverage as that used for Chapman, of £120. Also from Bowley, table A, pp. 124–25, and in the same coverage, we have $\varUpsilon = £$m.1445. Combining this with the values of the three other variables from Chapman, we can evaluate the approximation at 5·3 per cent. We have taken 5 per cent as the figure to use within the industrial sector in Germany and the U.S.A. But our estimates of capital in the U.K. cover the whole domestic economy outside agriculture, and here we have, as described in Appendix 2, U.K., F. II (e), $n_s = 4.011$m., $\bar{S} = £209·4$, $\bar{W} = £129·5$, $\varUpsilon = £$m.3270. These give an approximation of about 10 per cent, which we have adopted for use in the coverage of our capital estimates for the U.K.

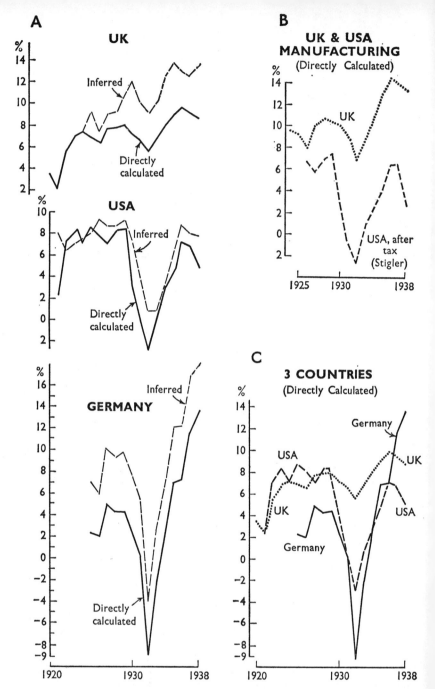

Fig. 43 Three countries, 1920s and 30s: Rates of profit in A, each country, directly calculated and inferred from the wage/income and capital/output ratios; B, U.K. and U.S.A., manufacturing only, directly calculated; C, three countries, directly calculated rates, in the coverage of A.

Sources: A. Directly calculated, appendix 2, F II (*d*); inferred, as described in Section 2.B.5. Tables 114, 138, 150.
B. U.K.: Appendix 2, F. II (*a*) (ii) and (*d*) ii. U.S.A.: G. J. Stigler, *Capital and Rates of Return in Manufacturing Industries* (1963), appendix B, table B.1.

obsolescence of equipment, to be set off, for instance, against gross investment in new equipment. But when it is set off against gross profits – which is how we have used it here – there may be double reckoning. Worswick and Tipping (1967, p. 11) point out that 'a considerable amount of the actual depreciation was met by allowances for repairs and renewals made in the process of arriving at Gross True Income. The greater part of the depreciation of gasworks and railways, for example, was dealt with in this way.' The Wear and Tear allowances made under British tax law avoid this difficulty. It is disturbing, however, that they come out much lower than the estimates of depreciation within the same coverage of industry – in 1927 and 1932 around a third, and after 1932, when they were raised, rather more than a half. This also reminds us that a change of regulation designed to relieve businesses of taxation would have the effect, if we used the allowances as our measure of depreciation, of lowering our estimated net profits.

We therefore cannot attach much significance to the comparative levels of the directly calculated rates of profit that are brought together under C in Fig. 43: even though the apparent similarity of the levels prevailing in the U.K. and the U.S.A. in the 1920s is interesting, and is probably not inconsistent with the difference between the rates calculated for manufacturing only and shown under B, for here the U.K. rate is *before* and the U.S. *after* tax. But the year to year movements can be compared with more confidence. Here the smaller U.K. fall to 1932 stands out. We also notice the terminal rise of the German and, to a less extent, the British rate of profit above their pre-depression levels. This agrees with what we have already seen of the wage/income ratios in those two countries, and is borne out by the movements of the inferred rates of profit accordingly.

The closeness of agreement between the directly calculated and inferred rates of profit in Germany and the U.S.A. lends some credence to our estimates. It will be remembered that the same figure for the capital stock is used in both methods, but it is combined in the direct calculation with an estimate of total profits, in the inferential reckoning with the estimates of wage-earnings and income generated. To the extent that the estimates used in the two methods are independent, the agreement of the outcomes is confirmatory; but it is always possible for divergences in the materials to be offset by an error in the approximation used for the reckoning by inference. In

I   B.B.C.P.

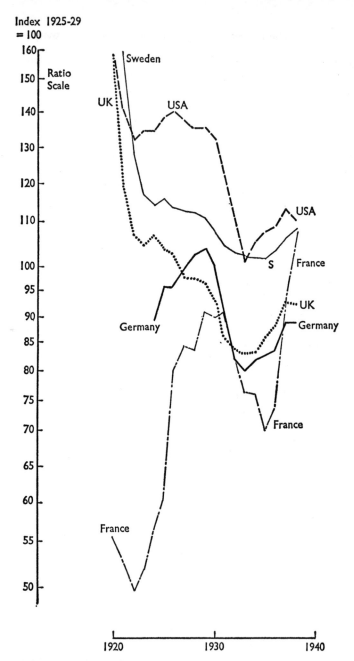

Fig. 44 Five countries, 1920s and 30s: Indexes of the cost of living, all as relative to U.K., 1925–29 = 100.
Sources: Appendix 3 and Table 15.

the U.K., moreover, the inferred rate, though it coincides with the directly calculated rate in its first year, proceeds to rise on a steeper trend, and finishes above 13 per cent when the directly calculated rate is below 9. Among other possibilities this may mark a downward bias in the estimates we have used for total profits; or – a likelihood already envisaged – an upward bias in our estimates of income generated.

6. The rise of real wages

The movements of money wage-earnings as those are portrayed in Fig. 33 were eventful, but their eventfulness was as nothing in comparison with the ups and downs of the cost of living that appear in Fig. 44. In all countries save Germany, where we begin only with the new currency, there was one steep descent from the peak of prices in the post-war boom, and another from 1929, with a subsequent rise. The course of events in France was additionally agitated by a rapid inflation in 1922–1926, and a rise of 50 per cent in prices within two years of the coming into power of the Popular Front in 1936.

None the less, Fig. 44 shows one systematic picture: save in France, the trend of the cost of living was clearly marked and it was downwards. This is so even if we abstract from the initial plunge. The trend was strong enough, moreover, when set over against the indecisive movements of money wages, to generate a marked upward trend in real wages; and where the cost of living moved the other way, in France, the rise of money wages at the same time was so far from indecisive that real wages moved up vigorously there too. These movements are shown in Fig. 45, in which we have drawn on the international comparisons of Section 2.A.3 to set the indexes for the five countries in a relation to one another that indicates the comparative levels of the wages in units of consumables, whose year to year changes within its own country each expresses by itself – thus the entry of near 160 for the U.S.A. in 1929 indicates that wages in units of consumables were then about 60 per cent higher in the U.S.A. than they were in the U.K. on the average of 1925–1929, as well as that U.S.A. wages so reckoned had risen, for example, by about 6 per cent from the level marked by the entry of 151 for 1926.

The annually compounded rates of rise that we calculate for spans

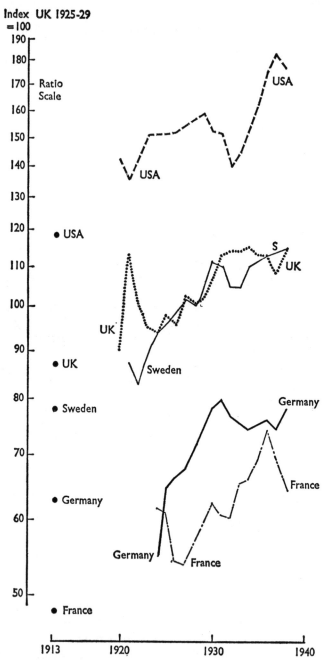

Fig. 45 Five countries, 1920s and 30s: Indexes of wage-earnings in consumption units, all as relative to U.K., 1925–29 = 100.
Sources: Appendix 3 and Table 15.

Table 23 Five countries, 1895–1913 and Period Two: Average annually compounded rate of rise of wage-earnings in composite units of consumables.

	France %	Germany %	Sweden %	U.K. %	U.S.A. %
1895–1913	0·38	1·27	1·48	a slight fall	1·33
1925–1927 to 1936–1938	1·92				
1925–1938		1·51			
1921–1938			1·65		
1920–1938				1·37	
1920–1938					1·25

Source: Appendix 3

so short and serrated as these depend much on the choice of terminal years, and we have used some perhaps arbitrary judgment in arriving at the rates shown in Table 23. None the less, the general finding of that Table is unmistakable: the rates of rise were high and, save in the U.S.A., a good deal higher than in the years before the war.

This improvement of the wage-earner's lot in years so much darkened for him by unemployment has been ascribed in part to a change that was adventitious, and even a cause of the unemployment – the fall of world commodity prices, and the improvement this brought in the terms on which the factory worker exchanged his own produce for foodstuffs and raw materials. Fig. 46 shows how those terms moved in the markets of each country, the curves being drawn so that a rise marks an increase in the amount of foodstuffs and raw materials obtainable in exchange for the unit of industrial products. These curves warn us against generalising from the experience of the U.K. Here, it is true, with relatively stable industrial prices and a high proportion of foodstuffs and raw materials imported at the prices of the day in world markets, the terms as we define them did move in favour of the factory worker by as much as 20 per cent between 1929 and 1938. Elsewhere, however, the prices of industrial products came down more, or food prices were not allowed to fall so much, or both: so that in all the four other countries the industrial worker was getting less food and raw material in exchange for a unit of his own product at the end of the period than at the beginning.

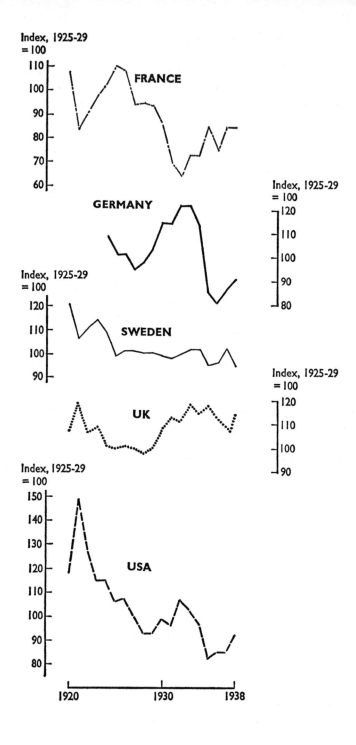

So far we have considered real wages only in their usual sense, of the quantity of goods and services purchasable by weekly wage-earnings. But if those wage-earnings have come to be obtained in a shorter working week, there is a gain of leisure to bring into account when we evaluate the rise in the worker's standard of living. In three of our countries there seems to have been little or no gain of this kind. In Germany the average hours actually worked in industry according to employers' returns were about 45 in 1928–1929 and approaching 47 in 1937–1938; in the intervening depression, of course, they had been lower. In Sweden daily hours remain close to 8 throughout. In the U.K. also there were very few changes after the wave of post-war reductions; in most industries the working week remained at 47 or 48 hours, though some reductions were negotiated by the miners, printers and boot and shoe operatives just at the end of the Period (McCormick, 1959). In France and the U.S.A., however, it was very different: the political revolution brought on by the depression in both countries joined with the cry for shorter hours as a means of spreading a limited amount of work over more men, to bring substantial reductions of hours by legislation. In the U.S.A. the codes promulgated under the National Industrial Recovery Act generally prescribed a maximum week of 40 hours, and this persisted even when the Act itself was declared unconstitutional. The weekly hours actually worked in manufacturing, which had been 48 or a little

---

Fig. 46 Five countries, 1920s and 30s: Quantity of agricultural products obtainable in exchange for a unit of industrial products, base 1925–1929.
Sources: (1) Food, (2) Industrial Products.
France. (1) *Annuaire Statistique Rétrospectif* (1961), ch. xxxii, table III 'produits alimentaires' in 'indices de prix de gros de 45 articles'. (2) *Annuaire*, as in (1), ch. xxxii, table iii, 'matières industrielles, 25 articles'.
Germany. (1) *Statistisches Jahrbuch 1939/40*, viii, table 6. (2) W. G. Hoffmann et al., *Das Wachstum der deutschen Wirtschaft seit der Mitte des 19 Jahrhunderts* (1965), part 2, table 151, export prices of manufactures.
Sweden. (1) *Historisk Statistik för Sverige, Statistiska Översiktstabeller* (1960). Table 94, wholesale prices of vegetable and of animal foodstuffs, combined by us with weights 25, 39, derived from G. Myrdal with S. Bouvin, *The Cost of Living in Sweden 1830–1930* (1933), pp. 161–2, standard budget for the cost of living index. (2) Wholesale prices of finished goods in *Historisk Statistik* as in (1), table 94.
U.K. (1) B. R. Mitchell & P. Deane, *Abstract of British Historical Statistics* (1962), ch. xvi, table 4. (2) Mitchell & Deane, as in (1), ch. xi, table 15, part B, Board of Trade index of average value of exports.
U.S.A. (1) *Historical Statistics of the U.S.* (1960), E.16. (2) *Historical Statistics*, as in (1), U.32, unit value of exports of finished manufactures.

below through the 1920s, were nearly 38 at the first peak of recovery in 1937, but dropped to 35 when activity fell back in the year following (Jones, 1963). In France the coming into office of the Front Populaire in 1936, with the Matignon agreements between employers and unions, were followed by the application of the 40-hour week to particular industries. The hours actually worked in 1937 in industry as a whole, excluding building, are reported as 40·2, as against 48 in 1930, a figure which probably holds for the later 1920s as well. The reduction in weekly hours was accompanied by two weeks' holidays with pay: France seems to have been the only one of our countries in which annual hours were thus reduced in greater proportion than weekly in this period.

In our earlier discussion of leisure we formed some estimate of its contribution to the rise in the worker's standard of living on the assumption that the hours gained for leisure could alternatively have added to his earnings at the same rate as the hours still worked. This assumption is reasonable in application to the choice open to workers in the long run, but can hardly be applied when the immediate reason for shortening hours was the lack of more work to give. We can calculate, however, by how much the rise in the real wage per hour exceeded that in the weekly real wage which we calculated above. In France it will have done so in the ratio of 48 to 40, or by a fifth; in the U.S.A. by rather more, the ratio of 48 to 38.

It is of interest to divide up the actual sources of improvement of real wages as we did in Period One. There, it will be remembered (Section 1.B.11), we quantified an identity: the annual percentage rise in real wages is approximately equal to the sum of the annual percentage changes in the product per wage-earner, the share of the wage-earner in the product, and the number of units of consumables obtained in exchange for a unit of the product. The results of a similar calculation for Period Two are set out, and compared with those for 1895–1913, in Table 24: here as before we cannot include France, for which we lack estimates of the value product in industry. It will be seen that the barter terms appearing here are not quite the same as those of Fig. 46: there we were considering the terms on which manufactures exchanged against foodstuffs and raw materials, whereas here we take industrial products generally over against the whole range of goods and services whose prices enter into our indexes of the cost of living.

Table 24 Four countries, 1895–1913 and Period Two: Average annually cumulated percentage rise in real wages as made up of average annual rates of change in (1) industrial productivity; (2) the wage/income ratio in industry, and (3) the barter terms between industrial products and the articles of wage-earners' consumption.
[Col. (1) does not always exactly equal the sum of cols. (2), (3) and (4), by reason of the rounding off of the original indexes whose rates of change are calculated here.]

Average annually cumulated percentage change in

	real wages	industrial productivity	wage/income ratio in industry	barter terms for industry[1]
	(1) %	(2) %	(3) %	(4) %
Germany				
1895–1913	1·27	1·93	− 0·45	− 0·20
1925–1938	1·51	2·60	0·18	− 1·26
Sweden				
1895–1913	1·48	2·13	− 0·24	− 0·40
1921–1938	1·65	3·86	− 1·09	− 1·09
U.K.				
1895–1913	− 0·11	0·03	− 0·32	0·16
1924–1938	1·68	1·79	− 0·63	0·49
U.S.A.				
1895–1913	1·33	1·49	− 0·77	0·61
1920–1938	0·65	1·91	0·29	− 1·54

[1] Number of composite units of wage-earner's consumables obtainable in exchange for a composite unit of industrial products, i.e. index of industrial product prices divided by index of wage-earner's cost of living.
Sources: 1895–1913, Table 12. Period Two, except as stated below for U.K. and U.S.A.: cols. (1)–(3), Appendix 3: col. (4), industrial product prices as under G.N.P. deflator and Table 107 in Appendix 2, and wage-earners' cost of living in Appendix 3. For the U.K. and U.S.A. col. (1) is calculated for wages in manufacturing only, to agree with the wage series used for col. (3): see Appendix 2, A. II (ii) for both countries. To reckon col. (4) for the U.S.A. we have used the index of industrial prices yielded implicitly by comparison of the industrial product at constant prices, used for col. (2), and at current prices, used for col. (3): see Appendix 2, U.S.A., D. I (c) and D. II (b).

Table 24 shows that in this period as in the last the outstanding contribution to the rise in real wages came from the rise of productivity: indeed in all four countries the sum of the other two factors is negative. In considering these other factors we must remember that we are only taking the change between one terminal year and another, and much depends here, especially for the wage/income ratio, on the

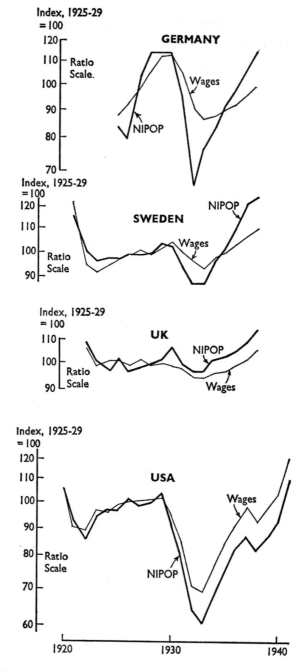

Fig. 47 Four countries, 1920s and 30s: Indexes of national income or net domestic product per occupied person (NIPOP) and of money wage-earnings, 1925–29 =100. Source: Appendix 3.

state of trade in those particular years; the initial years, moreover, are not the same for any two countries. None the less, any tilt given to the rate of change over the whole span by comparing a year of good trade, say, with one of bad, will not be big enough to hide any marked trend. It appears, then, that the distributive shifts indicated by the change in the wage/income ratio were generally small, save that in Sweden and the U.K. the recovery of the 1930s left the ratio lower in 1938 than it had been in the years after the First World War. The change in the barter terms for industry was generally of much more account, and only in the U.K. was it favourable to the industrial worker: in the other three countries the prices of industrial products fell more over this span than did the wage-earner's cost of living. It will further be seen in Table 24 that this period resembled the span of 18 years before the First World War in the predominance of the rise of productivity and the comparative unimportance of distributive shifts; but changes in the barter terms for industry, important for all countries in this period, were important in those pre-war years only for the U.S.A.

It remains to compare the movements of wage-earnings with those of income on the average of the whole economy – the average we obtain by dividing the total number of occupied persons into total domestic income. This comparison is made in Fig. 47. As in Period One, we notice the generally close agreement in the course of the two series, a closer agreement than we have found when we compared the movements of wages and the income generated per occupied person within industry or manufacturing alone. In Germany, Sweden and the U.K., however, we see a divergence already noted within industry in the concluding years, and here again we do not know whether this marks a displacement destined, but for the coming war, to be sustained, or the temporary aftermath of an exceptional depression. In the U.S.A., with the great drop of agricultural income, and the raising of wages under the New Deal, the divergence ran the other way.

Period Three
1946–1960

3A Levels of wages and incomes, 1953

The problems of principle and method raised by any attempt to compare the levels of incomes in different countries at a given date have been discussed in Section 1A. In the present period we have fixed these comparisons at 1953, because this was the year for which the estimates we rely on for the comparative costs of living in different countries were originally made by the Statistical Office of the Federal German Republic.

1. Earnings in money and in kind

We begin with estimates of the absolute monetary amounts of annual wage-earnings country by country in 1953: the coverages of these estimates are set out in Table 25.

Table 25 Five countries, 1946–1960: Coverages of the series for wages, pay of all employees, and income generated per occupied person in industry (IGPOPI). The wage and pay series include employers' contributions to social security, and other supplements paid by employers.

France
(1) Wage index   Annual earnings of manual workers in industry, commerce and services
(2) Av. annual wage earnings   As above
(3) Av. pay per employee   All wage- and salary-earners in the whole economy
(4) IGPOPI   Mining, manufacturing and utilities

Germany
(1) Wage index   Weekly earnings in mining, manufacturing, construction and utilities
(2) Av. annual wage-earnings   As above

(3) Av. pay per employee · All wage- and salary-earners in the whole economy

(4) IGPOPI · Mining, manufacturing, construction and utilities

Sweden

(1) Wage index · Hourly earnings in mining and manufacturing multiplied by annual hours worked in mining, manufacturing and utilities

(2) Av. annual wage-earnings · Mining and manufacturing (all workers) with private building (men only)

(3) Av. pay per employee · All wage- and salary-earners in the whole economy

(4) IGPOPI · Mining, manufacturing and utilities

U.K.

(1) Wage index · Average weekly earnings of all manual workers in mining and quarrying, manufacturing, construction, utilities, transport other than railways, storage and some services, with docks and railways

(2) Av. annual wage-earnings · As above

(3) Av. pay per employee · All wage- and salary-earners in the whole economy

(4) IGPOPI · Mining, manufacturing, construction, utilities, transport and communications

U.S.A.

(1) Wage index · Average weekly earnings in mining, manufacturing, 1st class steam railroads, local transport, construction, utilities and communications

(2) Av. annual wage-earnings · As above

(3) Av. pay per employee · All wage- and salary-earners in the whole economy

(4) IGPOPI · Mining, manufacturing, construction, transport, communications and utilities.

We have now to take account of an element previously neglected – that of 'employers' contributions' and other wage supplements. In all our countries we now find the employers under obligations, whether imposed by law or collective agreements, or accepted voluntarily, to make certain additional payments in respect of each period of employment for which they make a payment directly to the employee: there are contributions to insurance and other social funds administered by public agencies, and to funds – notably for pension and for supplementing unemployment benefit – maintained by the industry or firm. In addition there may be some benefits in kind which do not form part of the wage proper, but the cash value of which is included by the employer in the cost to him of a given unit of employment. Besides these there are generalised benefits such as recreational facilities, that form an overhead cost of employment and do not enter into its marginal cost, but these we shall not consider bringing into account here. The size of the contributions and supplements as a percentage of the payment made directly to the employee varies from country to country – in 1953 the percentages were about 20 in France, 10 in Germany, 0·5 in Sweden, 7 in the U.K., and 5·5 in the U.S.A.

How far we should include them in pay is evidently arguable. Hitherto we have not had to face this question, because the amounts at stake were small, and in any case were very partially recorded; but now the French 20 per cent confronts us with an inescapable decision. This concerns a range of contributions of differing kinds. At one end of the spectrum is the contribution, such as that to a pension fund or towards paid vacations, in which each week's work adds to the individual worker's entitlement, and the total entitlement thus accumulated will eventually be paid to him personally. It seems clear that a contribution of this kind forms part of the pay for the week's work, even though the payment is deferred. A contribution paid to a fund – such as for sickness or unemployment insurance – from which members of a group of workers can benefit should the occasion arise differs from the first kind in two ways: an additional week's work does not generally add to the worker's entitlement, and there is no assurance that any one worker's total receipts will ultimately equal the total contributions made in respect of his own work. None the less, if the fund is kept balanced taking one year with another, the total contributions will be paid out to the group as a whole, and the extra contributions made in respect of an additional week's work will be matched by extra payments to the workers. Thus though we cannot reckon a contribution of this kind as part of the pay for any one week's work by any one worker, for a group of workers as a whole we can so reckon it – provided always that the fund is balanced, and that it is maintained by and for them alone. It may be, however, that the fund is built up for some years together, or run at a loss and subsidised; or the contributors may include other persons than employers, and the beneficiaries other persons than their workers. In that case the flows through the circuit containing employers and workers commingle with the broad stream of public finance, from which they cannot be separated. Here we reach the other end of the spectrum, where the employer's contribution can be regarded only as a particular form of tax – a payroll tax – and the worker's benefits become part of the ambience of social welfare provided from public funds.

What parts of this spectrum we should include in our measure of pay depends on what the concept of pay is that we are seeking to quantify. There are at least three such concepts that we must distinguish:

(1) The pay accruing to a group of workers from their employers in respect of a particular amount of employment, whether paid to the workers directly or indirectly, currently or subsequently.

(2) The incomes of the workers as provided by (1) together with benefits which workers and their households receive in virtue of employment and not simply of citizenship, and which are paid for out of the general revenues of government.

(3) The cost to the employer of a particular amount of employment, as made up of (1) above together with any levy (such as a payroll tax or employment tax) not included in (1) but attached to each unit of employment.

Hitherto we have recorded only that part of (1) which is paid to the workers directly and currently. We have not included the rest of (1), viz. employers' contributions destined to accrue to their workers indirectly or subsequently; nor have we added the benefits provided out of the general fund of taxation that enter into (2). We have been able to follow this simple but arbitrary course only because in all of our countries down to the Second World War the omitted elements were relatively small.

If now it is concept (1) that we wish to quantify, then much the greater part of the employers' contributions ranks for inclusion, because in practice it lies near the first end of the spectrum. But to the extent that the contributions are made to funds that are not balanced or that receive contributions from and pay benefits to other persons, they merge into the tax revenues of the country at large, and should not be added to the pay. If it is concept (2) that we wish to quantify, then again we should include the greater part of employers' contributions, and we should also include benefits accruing to workers but financed from the general revenues of government; but the amount of these benefits calls for estimates of a kind not commonly available. If, finally, we wish to quantify concept (3), then it is simply the whole of employers' contributions and levies that we must include, whatever their form or destination.

Our problem has been to form from the available materials a measure of pay that would be as comparable as possible with the measure used in earlier periods, and as amenable as possible to international comparisons within Period Three itself. We decided that if in all countries we included the full amount of employers' contributions we should come close, if with some overspill, to quantifying concept (1), and thereby maintaining continuity with the measure of pay we have used hitherto; and we should also be quantifying concept (3), which is basic to our study of the division of the product of industry. But the element of overspill under concept (1) may be substantial where employers' contributions are as high a proportion of paid out wages as they are in France, and it may be that we have overestimated the comparative level of French pay accordingly. So far, moreover, as we are concerned with concept (2), we underestimate the comparative income of workers' households in those countries like Sweden which have financed the relevant benefits from general revenue rather than employers' contributions. We have therefore thought it well to show beside the pay as we reckon it for each country the amount of employers' contributions it includes.

One other basic difference distinguishes our treatment of pay in Period Three. Where in previous periods we have had to estimate annual wage-earnings from weekly, we have taken 'the year of normally continuous employment' as containing 49 paid weeks, after adding to the calendar year such paid holidays as there were, and deducting an average incidence of unpaid absence, including unpaid vacations and sickness. With the general extension of 'payment for hours not worked', whether under holidays with pay or sick pay, we have thought it appropriate to raise the ratio of annual to weekly earnings from 49 to 50.

With these qualifications in mind we may turn to the estimates of pay in Table 26. The main feature of rows 2 and 3 is the great change in the relative levels of money wage-earnings in different countries since the last such comparison in 1930/1931 – the U.K. level is now

Table 26 (1) Five countries, 1953: Comparison of average annual wage-earnings, excluding agriculture, and of average annual pay per employee, in money and in composite units of consumables.
(2) Five countries, averages of 1952–59: Comparison of income per occupied person in the whole economy and in industry, and wage/income ratio in industry.

(1) *1953* *Average annual wage-earnings*	France	Germany	Sweden	U.K.	U.S.A.
1. in own currency	398,500 frs	4337 M.	8,980 kr.	£427·5	$4062
1a. Employers' contributions included in (1)	67,500 frs	387 M.	45 kr.	£27	$210
2. (1) in £s at par of exchange[1]	£407	£373	£620	£427·5	£1451
3. (2) as relatives to U.K.	95	87	145	100	339
3a. (for comparison with row 3): the corresponding relatives in 1930/31	(57)	(77)	(117)	(100)	(194)
4. Relative cost of a composite unit of consumables	134	119	135	100	169
5. Relative annual wage-earnings in composite units of consumables, (3) ÷ (4)	71	73	107	100	201
5a. (for comparison with row 5): the corresponding relatives in 1930/31	(53 – 59)	(59 – 75)	(94–104)	(100)	(131–145)
Average annual pay per employee					
6. in own currency	516,000 frs	4352 M.	9,317 kr.	£440·7	$3835
6a. Employers' contributions included in (6)	87,400 frs.	388 M.	46 kr.	£28	$198
7. (6) in £s at par of exchange[1]	£527	£371	£643	£440·7	£1374
8. (7) as relatives to U.K.	127	84	146	100	312
9. Relative annual pay in composite units of consumables (8) ÷ (4)	90	71	108	100	185
(2) *Average 1952–59* *Whole economy, net domestic product per occupied person*					
10. in own currency	864,650 frs	7141 M.	13,610 kr.	£656·2	$5038
11. in £s at par of exchange[1]	£882	£609	£940	£656·2	£1805

Industry only, income generated per occupied person	France	Germany	Sweden	U.K.	U.S.A.
12. in own currency	780,600 frs	6904 M.	17,708 kr.	£632·2	$6015
13. in £s at par of exchange[1]	£797	£589	£1223	£632·2	£2155
14. Average annual wage-earnings	511,400 frs	5056 M.	10,597 kr.	£508·7	$4488
15. Industry only, wage/income ratio, (14)÷(12)	0·65	0·73	0·60	0·80	0·75
15a. (for comparison with row 15) : corresponding ratios in 1924–30					
industry		(0·61)	(0·61)		
manufacturing				(0·70)	(0·68)

[1] £1 = 979·9 frs = 11·724 M. = 14·48 Kr. = $2·791

lower than then relatively to all four other countries; and these have also diverged one from another, the rise of the French level relatively to the U.K. being by two-thirds and that of the U.S.A. being by substantially more than two-thirds, whereas the Swedish rise was by less than a quarter, and the German by only about an eighth. If the differences between the rates of exchange that we used at the two dates to convert the various sums into £s sterling corresponded closely with the relative changes in the purchasing power of money in the various countries, these changes between row 3a and row 3 in the relative levels of wage-earnings would mean just what they say – the average earnings of the French wage-earner, for example, would now have a purchasing power only 5 per cent less than those of his contemporary in the U.K., instead of more than 40 per cent less; but if the franc were overvalued in 1953, or the £ undervalued, then the true relative French improvement would be smaller.

In fact the estimates in row 4 of the comparative cost of living indicate that the current rates of exchange differed widely from purchasing power parity, so far at least as the prices of the objects of household outlay are concerned. The difference is greatest for the U.S.A.: the relative of 169 there means that though $2·79 were obtainable in exchange for £1 in 1953, it took 1·69 times as much as that, or $4·72, to buy as much of the objects of household outlay in the U.S.A. as £1 would buy in the U.K. As a whole, the divergences were much greater in 1953 than they had been at the dates of the two previous studies – 1905 or 1909, and 1930/1931. At all three dates the U.K. was the cheapest country to live in or (to say the same thing in another way) if purchasing power parity is reckoned within the range of household outlay alone, the £ was undervalued. But whereas in 1905 or 1909 the excess of the cost of living was about 10 per cent in France, 15 in Germany, and 50 in the U.S.A., and in 1930/1931 it was negligible in France and Sweden, about 7 per cent in Germany, and 40 in the U.S.A., in 1953 the excess percentages were near 35 for France and Sweden, 20 for Germany, and 70 for the U.S.A. If the £ had been revalued upwards in 1953 to an extent expressed by a dollar rate of about $3·50, the comparative costs of living in the other four countries would have been brought back to positions not very far from those of 1930/1931, but with France and Sweden a little higher than then, Germany and the U.S.A. a little lower.

The observed disparities might, it is true, be due not so much to an actual undervaluation of the £, as to an underestimation of the relative cost of the objects of household outlay in the U.K. in 1953. But this second possibility seems remote. The Statistical Office of the Federal Republic of Germany made its estimates for a large number of countries by forming relatives of average prices with weights first according to the German pattern of household outlay, and then according to the other country's pattern, and taking the geometric mean of the two relatives. In Section 3A below we shall show that the results stand in a generally consistent relation with those of the I.L.O. inquiry of Jan. 1931, when account is taken of the various changes in prices within each country meanwhile, as those changes are measured by each country's cost of living index.

If, then, we can accept the wide divergences in the relative costs of the objects of household outlay that row 4 of Table 26 indicates, we arrive in row 5 at the relative real wage-earnings. The level of real earnings in France and Germany alike appears to have been rather less than three-quarters that in the U.K.; that in Sweden rather higher than the U.K.; and that in the U.S.A. as much as double. Comparison in row 5a with 1930/1931 indicates a substantial advance over the span in the relative standing of France, no change in that of Germany, a moderate advance in that of Sweden, a great one in that of the U.S.A. We shall see later that our snapshot of 1953 records the momentary state of relations that were changing substantially over the decade; but our finding will stand, that real wage earnings in the

U.S.A. now ruled far higher than ever before relatively to those in our four European countries. It will be remembered that our estimates put them no higher than the British for most of the years between the Civil War and the 1890s: a progressive divergence since then, especially through the two World Wars, has lifted them to double the British.

Such a broad average as that of the earnings of all manual workers may be shifted by changes not only in the rates of pay but also in the relative numbers in different grades and occupations. In a labour force, for example, where women's average earnings are half those of the men, an increase in the proportion of women in the labour force from 30 to 40 per cent will lower average earnings by nearly 6 per cent. We know that in most western countries the proportion of women in the labour force has been increasing in recent years: do the average earnings reported here bear the mark of that? They prove not to, because they are drawn largely from industry, and among wage-earners in industry the proportion of women was generally a little lower in the 1950s than it had been in the interwar years: if we compare enumerations made at or near 1931 and 1950, the proportion falls from 25 to 24 per cent in France, from 20 to 19 per cent in Germany, from 19 to 15 per cent in Sweden, and from 26 to 23 per cent in the U.K. This may be attributed largely to the relative decline of the textile industry, in which the proportion of women was high. The growth in the absolute and relative numbers of women employees is to be found rather in the white-collar occupations, and the effect is to be looked for not in wages but in salaries.

Hitherto we have taken no direct account of these. The reason has been only lack of data. In earlier years, it is true, salaries bulked much smaller relatively to wage-earnings than more recently, but in the U.K. at least they still formed a considerable part of all earned incomes – Bowley (1937, p. 96) put total salaries as 27 per cent of total wage-earnings in 1911, and 46 per cent in 1924; and though those proportions fall far short of the two-thirds that rules at the present time, they are still big enough to make the omission of salaries a real shortcoming in any study of pay in those periods. The shortcoming, however, is unavoidable, because we lack annual series.

When in the present period such series become available, we can proceed to the estimates of average annual pay per employee that appear in row 6 of Table 26. It may be surprising to find that only in

France is this average pay much higher than average wage-earnings: in the U.S.A. it is actually lower. This finding reminds us that the expansion of the relative size of salaries as a whole has been accompanied by an even greater expansion of the numbers of the salaried. The expansion has been specially marked in the lower grades, and (as we have noted) among women; and this will have lowered the average salary relatively to the salary prevailing in any one grade or occupation. It may well have been the case, additionally, that rates of salary generally rose less than rates of wage-earnings, at least through and immediately after the war, and that some of the higher grades have never recovered their previous differential: but we need not invoke such changes in the structure of rates of pay in order to explain a fall in the average salary relative to the average wage. The increase in the numbers of salary-earners whose salaries are not far removed from the earnings of manual workers, and in recent years have often been smaller, has naturally been attended by some blurring of the line that used to mark off the white-collared from the blue-overalled, both at work and at home. There is an increasing tendency in the statistics, therefore, to cease distinguishing between categories that are interfused both economically and socially in practice, and instead to consider the earnings of employees as a whole.

When these are reckoned in real terms (row 9 of Table 26), the relative standing of the different countries is changed from that shown by real wage-earnings (row 5) according to the differences country by country in the relative levels of average salaries and average wages. In France, where salaries ruled highest relatively to wages in 1953, the real earnings of employees as a whole stood higher in comparison with other countries than did the real earnings of manual workers alone. In the U.S.A. cause and effect were the opposite. The positions of Germany, Sweden and the U.K. relatively to one another were hardly affected.

2. Hours of work

We have noted before that comparisons of real earnings concern only the quantities of goods and services that money earnings will buy, so that we leave an important element out of our assessment of the employee's lot if we take no account of the number of hours he worked to obtain the money. The element is not only important in principle, but varies widely between periods and countries.

We saw how the years after the First World War brought a general and substantial reduction in weekly hours: after the Second there was some more change of the kind, but it was not so general and it did not go so far. In Sweden the 48 hour week established in the 1920s remained usual in 1953. Germany and the U.K., which equally had adopted the 48 hour week in the 1920s, were now working weeks of around 46 hours. In France under the Popular Front government the 40-hour week had been promulgated in 1936–1937, though how far it had been adopted in practice is doubtful: in 1953 the prevailing week in French industry was of 44–45 hours. Similarly in the U.S.A. there had been a drive in the 1930s for the 40-hour week, and during the years of heavy unemployment the average hours actually worked had been even less; when the longer hours worked during the Second World War were cut back, it was again to less than 40 – the hours actually worked in manufacturing in 1953 have been put at no more than 38·6 (E. B. Jones, 1963). The U.S.A. thus stands out among our five countries by reason both of the extent of the change from the 1920s, and the shortness of the weekly hours of 1953.

There was another respect, however, in which hours began to be changed a great deal after the Second World War: it was then that paid vacations first became usual for the manual worker. American usage distinguishes between 'holidays', which are certain legally recognised general public holidays, mostly of one day at a time, and 'vacations', which are annual periods of leave forming part of the terms and conditions of a particular employment. By the 1930s it had become fairly general practice for employers to pay for a limited number of days, perhaps five or six in the year, such as Christmas Day, and Good Friday, with particular days in each country, like the 4th July in the U.S.A. and the Bank Holidays of the U.K.; but paid vacations remained, except in France, one of the privileges that set those on staff conditions apart from those 'on the clock'. After the Second World War this distinction began to break down. Generalisation is difficult, because here even more than in weekly hours practice varied from one industry to another, and most of our information relates to years after 1953. By 1960, however, French manual workers were generally entitled to 18 days' paid vacation after one year's service; the German had 12 days' legal entitlement, supplemented by collective agreements of which the great majority provided for at least 18 days; the Swedish likewise had 18 days, with four weeks under consideration; while the British generally had no more than 12 days (*Ministry of Labour Gazette*, Feb., 1962).

The effect is that we can no longer reckon the hours worked by a simple reference to weekly hours: henceforward we must cite the number of hours worked in the year. For 1956 the normal annual hours worked in industry, exclusive of overtime, have been given as follows (International Labour Conference, 1958, report viii, table v):

France	1920	Sweden	2212
West Germany	2296–2320	U.K.	2152–2192
	U.S.A.	1984.	

We can use these figures to make a rough estimate of the proportions in which the total gain available to the wage-earner since 1930/1931 was divided between additions to the real wage and to leisure. When we did this for an earlier span in Section 2.A.4 we assumed that if the hours worked at the terminal date were extended to equal those of the starting point, the real earnings would be increased in about the same proportion, and the increment of earnings might be taken as a measure, in the same terms as the actual gain in real earnings, of that part of the total available gain which was taken out in the form of added leisure. Let us take the annual hours just cited as holding for 1953, and let us assume that the annual hours worked in 1930/1931 were 50 times the weekly. Then in France, for example, we have annual hours of 50 times 48 or 2400 in 1930/1931, against 1920 hours in 1953, a reduction of 480 hours. Meanwhile, as we shall see in Table 28 (row 14) the gain in actual real earnings had been 73 per cent. On our assumption of proportionality, working the hours of 1930/1931 in 1953 would have provided a further increment of (480 ÷ 1920) 173, or 43 per cent. The total available gain can then be put at 73 + 43 = 116 per cent, divided in the proportions of about 7 to 4 between real earnings and leisure. Similar calculations for the other countries give us for Germany a total available gain of some 45 per cent, of which only about one seventh was taken out in the form of leisure; for Sweden, a total of about 77 per cent, of which rather less than one fifth was in leisure; for the U.K., a total of about 62 per cent, also with about one fifth in leisure; but for the U.S.A. a much greater total, some 154 per cent, in which added leisure made up nearly a third. We are a long way here from the assumption cited in Section 2.A.4 above that the total available gain would be divided about equally between real earnings and leisure. This assumption in fact agreed with the central tendency of our estimates of the division of the total available gain between 1905 or 1909 and 1930/1931, except in the U.S.A., where no more than a fifth seems to have gone to leisure. In our present reckoning it is only where the total available gain was largest, in France and the U.S.A., that the share of leisure exceeded one fifth, and even there it was only about one third.

The change of reckoning from weekly to annual figures is not the only change that the new circumstances of Period Three impose on the study of hours. We have also now to take much more account of overtime. To know how much there was of it we need comprehensive statements of normal hours as well as of hours worked, and they are not always available. We know, however, that overtime was insignificant in Sweden, and about 2 hours a week in U.S.A. manufacturing; but in U.K. manufacturing it came near to 8 hours. Its growth in the U.K. may be ascribed to several causes. In the short run, an excess of demand may be met by longer hours, but that managers should maintain higher output by systematic overtime can be ascribed only to the offsetting economies of a higher utilisation of equipment, and to the greater difficulty under full employment of obtaining additional trained workers as compared with more hours from those already there. Employers have been the more ready to use overtime, and have often provided it when not obliged to do so in order to get a given output by a given date, because it provides an expedient way of offering higher earnings in a competitive labour market: unlike a rise in the basic rate, the extra paid in overtime is offset by extra output, and it can be more easily withdrawn should the labour market become easier. Many workers for their own part welcome the opportunity to work overtime: whether or not the negotiated reduction of normal hours expressed the wishes of most workers, there have been many who prefer to take out a greater part of the total available gain in the form of real earnings.

One manifestation of this last preference has been the growth of 'moonlighting' – the taking of a second job in the time left, in the evenings and at weekends, by shorter normal hours. Such work may have the added attraction that the income evades tax. Most such work is unrecorded, but there is agreement in the U.K. and the U.S.A. that it has increased substantially with the coming of shorter hours. (For the U.S.A. see Ginsburg and Bergmann, 1958; Zeisel, 1958).

There are thus four variants now of the once straightforward notion of working hours: the normal hours to be worked annually; the recorded hours worked annually, including overtime; the hours paid for, including paid holidays and vacations and the overtime premium; and the actual total hours worked, including unrecorded second jobs.

3. The wage/income ratio in industry

The estimates set out in row 15 of Table 26 show that the ratio was higher in 1952–1959 in Germany and the U.S.A., and still more in the U.K., than in France and Sweden. The differences are large, but need not surprise us. One of their possible sources lies in the differing structures of the economies – the wage/income ratio is low in a capital-intensive industry like electricity supply, high in a labour-intensive industry like traditional housebuilding: in the economy as a whole it will be high or low according as the one type or the other predominates in the aggregate of industries. If the structures of the different economies did not change greatly between one period and another, the differences between their wage/income ratios are therefore likely also to persist. To some extent this was so here: the ratios of the U.K. and the U.S.A. were substantially higher than the others in 1924–1930, as they are seen to be now in 1952–1959.

But there were also shifts meanwhile. Only the Swedish ratio was virtually the same in the 1950s as it had been in the 1920s; in Germany, the U.K. and the U.S.A. the ratios of the 1950s were much higher. When did these shifts come about? Table 27 repeats the wage/income ratios already cited for 1924–1930 and 1952–1959, and inserts those of 1937–1938. Here it appears that in the U.S.A. alone was there little change through the thirteen years that followed 1938 and included the Second World War. In Germany and the U.K. the wage/income ratio stood lower in 1937/1938 than it had done in 1924–1930, so that the years after 1938 saw a rise even greater than that already noted over the longer span. Even more, it

Table 27 Four countries, Periods Two and Three: Wage/income ratios in industry (in Period Two, in U.K. and U.S.A. in manufacturing only).

	Germany %	Sweden %	U.K. %	U.S.A. %
1. Av. 1924–1930, industry	61	61		
manufacturing			70	68
2. Av. 1937–1938, industry	59	48·5		
manufacturing			63	73·5
3. Av. 1952–1959, industry	73	60	80	75

Sources: Rows 1 and 3, Table 26
Row 2, Tables for Period Two in Appendix 3.

seems, had the wage/income ratio fallen in Sweden by 1937–1938, so that here too we have to account for a big rise in the next thirteen years.

Part of it, but only part, can be accounted for by a discontinuity in our estimates of wage-earnings: in Period Three these include employers' contributions, but in Period Two they did not. The effect on the wage/income ratio of including them in 1938 is negligible in Sweden, but the German ratio would be raised by some $4\frac{1}{2}$ percentage points, the U.K. ratio by nearly 3, and the U.S.A. ratio by about $3\frac{1}{2}$ (see Tables for Period Three in Statistical Appendix 3). The U.S.A. ratio would thus actually stand higher in 1937–1938 than in 1952–1959, but in the other three ratios a large shift would remain.

It could have come about only if one or more of three other changes took place at the same time: (i) a fall in the average earnings of the salaried and self-employed, relatively to the average wage; (ii) a fall in the rate of profit; (iii) a fall in the capital/output ratio.

The first of these changes is relevant, we must remember, only in so far as it came about within industry: changes in the relative level of average salaries associated with the expansion of white-collar employment in the service industries and the public sector are not relevant here. That some effect of the kind was felt within industry in the years immediately after the war is possible, but it is unlikely to have persisted to any significant extent through the 1950s.

To assess the two other possibilities, those of falls in the rate of profit and the capital/output ratio, we must survey the statistical evidence. This survey should include the U.S.A., for though the wage/income ratio in industry does not seem to have risen here, this might have been due to compensating changes in the two factors now considered – as between 1937–1938 and 1952–1959 the rate of profit might conceivably have gone up while the capital/output ratio came down.

Unfortunately the statistical evidence is fragmentary. We lack estimates of the capital stock in Sweden altogether. For the U.K. two estimates of the capital stock in Period Three differ widely from one another (Redfern, 1955; Barna, 1957). Only Redfern's was constructed on the same principle as the estimates we have drawn from Feinstein for Period Two, and even here we have no assurance of agreement in the quantitative assumptions, particularly about the length of life of assets, such as affect so greatly the estimated size of the depreciated capital stock; perhaps, however, it is worth noting that Redfern's estimates yield on our reckoning a capital/output ratio for 1949–1953 somewhat higher than the 2·0 we obtained for 1937–1938.

For Germany alone do we have continuous series for both capital and profits. Hoffmann (1965) continues into our Period Three the estimates of the capital stock and the output of 'Gewerbe' – that is, industry with considerable elements of commerce, from which we derived a capital/output ratio of 2·2 for 1937–1938; we now derive one somewhat higher, at 2·5, for 1952–1959. From the same source we can also calculate the rate of profit on this capital: where before we found 12·8 per cent for 1937–1938, we now find, on the same way of reckoning, a closely similar rate for 1952–1959 – about 12·3 per cent. The problem of consistency is evident: unless there were a big fall in the average earnings of the salaried and self-employed, relatively to average wage-earnings, the wage/income ratio could not have risen as our estimates show it to have done without some fall in one or both of the capital/output ratio and the rate of profit. The explanation is likely to lie in disparities of coverage between the data we have used for wage-earnings, which are confined to industry, and those of Hoffmann's system. It is noteworthy that when we made estimates of the pay/income ratio, using Hoffmann's materials throughout, on each of two methods of estimate we found little difference between the ratios of 1938 and 1953.

Our materials for the U.S.A. are of special interest because they include a continuous series for the capital stock that proves to imply a sharp fall in the capital/output ratio. The estimates of the capital stock in industry by Kendrick (1961) extend through 1953: for 1937–1938 we derived from them a capital/output ratio of 2·15, but now we find a much lower ratio for 1952–1953 – no more than 1·36. With little change in the wage/income ratio, this suggests a marked rise in the rate of profit: how did this rate in fact behave? We are not able to continue into Period Three our previous estimates of the rate of profit, but we can draw some inference from the estimates of the rate of return after tax on the book values of the corporate assets in manufacture, provided by Stigler (1963, Appendix B). These show much the same rate in the 1950s as in 1936–1939 – about 6·0 per cent in the earlier years (if we omit the sharp but brief recession of 1938), 6·2 per cent over 1952–1958. But this is after tax, whereas our reckonings have been of profits before tax. Adding back the tax will raise the profits of 1936–1939 by about one-sixth (Barger, 1942, Table 38, and Bureau of Internal Revenue, *Statistics of Income 1938*, part 2, p. 48), whereas in the 1950s it will about double them (Graham & Bauman, 1962, Table 5). We may infer a rise, from about 7 to near 12 per cent, in the rate of profit as we reckon it here. Thus, so far at least as our present span of comparison extends, a sharp fall in the capital/output ratio in U.S.A. industry made possible a restoration of the profit rate to a much higher level than obtained at the stage of partial recovery from the great depression of the 1930s, without any reduction in the wage/income ratio being required at the same time.

A fall in the capital/output ratio at this time, though shown in our data only for the U.S.A., may well be significant of a major course of change operating on the distribution of the product of industry in recent years. We can give several reasons for expecting it, not in the U.S.A. alone. One is the more intensive utilisation of equipment at high levels of employment. Evidently this comes about when machines standing idle are brought back into use; but the extension of demand may raise the degree of utilisation beyond this. Suppose, to take an extreme but not unrealistic example, that a factory moves over from single-shift to double-shift working. Let the capital per worker on the old system be £200, the net output per worker £100, and the worker's pay be £80, leaving £20 to remunerate capital at the rate of 10 per cent. Neglecting the overhead elements in the labour force, let us further suppose that with the move to double-shift working the number of workers is itself simply doubled, so that the capital per worker is halved, and becomes £100: then with output per worker £100 as before, the worker's pay can go up to £90, and still leave a rate of return of 10 per cent on capital. The wage/income ratio has risen from 80 to 90 per cent. An effect of the same kind, though of smaller amount, is taken by overtime working. At the same time a high level of demand puts management under pressure to plan lay-outs and sequences of operations so as to raise the equipment utilisation factor: some of the techniques of management developed in recent years, such as critical path analysis, have this as one of their objects. Over and above the increased utilisation of given equipment are capital-saving changes in the form equipment takes. We have no measure of this technological factor of itself in recent years, but observation suggests that it has been common for improvements in design to raise the capacity of equipment more than its cost. Any increase in the capacity of equipment of given physical size, moreover, increases the output per unit of the building space containing it: it is noteworthy that on Kendrick's estimates the real stock of equipment in the private economy of the U.S.A. rose by 126 per cent between 1938 and 1953, whereas that of buildings other than dwellings rose by little more than 13 per cent. Technical advances of this kind not only raise output per worker, but enable the worker to receive a greater share of that output without reducing the rate of return to capital.

4. The relative levels at 1930/1931 and 1953, compared with the movement of our indexes between those dates

When we looked back from Period Two to Period One, we were able to ask (Section 2.A.6) whether the differences between average annual wage-earnings in each country's own currency, estimated by us at 1905 or 1909 and again at 1930/1931, agreed with the cumulated changes between those dates shown by our annual indexes of wage earnings, country by country. In the same way we took the comparative costs of living in the different countries at the earlier date, reckoned the changes in them that would have been brought about by the later date through the relative movement meanwhile of our annual indexes of the cost of living, and compared the outcome with the comparative costs of living actually found at the later date. We can now make similar comparisons over the span between 1930/1931 and 1953. They are set out in Table 28.

There is one respect in which the present check is less complete than the last. Whereas previously our comprehensive estimates of average wage-earnings at the terminal dates were generally made independently of the annual indexes of wage-earnings, which themselves usually had to be compiled from fragmentary evidence, the greater availability of data in later years has often provided comprehensive estimates of wage-earnings in every year, so that we have been able to take both our figures of wage-earnings in a country's currency at a given date, and our annual indexes of wage movements, from the selfsame series. If this were so in both periods the only disparity a check could reveal would lie in the appropriateness of our link between the two periods. This is in fact the case for the U.S.A. In the other countries, there is a common source in only one of the two periods: for Period Two in Sweden, for Period Three in France, Germany and the U.K.

We have just mentioned the link between our annual indexes of wage-earnings in the two periods: this also requires attention. The link embodied in the cumulated movement of the time series, set out in row 2 of Table 28, is not the same as that implied by the entry for 1938 (1952–1959 = 100) in our Tables for Period Three. We have estimated the latter on the same basis as the annual series in Period Three itself: that is, inclusive of employers' contributions, and – where weekly data had to be raised to annual – reckoning 50 paid weeks in the year. In Period Two itself, however, we did not include employers' contributions, and reckoned only 49 paid weeks in the year. In calculating the link appropriate to the purposes of Table 28 we have taken account of these differences, so that the link shows a bigger rise between 1938 and the 1950s than appears from the entry for 1938 in the indexes of wage movements in Period Three.

It will be seen none the less that in all five countries the annual wage-earnings we arrive at in 1953, through carrying the earnings of 1930/1931 forward by means of linked index-numbers, are lower than estimates we have made directly for 1953. The shortfalls range from 2·6 per cent in the U.K. to 5·9 per cent in Sweden. The most probable explanation is that increased earnings from overtime and payment by results have entered to a greater extent into our estimates of the level of earnings in 1953 than into our indexes of the year to

K   B.B.C.P.

year movements of earnings, and especially into the allowances we have made for the change between the two periods.

In rows 6–12 of Table 28 we check the consistency of the estimates we have drawn upon for the comparative cost of living in 1930/1931 and 1953, with the movements of our indexes of the cost of living within each country meanwhile. It will be remembered that the estimates for 1930/1931 are derived from the inquiry carried out by the I.L.O. for the Ford Motor Company, and those for 1953 from the inquiries of the Statistical Office of the Federal Republic of West

Table 28 Five countries, 1930/31 and 1953: Wage-earnings in money, comparative costs of consumables, and comparative real wage-earnings, as calculated for 1953 by carrying forward from 1930/31 by means of time series, and as estimated directly for 1953.

	France	Germany	Sweden	U.K.	U.S.A.
Wage-earnings in money					
1. in 1930/31	8347 frs	1870 M.	2517 Kr.	£118·8	$1121
2. 1953 as per cent of 1930/31, according to linked time series[1]	4595	218	336	351	351
3. Implied levels at 1953 (1) × (2)	383,545 frs	4077 M.	8452 Kr.	£416·6	$3935
4. As estimated directly for 1953	398,500 frs	4337 M.	8980 Kr.	£427·5	$4062
5. (3) – (4) as per cent of (4)	–3·6	–5·0	–5·9	–2·6	–3·1
Comparative cost of consumables					
6. in Jan. 1931	96–106	102–112	113–125	100	134–148
7. Cost in each country in 1953 as per cent of that in Jan. 1931, according to linked time series	2679	156	204	234	168
8. Comparative costs in 1953 implied by (6) × (7)	2572–2840	159–175	231–255	234	225–249
9. Ratio of no. of units of own currency per £ at par of 1953 to no. at par of Jan. 1931[2]	7·89	0·57	0·80	1·0	0·57
10. (8) adjusted for changes in par of exchange, i.e. ÷ (9)	326–360	279–307	288–319	234	295–436
11. (10) rel. to U.K. = 100, i.e. implied comparative costs at 1953	139–154	119–131	123–136	100	169–186
12. Comparative costs from inquiry at 1953	134	119	135	100	169

Comparative real wage-earnings

13. in 1930/31, rel. to U.K. = 100	53–59	69–75	94–104	100	131–145
14. Level 1953 as per cent of that of 1930/31 in each country, according to linked time series[1]	173	139	163	150	206
15. Comparative real wage-earnings in 1953 as implied by (13) × (14)	92–102	96–104	154–170	150	269–298
16. (15) rel. to U.K. = 100, i.e. implied comparative real wage-earnings in 1953	61–68	64–70	103–113	100	180–199
17. As estimated directly for 1953	71	73	107	100	201

[1] The rise between 1938 and Period Three that we have taken in linking the time-series of the two periods embodies the effect of our Period Three series including employers' contributions, as our Period Two series does not, and being based (in some countries) on a year of 50 paid weeks, against 49 in Period Two. It is therefore greater than that implied by the figure for 1938 in the Period Three tables of Appendix 3, as this figure has the same coverage as the Period Three series.

[2] Rates of exchange were, putting Jan. 1931 first and 1953 second for each country: £1 = 124·2, 979·9 frs = 20·45, 11·724 M. = 18·16, 14·48 Kr. = $4·87, 2·791.

Germany. We should be prepared for divergence, in a field where margins of error and dubiety are inherently wide, and in a time-span that includes the Second World War. Against these expectations, the extent of agreement in row 12 is remarkable: only for France does the comparative cost of living estimated directly for 1953 actually fall outside the bracket of rates obtained by carrying forward from 1930/1931, and then not by very much.

The remaining section of Table 28, in rows 13–17, provides no further check, but in effect combines the two preceding calculations by following the same procedure as they in terms of real wages. We have seen that for all five countries the estimate of money wage-earnings made directly for 1953 stood higher than the figure obtained by carrying forward from 1930/1931: whether the divergence of real wages will be greater or less than this depends on whether the comparative cost of living directly estimated for 1953 comes out lower or higher than that obtained by carrying forward. For France it does come out lower, and for Germany and the U.S.A., though within the bracket, it lies at the lower end: in these countries, therefore, the real wages (relatively to the U.K.) estimated directly for 1953 come out higher than those obtained by carrying forward (rows 16 and 17). In Sweden, on the other hand, the comparative cost of living obtained by carrying forward to 1953 falls at the upper end of the bracket and offsets the shortfall of the carried forward wage-earnings in money, to give close agreement between the two figures for real wage-earnings.

3B The course of wages, income and productivity

1. The course of money wages

Fig. 48 shows the rise of average wage-earnings, and of average pay (taking the earnings of employees of all grades and occupations), in each country's own currency. It also shows wage-earnings in the five countries on a common scale of dollars. Here the figures for each of the European countries have been turned into dollars at the rates of exchange prevailing year by year. This does not, of course, indicate the relative level of real wages in the different countries: we have seen already (Table 26) that in 1953 nearly 70 per cent more in dollars than the current rate of exchange would provide was needed to buy as much of the objects of household expenditure in the U.S.A. as the £ would buy in the U.K. Converting at the current rate of exchange also has the disadvantage, in one sense, of showing the wage-earnings of a country as falling when that country's currency is devalued against the dollar – Sweden and the U.K. after 1949, for example; and France after 1955. But the common scale is that in which costs and prices actually entered into international transactions.

The most conspicuous feature of Fig. 48 is the sustained rise of money earnings in all five countries. The average rate of rise is generally greater than that experienced before in all save rare years of high boom such as 1873 or 1919. The annually compounded rates of rise of the curves of Fig. 48 vary from 5·4 per cent in the U.S.A. to 11·2 per cent in France, with the U.K. at 6·7, Germany at 7·2, and Sweden at 7·8 per cent. In Period One, the highest annual rate of rise through the positive phase of the trade cycle was 3·6 per cent, in Germany (Table 7); in Period Two money wages rose at the annual rate of 6·1 per cent in Germany over 1925–1929, and at 6·6 per cent in France over 1926–1930 (Section 2.B.1). But even more unprecedented than the rate of the rise is its persistence for as much as

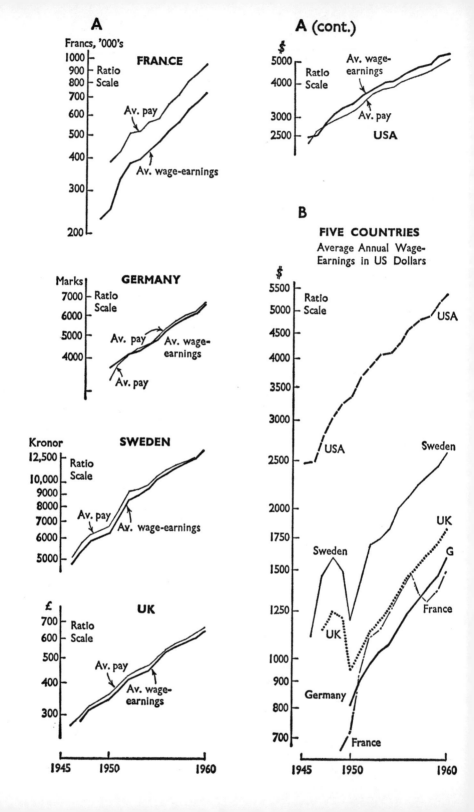

A

Francs, '000's

FRANCE

Ratio Scale

Av. pay

Av. wage-earnings

A (cont.)

$

Av. wage-earnings

Ratio Scale

Av. pay

USA

GERMANY

Marks

Ratio Scale

Av. pay

Av. wage-earnings

Av. pay

SWEDEN

Kronor

Ratio Scale

Av. pay

Av. wage-earnings

B

FIVE COUNTRIES

Average Annual Wage-Earnings in US Dollars

$

Ratio Scale

USA

USA

Sweden

Sweden

UK

G

UK

France

Germany

France

UK

£

Ratio Scale

Av. pay

Av. wage-earnings

1945   1950   1960

1945   1950   1960

15 years: hitherto it had been rare for rises to continue for more than five years together.

This new behaviour of money wages has been connected with what is also new in these years – the persistence of high levels of employment. Fig. 49 shows how low the ceiling was under which unemployment was contained in France, Sweden and the U.K. It also shows that in the U.S.A., where money wages rose less than in those three countries, unemployment ruled higher: this remains true even after allowance has been made for the U.S.A. method of counting the unemployed producing a bigger figure in a given situation than, for example, the British would (Zeisel, 1962). Yet for most of the span over which German money wages were rising at 7 per cent or more a year, unemployment in Germany, though diminishing, was severe. Even more, as unemployment diminished so did the rate of rise of money wages: in 1950–1955 when the unemployment rate (as reckoned here) averaged about 7 per cent, money wages rose at the annual rate of 7·4 per cent, but over 1955–1960, when the average unemployment rate was more like 3 per cent, money wages rose at no more than 6·9 per cent. Once again, therefore, we are precluded from taking unemployment as a sole or sufficient indication of the forces governing wage movements.

It does appear, however, that we can account for those movements within the same framework of pressures and expectations as we drew out to account for earlier movements (Section 1.B.10). The conditions of these post-war years have been like those of earlier phases of soft market environment, in which the consensus of expectations among employers has been that (up to a limit set by international competition) rises in unit wage costs imposed by higher money wages could be covered by higher prices without loss of sales. Here as there, the pressure for wage rises from the side of the workers has been intensified, and the expectations of employers have been strengthened, by the sight of wages being raised by the competitive bidding for labour by employers at particular points of excess demand for labour. But the general movement has depended on the willingness of

---

Fig. 48 Five countries, 1945–1960: A. Average annual money wage-earnings and average annual pay per employee, in each country's own currency. B. Average wage-earnings converted to U.S. dollars at current rates of exchange.
Sources: Wage-earnings and pay: Appendix 3. Dollar exchange rates: International Monetary Fund, *Financial Statistics*.

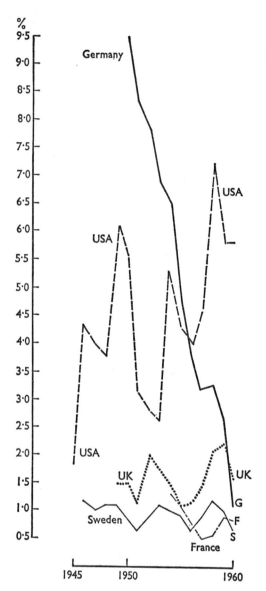

Fig. 49 Five countries, 1945–1960: Unemployment as a percentage of the non-agricultural labour force.

Sources: (1) Total occupied; (2) those in agriculture; (3) unemployed.

France

(1) 1954: *Census 1954, sondage au 1/20me.*, A1, p. 17; 1962: *International Year Book of Labour Statistics (I.Y.B.L.S.) 1965*, table 2A; with interpolations.

employers to agree to wage rises whether or not their own labour was in short supply; and this willingness in turn has depended on the sense of each that he is only doing what others will be doing, and his experience of how previous rises in money wages have not raised his unit wage costs relatively to those of his competitors.

Our studies of earlier periods have brought out the extent to which this last competitive constraint operates internationally: the movements of unit wage costs in different countries have been far more alike than those of their money wages (Figs. 2, 18; 33, 38). So it proves to be again here. Fig. 50 shows the indexes of unit wage costs which we have made by dividing our index of real output per occupied person in the industry of each country into that country's index of money wage-earnings. To bring the indexes together on a common scale, we have used the current rate of exchange of each country's currency against the dollar: thus, if, as between one year and another, a country's index of unit wage costs had risen by 32 per cent, but meanwhile the number of units of the currency given in exchange for the dollar had risen by 20 per cent, we should show its unit wage cost

---

(2) 1954: *Census 1954,* A1, table Pf1 ; 1962, and intercensal years: as for (1).
(3) *I.Y.B.L.S. 1955, 1961,* table 10, France vB.

Germany
(1), (2) and (3). 1950–1958: *Statistisches Jahrbuch (S.J.) 1960,* ch. vii, A, table i, Germany without the Saar and Berlin; 1959–1960: *S.J. 1962,* ch. vii, A, table i, including the Saar but excluding Berlin.

Sweden
(1) and (2). 1940: *Census 1940,* part iii, table i; 1950; *I.Y.B.L.S. 1960,* table 4; 1960: *I.Y.B.L.S. 1965,* table 2A; with interpolations for intercensal years.
(3) Appendix 2, E. III (*a*).

U.K.
(1) and (2). 1949–1959: *Annual Abstract of Statistics (A.A.S.) 1960,* table 132; 1960: *A.A.S. 1962,* table 131.
(3) Appendix 2, E III (*a*) (ii).

U.S.A.
(1) 1945–1957: *Historical Statistics of the U.S. (H.S.),* D. 13; 1958–1960: *Statistical Abstract of the U.S. (S.A.U.) 1963,* table 286.
(2) 1945, 1950–1960: *S.A.U., 1963,* table 286, those in jobs, to whom it was not possible to add those unemployed; 1946–1949, by interpolation.
(3) 1945–1947: *H.S.,* D. 46; 1958–1960, *S.A.U., 1963,* table 290.

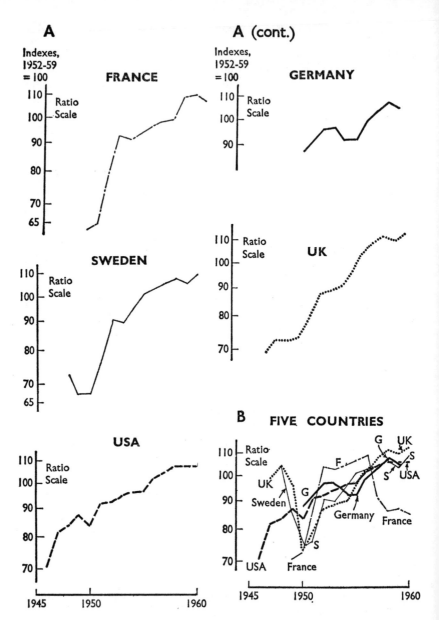

Fig. 50 Five countries, 1946–1960 : A. Index numbers of unit wage costs in industry, 1952–59 =100. B. Index numbers (1952 – 59 =100) of unit wage costs in industry expressed in U.S. dollars at the current rate of exchange.
Sources : Appendix 3, and International Monetary Fund, *Financial Statistics*.

in the bottom right-hand corner of Fig. 50 as having risen by a factor of $(1\cdot32 \div 1\cdot20)$ or 10 per cent. We are concerned here, that is to say, to trace the movement of unit wage costs as these impinge upon international trade in industrial products.

On this way of reckoning, we see how the faster rise of money wage-earnings in Germany and Sweden brought a rise of unit wage costs generally no greater than that of the U.S.A. The devaluation of 1949 dropped Swedish costs for a time relatively to those of the U.S.A., but the rapid rise in Swedish money wage-earnings that followed soon restored the previous relation. At that point the reaction of Swedish employers began to hold back the rise of money wage-earnings to a rate compatible with a rise of unit wage costs no greater than in Germany and the U.S.A., though the rapid advance of Swedish productivity still enabled money wage-earnings to rise faster in Sweden than in the U.S.A. In Germany, too, a rapid advance of productivity enabled money wage-earnings to rise rapidly without pushing unit wage costs above their internationally competitive course. The movements of the French curve of unit wage-costs are erratic, by reason of the successive devaluations of the franc – by nearly two-thirds between 1947 and 1949, and again by nearly 30 per cent of the remaining dollar equivalent, in 1956–1958. The U.K. like Sweden was quick to use up the elbow-room afforded by devaluation in 1949; and thereafter it had the benefit of no such advance of productivity as in Sweden, so that, though the rise of its money wage-earnings was comparatively moderate, its unit wage costs maintained a trend rising more steeply than those of Germany, Sweden and the U.S.A. To this, in part at least, may be attributed the endemic troubles of the British balance of payments. From 1957 it brought repeated endeavours by the British authorities to reduce the rate of rise of money wage-earnings.

If we were asked, then, to explain why money wage-earnings in any one of our countries rose at the actual rate, no more and no less, over these years, we should look not to any quantifiable system of forces within that country, but to the central international course of unit wage costs, in conjunction with the advance of the given country's productivity. But what, in turn, governed that central course of unit wage costs? Where potentially independent agents follow a common course, they may arrive at their consensus by an even process of interchange in which each influences the others as much as they influence him; or, at the other extreme, one may be the pace-setter, and all the others do but conform with him; or the process may be intermediate, with some influencing more than they are influenced, and some the other way about. In the present instance it is arguable that because international trade in industrial products bore a lower relation to the whole industrial product of the U.S.A. than of any of the other countries, it was the U.S.A. that was for the most part the pace-setter, though some reciprocal influence there must have been, and it will have increased as the dollar shortage of the 1950s began to give way to a passive balance of payments in the U.S.A. So far as the U.S.A. imposed the course of unit wage-costs unilaterally in the 1950s, we may infer that if U.S.A. domestic policy had held money wage-earnings down to a slower rate of rise, or if productivity in the U.S.A. had risen faster, money wage-earnings in the European countries could not have risen as fast as they did; and conversely.

2. Productivity

In the preceding discussion we have anticipated the findings of our inquiry into productivity, which we now present in Figs. 51 and 52.

Fig. 51 shows the rates of rise of the real output per occupied person in the whole economy. The series for different countries have been placed on a common scale by first expressing the income generated per occupied person in each country's own currency in constant prices at the average level of 1952–1959; and then converting this into dollars at the average rate of exchange prevailing over the same eight years. The drawbacks of such a procedure have been noted already: in particular we must note here that the current rate of exchange is likely to be much nearer purchasing power parity for internationally traded industrial products than for other parts of the national products, especially services and houseroom. The relative costs of different groups of products differ between one country and another, partly by reason of government action to keep some prices up by tariffs and keep others down by subsidies and controls, partly also through the general tendency of services to cost more relatively to industrial products, the higher a country's industrial productivity.

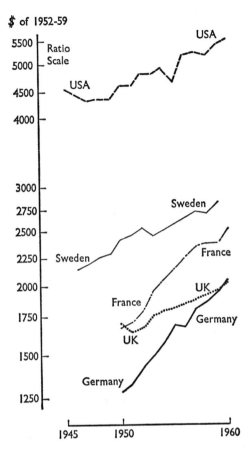

Fig. 51 Five countries, 1945–1960: Real output per occupied person, viz. national income, or net domestic product, per occupied person in own currency at average prices of 1952–1959, converted into dollars at average rate of exchange prevailing over 1952–1959.
Sources: Appendix 3, and International Monetary Fund, *Financial Statistics.*

It is likely on this last account that Fig. 51 overstates the relative level of the per capita product in the U.S.A. It may also overstate that of France: if the franc was overvalued during the earlier 1950s, and the appropriate rate of exchange was nearer that prevailing in 1959 than on the average of 1952–1959 as a whole, then the French curve would be largely coincident with the German, and show French per capita

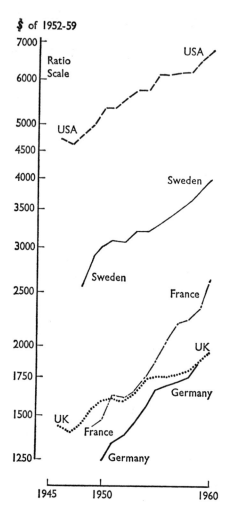

$ of 1952-59

Fig. 52 Five countries, 1946–1960: Productivity in industry, viz. net output per occupied person in industry, in each country's own currency at prices of 1952–1959, converted into dollars at the average rate of exchange prevailing over 1952–1959.
Sources: Appendix 3, and International Monetary Fund, *Financial Statistics*.

output as reaching equality with the British near the end of the 1950s instead of at their beginning. But with these reservations the comparisons made possible by the common scale of Fig. 51 seem useful as indications of relative attainments, and they gain credibility when regarded as continuations of similar comparisons attempted for previous periods (Figs. 15, 39). There seems no reason, for example, to doubt the substantially higher level of Swedish than of other European productivity.

In Fig. 52 the corresponding estimates of the real product per occupied person within industry alone are presented on the same plan, and subject to the same reservations.

These reservations do not affect the rates of rise shown by the curves of Fig. 52. They were remarkably high: Table 29 indicates

Table 29 Four countries: The annually compounded rate of rise of the real income generated per occupied person in industry in Period Three, compared with the corresponding rate in selected spans of years showing a high rate of rise in previous periods.

Germany	Period One	1894–1913	2·06
	Period Two	1931–1938	3·50
	Period Three	1950–1959	4·87
Sweden	Period One	1894–1913	2·31
	Period Two	1928–1938	4·81[1]
	Period Three	1948–1960	3·77
U.K.	Period Two	1928–1938	2·07
	Period Three	1946–1960	2·32
U.S.A.	Period One	1896–1914	1·96
	Period Two	1922–1929	3·17
	Period Three	1946–1960	2·52

Sources: Appendix 3.

[1] This high figure is derived from the same estimate of income generated per occupied person, at current prices, as yields the sharply falling wage/income ratio shown in Fig. 40. It seems possible that this estimate of ours rises too steeply.

that they were higher than in the previous spans recorded in each country, save for 1922–1929 in the U.S.A., and 1928–1938 in Sweden – though we have some reason to think that our estimates overstate this last rise. But the rates of Period Three also differ considerably from one another: the average annually compounded rates of rise over the spans shown in the Figure range from 2·3 per cent for the U.K., with the U.S.A. not far away at 2·5 per cent, up to the 5·9 per cent for France, with Sweden at 3·8 and Germany at 4·9 per cent in between.

Beckerman (1966) has derived from an analysis of the differences in the rates of rise of productivity in these and other economies in the post-war years an account of the mainsprings of growth which serves also to explain why these rates were generally higher than in earlier periods; it agrees with our own findings concerning the factors governing those earlier rates, especially the British standstill between 1900 and 1910. Productivity, as Beckerman sees it, rises more rapidly when expectations of a continuing extension of sales encourage managers to expand capacity: it is in these circumstances that a high proportion of equipment will come to embody technical innovations, and that the energies of the most efficient managers will have the greatest scope and encouragement. But in any economy that exports much of its produce, the expectation of widely extending sales that is the essential condition of this liveliness is generally possible only if exports are in process of rapid increase: the prospect of saturation is more remote in the international than in the home market. (That the French economy grew rapidly down to 1958 without rapidly growing exports may be explained by its having used devaluation and import controls to allow the internal expansion of demand to proceed unchecked.) A feedback from an achieved increase of exports forms a spiral: the expectation of extending sales engenders expansion, expansion raises efficiency, higher efficiency promotes exports, higher exports strengthen the expectation of extending sales. – To this we would ourselves add the factor of the varying rate at which technical improvements capable of widespread application become available: if most western economies today soon have access to such improvements wherever they are made first, this factor does not explain differences in the rates at which those economies advanced in this period, but it may help to explain why as a whole they advanced more rapidly in this than in earlier periods.

On these views, then, we should say that the rapid rises characteristic of Fig. 52 may be ascribed to the combination of a number of factors fostering expectations of progressively expanding sales, at a time when technology, its development accelerated by the Second World War, was making available great improvements in machines and methods. The example of France down to 1958 shows that the factors fostering expectations might be domestic – in particular, it was a major purpose of the French type of indicative planning to co-ordinate expectations about a high rate of growth, and the successive plans were valued by French managers as the most authoritative and, in their experience, reliable market research. The commitment of governments to maintain full employment, and the expectation it fostered that effective demand would never again be allowed to fall far below existing capacity, must have acted widely and powerfully in the same direction, the more so as the simultaneous commitment of many governments to the same policy made it visibly easier for each of them to maintain it. The same international consensus facilitated the expansion of international trade: full employment permitted the lowering of barriers that under-employment had raised; world trade in manufactures expanded more rapidly than world output. The effects on the rise of productivity were reduced in the U.S.A., where exports were a low proportion of output, and domestic demand was not unrestrained; and in the U.K., where a high propensity to import together with difficulties in redirecting activity toward expansive export markets brought recurrent deficits in the balance of payments, and hence restrictions on demand which in turn depressed expectations. But even in the U.K., as we have seen, the rise of productivity was faster than over either of the earlier recorded spans.

3. The course of distribution

Besides the estimates of the real product of industry which formed the basis of the figures of industrial productivity examined in the preceding section, our materials provide estimates of income generated in industry at current prices. As before, we can use the ratio of the average wage-earnings to the income generated per occupied person, both at current prices, as an indicator of any changes there may have been in the division of that product between pay and profits from time to time. Our estimates of the wage/income ratio are shown in Fig. 53.

In Section 3.A.3 we discussed possible reasons for the different levels at which the ratios of the different countries stood when this period opened, and for the changes they may have undergone since 1938. Data of capital and profits do not at present seem to be available to enable us to carry this kind of inquiry on to 1960. But we can ask what changes the wage/income ratios themselves showed as the period went on.

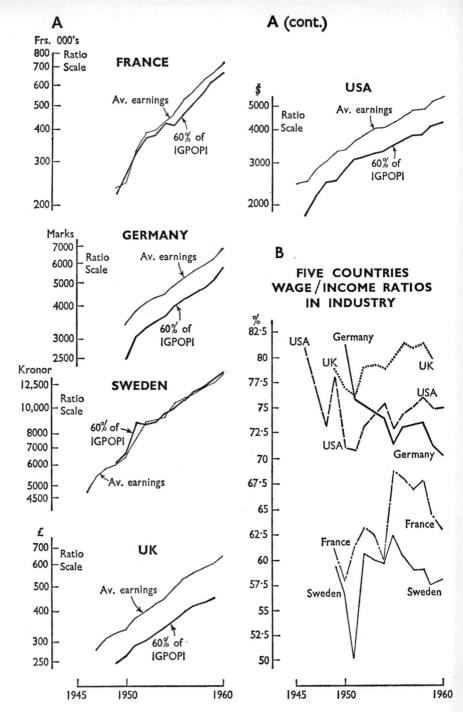

Fig. 53 Five countries, 1945–1960: A. Income generated per occupied person in industry (IGPOPI), reduced to 60 per cent of actual amount, compared with average annual wage-earnings, both at current prices in each country's own currency. B. Wage/income ratios in industry, viz. average annual wage-earnings as percentage of IGPOPI.
Source: Appendix 3.

One kind of year to year change appears here as in previous periods – the drop in the ratio when activity increases, and profits rise relatively to earnings; with the opposite movement in recession. But here only the boom set up by the Korean war of 1950–1951 was intense and general enough to set a mark on all our series. For the rest, save in France, what is remarkable is the smallness of the year to year fluctuations, which are no larger than the possible errors of estimate.

Though the period is short, it reveals movements which are something other than cyclical phases of the old kind, and may be regarded as trends. After the various movements of the years following the World War and going on to include the Korean war, the series for France, the U.K. and the U.S.A. show a rising trend; but the Swedish series trends downwards slightly, and the German markedly. The German trend may show a reaction against the narrow profit margins accepted deliberately in the early stages of recovery, when a minimum real wage had to be a first charge on a still small product: a similar reaction was recognised in the Netherlands from 1952. The upward trend of the ratio in the U.S.A. may be associated with the reduction in the share of profits in the product of industry (Graham & Bauman, 1962). Here as in France and the U.K. this might reasonably be attributed to a squeezing of profits between the rise of money wages under full employment and the restraints exerted by the authorities directly or indirectly on the raising of prices; but we have seen reason to believe that this was also a time in which the capital/ output ratio was likely to be reduced, so that a smaller share of profits would be compatible with maintenance of the rate of return on capital.

All in all, what is most remarkable in Fig. 53 is the smallness of the movements of the wage-income ratio, through a span of years in which money wage-earnings more than doubled in the U.S.A. where they rose least, and in France, where they rose most, more than trebled.

4. The rise in real wages

The rapidly rising productivity and the absence of distributive shifts that we have noted in the two preceding Sections assure us of rapidly rising real wages. That these came about in fact, is confirmed by

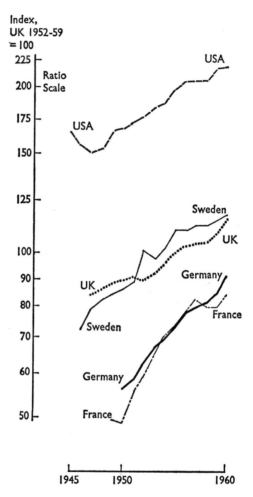

Fig. 54 Five countries, 1945–1960 : Indexes of wage-earnings in consumption units, all as relative to U.K. 1952–59 = 100.
Sources : Appendix 3 and Table 26.

Fig. 54. The indexes for different countries have been entered on a common scale by using the comparisons of absolute levels in Table 26 in order to set the level prevailing in each country through 1952–1959 in its relation to that prevailing in the U.K. through the same eight years. Implicit in this procedure is the use of the comparative costs of living reported in Table 26, instead of the current rates of exchange between currencies. These comparative costs are shown, together with the year to year movements of the cost of living in each country, in Fig. 55. Since the relative cost of living was so low in the U.K. and high in the U.S.A., the relative real wage comes out considerably higher for the U.K., and lower for the U.S.A., than did, for example, the real products of Fig. 52, which were reduced to a common scale by use of the current rate of exchange. By the same token, whereas Fig. 52 showed the real product per head in industry as generally higher in France than in Germany or the U.K., the French real wage now appears as lower than that of the U.K., and much the same as the German.

The salient feature of Fig. 54 is the high rate of rise of real wages in all five countries – also its continuity, for the apparent check to the French rise in the later years is imposed, on the procedure we have followed here, only by the devaluations of the franc. At its lowest in the U.K., the rise from end to end was by about a quarter; at its highest, in France, by nearly three-quarters. In Table 30 we shall see that in all five countries the average annual rate of rise was much higher than in either of the two spans there cited from the preceding periods.

How was this possible? One factor that had a powerful effect at times in Period Two was the quantity of primary products that the industrial worker could obtain in exchange for a unit of his own output. Fig. 56 presents indexes of these barter terms between farm and factory. The diversity of experience here is striking: more than ever before, the prices of farm produce have been set by domestic policies, and the variety of the curves of Fig. 56 reflects the variety of those policies. It appears first in the displacements through the war years. Already during the war it was foreseen that the adverse movement of those terms would oblige the U.K. to increase its exports greatly after the war if it was only to be able to bring in the same cargoes of foodstuffs and raw materials as before; and the drop between 1938 and 1950 in the U.K. index in Fig. 56 shows how this expectation was realised, even after the immediate post-war scarcities in the world commodity markets had been reduced, and the prices of British exports had risen rapidly. But the U.K. seems to have been the only one of our five countries to experience a displacement of this kind: in France and Sweden there was little change, in Germany and

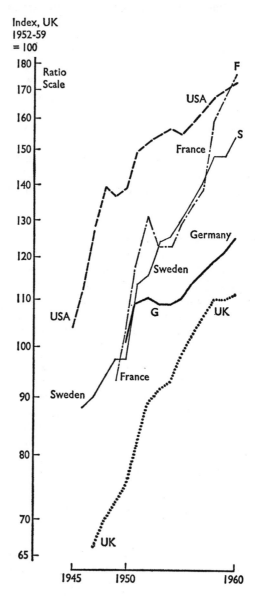

Fig. 55 Five countries, 1945–1960: Indexes of the cost of living, all as relative to U.K. 1952–59 = 100.
Sources: Appendix 3 and Table 26.

the U.S.A. the industrial worker of the 1950s could obtain much more agricultural produce in exchange for a unit of his own products than before the war. The course of change through the 1950s was also various. In France, Germany and Sweden the terms moved against the industrial worker; in the U.K., and much more so in the U.S.A. they moved in his favour. On these estimates it appears that by 1960 the British worker's standard of living owed even more to the terms of exchange between farm and factory than it had done in 1938 in an era of glut in world commodity markets. These movements in the U.K. and the U.S.A. will have been possible only because of the revolutionary technical progress of agriculture in those countries at this time.

But these terms of exchange between farm and factory enter into only one of the three elements which can, as we have seen, be regarded as composing the real wage. There is first industrial productivity, estimated by us in the form of the real income generated per occupied person in industry. Second, there is the wage/income ratio, which when multiplied against the first element gives us the real wage in units of industrial products. But the real wage as we reckon it here is in consumption units, and this is given when we multiply in turn by the third element, the rate at which industrial products can be exchanged for the articles of outlay by wage-earners' households: the movements of this rate of exchange are found by dividing an index of the prices of industrial products by our index of the cost of living. (This last index, it will be noted, covers many more objects of outlay than the agricultural products on which the curves of Fig. 56 are based, and indeed includes a number of the industrial products themselves.) In Table 30 we show how these three elements made up the rise of real wages in each country in the 1950s, and compare this with the corresponding composition in the two earlier spans.

We see that by far the largest part of the rise in real wages was provided by the rise of productivity. The distributive shift and the movement of the barter terms were, save in Germany, small in themselves, and in all four countries for which we can estimate them they were of opposite sign. That real wages now rose much faster in all countries than in either of the previous spans was clearly due to productivity likewise having risen faster than before, save only for its remarkable rise in Swedish industry in 1921–1938.

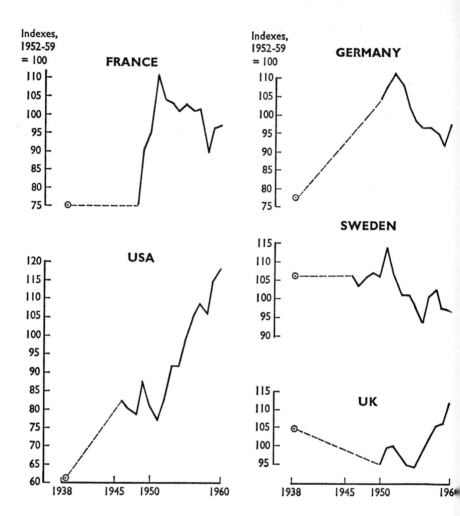

Fig. 56 Five countries, 1938, 1946–1960: Indexes of the barter terms between industrial and agricultural products (quantity of agricultural products obtainable in exchange for a unit of industrial products), 1952–59 = 100.

Sources: (1) agricultural products as food, (2) industrial products.

France, 1938, 1948–1960

(1) 1938: *Annuaire Statistique de la France, Rétrospectif* (1966), ch. 41, table vii, indexes of wholesale prices, 'produits alimentaires', spliced over 1948–1950 to ibid, table viii. A; 1948–1960: ibid, tables viii. A & viii. B.

(2) As for (1). 1938: 'produits demi-finis', spliced to table viii A, industrial products 'ayant subi une certaine transformation' and table viii. B.

The acceleration is most marked of all in France, but it happens that the earlier spans we have taken for all countries do the earlier rises in France much less justice. The terminal years 1911–1913 and 1938 both saw sharp drops in French real wages. If instead of 1895–1913 we took 1890–1892 to 1907–1909, we should find an average annual rise not of 0·38 but of 1·13 per cent; if instead of 1924–1938 we took the span from 1924 to 1935, the year before the upheavals of wages and prices under the Popular Front, we should find an average annual rise not of 0·32 but of 1·11 per cent. But the rise in Period Three is still by far the most rapid.

We noted that in this last span the signs of the distributive shift and the movement of the barter terms were opposite in all the four countries for which they have been estimated. Table 30 shows that the signs were also opposite in the earlier spans in these countries,

---

Germany, 1938, 1950–1960

(1) 1938: W. G. Hoffmann *et al., Das Wachstum der Deutschen Wirtschaft seit der Mitte des 19 Jahrhunderts,* part 2, table 137, col. (4), spliced over 1950–1954 to *Statistisches Jahrbuch (S.J.)* (1962), ch. xx. A, 'Landwirtschaftliche Produkte', given in crop years citing two calendar years of which we took the first; 1950–1960: *S.J.,* as above.

(2) 1938: Hoffmann, *op. cit.,* part 2, table 151, col. (1), index of export prices of manufactured goods, spliced to index of wholesale prices of manufactured goods; 1950–1960: *S.J.,* as above.

Sweden, 1938, 1946–1960.

(1) 1938, 1946–1950: *Historisk Statistik, Översiktstabeller,* table 95, indexes of wholesale prices, 1935=100, continued by *Statistisk Årsbok,* 'agricultural products', excluding forestry products.

(2) As for (1), 'mainly manufactured articles'.

U.K. 1938, 1950–1960.

(1) (*a*) Imported food – 1938: *Annual Abstract of Statistics (A.A.S.) 1938–1950.* Table 331, index of prices of imports of food, drink and tobacco, linked at 1950 with revised series 1950–1960 in *A.A.S. 1958,* table 272 and *A.A.S. 1961.* (*b*) Home-produced food – 1938, 1950–1960: index of wholesale prices of agricultural produce in England and Wales, 1938, *1938–1950,* table 329, *A.A.S. 1958,* table 354 and *A.A.S. 1961.* We combined (*a*) and (*b*) with weights 6, 4.

(2) 1938: *A.A.S. 1938–1950* table 331, index of prices of exports of manufactures, linked at 1950 with revised series, 1950–1960, in *A.A.S. 1958,* table 272 and *A.A.S. 1961.*

U.S.A. 1938, 1946–1960.

(1) 1938, 1946–1957: *Historical Statistics of the U.S. (H.S.),* E 27, continued 1958–1960 with *Statistical Abstract of the U.S. (S.A.U.) 1962,* table 461.

(2) 1938, 1946–1957: *H.S.,* U. 32, unit value of exports of finished manufactures, continued 1958–1960 with *S.A.U. 1961,* table 1212.

Table 30 Four countries, spans within all three periods; France, within Period Three only: Average annually cumulated percentage rise in real wages as made up of average annual rates of change in (1) industrial productivity; (2) the wage/income ratio in industry; and (3) the barter terms between industrial products and the articles of wage-earners' consumption.
[Col. (1) does not always exactly equal the sums of Cols. (2), (3) and (4), by reason of the rounding off of the original indexes whose rates of change are calculated here.]

| | Average annually cumulated percentage change in | | | |
	real wages (1) %	industrial productivity (2) %	wage/income ratio in industry (3) %	barter terms for industry[1] (4) %
France				
1895–1913	0·38			
1924–1938	0·32			
1949–1960	4·95			
Germany				
1895–1913	1·27	1·93	−0·45	−0·20
1925–1938	1·51	2·60	0·18	−1·26
1950–1959	4·66	4·86	−1·32	1·16
Sweden				
1895–1913	1·48	2·13	−0·24	−0·40
1921–1938	1·65	3·86	−1·09	−1·09
1949–1960	3·09	2·84	−0·16	0·43
U.K.				
1895–1913	−0·11	0·03	−0·32	0·16
1924–1938	1·68	1·79	−0·63	0·49
1949–1959	2·16	2·07	0·13	−0·02
U.S.A.				
1895–1913	1·33	1·49	−0·77	0·61
1920–1938	0·65	1·91	0·29	−1·54
1946–1960	2·46	2·52	−0·55	0·59

[1] Number of composite units of wage-earner's consumables obtainable in exchange for a composite unit of industrial products, i.e. index of industrial product prices divided by index of wage-earner's cost of living.

Sources: Spans in Periods One and Two, Table 23, or (France) Appendix 3. Spans in Period Three, cols. (1)–(3), Appendix 3; col. (4), indexes of cost of living from Appendix 3 divided into indexes of industrial product prices implicit in relation between cols. (8) and (10) of the table for each country in Appendix 3.

save only for 1895–1913 in Germany, and both the first two spans in Sweden. The Swedish experience in 1921–1938, indeed, appears exceptional: that industrial prices should have fallen more than the cost of living then was the experience of Germany and the U.S.A. as well as of Sweden, but the rise of productivity in Swedish industry was outstanding for its time, and it so outstripped the rise of wages that the wage/income ratio fell remarkably. We must expect that by 1937 pressure had been generated for a big rise in Swedish money and real wages, and we note that when our estimates of the wage/income ratio resume after the war, this ratio begins at and maintains a higher level than the less than 50 per cent to which it had apparently descended by 1937–1938. That elsewhere the wage/income ratio and the barter terms should have moved in opposite directions is intelligible. If a rise in the cost of living built up a greater head of steam behind wage claims, or brought them in earlier, a rise in that cost relatively to the prices of industrial products would put firms under pressure to accept a reduction in their profit margins; and conversely. It will be seen that this interpretation implies that the outcome of wage negotiations (whether or not conducted through combinations) depends not on market forces alone, but also on the parties' notions of what is their due, and their corresponding determination to press for it.

At the beginning of this section we spoke of the absence of distributive shifts in this period, but Table 30 reminds us that Germany was an exception. A large part of the fall in the wage/income ratio in German industry in fact came about in the first two years of our span – from the very high opening figure of 81 per cent in 1950 to 76 and 75 per cent in the two succeeding years. We have noted that a similar shift to profit came about in the Netherlands at the same time. In both countries we may attribute it to the rise of productivity in the course of recovery from the war making possible the widening of profit margins which at first had had to be squeezed between low productivity and a minimum real wage.

The rise of real wages in commodity units must be considered together with the rise in leisure. In Section 3.A.2 we saw that the end of the Second World War brought some reductions of weekly hours, and also more especially the extension of paid vacations among manual workers. The average hours worked in manufacturing in the early 1960s are shown in Table 31. Here the short hours in U.S.A.

Table 31 Five countries, early 1960s: Actual weekly hours worked in manufacturing, and prevailing entitlements of manual workers to paid holidays and paid vacations.

	Actual hrs. worked per week in manufacturing (1)	No. of paid holidays (2)	No. of days of paid vacation (3)
France	$46\frac{1}{2}$	1–5	18
W. Germany	$44\frac{1}{2}$	10–13	15
Sweden	45	11	18
U.K.	47	5–6	12
U.S.A.	$37\frac{1}{2}$	6–8	2 wks[1]

[1] Sometimes rising with length of service, to 3 weeks after 10 or 15 years' service.
Sources: France, Germany & Sweden: *Ministry of Labour Gazette*, Nov. 1964; *Intl. Yearbook Lab. Stat., 1966*; 'Hours of work in the U.S. and abroad', in *Monthly Labor Review*, 86, 8, Aug. 1963. U.K.: *Ministry of Labour Gazette*, Feb. 1962, Feb. 1967. U.S.A.: *Survey of Current Business, Business Statistics*, annually; *Ministry of Labour Gazette*, March 1962; National Industrial Conference Board, *Time Off with Pay* (Studies in Personnel Policy no. 196, 1965), pp. 26, 31.

manufacturing stand out: they make all the more remarkable the superiority of U.S.A. industrial productivity (Fig. 52) which is measured per man-year and not per man-hour. In the course of the 1950s the changes in weekly hours had been small in all our countries save Germany, in which the 48 hours of 1948 had come down to 42 by 1960. But by that date the pressure for shorter weekly hours was strong in Sweden, where the next decade was to see a progressive reduction from 48 to 40 hours; and in the U.K., where the 44 hours prevailing in 1959 were to be reduced to 42 by 1961 and to 40 in the later 1960s, though here as much as 8 hours' overtime continued usual. The movement towards paid vacations, moreover, had continued during the 1950s. Table 31 summarises the position reached by the early 1960s. The extent of paid vacations can be represented here only by a predominant or modal figure, for it was apt to vary from one collective agreement to another, and the entitlement under any one agreement might vary with the length of service – in the U.S.A., for example, where 2 weeks predominated, there was also frequent provision for a third week after 10 or 15 years' service. In general it seems that the extension of paid vacations, with some

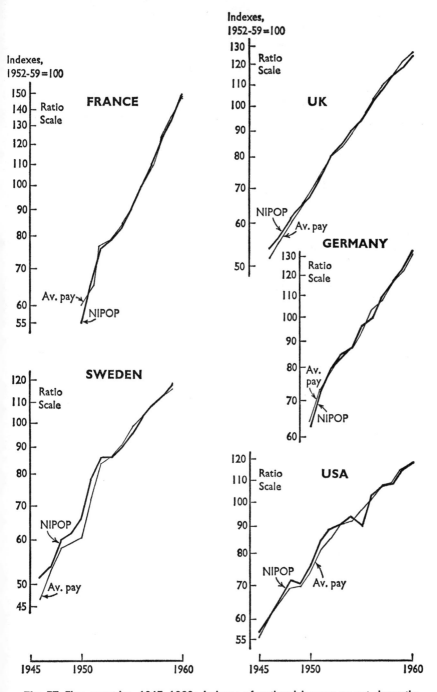

Fig. 57 Five countries, 1945–1960: Indexes of national income or net domestic product per occupied person (NIPOP) and of average pay per employee, 1952–59 = 100.
Source: Appendix 3.

increase also in the number of paid holidays, was now a major source of increased leisure. In the U.S.A. between 1940 and 1960 it had actually accounted for a greater reduction in annual hours worked than did the shortening of weekly hours: Henle (1962) puts this last effect at 75 hours a year, whereas 6 additional days of paid vacation, and 4 more paid holidays, together contributed 80 hours. Swedish legislation provided for four weeks of paid vacation from 1965.

In this study of real incomes it remains for us as before to set the movements of earned incomes over against those of the average income of the whole community. Fig. 57 displays indexes of the average pay per employee, taking wage-earners and salary-earners together, and the income generated per occupied person in the whole economy. More than ever before the movements of earnings and income per occupied person coincide in all five countries. There are two reasons for this. First, the relative contraction of 'the sector of unincorporated enterprise', the sector of self-employment, and the relative shrinkage also of rents under the impacts of inflation and public policy, have left profits as the only sector capable of expanding or contracting so as to lower or raise earned incomes substantially. But second, in a time of general inflation, when the soft market environment has been permissive towards the raising of costs and prices in most sectors, it has been hard to change relativities by holding one money income back while others advance. The changes from year to year in the wage/income ratio in industry have not been big enough, at least since 1952, to impart much divergence to the indexes of Fig. 57. It is understandable that the incomes policies which some of the economies have developed in recent years should have been concerned first and foremost with earned incomes alone.

Retrospect

4 Retrospect

1. The possibility of drawing conclusions from the record

'The extension of trade unionism made little difference to the movements of the general level of money wages'; 'the rise of real wages has depended mainly on that of productivity': these are the kinds of conclusion that we have drawn from the record and shall review here. We draw conclusions when we link cause with effect, and it is only in so far as we can do this that we make the course of events intelligible. But we can do it only in some measure. Drawing conclusions from the record is not a matter of proof, nor of eliminating all possibilities save one, but only of raising the probability of one hypothesis and reducing that of another.

For, at the outset, our insight into economic processes depends on our own notions of how men behave in business affairs. Only through these can we attempt to distinguish the significant association from the merely contingent. We saw how in the U.K. alone of our five countries productivity abruptly ceased to rise in 1900, and did not begin to transcend the level it had reached then until 1910. It happens that Queen Victoria died in January 1901, her successor King Edward VII in May 1910. Why do we dismiss out of hand the suggestion that it was the monarch who was responsible for the stasis, but are at least prepared to look further into the part played by the New Unionism? It is because the first suggestion does not agree with our stock of notions about the influences that bear on the behaviour of economic agents. An older generation was used to the thought of a King's misdeeds bringing down the wrath of God to afflict his people. 'And Ahab the son of Omri reigned over Israel in Samaria twenty and two years. And Ahab the son of Omri did evil in the sight of the Lord. . . . And Elijah the Tishbite . . . said unto Ahab, as the Lord God of Israel liveth, before whom I stand, there shall not be dew nor rain these years, but according to my word.' Minds reared on the

L

Bible would readily accept the possibility of a king's responsibility also for a drying up of the springs of economic progress. If we for our part doubt that, it is because a king's conduct has no place in the system of forces that we see as governing the advance of productivity – the rate of investment, for instance, the pace of technical innovation, the values and skill of management, the training and willingness of labour. The policy of trade unionism, on the other hand, and the punch behind it, clearly do enter into that system, and we therefore deem the rise of the New Unionism to be significant. But the essential is that we deem it so, we cannot observe it to be so. What we observe is only contingent: it is the notions we import that lend significance.

We may describe these imported notions formally as models built up out of envisaged propensities of the economic agents who work and manage, spend and save, and whose decisions check divergences from equilibrium, or carry chain reactions on. These propensities may be a matter of everyday knowledge, and even be yielded to introspection; or because they govern decisions that relatively few people have to take, they cannot be confidently assumed, or deduced from some simple premise of maximisation, but must be the object of special inquiry. But in one way or another we do form a picture of those reactions, so that in viewing them in the mind's eye we feel assured of tracing cause and effect; and out of them we build models of economic processes. It is these models that constitute economic theory. It is only by applying them that we can interpret the record of history.

But the traffic is not only one way. If it is by the models that we interpret the record, it is by the record that we test the models. For even when these have few components, they can lead with equal plausibility to the most various conclusions. We have already noted that much of the behaviour that provides their springs and gears is not a matter of everyday knowledge. Even in an everyday situation, we do not always know which of two opposite reactions will occur – will raising a piece-rate induce the worker to increase or decrease his output? In any interplay of forces, moreover, the outcome may depend in direction as well as size on their relative magnitudes. For all these reasons, when we attempt to follow a process through we set out on a journey in which whatever road we take at the first fork soon forks again, and from a common starting point we can arrive with equal plausibility at the most diverse destinations. The models, therefore, can only be provisional. They are built to be tested.

Inferences can be drawn from them about what will happen in practice, and if the record conflicts with such an hypothesis, the models that yielded it must be amended or discarded. If a model passes one test, it survives to the next.

But where the test is only by the record of history, passing and failing can only affect probabilities. Test by controlled experiment is a different matter. Here the number of variables can be limited, the extraneous and the accidental excluded; and within the guarded boundary, the variables can be changed one at a time. The record of history, by contrast, never presents a situation in which the number of variables is limited, or even known; and seldom if ever does it enable us to compare two situations that differ in only one important respect. We therefore cannot draw even negative conclusions from it with confidence. We have noted our finding that the coming of widespread trade unionism in a number of countries from the 1890s onwards was not accompanied by any change in the movement of the general level of money wages that would of itself lead us to infer the presence of a new factor in wage determination. Yet it is possible that the extension of unionism did make for a more rapid rise in money wages, but was offset by some other factor or factors coming into play about the same time – the greater organisation of the employers being one such. Again, strong unionism may have a marked effect on the movements of money wages in some circumstances but not in others: under sustained full employment, for instance, the rate of rise of money wages may be largely determined by trade union policy, even though through the ups and downs of the 8-year trade cycle collective bargaining did little more than alter the timing of wage changes that would have come about in its absence. We can establish no firm conclusions about the effects of union strength, therefore, by comparing the historical situations before and after the extension of unionism. Yet we are not reduced to nescience. If it is possible that variations in other factors supervened, we can always examine them, and judge what effect if any they are likely to have taken. Such judgments will indicate in turn what degree of probability attached to the initial finding that the extension of trade unionism did not make much difference to the movement of the general level of money wages. This finding increases the probability that models which predict such a result display the actual working of the economy, and decreases the probability that others do so; but by how much the probability is affected in each case can be only a matter for judgment after a review and appreciation of all the attendant circumstances.

In the attempt to assess the influence of a particular factor or trace the causes of a particular effect by comparing situations, we have an advantage in the present work through being able to compare different economies in the same period, as well as different periods in the same economy. In a number of respects – the trends of international commodity prices, the availability of new processes, the phases of the trade cycle, the movements of unit wage costs – the different economies were subjected to common influences at any one time. It is the most salient of our findings that the contemporary courses of our economies were so much alike. This similarity sometimes offers us more opportunity to 'keep other things equal' than was commonly offered by the degree of similarity between different periods in any one economy. Where one economy differed from its contemporaries in some one aspect, we can look for the cause in some other differentiation of the same economy.

None the less, we still cannot speak of models passing or failing the test of history. Our interpretation establishes probabilities, and is not built up out of rigorous conclusions. It is also subjective, in that it depends on the notions of behaviour we bring with us. Did the facts allow of only one conclusion, it would be impersonal; but though the interpreter is guided by the probabilities that the record establishes, the probable elements can still be arranged in different ways, and the picture he composes is his own. It is in this light that the following observations are to be viewed.

2. Population and employment

The growth of population that was so rapid in all our countries except France is to be regarded, at least in its origins, as exogenous to their economies. The subsequent development of those economies allowed it to continue, may even have fostered it in some places and periods; but it set in before the industrial revolution had gone far in any of them, it was as powerful in Southern Ireland, where there was next to no industrialisation, as in Great Britain, and we are bound to think it would have come about just the same if there had been no industrial revolution to follow. The last such exogenous increase, in the sixteenth century, had brought little but misery, and the Malthusian checks of hunger and disease. This time the increase of population could extend over vast natural resources in the United States, and both there and in our other four countries it was accompanied by great technical changes in agriculture, transport and manufacture, which provided ever increasing numbers with a continuing subsistence, and after a time even with a progressively rising standard of living.

Did the agrarian and industrial revolutions only impinge upon the growth of population as a fortunate coincidence, or were they stimulated by it, and carried farther where it went on more rapidly? Forceful arguments can be propounded *a priori* for the connection; but we must check them against our evidence.

That the growth of population stimulates productivity may be argued on the ground that, assuming the increased numbers find employment, total output grows faster. For any one industry or firm this fosters the expectation of more rapidly expanding markets, and this expectation in turn fosters the spirit of enterprise. In a more rapidly expanding industry, moreover, it is easier for the more efficient firms to expand relatively to the others; there will be less resistance to change; and a greater proportion of the equipment at any one time will be of recent installation and the most advanced design. A growing working population, again, is more adaptable than one in which the proportion of new entrants is lower and the average age higher.

We might therefore expect to find some tendency for productivity to rise more rapidly where the population of working age was growing more rapidly, even though this last was only one of many factors bearing on the rise of productivity. But this we do not find. France stands out from our countries down to 1914 by the extreme slowness of the rise of its working population (Fig. 1A): we lack estimates of industrial productivity for France, but the general agreement between the rates of rise of productivity and real wages allows us to take the latter as a fair indication of the former, and it is noteworthy that over 1860–1900 in France, where the working population was rising at less than half of 1 per cent per decade, real wages rose at an average annually compounded rate of over 1·25 per cent, whereas in the U.S.A., where the working population was rising at 25 per cent or more in a decade, the annual rise of real wages was still only of the order of 1·65 per cent. We shall see that over the whole span from 1860 to 1960 the rise of real wages was much the same in France as in Germany and the U.K. In the twenty years before the First World War the most rapid rise of industrial productivity was in Sweden, but here the working population was growing at little more than half the rate of the German, and two-thirds that of the British (Table 8). In most countries the working population grew more slowly in Period Two, but in all four countries for which we can make the comparison industrial productivity rose a good deal faster in the twenty inter-war years than it had done in the twenty years before the war. The still higher rates of rise of productivity after the Second World War were linked in the European economies with an industrial expansion that, so far from responding to the growth of numbers, set up a labour shortage that drew immigrants in.

We are therefore inhibited from regarding the growth of population as a dominating influence for industrial development: this has gone on where the increase of population has been negligible, and variations in the rate of development have not been directly associated with those of population growth. It remains possible, indeed probable, that at least in some circumstances a rapid growth of the working population promotes the rise of productivity, but evidently it is only one factor among many, and not so strong as to outweigh the others. What seems most probable is that if those other factors are making for a rapid development, a rising working population will not only obviate checks to the development but actually increase the rise of productivity; but in the absence of those other factors it can do nothing for its own part, and may even imprison the economy within a vicious circle of low consumption and low productivity, as in some underdeveloped countries today.

The *a priori* arguments we set out assumed that the extra hands seeking work year by year would in fact find it. It is one of the most obvious yet significant features of our evidence that this assumption is justified: however fast and cumulatively the numbers seeking work increased, there was no cumulation of unemployment, and over any long span of years the number of vacancies increased in the same proportion as that of applicants. This is in striking contrast with the experience of not a few underdeveloped countries in which population has grown rapidly in recent years. It also appears downright paradoxical, when we consider the severity of unemployment in the inter-war years, and the experience of recurrent unemployment even before then, which implanted in the minds of wage-earners a sensitivity to any threat of redundancy that remains morbid even after a quarter-century of full employment.

How were the additional vacancies created? If we suppose the problem solved, and look back at the end of a decade in which the number of working age and the number gainfully occupied have both risen by say 15 per cent, we can see that the extra hands have really given employment to one another: the extra income generated by the activity of all provides the market for the output of each. Formally, an increment of the Gross National Product of the order of 15 per cent requires changes in the outputs of the various products, and of the numbers engaged in making them, that will most of them be increases, some more and some less than 15 per cent, though with these perhaps will go a few actual decreases. The pattern of development of the additional manpower will be determined by the consumers' choices that govern the allocation of the additional income; the input-output relations through which the demanded increments of final products are translated into increments of intermediate products; the participation of the economy in international trade; and the technical change that is going on meanwhile. Such a pattern is internally consistent, in the sense that the different groups of workers composing it will be able to exchange their outputs with one another without residue, and so maintain themselves in employment. The problem then is, how are the newcomers to be marshalled into the required pattern? Somehow this problem was solved, without a widening margin of error, long before governments concerned themselves with manpower policies and national economic development.

The solution can have been found only by a process of *tatonnement*, of probing here and there; of pushing forward as far as one could get all along the line. We can see those young people who cannot take over a parent's place in the economy but must find a place of their own, looking out around them for something they could do, moving afield if there is no opening at hand. They will not do this unless they live in a culture that extrudes them from the family when they grow up, expects them to maintain themselves, and allows them freedom of movement and of entry into many occupations if not all. But granted these conditions, each will look for something he can do, by working for someone who is expanding a line of output, or starting some line of his own. How this comes about has been illustrated in recent experience by the way in which the coming of the motor-car brought a network of garages, the coming of radio and television a network of service shops, not by direction from above but by the initiative of countless people throughout the length and breadth of the land. Some initiatives will soon be checked by a saturation of their particular market for the time being, while others can be pushed farther on: the pattern of deployment changes as the total working population and the total product increase. But the essential requirement is that whatever resistance or encouragement the initiatives meet with point by point, their pressure shall be kept up all along the line: for each increment of output will find a market only if the other increments are being added at the same time.

Evidently this process depends upon a culture that favours individual enterprise, especially if it brings forward a number of men of outstanding vigour and capacity who create jobs for their less enterprising neighbours. It is also promoted by improved communications. The point for our present purpose is not just that the growth of population within any one region that cannot provide increasing quantities of the necessities of life from its own natural resources depends on the exchange of produce with other regions. It is rather that within a given increase in the number of bodies subsisted, the number of jobs will grow more readily if the localised natural resources can be exploited intensively, or the inhabitants specialise in a particular industry: but 'the division of labour depends upon the extent of the market', and jobs will open faster in these ways where transport is cheaper. We might also think that the process will be facilitated by a high rate of saving making possible the liberal equipment of the new hands with buildings and machinery; but the record does not show that the process in fact went worse in periods of relatively low investment, nor does it seem to have gone better in the U.S.A., where population could extend over a vast and vacant domain, than within the sometimes already close-packed curtilages of Europe.

But it does appear that the creating of new vacancies overall was powerfully assisted from time to time by a process which did not depend on the simultaneity of local initiatives and their mutual support. That process, it is true, might go on while the total flow of monetary payments remained unchanged, and each increment of real output edged its way into the market by bringing prices down a little: that does seem to have been the trend of affairs for twenty years or so after the mid-70s. But the process will be easier if the monetary flow rises in the same proportion as the real output, so that this can be sold at unchanged prices. And more than this: if the monetary flow takes the lead, the first effect will be a margin of excess demand, creating jobs to satisfy itself. Here a new mechanism is brought into play: we do not have to rely on the simultaneity of various and widespread initiatives creating in the aggregate the market for the output of each, but the market is now created initially by higher spending. The effect will be stronger if the increase in the monetary flow exceeds the increase in real output that will be achieved by setting all additional hands to work: there will then be unfilled vacancies in most industries and places, and the chances of any one man with given qualifications and residence soon finding a job he can do will be raised. In Period Three it was very generally this that came about. In the earlier periods the monetary flow fluctuated with the trade cycle. The positive phase of the cycle therefore saw big increases in the number of jobs; in the negative there might be a small increase or none, or, though this only in the most severe depressions, a decline. Typically, for example, in the U.K. in Period One, those available for jobs were increasing at the rate of $1\frac{1}{4}$ per cent a year, so that in four years the increase would be rather more than 5 per cent. In the same span, from a cyclical peak to a trough, the unemployment rate might rise by about 5 percentage points, so the number in jobs would change little; but in the following four years it would rise by around 10 per cent.

In this last argument we have touched by inference on two of the main sources of unemployment – the cyclical and the structural. Down to the Second World War the trade cycle brought rising unemployment in some four years out of every eight. We must realise what this meant to the workers. In a bad year, though not the worst ever, the unemployment rate might be about 7 per cent: this might mean, at the one extreme, that 93 per cent of the workers were continuously employed and the remainder as continuously un- employed, or at the other extreme that every worker was unemployed for nearly one month in the year. The actual state of affairs will have lain somewhere between, but near enough to the second extreme for

L2   B.B.C.P.

most workers to have cause to worry. That anxiety, extending far more widely than the actual incidence of unemployment, goes far to explain why it was the failure of the economic system to provide work for all that stood out rather than its proven ability to match the rising trends of population with one of jobs. But not this alone: in the inter-war years especially, the German, Swedish and British workers experienced high rates of unemployment persisting through the positive phase of the trade cycle. This unemployment was structural. The problem here was different from that of finding jobs for those whom the growth of population was injecting into the labour force year by year. These last were young people, and they were spread fairly evenly over different regions and the different occupations with which their families were already in touch; but the structurally unemployed were most of them older, and they were concentrated in particular regions and occupations. The system that had long coped well with the first problem unaided proved unable to get far with the second. Experience in Period Two, and still more in Period Three, has shown that higher levels of aggregate demand enable more of the structurally unemployed to find work, but by no means all of them. The readiness with which governments can lower the national rate of unemployment by increasing the flow of spending stands in contrast with the slow progress of their plans for regional employment.

So it has come about that economic systems which have doubled and re-doubled the number of jobs they have provided for their peoples have inspired in them at the same time a dread of unemployment. The grounds are intelligible, and the dread is not to be dismissed by those whose own security enables them to take the longer view. But on that view, what is outstanding in the working of these systems is their ability to match the trends of population and jobs. This performance stands out in contrast with the failure of many contemporary societies to achieve it. It is therefore pertinent to ask how it was achieved here. We have found the answer in a culture that favoured individual enterprise; the improvement of transport; and the irregular expansion (for all its attendant disorders) of the flow of spending.

3. The rise of productivity

To the early economists it would have been a great surprise that productivity rose at all. They expected the growth of population to carry the economy into zones of diminishing returns. That it did not do so, but instead was accompanied by progressively increasing output a head, we can now explain as due to a number of factors: the list is familiar. The improvements of transport enabled economies to escape from the limitations of natural resources within their own borders, while technical progress in agriculture continued to push back the limits of food supply. In industry, no less, technical progress continued to develop new processes and devices, and these were embodied in equipment with which the worker was provided in ever-increasing amount. When these improvements were applied to the generation of energy they made it possible also to put ever more horse-power at his disposal. Investment went on besides in the quality of the labour force, through general education and specialised training. These developments were promoted and administered by men of enterprise in cultures that favoured enterprise. In these ways a rise in productivity was initiated and sustained, on a scale to which we know of no counterpart since the Neolithic Revolution.

But the listing of these processes has not proved of much help to many contemporary countries seeking to follow them: they describe the 'how', rather than analyse the 'why'. In such a study as ours, cannot we find out more about the really governing factors, the initiating causes as distinct from the required conditions, by surveying the different rates at which productivity rose in the various periods and places, to see whether those differences are significantly connected with those in attendant circumstances?

Our estimates of real income generated per occupied person in industry show various rates of change, but some differences are outstanding: the sudden check in 1900 to the rise of the British series, lasting until at least 1910; the higher rates of rise in Period Two than before; the yet higher rates again of Period Three. The search for possible causes of these differences yields at least some negative findings. We have already seen that any influence the rate of growth of population may have had upon them is not big enough to stand out by itself. Nor does there seem to be any decisive influence from the tide of rising and falling prices. British industrial productivity rose during the twenty years of prevailing monetary stringency and downward trend of prices from the mid-70s, but stopped rising when the tide of prices turned. It is true that the rates of rise of productivity in Period Three, unprecedentedly high in all our countries save Sweden, went with a sustained rise of prices that was generally also unprecedented, but we shall argue later that this was only a side-effect of the really effective difference in the circumstances of this period. Some recent discussion has laid stress on incentives, on the size of the increments of income after tax that can be gained by making the effort and taking the risk of innovation: but the British stasis occurred when income tax ruled under a shilling in the £ and there was no surtax or capital gains tax; and rates of taxation were generally higher in Period Two than before, but productivity rose faster. Nor can any association be traced with another factor on which recent discussion has laid stress, the size of investment as a proportion of the national product. The cumulative rise in the amount of capital per worker has certainly been a necessary condition of the rising trend of productivity, but variations from time to time in the rate of annual investment have not been clearly associated with corresponding changes in the rise of productivity. This implies that the incremental capital/output ratio has varied widely, so that we cannot be at all sure of obtaining a given increment of output by adding a given amount to our capital stock; and comparison of the performance of the western economies over a wider range than ours in recent years has borne this out.

When these possibilities have been excluded there remains an explanation in part indicated by the record, in part suggested by direct knowledge of affairs and acceptable as not incompatible with the record. The essentials of this explanation were arrived at in our study of the British stasis of 1900–1910, but they can be tested against the further differences in the rise of productivity in Periods Two and Three.

Foremost here is the rate at which technical advances have been made that are capable of and have reached the stage of widespread application. Some technical advances concern the forms of products rather than of processes. Others, though they do improve processes, are peculiar to particular industries: in any one industry they are likely to be made irregularly, and some differences in the advance of productivity in the whole economy may arise from the contemporary fluctuations industry by industry being sometimes compensatory of one another and sometimes cumulative. But the larger movements of the aggregate are likely to depend on technical advances of wider application. Such advances may be made in common services, especially transport and energy; or in the production of basic materials, such as steel; in widely used equipment, like the steam engine in earlier days and the electric motor later; and in methods of management also of widespread application, such as the mass production of the early 1900s and the computerisation of the 1960s. There is no reason why advances of these kinds should come forward at a steady rate: indeed, what seems remarkable in the record is not that the rate of rise of industrial productivity varied as it did, but that the variations were not bigger. Nor are we likely to find any statistically recorded factor to which those variations are attributable. But it does appear that the higher rates of advance achieved successively after the two World Wars owed much to the intensification of research, and more especially to the acceleration of development from the laboratory through the pilot plant to quantity production that had been brought about in the course of the war efforts. Some have held that what was done in war can continue to be done in peace, by allocating sufficient resources to research and development, and that the cultivation of innovations can proceed like that of corn, subject only to minor variations of the harvest from year to year. Others agree that an initial increase in the allocation of resources can draw on a backlog of ideas, and expedite the development of those already being worked up; and that maintaining a large allocation will prevent another backlog building up, and may bring more new ideas to birth; but they doubt whether the sequence of discovery can be expedited beyond certain limits, and indeed ultimately whether the vein of technology that was opened up two hundred years ago may not ultimately be worked out.

The other main component of our explanation of variations in the rate of rise of productivity lies in the outlook of businessmen. This outlook depends in part on the values of the culture in which they have grown up, on what they have learned to admire, and the standards of achievement by which they believe their fellows judge them. All these vary between countries in any one period, and between periods in any one country. But with a given attitude towards enterprise, the degree of enterprise actually shown depends on the perceived prospects of its success. Here we return to variables of the kind our record contains. The prospects of the expansion of the output of any one product depend on those of the market for it at home and abroad, and these in turn depend on recent experience. A high rate of growth of the national product already achieved will encourage expectations of a continuance of expansion of the home market. Here, as so often, nothing succeeds like success; in technical language, there is positive feed-back: where expansion and innovation are vigorous already they are most likely to continue so, and enterprise achieves growth at the same time as growth fosters enterprise. But even in a rapidly growing economy, and with a product that may expect to command an increased share of final outlay, the prospects of expansion of sales in the home market must be limited in comparison with those that open if the market is international. Hence the particular importance that attaches to the expansion of exports in industries in which innovations can be developed and applied more rapidly under more enterprising management. But here again, as has been emphasised by Beckerman (1966), there is a virtuous spiral: if it is the countries that have expanded their exports most that have achieved the greatest economies in their manufacture, it is because they have achieved the economies that they have been able to effect the expansion.

The higher rates of rise of industrial productivity of Period Two must be attributed largely to the acceleration of research and development during the First World War, and to the existence – as it happened – of a concentration of technical advances still in the pilot plant stage on the eve of the War. The rates of rise generally achieved since the Second World War will equally have owed much to that War itself; but that they were generally greater than ever before can be ascribed, on the explanation offered here, to the rapid expansion of world trade in manufactures, and the unprecedented effect on the expectations of businessmen of their governments' unprecedented but proven ability to maintain substantially full employment. If in wage negotiations these expectations have conduced to inflationary settlements, in the management of industry they have not merely reduced the risks of innovation but exerted a positive pressure to find ways of getting a greater output from limited available resources; and they have fostered a professional emulation, a consensus on the standards of performance by which a manager is judged among his fellows. In France and Sweden the expectations of managers have been strengthened and aligned by the indicative planning designed by Jean Monnet. That industrial productivity has risen more slowly in the U.K. than in our other four countries – and not a few more besides – may be explained by a vicious circle: the innovation needed to redeploy its industrial resources towards the currently expanding international markets has taken too long for a recurrent imbalance of international payments to be avoided meanwhile, and the setbacks thereby imposed on domestic activity have shaken the confidence of businessmen so as to slow down the needed innovation.

As so often in the argument of this work, our account of the springs of productivity has stressed the importance of consensus. We have shown how the expectations generally entertained by the business community are shaped by events; but a consensus can also exist in its own right. It is formed by a process in which each adjusts his own expectations to what he believes the others are expecting, while they for their part are adjusting theirs to his. Once formed it tends to strengthen itself, because – in the nature of things – the decisions it leads to are of a kind that will justify it in the event. There may be external constraints or exogenous impacts that prevent this, and then it will break up, and in time some new consensus will form. But in the absence of such jars, once formed it tends inherently to maintain itself; and one of the reasons for differences in the rate of rise of industrial productivity may well lie in differences between prevailing consensuses of expectations.

4. The course of distribution

To trace the course of distribution distinctly we need more detail than we have been able to provide. It is true that because shares in the whole national product have depended much on the relative sizes of different sectors, and especially that of the sector of self-employment, we have confined our study to industry – that is, generally, to mining, manufacturing, transport, public utilities and construction. But even within industry alone, the division of the aggregate product depends on the relative sizes of the particular industries, as well as on changes in the shares of pay and profit in the value added by any one of them. Industries differ widely in the amount of capital per worker, but not nearly so much in the rate of profit on capital: so changes in the relative sizes of different industries will raise or lower profits relatively to pay in industry as a whole. It is probable that differences in the proportionate composition of the aggregate industry of different countries account for some of the differences we have found between their wage/income ratios; and that, in any one country, changes in that composition account for some of the observed movements of the wage/income ratio over time. It seems unlikely, however, that they can account for so much movement as we find. This must also be due to changes in the rate of profit relatively to the pay per man that run through a number of industries at the same time. What account of the process of distribution does our evidence suggest?

It will be remembered that our materials have lent themselves to arrangement within the identity

$$s \equiv 1 - rk,$$

where s is the share of labour in the product, r is the rate of profit on capital, and k is the capital/output ratio. (We shall follow convenient precedent here in using 'labour' to comprise all employed, which in turn, within industry, we take as virtually equivalent to all occupied; and in denoting all earned incomes by 'wages'.) We have not directly estimated the share of labour, but can take the year to year movements of our wage/income ratio in industry as a sufficiently close indicator of the corresponding movements of the share of labour as here defined – the two will differ only to the extent that the proportion of wage-earners among all employed changes, and this will be small in the short run. We can therefore obtain a synoptic view of the course of distribution, by following the movements of the wage/income ratio in industry, the rate of profit, and the capital/output ratio. Unfortunately all three are available only for Germany, the U.K., and the U.S.A., and that only in the first two periods, for we have not been able to draw on continuous estimates of the capital stock throughout Period Three. Period Two, moreover, is too short, and within its limits too much affected by the great depression of the 1930s, to throw much light on distributive trends.

The purpose of Table 32 is to survey the prevailing levels of these three variables and the extent of their variability, by citing the lowest and highest values of each in each period. Because the annual series were moved about so sharply by the trade cycle in the first two periods, we have removed most of that fluctuation by taking a seven-

Table 32 Five countries, three periods: Lowest and highest value of 7-year moving averages in Periods One and Two, and annual entries in Period Three, of the wage/income ratio in industry (in U.K. Period 2 , in U.S.A. Periods 1 and 2 manufacturing only), and of the rate of profit and the capital/output ratio in the mainly industrial sector.

	France	Germany	Sweden	U.K.	U.S.A.
Period One					
Span begins		1860[1]	1870	1870	1889
1. Wage/income ratio, %		62–67	51–67	63–73	59–71
2. Rate of profit, %		9·0–12·0[3]		11·5–14·7[4]	8·4–14·1[3]
3. Capital/output ratio		2·14–3·27		2·16–3·17	2·52–2·88
Period Two					
Span begins		1925	1920	1924	1921[2]
1. Wage/income ratio, %		62–64	56–62	68–71	68–80
2. Rate of profit, %		0·29–4·35[4]		9·2–11·7[3]	2·3–7·9[4]
3. Capital/output ratio		3·11–3·82		2·07–2·30	2·31–2·97
Period Three					
1950–1960					
1. Wage/income ratio, %	58–69	70–81	50–62	76–82	71–76

[1] Wage/income ratio, 1880   [2] Wage/income ratio, 1920
[3] Inferred rate   [4] Directly calculated rate

Sources: Rows 1 & 3, Appendix 3. Row 2, Germany, Tables 113, 114; U.K., Tables 137, 138; U.S.A., Tables 149, 150.

year moving average, and it is the lowest and highest entries of this that we have taken. Period Three suffered fewer fluctuations and we cover only eleven years, so here we have taken simply the lowest and highest annual entries.

Table 32 reveals some differences between periods and countries. That the rates of profit lie in a zone that is altogether lower in Period Two than in Period One is due partly to the downward displacement of the early 1920s (Section 2.A.5) but even more to the impact of the deep and protracted depression of the early 1930s. In Germany and the U.K. the wage/income ratio ruled higher in Period Three than ever before, and in the U.S.A. it remained around the high level reached under the New Deal, which likewise appears to have been without precedent; but there seems to have been no such shift in the zone containing the Swedish ratio. We have already (Section 3.A.3) discussed the possible reasons for higher wage/income ratios appearing in Period Three; unfortunately we lack estimates of the associated levels of the rate of profit and the capital/output ratio. In all three Periods, the Swedish zone lay lower than the others.

But these differences apart, what Table 32 brings out is the extent to which each variable has lain within the same not very wide zone throughout a number of years and in more than one country. Through most of Periods One and Two, and in four countries, the wage/ income ratio appears to have lain in the region of 60 to 70 per cent. Throughout the long span of Period One, the range of 8 to 15 per cent contains the variations of the rate of profit, after cyclical fluctuations have been removed, in all three countries for which we have estimates. The capital/output ratio, taking Periods One and Two and the three countries together, lay between extremes of 2·07 and 3·82; but the 3·82 is due to the catastrophic fall of output in Germany in 1931–1933, and if we except this the maximum becomes 3·27.

It appears, then, that each of the three variables remained for the most part within a determinate and limited zone of values that was common to different countries. The numerical values of these zones are familiar to us: we commonly expect, for instance, that the prevailing rate of profit, on capital bearing the risks of enterprise, will be of the order of 10 per cent, and not 3 per cent, or 23. But what seems part of the natural order of things requires all the more to be accounted for. There is no immediately apparent reason why an economy should not be found in which pay of all kinds absorbed only half the product, the remainder accruing to capital as a rate of profit of $12\frac{1}{2}$ per cent on a capital stock amounting to four times the output –

$$0\cdot5 = 1 - (0\cdot125 \times 4);$$

or in which the share of pay was nine-tenths, with a 5 per cent rate of profit and a capital/output ratio of two –

$$0\cdot9 = 1 - (0\cdot05 \times 2).$$

How can we account for the actual values being those we commonly find, such as

$$0\cdot75 = 1 - (0\cdot10 \times 2\cdot5)?$$

We can offer an explanation in two stages. First, formally, we can draw on the findings of the mathematical economists who have built models of economies that are developing through the growth of the working population, the accumulation of capital, and technical progress (R. G. D. Allen, 1967). Among these models the neo-classical have been designed so as to generate a behaviour over time which in three respects reproduces salient features of the actual course of western economies: the real rate of return per man-year rises in proportion to the output per man; the rate of profit is steady; the capital/output ratio is steady. This behaviour flows from assumptions built into the model, of which the chief again are three. First, there is a market for the factors of production labour and capital, in which the demand for each is derived from its marginal productivity, and the rate of return on each is brought into equality with the marginal productivity of the quantity employed. Second, production is carried on under technical conditions such that there are constant returns to scale, and technical progress affects the relation of inputs to output in certain defined ways. Third, a condition is formulated by which the amount of investment is determined: one such is that investment must equal the amount of savings made out of the income currently generated according to fixed propensities to save.

The macro-economic theorist, then, shows us how the share of pay in the product, the rate of profit and the capital/output ratio will behave as we have seen them to have done in the western economies, if their factor markets, technical conditions and investment determination conform with the assumptions out of which his models are built. In this there is a great gain of understanding. True, we do not know that it is the mechanism of these models and these alone that can generate behaviour like that of the western economies, but we do see one intelligible way in which that behaviour could have been generated: we see how our variables can have been kept within certain zones common to different countries, because the markets and techniques of those economies had certain basic traits in common.

Yet so far this is only in general terms: it shows us in what conditions, for instance, the rate of profit will lie within a certain zone, but for all we know this zone might as well be centred on 50 as on 10 per cent. In the second stage of explanation, however, the actual numerical values can be accounted for if it is the case that investible funds have generally been in elastic supply at prospective rates of profit not far removed from 10 per cent, and that enterprise has been persistent and pervasive in carrying investment into openings that held this prospect forth. In that case we can formulate a new equation to govern the flow of investment: instead of setting this equal to the flow of savings that arises when savings are a fixed proportion of income, we require it to be such as to adjust the stock of capital so that the marginal productivity of capital shall be equal to a rate of profit, say 10 per cent, which is given as a parameter of the system. The marginal productivity of capital being maintained at this rate, the capital/output ratio will also be determined numerically. Thus supposing the production function is of the Cobb–Douglas form and, with suitable choice of units, can be written

$$Y = L^{0.75} C^{0.25} \tag{1}$$

then the marginal productivity of capital, held say at 10 per cent, will be a quarter of its average productivity, and this puts the capital/output ratio at $2\frac{1}{2}$ –

$$\frac{\partial Y}{\partial C} = 0.25 \frac{Y}{C} = 0.1,$$

$$\frac{C}{Y} = 2.5 \tag{2}$$

The basic assumption here is of a stream of investible funds available at prospective rates of return lying within a zone around 10 per cent, and channelled by enterprise into expanding production at many points in the economy. This assumption is not merely heuristic, but is substantiated by a fact of experience. Save for France, the western economies had to find jobs for working populations that were growing at rates of from 10 to 15 per cent per decade: but they solved the problem – as the numbers seeking jobs grew, so did the number of jobs. There was cyclical unemployment, and much unemployment at all times among the unskilled; but over a span of fifty or sixty years in which the numbers needing jobs would double, the margin of unemployment did not widen. This can have been so only if new jobs were being opened as new hands were looking for them, if existing businesses were expanding and new ones starting up in so far as labour was available. There was no invisible hand to match applicants with vacancies place by place, and from one year to another the balance between them tilted now this way and now that. But in the aggregate the match was made. It has not been made in some of the poor countries whose population has been rising in recent years. That it was made in the western economies is best explained by the pervasive pressure of enterprise and investible funds in them towards the expansion of activity and the creation of employment.

So far, then, we account for the rate of profit, the capital/output ratio and the share of pay in the product all remaining within certain not very wide zones, as follows. At a prospective rate of profit in the region of 10 per cent the supply of investible funds has been so elastic that investment has adjusted the capital stock so as to keep its marginal productivity within the region of 10 per cent. This steadying of the rate of profit has gone on while the labour force has been growing and technique has been changing; but the form of the aggregate production function has ensured that the growth of the capital stock which in these changing circumstances will steady the rate of profit will also steady the capital/output ratio. Thereby and necessarily the share of pay in the product is steadied too. The outcome depends in part on the technical relations of inputs and output expressed by the aggregate production function, in part on the decisions made by economic agents. These decisions are of two kinds. There is first the decision to invest – a combination of the willingness to provide funds with the initiative of the entrepreneur in seizing or creating an opening for investment, wherever the prospective rate of return is not less than that which is generally looked for and at which the funds are available. Second, and no less necessary to the outcome, there are the decisions taken in the labour market, which similarly check any divergence between the marginal productivity of labour and the prevailing rate of pay. If it is the marginal productivity that for the moment is the higher, more workers may be employed so that the marginal productivity is reduced; and/or, to the extent that the supply of labour is inelastic, competition between employers will raise the rate of pay.

Evidently there is room here for some shifting of the zones from time to time, and for some wandering within them. The zones will shift if the technical conditions of production change, or if there is a change in the rate of profit that is sufficient to attract investible funds. There will be wanderings within the zones, and occasional excursions outside them, if the adjustments between marginal yields and the intakes or prices of factors are sluggish and lag behind the

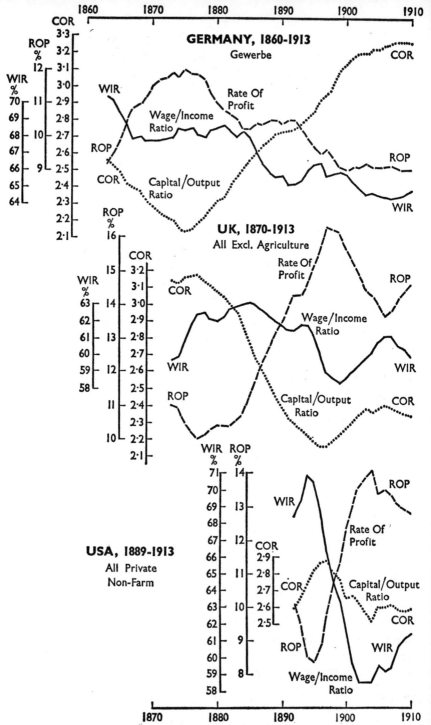

Fig. 58 Three countries, 1860–1913: (1) Wage/income ratio. (2) Capital/output ratio. (3) Rate of profit inferred from (1) and (2). 7-year moving averages.
Sources: (1) Germany: Appendix 2, Table 113; U.K.: Appendix 2, Table 137; U.S.A.: Appendix 3. (2) Appendix 3. (3) Appendix 2, Tables 113, 137, 149.

course of change, or on the other hand overshoot the mark; and if they respond only to big divergences.

Table 32 indicated the extent of the stability of the zones, but also – notably in the rate of profit in Period Two – the possibility of their shifting. What also of the wanderings in and around them? These are illustrated in Figure 58. The sharp fluctuations of the 8-year cycle have been largely eliminated here, in all but the most severe cycles, by the use of moving averages. The remaining movements are still marked. Three variables are shown, but because (if the wage/income ratio can be taken as varying closely with the share of pay in the product) they are locked into the identity $s \equiv 1 - rk$, only two of them are capable of independent movement. The most conspicuous feature is the inverse movement of the rate of profit and the capital/output ratio in Germany and the U.K., a relationship which appears also in the U.S.A., though less strikingly, for here the movements of the capital/output ratio are smaller. This inverse relation can have a number of explanations.

The simplest would be that it arises from errors in the estimates of the capital stock. It is these estimates that are suspect rather than those of profits, partly because they are inherently more difficult and hazardous, partly because they stand largely on their own whereas the estimates of profits have to fit into those of pay and product. If the estimates of capital stock do have a steady bias upwards, we shall find – what Germany shows from the 1870s onwards – a rising capital/output ratio and a falling rate of profit; and if, conversely, their bias is downwards, that would account for the fall of the capital/output ratio and the rise of the rate of profit in the U.K. between the mid-70s and the mid-90s. But the extent of the error needed to make those movements appear when the capital/output ratio had actually been constant is improbably great. In Germany, for instance, our estimates (taking the values for single years) show the capital/output ratio as rising from 2·09 in 1874 to 3·32 in 1908, and the stock of capital itself as rising at an average annually compounded rate of 4·76 per cent. To keep the capital/output ratio constant the stock would have had to rise at no more than 3·39 per cent a year, and if this was the rate at which it actually did rise the estimates have overstated annual net investment by an average of 40 per cent. In the U.K. the extent of the error required to reconcile the apparent fall of the capital/output ratio from 3:21 in 1874 to

2:10 in 1895 with an actually constant ratio is even greater: the estimate of the capital stock shows it rising at less than one per cent a year, but if the capital/output ratio were actually constant the stock must have been rising at nearly 3 per cent a year. It is unlikely that the estimates are out so far as that. Part at least of the movements of Fig. 58 must be accepted as significant. They call for other explanations.

One such can be provided on the assumption of rigorous determination and close adjustment by the mechanism of the model. It is that progressive changes were taking place in the technical conditions of production expressed in the aggregate production function, and/or in the prospective rate of profit at which investible funds are readily forthcoming. It might be, for instance, that in Germany between 1874 and 1908 the course of technical change was raising the amount of capital required per unit of output, while it was lowering that amount in the U.K. between 1874 and 1895. But there seems little support for that in what we know of the two economies, and it is specially hard to see why the types of technical change their industries experienced at this time should have been opposite. The explanation by shifts in the supply of funds seems more probable. In Germany there was a willingness, conspicuous to contemporary observers, to invest in equipment and operate it at a lower rate of return than was looked for in the U.K., and this may have made it possible for the capital stock to be so expanded that its average and marginal productivities fell, and with the marginal the rate of return, without checking investment. In the U.K., on the other hand, where the market for funds was international, the higher rates of return offered overseas may have kept up the rate expected from investment at home and so reduced its amount. Between 1870 and 1900 capital per head failed to rise in U.K. industry, whereas in German industry it nearly doubled.

There remain some explanations that rest upon the possibility of the adjustment between marginal productivities and factor prices having been tolerant of divergences. Suppose, for instance, that a general rise in pay per man raises total pay, and this is compensated by an equal fall in profits. The total product, as valued at the sum of payments to factors, is unaffected, so that the capital/output ratio is unchanged, but the wage/income ratio goes up and the rate of profit down. The effects will be of the same kind if the increase in total pay is not offset, or is offset only partially, by a fall in profits: the total product at current prices will now be raised, but the capital stock valued at current prices will rise in the same proportion, and the capital/output ratio will remain unchanged, while again the wage/income ratio goes up and the rate of profit down. Another possibility with the same kind of outcome is that total profits are reduced without a compensating increase in total pay. To each of these possibilities there corresponds an opposite case in which it is profits that gain on pay: once again the capital/output ratio will be unchanged, but here it is the wage/income ratio that goes down and the rate of profit that rises.

We cannot hope simply by inspection of Fig. 58 to identify phases in which one or other of these various possibilities has predominated. The shifts we have just noticed that originate in factor shares may, and very probably will, have been taking place at the same time as those noticed earlier that originate in the technical conditions of production and the supply price of investible funds; and their influences may have offset or reinforced one another. But the most striking feature of Fig. 58 is the wide and opposite movements of the capital/output ratio and the rate of profit in Germany and the U.K. They go too far to be explained by lack of adjustment between marginal productivities and factor prices. We have seen that a possible explanation lies in the different conditions of the supply of investible funds in the two countries.

At the end of this discussion of variations we must remind ourselves that the shifts of the zones are less remarkable than their persistence over time and similarity between different economies, and that the wanderings of the variables are less remarkable than the narrowness of the zones that contain them. We are brought back to the neo-classical models of the growing economy as indications of what sort of technical conditions and human propensities may be doing the steadying in the actual world. Chief of these propensities for our present purpose seems to be the influx of enterprise and investible funds.

5. The rise of real wages

'The real wage' is a more comprehensive term than 'the average wage reckoned in composite units of commodities' to which alone the limited coverage of our index-numbers of the wage-earner's cost of living allows us strictly to refer. But these index-numbers do at least serve to measure changes in the wage-earner's power to command the staples of consumption with the unit of the money in which he is paid. They therefore enable us to trace the rise in the wage-earner's material standard of living, at least in the sense of the quantities of the principal objects of household expenditure that average wage-earnings will buy.

Table 33 Five countries, three periods: Percentage increase from end to end of each period of average wages reckoned in composite units of commodities; and factor by which the wage so reckoned was multiplied over the whole span 1860–1960.

	France	Germany	Sweden	U.K.	U.S.A.
% increase,					
1860–1913	57	84	171[1]	91	79[2]
1913–1938	33	24	47	32	49[2]
1938–1960	97	77	88	67	98
1860–1960					
X factor of	4·1	4·0	7·5	4·2	5·3

[1] from 1861   [2] terminal date is 1914

Source: Appendix 3.

This rise is summarised in Table 33. Over the hundred years of our full span, the real wage was increased fourfold in France, Germany and the U.K., and more than fivefold in the U.S.A.; in Sweden it was multiplied by a factor of as much as 7·5, though this was due to the great advance down to 1913, from the low initial level of Swedish real wages on the eve of industrialisation, rather than to any exceptional progress thereafter.

The sources of this very great advance admit of a less qualified statement than most of the changes reviewed here. Our analysis of the components of change period by period (Tables 13, 24 and 30) has shown that the rise in real wages was made possible almost entirely by the rise of productivity in industry. Shifts in the share of the product allotted to the worker, and in the terms on which he could exchange his own produce against foodstuffs and raw materials, were both relatively small in themselves, and more often than not in opposite directions. That the economies of these five countries have been able to achieve this advance in productivity while absorbing into employment within their own bounds an ever-increasing – and except in France a rapidly increasing – number of workers, marks the uniqueness in all history since the Neolithic Revolution of the capacity for development first manifest only two hundred years ago in the Industrial Revolution.

The significance of this rise in real wages has been enhanced by two attendant changes. One is a general reduction in the size of the family: in the U.K., for instance, whereas in 1860 the wage of a manual worker in the middle years of life would typically have to support six children, a hundred years later he would typically have two or three. The other change is the reduction in weekly and annual hours of work. The particulars we have brought together of these hours, period by period, have shown how difficult it is to generalise, even within one country. But it may be said that in 1860 few industrial wage-earners were working less than a 60-hour week, save for those in the U.K. who had recently got down to 54 hours; and public holidays did not exceed four or five days. By 1960 the week actually worked ranged downwards from 47 hours to under 40, the number of holidays had been somewhat increased, and paid vacations had come in, generally of two or three weeks. We calculated that down to the Second World War the wage-earner had taken out his gains about equally in the forms of purchasable goods and leisure. Since then there have been signs of different valuations of increased leisure as against increased purchasing power on the part of different wage-earners: evidently there are some who are willing to work longer hours for more purchasing power. There is no difficulty moreover, in seeing how a manual worker's household could use double the purchasing power it enjoys today – use it, namely, as its neighbours not far removed in space or social standing are using purchasing power on that scale now. The wage-earner is increasingly aware of the possibilities of obtaining a higher income, and knows what he could spend it on. It may be, therefore, that further advances in productivity will be used more than in the past to raise the real wage, and less to reduce weekly hours. But one form of consumption that higher real incomes make possible is the vacation, and it may be expected that annual vacations will be extended.

In these conjectures we have passed beyond the reckoning of

purchasing power, to consider wage-earning as a way of life. If at the last we look back over these hundred years to ask how this has changed, we find some major drawbacks to set against the rise of the real wage. Industrialisation has created many jobs which do not engage the whole man, and hold his interest, nor do they give him the satisfaction of achievement, and sustain his self-respect and his standing with his fellows. Whatever the job, it usually requires the man who does it to adopt the status of employee, with its loss of independence and its need for self-defence in the wage bargain and in daily relations with the authority of management. In neither of these respects is any sweeping indictment to be made out: most men have jobs in which they find some satisfaction and take some pride, and most industrial relations are tolerable, for all that we hear of the exceptions; yet there is anomie, there is resentment. Industrial productivity has also drawn on the external economies of urbanisation, and that in turn has imposed a cribbed and drab setting on too many childhoods – a deprivation of the freedom and activity as well as of the beauty of the countryside. It is perhaps the combination of this imprisonment with higher purchasing power to which contemporary urban manifestations of juvenile discontent are largely attributable. The achievement of a better life for the worker will continue to depend, now as before, on the advance of productivity; but more than before this needs to be accompanied by improvements in the design of jobs and the human relations that go with them, and of the environment in which the worker's child must attempt the harrowing task of growing up.

Appendixes

1 International comparisons at 1905 or 1909, 1930/1931, and 1953: sources and methods

1. 1905 or 1909

A. AVERAGE WAGE-EARNINGS IN MONEY

1. *France*
(*a*) Ministère du Travail, Statistique Générale de la France, 1911: *Salaires et Coût de l'Existence à diverses époques, jusqu'en 1910*, at pp. 22, 23 gives daily rates prevailing in 1906, as reported by the Conseils de Prud'hommes, in 36 M and 7 F occupations. (*b*) *Annuaire Statistique de la France, Rétrospectif, 1961*, p. 256, tableau vi, daily wages of coal-miners. (*c*) *Résultats Statistiques du Recensement Général de la Population effectué le 4 mars 1906*, tome i, 2me partie, tableau vii, p. 194 *et seq.*, France entière; tome ii, tableau vii, p. 23, Paris and p. 37, banlieue de Paris. From (*a*) we selected 20 M occupations that could be assigned to one of the categories (1) unskilled, (2) operative, (3) craftsmen. We took the provincial wage-rate for all except, in (3), the tourneur en métaux, for whom we took the Paris rate. We made a weighted average for each category, using as weights the numbers occupied reported in (*c*). These were numbers of wage-earners in all France except for the number used to weight the Paris metal-worker's rate, which was that of wage- and salary-earners together in the metal trades of Paris et banlieue. We combined these three averages with the coalminer's daily wage given in (*b*), using weights provided by our estimates, based on (*c*), of the total numbers of wage-earners occupied in each of the four categories. For F, we took the unweighted AM of the 7 wage rates reported in (*a*). To move from daily to annual earnings, we noted that comparison of hourly and daily rates in (*a*) shows that in the great majority of cases the day was of 10 hours: assuming a 54-hour week, we therefore multiplied our daily rate by 5·4 to get a weekly rate; this in turn we multiplied by

49 to get annual earnings. The estimates so far are for the earnings of adults only. To take account of juveniles, we took 45 per cent as the prevailing ratio of juvenile to adult earnings, on the evidence of E. Levasseur, *Questions ouvrières et industrielles en France sous la troisième république* (Paris, 1907), pp. 533, 547, and the British Department of Labour's *Third Abstract of Foreign Labour Statistics* (Cd 3120 of 1906), p. 53. From *Recensement 1906*, tome i, 3me partie, table iv, pp. 96–97, we took the proportions of juveniles as 15 per cent of all M and 30 per cent of all F. Combining these ratios, we find that the average earnings of all M wage-earners will be 91·75 per cent, and those of all F wage-earners 83·5 per cent, of those of adults only. We applied these percentages to the average earnings already calculated for M, F, and combined the outcomes with the weights 3, 1, representing approximately the relative numbers in the working population as reported in (*c*) above. To move from 1906 to 1905 we applied our index of wage-rates.

2. *Germany*

A. V. Desai, *Real Wages in Germany 1871–1913* (1968) takes from the returns of employers under the insurance scheme for workmen's compensation the average annual earnings of all employees earning not more than (in most industries) 3000 marks a year, in twenty-seven industries. Through 1902, and in some industries after that, the reported earnings were distorted by the practice of entering at the locally prevailing wage for the unskilled adult the earnings of juveniles who actually earned less; and by the deduction of two-thirds of the excess of actual earnings over 1200 marks (1500 marks from the last quarter of 1900). Dr Desai adjusted the reported earnings to obtain estimates nearer actual average earnings. He says that the number of non-manual employees included is small. The twenty-seven industries are made up of eighteen in manufacturing, with printing, mining, quarrying, building, four kinds of transport, and warehousing. Dr Desai divides these industries into two sections, of which one contains those whose reported earnings are less reliable, but we have excluded only the four – quarrying, building, glass and bricks – for which comparison with the Census gave Dr Desai reason to believe that employers had been reporting not the average number of employees but the (often much greater) number whose names appeared on their books in the course of the year. Dr Desai gives an annual average for the two sections combined: we adjusted this average for the exclusion of the four industries, using as weights the numbers of employees at the time of the Census in June 1907 (*Statistisches Jahrbuch 1910*, Gewerbe v, Table 1a). We estimated these numbers by deducting the number of establishments, as a measure of the number of employers, from the total occupied.

3. *Sweden*

We combined the data for M described in Appendix 2 with a rough estimate for F formed by combining average earnings in food products and textiles (G. Bagge *et al.*, *Wages in Sweden, 1860–1930* (1933), part i, tables 18, 20) with weights 1, 3. We combined the average earnings of M, F with weights proportional to the total number of each (age 18 and over) in employment (Bagge, op. cit., part ii, table 187). The resultant annual earnings of 915 kronor will be higher than the average for all wage-earners because the component for M relates 'primarily to the more permanently employed and more skilled' (Bagge *et al.*, op. cit., part ii, p. 286). We have average annual earnings of all wage-earners, in *Lönestatistisk Årsbok för Sverige, 1934*, table 13, p. 52, but not before 1913; the mean for 1913, 1914 is 93 per cent of that obtained for those years from Bagge *et al.* in the same way as we obtained the 915 kr. for 1905, and we applied this ratio to the 915 kr.

4. *Great Britain*

To obtain estimates excluding agriculture, for 1905 and 1909, we (*a*) estimated average earnings of M in agriculture – we were unable to make an estimate for the F, but they will not have been numerous; (*b*) estimated the average annual earnings of M manual workers excluding agriculture; (*c*) formed a weighted average of (*b*) with average earnings of F, excluding those in domestic and personal service. (*a*) A. L. Bowley, *Wages and Income in the United Kingdom since 1860* (1937), pp. 106, 113, gives average earnings of M in agriculture in 1906 in England and Wales, and says that including Scotland 'could not affect the averages seriously'. At col. 1 of table ii, p. 8, he gives an annual index for wages in agriculture, by applying which we also obtained weekly earnings in 1911. (*b*) We had now to estimate the total wages of M in agriculture in Britain in 1906, 1911, for deduction from the total wages of M in all industries in Britain,

M   B.B.C.P.

which we derived for those two years from Bowley. To arrive at his figures for annual earnings, Bowley took a year of 50·6 weeks but made further allowances for unemployment, sickness, casual work and superannuation: we put back these allowances but took a year of 49 weeks. We obtained the number of M wage-earners in agriculture from the Censuses for 1901 and 1911: *1901* for England and Wales, Summary table xxxv; for Scotland, we applied the percentage that wage-earners formed of all M in Scottish agriculture in 1911 to the corresponding total in 1901; *1911*, England and Wales, vol. x, table 13; Scotland, vol. ii, table xxvii. We made an estimate for 1906 by linear interpolation. We multiplied the numbers so obtained by the average wages obtained in (*a*) to arrive at total weekly wages of M in agriculture in 1906, 1911, with corresponding annual wages on the assumption of 49 weeks paid for. We deducted these from the corresponding totals for all industries obtained by multiplying the number of M (Bowley, op. cit., p. 136, and linear interpolation) by their average earnings (ibid., pp. 52, 53). We divided the residual by the number of M in industries other than agriculture to obtain the average annual earnings of the latter in 1906 and 1911. (*c*) We combined these earnings of M with those of F in the same two years: Bowley, at p. 16, gives the average earnings of F in industry in 1906 as 43 per cent of those of M, and at p. 53 he gives earnings of all F in 1911 – we took this last figure without attempting adjustment for the shop assistants and domestic servants it includes. As weights we took numbers occupied: M outside agriculture, as above; F, Bowley, p. 136, less those in domestic and personal service, G.B. only, from B. R. Mitchell and P. Deane, *Abstract of British Historical Statistics* (1962), p. 60. To obtain estimates for 1905, 1909 we extrapolated with an index of the required coverage formed by extracting from Bowley's index for all industries (table i, col. 1, with numbers at p. 136), the component for agriculture (table ii, col. i, with numbers as in (*b*) above). We extrapolated from both 1906 and 1911, and in each of 1905, 1909 took the average of the two results.

5. *U.S.A.*

Average annual earnings of full-time equivalent workers in manufacturing, in table 10 of A. Rees, *Real Wages in Manufacturing 1890–1914* (N.B.E.R., General Series, no. 70, 1961).

B. COST OF LIVING

   1. *France with Britain, October 1905*
(i) *Report of an Enquiry by the Board of Trade* (Cd 4512 of 1909) gives 'the expenditure of the average British working man (with an average family) on certain standard articles of food and fuel, and on rent at the prices and rents ruling in France' as 14 per cent above his corresponding expenditure in England when rates are excluded from his rent (p. xlvi). (ii) To find the corresponding ratio for a French wage-earner's budget we need first to know what weight to give to rent in this: at p. xxv rent is taken as one-sixth of the combined outlay on food and rent, but from the table on p. xviii a proportion of one-seventh seems nearer the mark. We are told that the 'cost of the average French working man's budget (excluding fuel and commodities for which no comparative prices can be given)' was 6 per cent greater at French than at English prices (p. xlii); and that 'net rents of working class dwellings in France are to the net rents of working class dwellings in England (excluding that portion of English rents which represents local taxation) as 98 to 100' (p. xlvi). We then have

$$(1 \times 0{\cdot}98 + 6 \times 1{\cdot}06) \div 7 = 1{\cdot}05$$

   2. *Germany with Britain, October 1905*
(i) *Report of an Enquiry by the Board of Trade* (Cd 4032 of 1908) gives the cost of the items making up a British wage-earner's budget for food, fuel and housing as 19 per cent greater in Germany than in England (p. lii). (ii) To find the corresponding ratio for a German wage-earner's budget we need first to know what weight to give rent in this budget. The rent (apart from local taxation) for a given number of rooms was about 23 per cent higher in Germany than the U.K. (p. xlii), but the British workman for the most part had 4–5 rooms against the German's 2–3: $(2{\cdot}5 \div 4{\cdot}5) \times 1{\cdot}23 = 0{\cdot}68$. German weekly wages were about 0·83 of the British (p. lii). The British weight for rents was one-fifth. So we have

	Rents	Food and Fuel	All Items
Britain	20	80	100
Germany	13·6	69·4	83

and the German weight for rent may be put at one-sixth. This seems likely to be nearer the mark than the one-fifth taken on p. xxviii. We then have:

(p. xlv) Cost in Germany of German wage-earner's Budget of food and fuel bears to its cost in England the ratio   1·08

(p. xlii) Rent in Germany of given number of rooms bears to rent in England the ratio   1·23

$$(1 \times 1{\cdot}23 + 5 \times 1{\cdot}08) \div 6 = 1{\cdot}105$$

3. *U.S.A. with Britain, February 1909*

(i) *Report of an Enquiry by the Board of Trade* (Cd 5609 of 1911) gives the cost of the items making up a British wage-earner's budget for food and rent as 52 per cent greater in the U.S.A. than in England and Wales (p. lxxvi). (ii) To find the corresponding ratio for the American wage-earner's budget we need to know the weight of rent in this budget: we are told (p. xxxvi) that rent amounted to one-quarter of the combined expenditure on food and rent, and this is borne out by the table on p. xlix. The average American–British (Northern) working man's budget of food (excluding commodities for which prices could not be given) cost 25 per cent more in America than in England and Wales (p. lxvii). The ratio of '207:100 may be taken as representing with approximate accuracy the level of rents paid by the working classes in the United States and England and Wales respectively' (p. lxiii). Then we have

$$(1 \times 2{\cdot}07 + 3 \times 1{\cdot}25) \div 4 = 1{\cdot}45.$$

C. INCOME PER OCCUPIED PERSON, AND WAGE/INCOME RATIO

The entries in rows 6, 7 and 8 of Table 2 were taken from the series of national income, income generated in industry, numbers occupied in whole economy and in industry, and average wage-earnings, compiled as described in Appendix 2. In U.S.A. 'industry' covers manufacturing only.

D. HOURS OF WORK

1. *France*
Report of an Enquiry by the Board of Trade (Cd 4512 of 1909). J. H. Clapham, *Economic Development of France and Germany* (3rd edn, 1928), p. 405. H. Sée, *Histoire Économique de la France*, vol. 2, *Les Temps Modernes 1789–1914* (1951), pp. 346–7.

2. *Germany*
Report of an Enquiry by the Board of Trade (Cd 4032 of 1908). J. H. Clapham, *Economic Development of France and Germany* (3rd edn, 1961), p. 405. G. Bry, *Wages in Germany 1871–1945* (1960), p. 46.

3. *Sweden*
G. Bagge *et al.*, *Wages in Sweden 1860–1930, Part i* (1933), p. 59.

4. *U.K.*
A. L. Bowley, *Wages & Income in the U.K. since 1860* (1937), pp. 25–26. E. C. Ramsbottom, 'Changes in Labour Conditions during the past Forty Years', Manchester Statistical Society, *Transactions*, 1941–1942. B. McCormick, 'Hours of Work in British Industry', *Industrial & Labor Relations Rev.*, 12, 3, April 1959.

5. *U.S.A.*
Report of an Enquiry by the Board of Trade (Cd 5609 of 1911). Leo Wolman, *Hours of Work in American Industry* (N.B.E.R. Bulletin 71, Nov. 1938), pp. 4, 8. C. D. Long, *The Labor Force under Changing Income & Employment* (1958). A. Rees, *Real Wages in Manufacturing 1890–1914* (1961), tables 10, 13, 16. S. de Grazia, *Of Time, Work and Leisure* (1962), pp. 441–443. E. B. Jones, 'New estimates of hours of work per week and hourly earnings, 1900–1957', *Rev. Econ. & Stats.*, Nov. 1963.

2. January 1931 or average 1930/1931

A. AVERAGE WAGE-EARNINGS IN MONEY

1. *France*

We used the estimate of weekly wage-earnings described in Appendix 2, except that the earnings of craftsmen (OQ) in Appendix 2 were those only of Paris metalworkers and ten crafts in the provinces, whereas here we included those of the same ten crafts in Paris, as follows. On the average of 1930, 1931, we took the median of the hourly wages given for the ten crafts in Paris in *Annuaire Statistique de la France, Rétrospectif, 1961*, ch. xxiii, A, tableau i. To combine this median with the provincial average for the same crafts, we used as weights the number of 'employés et ouvriers' (it was not possible to separate them) in manufacturing industry, in the Paris region, and in the provinces, obtained from *Résultats Statistiques du Recensement Général de la Population, 1931*, tome i, 3me partie, table vii, and tome ii, table vii; we took 'tisserands' out from the total for all France, and metalworkers from the figure for the Paris region. This gave us the weights, Paris region 4, provinces 27, and we used these to obtain an average wage for craftsmen in all France. Using the rates and weights described in Appendix 2 we then combined this average for craftsmen with averages for the semi-skilled (OS), weavers, labourers, Paris metalworkers, miners, and women, all expressed as weekly rates. We obtained average annual earnings on the assumption of 49 paid weeks in the years. These earnings are for adults only. To take account of juveniles, we noted that at p. 849 of 'Statistics of the Working of the Social Insurance Act in France from 1932 to 1935', *International Labour Review*, xxxv, June 1937, the daily wages of juveniles appear as very closely two-thirds of those of adults aged 25–44, in both cases taking M and F together, and that *Recensement 1931*, tome i, 4me partie, table iv, shows workers under 20 as 18·9 per cent of all workers. Putting these ratios together we obtained $6\frac{1}{3}$ per cent as the reduction required to adjust average earnings of adults to those of all workers.

2. *Germany*

We multiplied by 49 the average weekly gross earnings in 1930, 1931 given by G. Bry, *Wages in Germany 1871–1945* (1960), table 16, col. 2 for wage-earners in iron, metal trades, chemicals, construction, wood and furniture, paper production, printing, textiles, shoes, confectionery and brewing. We took the A M of 1930, 1931.

3. *Sweden*
We took the A M of the average annual earnings in 1930, 1931 of all wage-earners, including juveniles, in industry, handicrafts, commerce and transport, given in *Lönestatistisk Årsbok för Sverige, 1934* (Sveriges Officiella Statistik, K. Socialstyrelsen), table 13.

4. *U.K.*
A. L. Bowley, *Wages and Income in the U.K. since 1860* (1937) using the Wage Census of 1931, table xvi, p. 105, gives average actual earnings of all manual workers employed in industries covered by unemployment insurance, together with railways, as 48·5s per week, and we have taken 49 weeks to the year.

5. *U.S.A.*
See Appendix 2, U.S.A., A.2(i).

B. CONSUMER PRICES
From *A Contribution to the Study of International Comparisons of Costs of Living* (I.L.O. Studies and Reports, N.17, 1932), we drew particulars of the costs of (*a*) food, (*b*) clothing, in Paris and Marseilles; Berlin and Frankfort; Stockholm; and Detroit. (*a*) The report gives the cost in each city of the articles of food consumed in 1929 by Detroit households whose head was earning about $7 a day in the employ of the Ford Motor Co. (annex i, table iv, pp. 160–3), and the cost in Detroit of the articles of food consumed by wage-earning households in each of the other cities; we have used the G.M. of the relatives on these two bases. (*b*) A sample collection of articles of clothing bought by the Detroit households was priced in each city; we have used the results omitting children's clothing, which in the American form had little counterpart in some other cities. We used the average relation of the price level in each city to that in Detroit, for food and for clothing, to calculate relatives to Manchester, and we combined these relatives with (i) Manchester weights throughout, (ii) in the comparison of

each other city with Manchester, the other city's weights. The weights were:

	Manchester	Paris	Marseilles	Berlin	Frankfurt	Stockholm	Detroit
Food	84·0	82·6	80·0	79·5	79·3	74·5	81·1
Clothing	16·0	17·4	20·0	20·5	20·7	25·5	18·9

We obtained them as follows: Manchester, *The Social Survey of Merseyside*, D. Caradog Jones, ed., vol. i (1934), table vii, p. 227, and p. vii; Paris, J. Singer-Kérel, *Le Coût de la Vie à Paris de 1840 à 1954* (1961), pp. 427–8, weights for 1909–1939, Ouvrier A; Marseilles, *Mouvement Économique en France 1929 à 1939* (Statistique Générale et Institut National de la Statistique, 1941), p. 55; Berlin, Frankfurt, *Die Lebenshaltung von 2000 Arbeiter-, Angestellten- und Beamtenhaushaltungen* (Statistisches Reichsamt, Berlin, 1932), part ii, pp. 13–14, 58–59; Stockholm, *Levnadsvillkor och Hushållsvann i Stader och Industriorter omkring år 1933* (Sveriges Officiella Statistik, K. Socialstyrelsen, Stockholm 1938), table LL, p. 138; Detroit, above-cited I.L.O., N.17, 1932, annex ii, excl. children's clothing.

Where the comparisons obtained with the two sets of weights differed, as they did for every city except Frankfurt, we treated them as a bracket.

To adjust the bracket for a given city so as to make it more representative of the whole country concerned, our only evidence was the relation of food prices in the city and the country as far back as 1905 or 1909 (inquiry by British Board of Trade described in Appendix 1, 1.B.: Cd 3864, table at p. xxxi; Cd 4032, table C, p. lv; Cd 4512, table C, p. lii; Cd 5609, table I.C., p. lxxx). The effect of applying this relation city by city appears in row 2 of Table 16 in the main text.

Table 16 also gives, with sources, estimates of the relative costs of food and clothing in 1931 made by carrying estimates of relative costs in 1905 or 1909, 1950 and 1953 forward or back to 1931 in accordance with the movement over the relevant spans of the indexes of the cost of food, clothing and fuel within each country. The method is described in principle in the text adjoining Table 16. Where levels in a number of places are expressed as relatives to the level in one of them, an error in that one will appear as an opposite error in all the relatives, and when we are seeking to deduce the relatives at one date from those at another this is vexatious, unless the same error in the place chosen as base should occur at both dates. In Table 16 we have therefore expressed the cost in each place as a relative to the average of all. We formed this average simply as the mean of the relatives as originally expressed, Manchester = 100. It may therefore be conceived as an average of the costs, recorded country by country but all expressed in £s at the current rates of exchange, of a bill of goods which cost £100 in Manchester.

How we reached final estimates from the array in Table 16 is also described in the text adjoining that table.

C. INCOME PER OCCUPIED PERSON, AND WAGE/INCOME RATIO

The entries in rows 6, 7 and 8 of Table 15 were taken from the series of national income, income generated in industry, numbers occupied in the whole economy and in industry, and average wage-earnings, compiled as described in Appendix 2.

D. HOURS OF WORK

1. *France*
International Yearbook of Labour Statistics (I.Y.B.L.S.), 1935–1936, table viii. *I.Y.B.L.S., 1941*, table 9.

2. *Germany*
I.Y.B.L.S., 1935–1936, table vii. G. Bry, *Wages in Germany 1871–1945* (1960), pp. 46–47.

3. *Sweden*
Lönestatistisk Årsbok för Sverige, 1932, table 8; *1936*, table 12; *1939*, table 27.

4. *U.K.*
A. L. Bowley, *Wages and Income in the U.K. since 1860* (1937), pp. 25, 26. E. C. Ramsbottom, 'Changes in Labour conditions during the

past forty years', Manchester Statistical Society, *Transactions 1941–1942*. B. McCormick, 'Hours of work in British industry', *I.L.R.R.*, 12, 3 April 1959.

5. *U.S.A.*

S. H. Slichter, *Union Policies and Industrial Management* (1941). H. R. Northrup and H. R. Brinberg, *The Economics of the Work Week* (N.I.C.B., Studies in Business Economics No. 24, 1950). G. Brooks, 'History of union efforts to reduce working hours', *Monthly Lab. Rev.*, Nov. 1956. C. D. Long, *The Labor Force under Changing Income and Employment*. E. B. Jones, 'New estimates of hours of work per week and hourly earnings', *Rev. Econ. & Stats.*, Nov. 1963. *Historical Statistics of the U.S.*, D.636, D.639, D.643, D.670.

3. 1953

A.I. AVERAGE WAGE-EARNINGS IN MONEY

1. *France*
We took the salaire brut annuel, ouvrier, in tableau iii of: Institut des Sciences Économiques Appliquées, *Masse de Salaires versés dans les secteurs de l'industrie, du commerce et des services* (April 1963); and raised this figure by the percentage of cotisations (20·4) reckoned as in Appendix 2.

2. *Germany*
We took the gross weekly earnings in DM. in industry including mining, at 1956, in *Statistisches Jahrbuch 1957*, xxi A, table 1, and extrapolated to 1953 using the index with the same coverage in the corresponding Table in *Statistisches Jahrbuch 1961*. We added employers' contributions to social security (9·8 per cent) reckoned as in Appendix 2. We multiplied by 50 to get annual earnings.

3. *Sweden*
Sources: *Löner, 1953*, Del ii, (L); *International Yearbook of Labour Statistics 1960*, (I.Y.); *Statistisk Årsbok 1955* (S.A.); Per Holmberg, *Arbete och Löner i Sverige* (1963) (P.H.). (i) *All workers in manufacturing*

and mining. L, p. 45, tells us that most adult M workers were on a 48-hour week; excluding those on a 42- or 40-hour week, average hourly earnings were 4·07 kr., and we took annual earnings of adult M as given by 4·07 kr. × 48 × 50. We reduced this in the proportion 4·01 to 4·11, given by L, p. 44, as the ratio of the hourly earnings of all M wage-earners to those of adult M. P.H., table 10, states that in 1961 average weekly hours of M wage-earners were 46·5, of F 38·4: we raised the 38·4 by 1·5 hours, to correspond with 48 hours for M in 1953. Taking hourly earnings of all F from L, table Z, we had 2·77 kr × 39·9 × 50 for annual earnings of adult F. We combined earnings of M and F, using as weights their numbers given in L, table Å, and rounded to M 400, F 92·6. (ii) *Private building, adult M.* L, table 30, concept C, gives average hourly earnings. S.A., table 269, gives total man-hours in 1956, and I.Y., table 16, gives total numbers covered by the survey, also in 1956; we calculated average annual man-hours per wage-earner in 1956, and assumed the figure was the same in 1953. (iii) We combined average annual earnings in (i) and (ii) with weights 526, 63, corresponding to the numbers of wage-earners in the survey of 1953, given by L, tables V and 30. We raised the outcome by 0·5 per cent to include employers' contributions to social security, reckoned as in Appendix 2.

4. *U.K.*

(*a*) We took the mean of the average weekly earnings of M, F, in April and October 1953, among all manual workers within the Ministry of Labour's survey, as reported in the *Ministry of Labour Gazette* (*M.L.G.*), and avoided the overweighting of M in the survey by forming a combined average with weights M 9533, F 3863, these being the numbers within the scope of the survey as estimated by us from *Annual Abstract of Statistics 1954*, table 123. We also took from *M.L.G.* the average weekly earnings of: (*b*) Adult M wage-earners of British Railways, conciliation and workshop grades; (*c*) coal mines, all wage-earners; (*d*) dockers, registered male workers. We formed a weighted average with weights (*a*) 1317, (*b*) 52, (*c*) 80, (*d*) 8, proportional to numbers occupied in 1953, derived from the sources in Appendix 2, U.K., A. 3 (i), and multiplied by 50 to reach annual earnings. We raised the product by 6·74 per cent to include employers' contributions to social insurance, also reckoned as in Appendix 2, loc. cit.

5. *U.S.A.*
See Appendix 2, U.S.A., A. 3 (1).

A.2. AVERAGE PAY (ALL EMPLOYEES) IN MONEY
For all countries we took the figures originally calculated in money
for our annual series, as described in Appendix 2.

B. COST OF LIVING
For all countries we took the estimates in Federal Republic of
Germany, Statistisches Bundesamt, *Preise, Löhne, Wirtschaftsrechnung-
en, Reihe 10, Internationaler Vergleich der Preise für die Lebenshaltung,*
Stand Januar 1960. The Bundesamt's procedure is described by
G. Fürst and P. Deneffe in *Wirtschaft und Statistik,* 6, 11, Nov. 1954,
p. 516.

C. INCOME PER OCCUPIED PERSON, AND WAGE/INCOME
    RATIO
For all countries we used the series of national income, income
generated in industry, numbers occupied in the whole economy and
in industry, average wage-earnings and average pay, compiled as
described in Appendix 2.

2 Five countries, in each period: sources and methods for main time-series

France

A. PAY

1. *1860–1913*

Content. Average annual wage-earnings of all wage-earners in 1905, extrapolated by an annual index of hourly and daily wage-rates in industry, mostly for men.

Sources & Method. We estimated average annual wage-earnings in 1905 as in Appendix 1, 1.A.1. In that estimate we used one factor to reduce the average earnings of adults to those of all wage-earners including juveniles, and another to raise daily to annual earnings. On the assumption that these factors did not change substantially over time, we extrapolated the average annual wage-earnings of 1905 by applying an annual index of wage-rates based on the only available materials, and formed as in E. H. Phelps Brown and S. V. Hopkins, 'The Course of Wage-rates in Five Countries, 1860–1939' in *Oxford Economic Papers*, ii, 2, June 1950. After graphical comparison of series from 12 sources, we took two as tracing the central tendency – F. Simiand, *Le salaire, l'évolution social et la monnaie*, vol. iii, annexe 22, pp. 99–100, 'Industrie, indice du salaire'; and *Salaires et coût de l'existence à diverses époques, jusqu'en 1910* (Statistique générale de la France, Ministère du Travail, 1911), index at p. 20. We filled in the year to year movement between points fixed in the light of the above series according to *Bulletin of U.S. Dept. of Labor*, Sept. 1898, 668, average daily wages in gold of 21 occupations in Paris, 1870–1898; and J. Kuczynski, *Die Entwicklung der Lage der Arbeiterschaft in Europa und Amerika 1870–1933* (Philographischer Verlag, Basel, 1934), index at p. 45. The earnings or rates mentioned in the text, 1.B.1, as having risen faster than the average from 1896 to 1911 are given in Simiand (as above), vol. iii, tables i, iii and iv, and *Annuaire Statistique de la France, Rétrospectif, 1961*, ch. xxxiii A, tables i, ii and vi.

2. *1913, 1924–1938*

Content. Average annual earnings of all industrial wage-earners in 1930/1931, extrapolated by an index of weekly earnings of adult industrial wage-earners.

Sources. Annuaire Statistique de la France, Rétrospectif, 1961, ch. xxxiii (*A.S.F.*). *International Yearbook of Labour Statistics, 1941*, table 9 (*I.Y.B.L.S.*). *Résultats Statistiques du Recensement Général de la Population*, 1931 (*R.G.* 31). *Recensement Général de la Population, 1954. Sondage au 20me*, France Entière, 1ère partie A.1 (*R.S.* 54). *Recensement Général de la Population, 1954*, Départements No. 75, Seine incl. Paris (*R.G.* 54). A. Chabert, *Les Salaires dans l'Industrie Française* (*La Métallurgie*) (1955), (A.C.).

Method. (i) *Men.* We built up our national average from the following groups:

1. Skilled workers in provincial towns (ouvriers qualifiés, OQ)
2. Semi-skilled workers, other than those in (4) and (5) below (ouvriers spécialisés, OS)
3. Unskilled workers in provincial towns (manœuvres, OM)
4. Metal workers of the Paris region
5. Weavers
6. Workers in coalmines, above and below ground.

(*a*) *Numbers.* Comparison of *R.G.* 31, i. 3. vii, with *R.S.* 54, Sf. 1, suggested that *R.G.* 31 included under OQ a considerable number who were not in fact craftsmen. We therefore estimated the numbers of OQ, OS, OM in 1931 by applying to the relevant total in 1931 the proportions reported for 1954. We obtained the relevant totals in 1931, 1954 by deducting from all M wage-earners those in agriculture, fishing, domestic service, with (in 1954) apprentices (*R.G.* 31, i, 3, table vii; *R.S.* 54, table Sf. 1), and also those in groups (4), (5), (6) above. We found the numbers of OQ, OS and OM left within the total thus arrived at for 1954, and applied the proportions of these three groups to the corresponding total for 1931. (While our earnings for OQ and OS are drawn from industry alone, the numbers arrived at in this way to weight them include some wage-earners in other sectors.) For the number in (6) in 1954 we had to take the number in all mining and not coalmining alone. To estimate the number of wage-earners within the totals of employees reported for (4) in *R.G.* 31, tome ii (Départements), Paris, table vii, and Seine (banlieue de Paris) table vii, and in *R.G.* 54, A1. B, we applied to those totals the proportion of wage-earners among all employees in 'industries mécaniques', all France, private industry, in *R.S.* 54, table A.Sf.2. For (4), we estimated the numbers of OQ, OS, OM by applying the percentages given for about 1953 by A.C., p. 99. For (5), we compiled a total from the various textile industries in *R.S.* 54, A.Sf.2. The number in (6) is reported separately in *R.G.* 31. We thus reached the following weights for 1931: (1) 219; (2) 116; (3) 79; (4) 26; (5) 16; (6) 29.

(*b*) *Average hourly earnings*, by groups. (1) From the 38 occupations for which provincial wage-rates are given in *A.S.F.*, table ii, we selected 10 whose classification agreed closely enough with that of the census, and whose numbers (after adjustment in the light of the proportions reported in *R.S.* 54, A.Sf.2) were each not less than 10,000. We formed an average of the rates given for these 10, with weights (proportional to numbers) in brackets: charpentier (22), menuisier (65), scieur (21), plombier (30), couvreur (15), maçon (92), peintre en bâtiment (40), carrier, pierre (28), imprimeur (48), tailleur d'habits (14). (2) *A.S.F.* provides no typical wage-rate. In Paris metals, we took the ratio of the OS rate (1924–1938, *A.S.F.*, table v) to the rate for 'manœuvre à temps' (1926–1938, *A.S.F.*, table iv; 1924–1925, the series for 1926–1938 extrapolated proportionally to the provincial rate for OM, (3) below). We took this ratio as 1·20 through 1924–1930, 1·26 through 1931–1935, and 0·97, 1·17 and 1·19 in 1936, 1937, 1938; and applied it to the series for provincial OM [(3) below]. (The alternative, of applying the ratio of OS to OQ in Paris metals to the provincial rate for OQ [(1) above] gave rather lower estimates for OS, which we thought due to the OQ of Paris metals including some exceptionally highly paid occupations.) For 1911, we assumed the same ratio as in 1924; applying the average ratio of OS in Paris metals to the weavers' rate through 1924–1927 to the weavers' rate in 1911 gave almost exactly the same result. (3) Manœuvres, *A.S.F.*, table ii, (4) 'Ensemble des ouvriers' in *A.S.F.*, table v. We estimated 1911 by applying the ratio of 1911 to average 1924–1927 in (1) above. (5) *A.S.F.*, table ii. (6) *A.S.F.*, table vi (daily rate). (*c*) *Index of weekly earnings.* We averaged the hourly rates of (1)–(5), using the weights estimated in (a). We multiplied the average, through 1930–1938 by the weekly hours worked (*I.Y.B.L.S.*), and through 1924–1929 by 48, as in 1930. In the absence of information about coalminers' weekly hours we multiplied the daily rates of (6) by 6 throughout. We combined the resultant weekly rate with the average weekly rate of (1)–(5), with weights as in (a).

(ii) *Women.* A.S.F., table ii, gives the AM of hourly rates in 7 occupations: repasseuse, couturière, lingère, giletière, dentellière, brodeuse, modiste. This is clearly an inadequate basis – there were, for instance, some 190,000 women weavers, and some 1·2m. women in all in 'industries de transformation'; but in the absence of other information we could but take it. We multiplied by weekly hours worked (*I.Y.B.L.S.*).

(iii) *Combined index.* We combined the series in (i), (ii) with weights 4, 1. We extrapolated 1913 from the estimate now obtained for 1911, by reference to our index for Period One.

3. *1938, 1949–1960*

Content. (1) Average annual earnings of all wage-earners, plus social contributions by employers.

(2) Average annual earnings of all employees, plus social contributions by employers.

Sources and Methods. (1) For 1950–1960 we took the series of gross annual wage-earnings (before deduction of employees' contributions to insurance) in Institut de Science Économique Appliquée, April 1963, *Masse de salaires versés dans les secteurs de l'industrie, du commerce et des services*, table iii. To estimate 1949, we applied to this series over 1950–1954 a series we constructed from *International Yearbook of Labour Statistics* (*I.Y.B.L.S.*), 1955, table 16(*b*). This gives average hourly earnings in manufacturing, construction, commerce, and some transport and services, at September from 1952 onwards, but in 1949, 1950, 1951 at December, November, December, and as earnings in these months may have been seasonally higher, we substituted estimates made by raising the average hourly rates reported in *I.Y.B.L.S.*, 1953, table 16, by the ratio of earnings to rates over 1952–1954. We multiplied the hourly earnings so obtained by average weekly hours worked, reported in *Annuaire Statistique de la France, Rétrospectif, 1961* (*A.S.F.*), table x. For 1938, we adjusted our weekly earnings estimated for 1938 in Period Two for a small dif-

ference between the weekly hours there taken and those given in
A.S.F.; and multiplied the adjusted weekly earnings by 49. For
employers' contributions we applied to average wage-earnings a ratio of
total contributions to total pay, obtained as follows. Sources: 1938,
Ministère des Affaires Économiques et Financières, *Les Comptes
Économiques de l'Année 1938* (1957), pp. 10, 12; 1949–1953, Ministère
des Finances, des Affaires Économiques et du Plan, *Rapport sur les
Comptes de la Nation, 1949–1955,* vol. i, pp. 142–47; 1954–1955,
Ministère des Finances, *Statistiques et Études Financières*, no. 130,
October 1959, pp. 1248, 1258, 1262–1263; 1956–1960, *Statistiques et
Études Financières*, Supplement no. 140, August 1960, table 70, and
similar tables in full issues nos. 151, July 1961, and 163–4, July–
August 1962. For 1949–1955 we added the 'cotisations' paid by
'entreprises' and 'administrations' together with two-sevenths of
those paid by 'ménages', this being the proportion of all payments by
'ménages' made in respect of wage-earners in 1952 (see above
Rapport, vol. ii, p. 92). For 1956–1960 the sources give directly the
total 'cotisations' paid by employers in respect of wages and salary-
earners. We expressed total 'cotisations' as a proportion year by year
of total wages and salaries as given by the above sources.

   (2) We took total pay from *Annuaire Statistique Rétrospectif, 1966*,
Part vii, ch. 53, table x, and divided it by our estimates of the total
number of employees, obtained as in (E) below. For employers'
contributions, we applied the same ratio as in (1).

B. COST OF LIVING, 1860–1960

Content. Prices of objects of outlay by wage-earning households in
Paris, with weights as in Table 101. Where an index for Paris can be
compared with one for the provinces, there is little divergence, except
that the provincial index runs higher in 1927–1934 and lower in
1953–1955, 1959–1960.
Sources and Method. Through 1860–1954 we have used the index
'Ouvrier A' in J. Singer-Kérel, *Le Coût de la Vie à Paris 1840–1954*
(Paris, Armand Colin, 1961) p. 141, and annexe iv, table 42. To this
we spliced at 1949–1954 the index in *Annuaire Statistique 1961*, ch.
xlviii, table 1, col. 7. In 1950–1956 this index combines the INSÉE
index of 213 articles plus fruit and vegetables in Paris (1949 weights;
Annuaire Statistique 1958, p. 296) with the INSÉE index of 250 articles

Table 101 France, 1860–1954: Weights of components of index of cost of living in five periods.

	1860–1880[1]	1870–1900[1]	1900–1919	1913–1939	1938–1939 1949–1954
Food	70·66	65·02	63·65	60·00	58
Rent & household expenditure[2]	15·19	15·73	17·15	17·84	
Clothing	12·24	12·64	10·52	12·60	
Miscellaneous	1·91	6·61	8·68	9·56	3[3]
Heat & Light					4
Manufactured goods					20
Services[4]					15
	100·00	100·00	100·00	100·00	100

[1] In 1870–1880 the weights used are a blend of those given in the first two columns.
[2] Incl. heat, light, kitchen equipment, furnishings, cleaning materials.
[3] Tobacco, newspapers.
[4] Incl. rent, taxes, water, transport, laundry.

in Paris (base 1956–1957; *Bulletin Mensuel de Statistique*, N.S. 6, June 1961, table 11); in 1957–1960 it follows the index of 250 articles alone.

C. G.N.P. DEFLATOR

Content. With weights in brackets, indexes of: (*a*) money wages, or pay of all employers (1·5); (*b*) cost of living (7); (*c*) wholesale industrial prices (1·5). *Sources.* (*a*) A.1, A.2, and A.3 (ii) above. (*b*) B above. (*c*) *1860–1913: Annuaire Statistique de la France (A.S.F.) Rétrospectif 1961*, ch. xxxii, table i, p. 217, 'indices de prix de gros de 45 articles, (1901–10 = 100), calcul rétrospectif, 'produits industrielles' 1860 to 1900; table ii, indices de prix de gros de 45 articles (1901–1910 = 100) matières industrielles', 1901–1913. Table i is a retrospective calculation but provides no link: we have treated these two series as continuous. *1913, 1924–1938: Annuaire Statistique de la France (A.S.F.) Rétrospectif 1961*, ch. xxxii, table iii, p. 219, 'indices de prix de gros', 'Matières industrielles, ensemble (25 articles)', minerals and metals, textiles, miscellaneous. *1938, 1948–1960:* 1938, 1948–1959, *A.S.F. Rétrospectif 1961*, ch. xxxii, table vii, 'produits industriels' 1938–1950;

table viii, 'produits industriels, ensemble'. For 1938, we spliced the series of table vii to that of table viii over 1948–1950. 1960, *A.S.F. 1962*, ch. xxxix A, table vi.

D. INCOME

1. *1860–1913*

(*a*) *National income.* The available estimates are surveyed in *La Croissance du Revenu National Français depuis 1780* (Institut de Science Économique Appliquée, Cahiers, série D, 7, 20 Dec. 1952) and in International Association for Research in Income and Wealth, *Income and Wealth, Series III (1953) 3, La Croissance Économique Française.* For 1901–1913 annual estimates of G.N.P., in 1938 francs, are given by A. Sauvy in 'Rapport Général sur le Revenu National' (Journal Officiel, 7 April 1954: Conseil Économique, Avis et Rapports, 14, p. 386). L. A. Vincent, 'L'évolution de la production intérieure brute en France 1896–1938. Méthodes et premiers résultats' in *Études et Conjoncture*, Nov. 1962, gives estimates of G.D.P. by volume in 1896, 1913. Estimates for net national product in current francs in 1898, 1909 are given by F. Perroux, 'Prise de Vues sur la croissance de l'économie française 1780–1950' in *Income and Wealth V* (International Association for Research in Income and Wealth, 1955).

(*b*) *Sector income.* Estimates of gross output per occupied person, in current francs, are given for agriculture and industry, by decades 1865–1914, in J. Marczewski, *Introduction à l'Histoire Quantitative* (1965).

(*c*) *Real product of industry.* (i) An index of production in manufacturing, 1894–1913, is given in League of Nations, *Industrialization and Foreign Trade* (1945), pp. 132, 134. The entries for 1894–1897 are extrapolations based on J. Desserrier, *Statistique Générale de la France*, Oct.–Dec. 1928, and cover mining. (ii) An index of production in mining, manufacturing and utilities, 1901–1913, is given in O.E.E.C., *Industrial Statistics* (1955), p. 4. We spliced (i) to (ii) over 1901–1910 to extend (ii) back to 1894.

2. *1913, 1921–1938*

(*a*) *National income.* (i) R. Tavitian, *La part des salaires dans le revenu national* (1956) gives national income in current francs in 1913, 1921, 1926, 1928–1938, as estimated by the Commissariat du Plan on the basis of net domestic product at factor cost. (ii) A. Sauvy (as under 1 above) gives annual estimates for 1920–1939 in 1938 francs.

(*b*) *Income generated in industry.* (i) R. Froment and F. Gavanier, 'Le revenu national français' in *Revue d'Écon. Politique*, Sept.–Oct. 1947, estimate the net product of industry in 1938 as 127 md. francs. (ii) L.-A. Vincent, 'Évolution de la production intérieure brute en France 1896–1938' in *Études et Conjoncture*, Nov. 1962, puts the gross domestic product of industry in 1938 at 176·6 md. francs; he includes 'agricultural and food industries' with agriculture, and we have estimated that transferring them to industry would raise the estimate for the gross domestic product of industry to 187 md. francs. (iii) J. Marchal, *La Comptabilité Nationale Française* (1959), p. 89, gives the income generated in 1952 by manufacturing, with fuel and power, at 3253 md. francs. We tried carrying this back to 1938 using an index of industrial production, 1938 = 100, 1952 = 138 (O.E.E.C., *Industrial Statistics 1900–1955* (1955)), and a price index, 1938 = 100, 1952 = 3547, which we made by combining with weights 2, 3, indexes of the retail prices of manufactured goods (J. Singer-Kérel, *Le Coût de la Vie à Paris de 1840 à 1954* (1961), annexe iv, table 1) and of industrial wholesale prices (*Annuaire Statistique de la France Rétrospectif, 1961*, ch. xxxi, tables v, vii, viii). The result was a figure of 66·5 md. francs for income generated by industry in 1938. (*c*) *Discussion.* The estimates of income generated in industry, in (*b*), (i), (ii) and (iii), are wide apart. Only (iii) gives a wage/income ratio in industry that does not seem improbably low, but it also gives an income generated per occupied person in industry that seems improbably low in comparison with the national income per occupied person yielded by (*a*) (i). This last figure seems too high relatively to the average wage in France – it implies a wage/income ratio in the whole economy of only about 0·40. – We have therefore been unable to adopt any estimates of national income or income generated in industry for the period.

3. *1938, 1949–1960*

(*a*) *National income, Annuaire Statistique Rétrospectif, 1966*, viii, ch. 53, table x, national income at factor cost. (*b*) (i) *Income generated in mining, manufacture and utilities.* We omitted construction because we have no corresponding series for numbers occupied before 1954. From J.

Marchal, *La Comptabilité Nationale Française* (1959), p. 8, we took the 'revenue intérieure net' at current prices in the above sectors in 1952, and we extrapolated by using as index the annual series for the gross product of industry excl. construction and transport in *Annuaire Statistique Rétrospectif 1966*, viii, ch. 53, tables 1A, 1B. (This index agreed closely with that obtained by reflating the index of production in mining, manufacture and utilities, in O.E.C.D. *Industrial Statistics 1964*, p. 4, by an index of industrial prices compiled from *Annuaire Statistique Rétrospectif 1961*, ch. xxxii, table vii, and *Annuaire Statistique 1962*, ch. xxxixA, table 6.) (ii) *Real product*. O.E.C.D. op. cit. p. 4.

E. OCCUPIED POPULATION

1. *1860–1913*

We obtained the estimates shown in Fig. 1, and set out here in table 102, as follows: In accordance with C. Vimont, *La Population Active* (1960), pp. 20–21, we took it that (i) for F in agriculture, 'activity' was subject to wide variations of definition; (ii) in the censuses before 1896 the enumeration of the 'active' is not reliable; (iii) the classification of the 1911 census is not comparable with that of 1901, 1906. We dealt with these points – (i), by assuming that in 1896, 1901, 1906 the 'active' F in agriculture were 45 per cent of the M; (ii), by applying to the whole population aged 15–64 in censuses before 1896 the ratio which our estimated total occupied bore to the population aged 15–64 in that year, viz. 75 per cent; (iii), by applying to the population aged 15–64 in 1911 the ratio which our estimated total occupied bore to the population aged 15–64 in 1906, viz. 78 per cent. We took the census figures from *Annuaire Statistique de la France, Rétrospectif 1961 (A.S.F.).* Our estimates show a drop between 1866 and 1872 additional to that due to the loss of Alsace-Lorraine:

Table 102 France: Estimated total occupied population in census years 1861–1911.

	Occupied population m.		Occupied population m.		Occupied population m.		Occupied population m.
1861	18·5	1876	18·0	1891	18·7	1906	19·9
6	18·7	81	18·3	6	18·8	1911	20·1
1872	17·7	1886	18·5	1901	19·6		

E. Levasseur, *La Population Française* (1889–1892), vol. i, p. 306, says that death and emigration caused an additional loss of 700,000 at this time. Through 1876 the censuses enumerated the 'population légale', from 1881 onwards the 'population présente'. The difference in 1881 was under 300,000; we have not corrected for it.

We drew estimates of the numbers occupied by sector from INSÉE, 'Évolution de la population active in France depuis cent ans d'après les dénombrements quinquenniaux' in *Études et Conjoncture*, May–June 1953, but for the numbers given there of F in agriculture we substituted numbers equal to 45 per cent of M in agriculture throughout. The above source tells us that the censuses, except perhaps that of 1901, probably counted the unemployed as 'active'; we made annual estimates by interpolation without adjustment for unemployment. We took the numbers in building through 1906 from the retrospective table in the Census of 1906, tome i, 2me partie, p. 58. For 1911 we estimated the numbers in both building and transport by extrapolation from 1901–1906. In table 103 we compare our estimates with those of C. Vimont, *La Population Active* (1960), table 7, and L.-A. Vincent, 'Population active, production et productivité dans 21 branches de l'économie française (1896–1962)' in *Études et Conjoncture*, Feb. 1965; this revises estimates by the same author in the same journal for Nov. 1962, which we also used. Vincent states that his estimates of both occupied population and output 'have been raised to take account of Alsace-Lorraine': in most branches the increase is about 4 per cent, but more detailed adjustments were made for mining and the production of metals.

2. *1921–1936*

For estimates shown in Fig. 1.A, we took the 'population active' in INSÉE, 'Évolution de la population active en France depuis cent ans d'après dénombrements quinquenniaux', *Études et Conjoncture*, May–June 1953, except that for the numbers given for F in agriculture we substituted a number equal to 45 per cent of the M throughout. See our table 104.

3. *1938, 1950–1960*

1938: We based an estimate on the Census of 1936, after deduction of estimated numbers of unpaid family workers and unemployed.

1950–1960: *Sources. Recensement général de la population de mai 1954,*

Table 103 France, 1896–1913: Estimates of the occupied population by sector and in total.

	Vimont	Vincent	Present Authors
	m.	*m.*	*m.*
1896			
1. Agriculture	8·46	8·44	8·32
2. Industry	5·45	5·20	5·66
3.　of which building		(0·82)	(0·80)
4. TOTAL	18·93		18·8
1906			
5. Agriculture	8·85	7·91	8·01
6. Industry	5·94	5·73[1]	6·34
7.　of which building	(0·77)	(0·79)	(0·79)
8. TOTAL	20·72		19·9
1913			
9. Agriculture		7·52	7·62
10. Industry		5·89	6·48
11.　of which building		(0·91)	(0·80)
12. TOTAL			20·2

[1] From Vincent 1962, with addition of food industries from Vincent 1965.

résultats de sondage au 1/20me A.1 (*R.G.S. 54*); *International Year Book of Labour Statistics 1962* (*I.Y.B.L.S. 62*) and *1965* (*I.Y.B.L.S. 65*); *Annuaire Statistique de la France 1952* (1953) (*A.S.F. 52*); *Annuaire Statistique de la France Rétrospectif 1966* (*A.S.F.R. 66*); *Études Statistiques* (quarterly supplement of *Études et Conjoncture*) (*É.S.*), January/March 1951, October/December 1952, October/December 1954; *Statesman's Year Book* 1950 and 1957 (*S.Y.B. 50* and *S.Y.B. 57*); Groupe d'Études des Problèmes du Contingent, *Service Militaire et Réforme de l'Armée* (1963), annexe 1, p. 230 (S.M.).

Method. (i) Total gainfully occupied in jobs. *1950–1953.* The sum of (*a*)–(*d*) as follows. (*a*) From the *Enquête Emploi* (*A.S.F. 52* and *É.S.*) we took the numbers of employees. This series covers only those in jobs and living in private households: we added estimates of (*b*) employees living in hospitals, hotels etc. (with help from *R.G.S. 54*), (*c*) the call-up, and professional soldiers in barracks or abroad (using *R.G.S. 54*, p. 17, *S.Y.B.*, and *S.M.* which gives length of

Table 104 France, 1921–1936 : Estimated total occupied population in census years.

	m.		m.
1921	20·0	1931	20·4
1926	20·2	1936	19·3

service). (*d*) For employers and self-employed, we noted that the number of 'non-salariés' in *A.S.F.R. 66*, ch. 3, table ii tallied in 1954 with the sum of unpaid family workers and employers and self-employed given in *R.G.S. 54*, table Sf.1, and the number in 1962 is also near that given in *I.Y.B.L.S. 65*: we therefore deducted our series for unpaid family workers (*R.G.S. 54*, Sf.1, and *I.Y.B.L.S. 65*) from the 'non-salariés', and extrapolated the remainder through 1950. *1954–1960*, total occupied less unpaid family workers, both from *R.G.S. 54*, table Sf.1, and *I.Y.B.L.S. 65*, with interpolations, and less the unemployed, *I.Y.B.L.S. 62* and *65*, table 11. (ii) Total employees. *1950–1953*, the sum of (*a*), (*b*), (*c*) under (i) above. *1954–1960*, total in (i) for these years less employers and self-employed as in (*d*) under (i) above. See our table 105. (iii) Occupied persons in mining, manufacture and utilities. For 1954–1960 the numbers are given in *Annuaire Statistique Rétrospectif 1966*, ch. 3, table ii, and we retropolated through 1949 using the index of employment in manufacturing in *Bulletin of General Statistics*, O.E.E.C., March 1957, p. 11, and O.E.C.D., Jan. 1965, p. 13.

Table 105 France, 1938, 1950–1960: (1) Estimated total gainfully occupied population in jobs. (2) Estimated total employees in jobs.

	(1) m.	(2) m.		(1) m.	(2) m.		(1) m.	(2) m.
1938	15·80	11·40	1953	16·71	12·56	1958	17·41	13·54
			4	16·79	12·69	9	17·49	13·69
1950	16·28	11·98	5	16·94	12·86	1960	17·63	13·81
1	16·46	12·21	6	17·13	13·05			
1952	16·58	12·38	1957	17·29	13·31			

Germany

A. PAY

1. *1860–1913*

Content. Average annual wage-earnings in 1905 in mining, manufacturing, transport and warehousing; extrapolated by an annual
index of wage-rates or earnings with coverage from time to time as
shown below.

Sources and Method. We calculated average annual wage-earnings
within the above coverage in 1905 as in Appendix 1, 1.A.2. We
extrapolated by an index we formed as follows. *1860–1871:* We used
(*a*) the index of money wage-rates outside agriculture in J. Kuczynski,
*Die Geschichte der Lage der Arbeiter in Deutschland von 1800 bis die
Gegenwart*, Band 1 (1947), pp. 100, 170–71, as revised for 1871–1900
at pp. 297–98 of the same author's *Die Geschichte der Lage der Arbeiter
unter dem Kapitalismus*, Band III (1962). This index combines at fixed
weights, proportional to the industries' wage bills, a number of daily,
shift, weekly and annual wage-rates, principally in larger firms and
higher-paying localities, in building, mining, metals, textiles, wood,
printing and (1871 only) cement. We spliced this index at 1890/1899
to (*b*)that given by F. Grumbach and H. König, 'Beschäftigung und
Löhne der deutschen Industriewirtschaft 1888–1954', *Weltwirt-
schaftliches Archiv*, Band 79, Heft 1, 1957. Their index is based on the
aggregate wages paid and numbers employed annually as reported
under the scheme of insurance against industrial injuries introduced
in 1885. (*c*) *1872–1913:* A. V. Desai, *Real Wages in Germany, 1871–
1913* (1968), adjusts the returns used by Grumbach and König
for certain limitations, and constructs an annual average for 1887–
1913 which he retropolates, using available series for six industries,
to 1871. The average is of the annual earnings of all employees
earning for the most part not more than 3000 marks per annum,
through 1872–1886 in coal mining, steel, engineering, cotton,
printing and building, and through 1887–1913 in those six industries together with transport by land and water and the rest of
manufacturing; the averages by industry are combined with variable
weights proportional to the numbers employed by industry annually.

We adopted Kuczynski's index, as spliced, for 1860–1871; its value in 1872 is almost the same as that of Desai's index, which we adopted for 1872–1913.

2. *1913, 1924–1939*

Content. Average annual wage-earnings in 1930–1931 in iron, metal trades, chemicals, construction, wood and furniture, paper, printing, textiles, shoes, confectionery and brewing; extrapolated by an index of annual wage-earnings in mining and quarrying, manufacturing, utilities and transport.

Sources and Method. We took gross weekly wage-earnings in 1930–1931 from G. Bry, *Wages in Germany 1871–1945*, p. 58, and multiplied by 49 to get estimated annual earnings. The index used for extrapolation is that described under (*b*) in Period One, *Sources and Method*, above. It may be compared with indexes given by J. Kuczynski, op. cit. in 1 above, for 1924–1932 in his Band I, p. 320, and for 1932–1939 in his Band II (1947), pp. 127, 199; and with indexes of hourly rates, weekly rates, and hourly and weekly earnings, at table A.2, p. 331, of G. Bry, *Wages in Germany, 1871–1945* (1960).

3. *1938, 1950–1960*

Content. (i) In 1938, industry including coal-mining. In 1950–1960, average actual weekly earnings in industry, with mining and construction, but excluding transport and services.

(ii) Average annual earnings per employee at work.

Sources and Method. (i) For 1950–1960 we used the index of average gross weekly earnings in industry in *Statistisches Jahrbuch* (*S.J.B.*) *1961*, xxi. A, table 1, to extrapolate from the figure in marks in 1956 given for the same coverage in *S.J.B. 1957*, xxi. A, and multiplied by 50 by us to give estimated annual earnings. We adjusted the resultant series for employers' contributions to social insurance by the ratio of these contributions to the gross income of wage- and salary-earners year by year in *S.J.B. 1960* and *1963*, xxiii, table 7. For 1938, we had to take account of the change of frontiers, which seems to have had a considerable effect on average weekly earnings in industry: these in 1938 are put at 39·68 DM. within the boundaries of the Bundesrepublik by *S.J.B. 1957*, p. 31, and at 38·23 DM. within the Reich by *S.J.B. 1957*, xxi, A.1. We decided that the balance of advantage lay in taking for our link with Period Two the average earnings within the boundaries of 1938, and used the average gross weekly earnings in 1938 given for all industry including coal-mining, within the boundaries of the Reich (but excluding the Ostmark) by G. Bry, *Wages in Germany 1871–1945* (1960), table 16. We multiplied these weekly earnings by 49.

(ii) We divided total pay (sources as in D.3 (*a*) below) by total employees (sources as in E.3 (*a*) below).

B. COST OF LIVING

1. *1860–1913*
Sources and Method. 1860–1871: J. Kuczynski (as in A.1 (*a*)), Band 1 (1947), gives at pp. 145, 265, indexes of retail food prices 1850–1914, and at p. 266 an index for rent, 1820–1914; this latter index is revised at p. 437 of his Band III (1962). A. Jacobs and H. Richter, *Die Grosshandelspreise in Deutschland von 1792 bis 1934* (Deutsche Institut für Konjunkturforschung, Sonderheft 37, 1935), give indexes of the wholesale prices of the principal groups of commodities. We combined Kuczynski's index of retail food prices and of rent with four series of wholesale prices, with weights: food, 60; rent, 16; textiles, 12; coal, 8; iron, 2; wood, 2, corresponding to those of the U.K. Ministry of Labour's cost of living index based mainly on household budgets of 1904. Through 1850–1886 Kuczynski's index for rent is in the form of single figures each covering a period of eight or nine years; we made annual estimates by linear interpolation. *1872–1913:* A. V. Desai, *Real Wages in Germany, 1871–1913,* has combined mainly retail with some wholesale prices, and rents, collected by the governments of the Reich, Prussia, Bavaria and some cities, at fixed weights based on a household budget inquiry reported in the Reichsarbeitsblatt, supplement 2, 1909, to form an index for 1871–1913. For 1872 this index has nearly the same value as that made by us for 1860 onwards as above, and we adopted it from 1872 onwards.

2. *1913, 1924–1938*
Sources and Method. G. Bry, *Wages in Germany 1871–1945* (1960), at p. 254, table 68, gives (col. 4) the official index from *Statistisches*

Jahrbuch, and (col. 5), adjustments designed to correct an understate-
ment by the official index of the actual rise in 1937–1939. Bry dis-
cusses the validity of the official index at op. cit., p. 260. We have used
the official index with Bry's adjustments in 1937–1938.

3. *1938, 1950–1960*
Source and Method. Statistisches Jahrbuch at xx, C gives an official index
for each of three levels of income. We took the middle level, which
is that of a monthly household income of about 360 DM. in 1950.

C. G.N.P. DEFLATOR

1. *1861–1913,* and 2, *1913, 1924–1938*
We calculated the implicit deflator from W. G. Hoffmann with F.
Grumbach and H. Hesse, *Der Wachstum der deutschen Wirtschaft seit
der Mitte des 19 Jahrhunderts* (1965), part ii, table 122 (14), net
domestic product at current prices, and Table 103 (10), total output
at 1913 prices.

3. *1938, 1950–1960*
Content. With weights in brackets, indexes of: (*a*) pay of all employees
(1·5); (*b*) cost of living (7); (*c*) industrial wholesale prices (1·5).
Sources. (*a*) A.3 (ii) above; (*b*) B.3 above; (*c*) *Statistisches Jahrbuch*
(*S.J.*) *1962,* xx, A.1, for 1950–1960, linked at 1950 with the same
series in *S.J. 1957,* xx, A.1, to provide an entry for 1938.

D. INCOME

1. *1860–1913*
(*a*) *National Income.* Net domestic product at factor cost, within the
boundaries of the Reich of 1913, but excluding Alsace-Lorraine
1860–1870. W. G. Hoffmann *et al., Das Wachstum der deutschen
Wirtschaft,* part 2, table 122.
(*b*) *Sector income.* Hoffmann, loc. cit. in (*a*), gives net domestic product
in (i) agriculture, forestry and fishing; (ii) 'Gewerbe', which comprises manufacturing and handicrafts, mining, transport excluding

railways and postal service, commerce, banking, insurance, hotels; (iii) residual, including rent of dwellings.

(c) *Income generated in industry.* (i) *Real product.* Hoffmann, op. cit., part 2, table 103, cols. 2, 3, gives net product in constant (1913) prices. (ii) *Value product.* We reflated (i) by an index which we formed by combining the following price-indexes: (a) Hoffmann, op. cit., table 139, building and construction, industrial inventories and equipment; agricultural machinery; railway building: we combined these

Table 106 Germany, 1880–1913: Index of industrial prices.

	1913 =100		1913 =100		1913 =100		1913 =100		1913 =100
1880	93	1887	84	1894	79	1901	93	1908	95
1	90	8	86	5	80	2	91	9	92
2	92	9	90	6	83	3	91	10	94
3	91	90	94	7	84	4	92	11	94
4	89	1	90	8	85	5	93	12	97
5	84	2	84	9	92	6	97	1913	100
1886	83	1893	80	1900	100	1907	100		

three series with equal weights. (b) Hoffmann, op. cit., table 148, combined index for furniture, household equipment and heating. (c) Source as for (b), combined index for clothing, textile, fabrics and leather goods. (d) Hoffmann, op. cit., table 151, exports of manufactures. (e) A. Jacobs & H. Richter, *Die Grosshandelspreise in Deutschland von 1792 bis 1934* (Deutscher Institut für Konjunkturforschung, Sonderheft 37, 1935), coal. We combined these with weights: (a) and (d), each 3·5; (b), (c) and (e), each 1. This index is available only from 1880, the year in which (d) begins. We show it here in our table 106.

2. *1913, 1925–1938*

(a) *National income.* Net domestic product at factor cost, within the boundaries of: 1913, the Reich of 1913; 1925–1934, the Reich of 1925; 1935–1938, the same with the addition of the Saar. Source as for Period One.

(b) *Income generated in industry and mining.* As in Period One. In component (a) of the price index, inventories and equipment are now given separately, and we combined them with weights 1, 5. We give the index in Table 107. (*c*) *Real product*: as in Period One.

3. *1938, 1950–1960*

(*a*) *National income*. Net domestic product at factor cost, within the boundaries of the Federal Republic, excluding Berlin throughout, but in 1960 including the Saar. For 1938, *Statistisches Jahrbuch* (*S.J.*) *1960*, xxiii, A1, gives net national product at factor cost estimated for

Table 107 Germany, 1925–1938 : Index of industrial prices.

1913 = 100		1913 = 100		1913 = 100		1913 = 100	
1925	146	1929	151	1933	111	1937	112
6	143	30	146	4	110	1938	115
7	143	1	133	5	109		
1928	150	1932	117	1936	108		

the territory of the Bundesrepublik: we adjusted this to obtain net domestic product by applying the ratio of N.D.P. to N.N.P. in the territory of the Reich of 1938, as given by Hoffmann *et al.* (loc. cit. in 1 above). For 1950–1954, *S.J. 1960*, xxiii, A2; 1955–1960, *S.J. 1963*, xxiii, 3.

(*b*) *Income generated in industry.* (i) *Value product.* Total net product at factor cost in mining and power; manufacturing industry; building and construction. The Saar is included in 1960. 1950–1957: *S.J. 1960*, xxiii, A3. 1958–1960: corresponding table in *S.J. 1963*. (ii) *Real product.* As in D.1 (*c*) (i).

E. OCCUPIED POPULATION

1. *1860–1913*

(*a*) *Total* within the boundaries of the Reich of 1913, but excluding Alsace-Lorraine 1860–1870. W. G. Hoffmann with F. Grumbach and H. Hesse, *Das Wachstum der deutschen Wirtschaft seit der Mitte des 19 Jahrhunderts* (1965), part 2, table 20, all classified as occupied. We interpolated between 1858 and 1861 for 1860, and between 1861 and 1867 for 1862–1866, and extrapolated from 1861–1867 for 1868–1870. We interpolated between 1871 and 1875 for 1872–1874.

(*b*) *By sector.* Hoffmann, op. cit., table 20, occupied population in (i) agriculture, (ii) mining, industry, transport, and commerce; (iii) residual. For 'Gewerbe', we took (ii) less those in railways and postal services (table 16). Interpolations as in (*a*). See our table 108. (*c*) For *industry and mining*, Hoffmann, op. cit., table 20.

Table 108 Germany, at 10-year intervals 1871–1911, occupied population by sectors.

	(1) Total Occupied '000s	(2) Agriculture '000s	(3) 'Gewerbe' '000s	(4) Residual (1)–(2)–(3) '000s
1871	17337	8541	6223	2573
81	19745	9609	7327	2809
91	22485	9551	9722	3212
1901	25617	9825	12110	3682
1911	30034	10627	15046	4361

2. *1913, 1924–1939*
(*a*) *Total.* All gainfully occupied, excluding the unemployed and unpaid family workers, within the Reich of 1925 but including the Saar with effect from 1935. (i) *Occupied population excluding unpaid family workers.* We took Census figures of the whole occupied population excluding the Saar, for 1925 and 1933 from *Statistik des deutschen Reiches*, Band 408, p. 9, and Band 453/2, p. 11, and for 1939 from the *International Yearbook of Labour Statistics 1945/1946*. We deducted figures of unpaid workers obtained for 1925 and 1933 from *Statistik des deutschen Reiches*, Band 408, p. 9, and Band 453/2, p. 11, and for 1939 from the *International Yearbook*, which excludes Austria. We obtained annual estimates through 1925–1934 by linear inter- and extrapolation. For the Saar, we took figures of all occupied and of unpaid family workers in 1935 and 1939 from *International Yearbook of Labour Statistics 1941* and *1945/1946*. We added the net figures already obtained for the boundaries of 1925, and made estimates for 1936–1938 by linear interpolation. (ii) *The unemployed. Statistisches Jahrbuch 1928*, ix, B, table 10, with similar tables in later volumes, give the percentages of trade union membership unemployed annually in 1924–1931. From 1928 onwards these percentages overlap with

figures of the absolute number of all unemployed given in *Statistisches Jahrbuch 1936*, x, table 12, and similar tables in later volumes. We took the relation of 1929, when a percentage of 13·1 corresponded with an absolute number of 1·9 m., applied this to the percentages of 1913 and 1924–1927, and then reduced the resultant numbers in the ratio of the estimated total of all employees in each year to that in 1929. We obtained these figures of all employees from J. and M.

Table 109 Germany, 1913, 1925–1938: (1) Estimated total gainfully occupied population in jobs. (2) Estimated unemployed.

	(1) Occupied in jobs m.	(2) Un- employed m.		(1) Occupied in jobs m.	(2) Un- employed m.		(1) Occupied in jobs m.	(2) Un- employed m.
1913	25·67[1]	0·3[1]	1929	25·90	1·9	1935	25·70[2]	2·1[2]
			30	23·75	3·1	6	26·50[2]	1·6[2]
1925	25·70	0·9	1	22·40	4·5	7	27·50[2]	0·9[2]
6	24·25	2·4	2	21·35	5·6	1938	28·30[2]	0·4[2]
7	25·50	1·2	3	22·20	4·8			
1928	25·35	1·4	1934	24·60	2·7			

[1] Within the frontiers of 1913.   [2] Including the Saar.

Kuczynski, *Die Lage des deutschen Industrie-Arbeiters 1913–1914 und 1924 bis 1930* (1931). The resultant estimates, together with the absolute numbers reported from 1928 onwards, gave us an annual series which we deducted from the totals obtained under (i) above. (iii) *The link with 1913*. In 1907 the census gave the number of unpaid family workers as 4·3 m., for a wider area than in 1925, when the census gave 5·4 m.: this suggests a change of definition, and we estimated 5·0 m. for 1913. We now also deducted the unemployed in 1913, as we did not in Period One. For both these reasons the figures of occupied population and of national income per occupied person in 1913 that we use as a link with the 1920s differ from those we used in Period One. Our final estimates are shown in our table 109. (*b*) *In industry and mining*. Hoffmann, op. cit., part 2, table 20; these figures exclude the unemployed. We deducted unpaid family workers, as given in Censuses of Population, with interpolation for annual estimates. See our table 110.

Table 110 Germany, 1925–1938: Estimated gainfully occupied in jobs in industry.

	'000s		'000s		'000s		'000s
1925	12231	1929	12743	1933	8437	1937	13259
6	10959	30	11151	4	10342	1938	14134
7	12800	1	9230	5	11253		
1928	13144	1932	7713	1936	12299		

3. *1938, 1950–1960*

(*a*) *Total.* All gainfully occupied, excluding the unemployed and unpaid family workers, within the Federal Republic of 1950 excluding Berlin throughout and in 1960 including the Saar. *1938: Statistisches Jahrbuch (S.J.) 1954*, vii, A, table 2, gives the occupied population (less unpaid family workers) in 1939 as adjusted to the boundaries and census classification of 1950. We estimated the corresponding figure for 1938 according to our estimates of the occupied population within the then boundaries in 1938, 1939; and deducted half the 0·4 m. unemployed of 1938. *1950–1958: S.J. 1960* vii, A, table 1, gives annual figures of the total occupied population, unpaid family workers, and unemployed. *1958–1960: S.J. 1963*, vii, A, table 1, gives figures under the same three heads but including the Saar. To match our estimate for national income we had to include the Saar from 1960 only. We excluded the Saar from the figure given for 1959 by using the percentage difference between the figures for 1958 with and without the Saar. We took the total number

Table 111 Germany 1938, 1950–1960, as within the frontiers of 1950 (excluding Berlin) throughout; in 1960 including the Saar: (1) Estimated total gainfully occupied population in jobs. (2) Estimated number of employees in jobs.

	(1) Total Occupied '000s	(2) Employees '000s		(1) Total Occupied '000s	(2) Employees '000s		(1) Total Occupied '000s	(2) Employees '000s
1938	16300	13400	1953	18513	15344	1958	21480	18240
			4	19137	15968	9	21828	18580
1950	16875	13675	5	20008	16840	1960	22770[1]	19530[1]
1	17475	14286	6	21408	17483			
1952	17932	14754	1957	21210	18020			

[1] Including the Saar.

Table 112 Germany, 1950–1960, excluding Berlin throughout; in 1960 including the Saar: Gainfully occupied population in industry.

	'000s		'000s		'000s		'000s
1950	8355	1953	9350	1956	10917	1959	11422
1	8725	4	9847	7	11130	1960	11995[1]
1952	8972	1955	10460	1958	11280		

[1] including the Saar.

of employees from the sources cited above and excluded employees in the Saar in 1959 by using *S.J. 1960*, vii, B, table 2. Our final estimates are shown in our table 111.

(*b*) *In industry.* Employment in 'produzierendes Gewerbe', *S.J. 1960*, vii, A.1, and corresponding table in *S.J. 1963*. We excluded the Saar from the figure given for 1959 by the method used for the total occupied. See our table 112.

F. CAPITAL, CAPITAL PER OCCUPIED PERSON, CAPITAL/OUT-
   PUT RATIO, AND PROFITS

   1. *1860–1913*
(*a*) *Capital.* W. G. Hoffmann with F. Grumbach and H. Hesse, *Das Wachstum der deutschen Wirtschaft seit der Mitte des 19 Jahrhunderts* (1965), part ii, table 40, capital stock including inventories, within 'Gewerbe', at current prices, and table 39, in 1913 marks.
(*b*) *Occupied population within coverage of estimates of capital.* As for 'Gewerbe', see E.1 (*b*) above.
(*c*) *Output, for capital/output ratio.* Hoffmann *et al.* (as in (*a*)), table 122, income in 'Gewerbe' in current prices in 1913, extrapolated by value added at 1913 prices in wider coverage of table 103.
(*d*) *Wage/income ratio* within (approximately) 'Gewerbe', for inferred rate of profit: wage-earnings as in A.1; income per occupied person, Hoffmann *et al.*, table 122, and (*b*) above. See our table 113.

   2. *1925–1938*
(*a*) *Capital.* As in 1 (*a*).
(*b*) *Occupied population within coverage of estimates of capital*, including the unemployed and excluding unpaid family workers. (i) *Industry.* 1925, *Statistisches Jahrbuch (S.J.), 1930*, table 17; 1933, *S.J. 1935*, table 18; 1939, *International Yearbook of Labour Statistics (I.Y.B.L.S.) 1945/1946*, table ii. (ii) *Commerce.* Including hotels, banking and

Table 113 Germany, 1860–1913, Gewerbe: (1) Inferred rate of profit. (2) Wage/income ratio used for the calculation of (1).

	(1) %	(2) %		(1) %	(2) %		(1) %	(2) %
1860	8·8	70·8	1878	11·3	69·5	1896	9·6	66·4
1	8·3	72·1	9	11·3	68·9	7	8·9	67·7
2	8·3	71·2	80	11·2	67·6	8	8·9	66·8
3	9·8	69·1	1	11·1	67·8	9	8·9	66·0
4	9·4	70·0	2	9·7	70·5	1900	10·2	62·3
5	10·0	69·6	3	10·8	68·0	1	8·6	65·9
6	9·8	70·2	4	10·4	68·5	2	8·7	66·3
7	10·8	68·4	5	10·5	67·0	3	9·1	65·3
8	11·5	67·3	6	10·1	66·6	4	9·1	64·8
9	12·4	66·0	7	9·1	69·6	5	9·2	64·1
70	12·3	64·1	8	10·6	65·3	6	9·4	63·5
1	10·1	70·1	9	11·4	63·8	7	9·7	63·0
2	11·7	67·7	90	10·9	64·3	8	8·7	65·1
3	11·5	70·0	1	10·7	64·5	9	8·6	65·4
4	12·2	68·5	2	10·5	65·1	10	8·8	65·2
5	12·3	67·9	3	9·6	67·1	11	8·9	65·1
6	12·9	66·5	4	10·1	65·6	12	9·1	64·9
1877	11·8	68·1	1895	10·4	65·4	1913	9·1	64·6

Table 114 Germany, 1925–1938, Gewerbe: (1) Rate of profit directly calculated. (2) Inferred rate of profit. (3) Wage/income ratio used in the calculation of (2).

	(1) %	(2) %	(3) %		(1) %	(2) %	(3) %
1925	2·29	6·8	71·9	1932	−9·12	−4·2	124·2
6	2·05	5·9	74·5	3	−2·14	2·7	83·2
7	4·99	10·2	66·7	4	2·12	7·4	70·6
8	4·16	9·6	68·4	5	6·89	12·0	62·2
9	4·18	9·8	68·4	6	7·16	12·2	63·4
30	2·39	7·7	71·7	7	11·74	16·6	57·1
1931	0·43	5·3	75·6	1938	13·83	17·8	56·2

transport, excluding railways and post: Statistiches Reichsamt *Statistik des deutschen Reichs*, Band 402 (1925), II, p. 223, less III, W.129–131; Band 453 (1933), 2, p. 211, less W.G.R. 44; 1939, *I.Y.B.L.S. 1945/1946*, less an estimate for railways and post. These figures are exclusive of the Saar and Austria. We added numbers for the Saar in 1935 and 1939, from *I.Y.B.L.S. 1941* and *1945–1946*, table ii, without adjustment for railways and post. We obtained annual estimates by interpolation.

(*c*) *Output, for capital/output ratio.* Hoffmann *et al.* table 122.

(*d*) *Profits*, Hoffmann *et al.*, as in 1 (*a*) above, table 122, 'Gewerbe', col. 5. For rate of profit, see our table 114.

(*e*) *Price index.* To convert 1913 into 1929 marks, Hoffmann *et al.*, as in 1.(*a*) above, table 139, price indexes combined by us with weights as shown: buildings (1), industrial equipment (4).

(*f*) *Wage/income ratio*, for inferred rate of profit: wage-earnings as in A.2; income per occupied person, Hoffmann *et al.*, table 122, and tables 16, 20 less unpaid family workers. See our table 114.

Sweden

A. PAY

1. *1861–1913*

Content. Average annual wage-earnings in 1905, as in Appendix 1, 1.A.3, extrapolated by index of annual earnings of adult male workers in mining; iron and steel; metal manufacturing and engineering; mineral and stone; saw mills (from 1884); wood-pulp (from 1894); paper mills; food products; textiles (from 1865); leather, rubber and chemicals (from 1870).

Source and Method. Institute of Social Sciences, University of Stockholm, *Wages, Cost of Living and National Income in Sweden, 1860–1930*, vol. ii, *Wages in Sweden 1860–1930* by G. Bagge, E. Lundberg and I. Svennilson (London, 1933), part i, table 1, p. 48, average i and table 2, pp. 50–51. Average annual earnings in each industry are weighted by the number of employees at about 1913. The weights are: mining, 1; iron and steel, 3; metal and engineering, 4; mineral and stone, 3; saw mills, 3; woodpulp, 1; papermills, 1; food products, 3; textiles, 3; leather, rubber and chemicals, 2. The authors state that they selected firms with good continuous wage records, and in each firm 'the investigation has been confined to a small number of selected workers from representative occupations'. These individual series were combined to give an average series for the firm: 'according as such series show a concordant tendency, they have been combined into averages' (Bagge *et al.*, op. cit., bk. i, ch. ii).

2. *1913, 1921–1938*
Content. Annual earnings of all manual workers in industry and handicrafts, with some in commerce, transport and services.
Source. Lönestatistisk Årsbok, 1934, table 13; *1939*, table 27.

3. *1938, 1946–1960*
Content. (i) Estimated annual wage-earnings (including overtime and all supplements) of manual workers in mining, manufacturing and building.
(ii) Average annual earnings per employee at work.
Sources and Methods. (i) We took annual wage-earnings in 1953 estimated as in Appendix 1, 3.A.3, and extrapolated by an index formed as follows. We took the annual series for average hourly earnings of all workers in mining and manufacturing, in *Löner 1959*, Del II, table 16, and *Statistisk Årsbok 1962*, table 257. This begins only in 1939, and for 1938 we made a weighted average of the hourly earnings and numbers at work given separately for men, women and juveniles (but excluding foremen) in *Lönestatistisk Årsbok 1938*, table 27, after adjusting the earnings and numbers of men to include foremen. We estimated the earnings of foremen by comparing earnings including foremen in *Löner 1959*, table 16, with earnings excluding foremen in ibid. tables 14, 15; and the number from that given for 1939 in *Lönestatistisk Årsbok 1939*, table 30. We multiplied the series for average hourly earnings by the average annual hours per worker in mining, manufacturing and utilities given for 1938, 1946–1960 in the annual volumes of Sveriges Officiella Statistik, Kommerskollegium or Statistiska Centralbyrån, *Industri, 1938, 1946–1949, 1951:* table 3; *1950:* table 5; *1952–1960:* table 9. In 1960 the average excludes utilities but comparison with earlier years shows that the

difference is negligible. We raised the continuous series throughout by annual estimates of employers' contributions to social insurance as a percentage of total pay, provided by Docent K.-O. Faxén.

(ii) We divided the total of wages and salaries given annually in *National Bokföring för Sverige 1938/1939, 1946/1959* (Konjunkturinstitutet, Stockholm, Meddelanden B.30, 1960), table 15, iv, 4 (taking the figures for financial 1938/1939 to represent calendar 1938) by the total number of employees in jobs annually, estimated as stated under *Occupied Population*. We added employers' contributions to social insurance.

B. COST OF LIVING

1. *1861–1913*
Institute for Social Sciences, University of Stockholm, *Wages, Cost of Living and National Income in Sweden*, vol. i, *The Cost of Living in Sweden 1860–1930*, by G. Myrdal with S. Bouvin (London, 1933), table A at pp. 197, 199, Budget B, based on national average consumption for 1881–1890, with weights: foodstuffs 55, fuel 3, lighting $1\frac{1}{2}$, clothing 12, housing 10, misc. $18\frac{1}{2}$.

2. *1913, 1921–1938*
Statistisk Årsbok för Sverige, 1962, table 217, with corresponding tables in earlier issues: cost of living index based on the outlay of a normal urban household with a budget of 3,500 kroner in 1935. Changes in the index are described in A. van Hofsten and M. Gustaveson, 'Le nouvel indice suédois des prix de la consommation', *Revue Économique et Sociale*, Oct. 1956. We obtained an entry for 1913 by extrapolating from 1914 with the aid of the index cited in 1 as continued after 1913 in op. cit., vol. iii (by E. Lindahl *et al.*), part i, table 51.

3. *1938, 1946–1960*
Statistisk Årsbok för Sverige, 1962, table 216, gives an index of consumer prices, based on the consumption of households of all incomes throughout the country, for 1949–1960. Van Hofsten and Gustaveson, op. cit., p. 279, point out that from 1949 to mid-1954 the old cost of living index, base 1935 = 100, followed the same course as the new, in spite of their difference of construction. For 1938, 1946–1948, we therefore took the old index, given in *Statistisk Årsbok 1962*, table 217.

C. G.N.P. DEFLATOR

Content. With weights in brackets: indexes of (*a*) money wages, or pay of all employees (1·5); (*b*) cost of living (7); (*c*) industrial wholesale prices (1·5).

Sources. (*a*) A.1, A.2, A.3 (ii) above. (*b*) B.1, B.2, B.3, above. (*c*) *1861–1913:* G. Bagge *et al.*, *Wages in Sweden*, part 2, table 190, col. 8, industrial raw materials. *1913, 1920–1938: Historisk Statistik för Sverige, statistiska översiktstabeller* (1960), table 94, Produktions-förnödenheter. *1938, 1946–1960:* 1938, *Historisk Statistik*, table 95, Industrial products spliced at 1949, 1951–1953 to following series for 1945–1953. 1945–1953, *Statistisk Årsbok 1947*, table 173, and corresponding table in later issues, spliced over 1949–1953 to *Statistisk Årsbok 1962*, table 218, and corresponding table in earlier issues.

D. INCOME

1. *1861–1913*

(*a*) *National income:* E. Lindahl, E. Dahlgren, K. Kock, *National Income of Sweden 1861–1930*, part i, p. 234, alternative i.

(*b*) *Sector income:* E. Lindahl *et al.*, op. cit., tables 48 (1861–1930) and 49 (1896–1930) give incomes generated in the sectors of agriculture; manufacture, mining and handicrafts; transport and communications; commerce; service of consumers' durables; domestic service. In table 48 these sectors comprise building; in table 49 it appears separately. The incomes are stated gross of 'joint debit items' and 'raw materials and services for building' in table 48, and the first of these alone in table 49. We distributed these deductions between the

Table 115 Sweden, at 10-year intervals, 1870–1910: Estimated income generated by sector, at current prices.

	Total	Agri-culture	Industry mining & crafts	Residual (1)–(2) –(3)		Total	Agri-culture	Industry mining & crafts	Residual (1)–(2) –(3)
	(1) m.Kr.	(2) m.Kr.	(3) m.Kr.	(4) m.Kr.		(1) m.Kr.	(2) m.Kr.	(3) m.Kr.	(4) m.Kr.
1870	811	353	133	325	1900	1988	570	617	801
80	1163	475	207	481	1910	2966	688	1070	1208
1890	1298	440	285	568					

sectors other than domestic service, in proportion to their incomes as stated gross of the deductions. See our table 115.

(*c*) *Income generated in industry from 1870.* (i) *Value product.* We took the income from manufacturing, mining and crafts in Lindahl, op. cit., table 48 for 1870–1913, and the corresponding item together with building in table 49 for 1896–1913, both after deductions allocated as above. Because only a small part of building was comprised in manufacturing etc. in table 48, our resultant series from table 48 runs well below that from table 49, and in adopting the former for 1870– 1895 we raised it throughout by 20·6 per cent, the median of the difference through 1896–1913: we should as it happens have made the same adjustment if we had spliced over the first five years of overlap, 1896–1900. See our table 116. (ii) *Real product.* We deflated

Table 116 Sweden, 1870–1913: Estimated income generated by industry including handicrafts, at current prices.

	Income m.Kr.		Income m.Kr.		Income m.Kr.		Income m.Kr.		Income m.Kr.
1870	133	1880	207	1890	285	1900	617	1910	1070
1	156	1	230	1	300	1	615	11	1116
2	192	2	240	2	314	2	631	12	1168
3	206	3	232	3	329	3	694	1913	1287
4	230	4	234	4	346	4	723		
5	247	5	233	5	382	5	755		
6	222	6	230	6	454	6	889		
7	227	7	230	7	493	7	998		
8	195	8	240	8	545	8	961		
1879	182	1889	270	1899	595	1909	908		

the series obtained under (i) by an index of prices which we made by combining the following, with weights (*a*) 65; (*b*), (*d*), (*e*), each 5; (*c*), 20; (*a*) manufactured exports – C. P. Kindleberger, 'Industrial Europe's Terms of Trade on Current Account, 1870–1953' in *Economic Journal*, 65, March 1955, table 1; we made a correction for the cumulative error of 12 per cent, 1897–1913, noted at loc. cit., p. 32. (*b*) Fuel (birch and pine), (*c*) Clothing, (*d*) Lighting, (*e*) Coke in Stockholm – retail prices from G. Myrdal with S. Bouvin, *The Cost of Living in Sweden 1830–1930* (1933), appendix table A, cols. 13, 14 (Budget B), 15; appendix table C.17. See our table 117.

Table 117 Sweden, 1892–1913 : Index of industrial prices.

1892–97 =100		1892–97 =100		1892–97 =100		1892–97 =100		1892–97 =100	
1892	110[1]	1897	99	1902	102	1907	112	1912	114
3	105	8	100	3	102	8	113	1913	116
4	97	9	103	4	101	9	109		
5	96	1900	109	5	101	10	111		
1896	96	1901	104	1906	105	1911	110		

[1] Extrapolated by comparison with Germany.

2. *1913, 1921–1938*
(*a*) *National income.* E. Lundberg, *Oversikt av Inkomst- och Konsumtionsläget* (Konjunkturinstitutet, Stockholm, Meddelanden B.3, 1945), p. 14, for 1923–1938. To this series we spliced the series in 1(*a*) above, over 1923–1927, to make estimates for 1913, 1921, 1922.
(*b*) *Income generated in industry.* (i) *Value product.* (1) From E. Lindahl *et al.*, *The National Income of Sweden 1861–1930*, Pt. I, table 49, we took the sum of income from manufacturing, mining and handicrafts, and building and construction, through 1925–1929, and deducted from it a part of the joint debit items in the same table proportionate to its share in total income gross of these items. (2) From O. Lindahl, *Sveriges Nationalprodukt 1861–1951* (Konjunkturinstitutet, Meddelanden B.20, 1956) we took G.D.P. in manufacturing, mining and handicrafts, and building and construction, through 1920–1938, and reduced it throughout by the factor 0·908 which made its sum over 1925–1929 equal to that of (1) in those years. See our table 118.

Table 118 Sweden, 1920–1938 : Estimated income generated by industry including handicrafts, at current prices.

	m.Kr.		m.Kr.		m.Kr.		m.Kr.
1920	4251	1925	2862	1930	3563	1935	3779
1	3030	6	3024	1	3120	6	4150
2	2591	7	3172	2	2751	7	4857
3	2709	8	3211	3	2689	1938	5270
1924	2834	1929	3541	1934	3380		

(ii) *Real Product*. We deflated (i) by an index which we made, with weights as in brackets, from the indexes of the wholesale prices of: finished goods (2); semi-manufactured goods (1); production goods (1), given in *Historisk Statistik för Sverige, Statistiska Översiktstabeller* (Statistiska Centralbyrån, Stockholm 1960), table 94. See our table 119.

Table 119   Sweden, 1920–1938 : Index of industrial prices.

	1925–29 =100		1925–29 =100		1925–29 =100		1925–29 =100
1920	246	1925	108	1930	83	1935	78
1	156	6	100	1	75	6	81
2	118	7	98	2	73	7	95
3	111	8	99	3	72	1938	89
1924	109	1929	94	1934	77		

3. *1938, 1946–1960*

(*a*) *National income: National Bokföring för Sverige, 1938/39, 1946–1959.* (Konjunkturinstitutet, Stockholm: Meddelanden B.30, 1960), table 2 (4) gives G.N.P. at factor cost. To get an estimate of national income, we deducted depreciation as given in table 15, vi, (8). The figures deducted are at market prices, so there is some over-deduction. See our table 120.

(*b*) *Income generated in industry*. From annual volumes of Sveriges Officiella Statistik, Kommerskollegium or Statistiska Centralbyrån, *Industri*, table 1, we took value added in mining, manufacturing and utilities, in current Kronor, 1952–1960; in 1960 the series excludes utilities, which we covered on the assumption that their value added bore the same proportion to that of mining and manufacturing as in 1959. To cover 1949–1951, we took from L. Fridén, *Inkomsfördelningen under Efterkrigstiden* (Industriens Utredningsinstitutet, Stockholm, 1964), table 7, the value added in industry excluding utilities and dairies, in current Kronor, 1947–1961, and spliced this over 1952–1956 to the above series for 1952–1960. *Industri 1952*, p. 59 tells us that 'value added' has been calculated gross of interest, rent, taxes and depreciation. To estimate depreciation, we used the

Table 120 Sweden, 1938/1939, 1946–1959: Estimated national income, and pay of all employees, at current prices.

	Income m.Kr.	Pay m.Kr.		Income m.Kr.	Pay m.Kr.		Income m.Kr.	Pay m.Kr.
1938/39	10851	5761	1950	26605	15583	1956	43803	28891
			1	32455	18896	7	46936	31096
1946	19527	11292	2	35462	22271	8	48644	32534
7	21121	12891	3	35770	23116	1959	51452	33975
8	23569	14383	4	37525	24538			
9	24752	14886	1955	40373	26893			

German *Statistisches Jahrbuch 1961* and *1962*, ch. xxiii, table 4: taking five years within 1954–1960, we found that depreciation as a percentage of gross product averaged 17·8 per cent in mining and energy and 7·6 per cent in manufacturing. We applied these rates to the relevant sectors in *Industri*, table 1, over 1952–1960. In 1949–1951, for which we have sectoral figures for sales value but not for gross value added, we applied the following figures, taken from *Industri*, table 1, of gross value added as a percentage of sales value in 1952–1954: mining, 85; utilities, 70. Deducting the resultant estimates of gross value added in those sectors from our estimates of the total gave gross value added in manufacturing. We then deducted depreciation according to the above percentages, 17·8 and 7·6.

(*c*) *Real Product:* O.E.C.D., *Industrial Statistics 1900–1962* (1964), p. 4, index of production in mining, manufacturing and utilities.

E. OCCUPIED POPULATION

1. *1861–1913*
(*a*) *Total.* We applied to the total numbers of M and F aged 15 and over in census years 1860–1920, given in *Historisk Statistisk för Sverige, I, Befolkning 1720–1950*, table A 17, the participation rates given for census years 1890–1920 in the table at *Folkräkningen 1930, Part VIII*, p. 10. The rate given for F in 1920, namely, 36·2 per cent, has been considered too high, and we reduced it to 32 per cent: the rate for 1910 is 30·4 per cent. For both M and F, we carried the participation rates given for 1890 back unchanged through 1860, and we made

Table 121 Sweden, census years, 1860–1920: Estimated total occupied population aged 15 years and over.

	'000s		'000s		'000s		'000s
1860	1417	1880	1696	1900	1969	1920	2516
1870	1512	1890	1755	1910	2192		

annual estimates by linear interpolation. We were not able to deduct unpaid family workers or the unemployed. See our table 121.

(*b*) *By sector.* G. Bagge *et al.*, *Wages in Sweden 1830–1930*, Pt. II (1935): agriculture, table 186; industry, p. 209, line b. See our table 122.

(*c*) *Industry.* G. Bagge *et al.* (as in (*b*)): (i) p. 209, line b, occupied population in census years in manufacturing, mining and handicrafts, including unallocated urban labourers; and (ii) table 187, annual estimates of workers in manufacturing and mining. We formed an annual series from (i) by spreading the difference between each two census years over the intervening years in proportion to the movements of (ii). See our table 123.

2. *1913, 1921–1939*

(*a*) *Total.* We estimated the number of gainfully occupied in jobs by (i) taking or estimating the number of occupied aged 15 and over excluding unpaid family workers (U.F.W.), then (ii) deducting the unemployed. (i) The required numbers are given for 1930 in *Folkräkningen* 1930, viii, table i; and for 1940 in *Folkräkningen 1940*, iii,

Table 122 Sweden, census years, 1870–1910: Estimated occupied population aged 15 years and over, by sectors.

(1)	(2) Agri- culture	(3) Industry mining & crafts	(4) Residual (1)–(2) –(3)		(1)	(2) Agri- culture	(3) Industry mining & crafts	(4) Residual (1)–(2) –(3)
Total					Total			
'000s	'000s	'000s	'000s		'000s	'000s	'000s	'000s
1870 1512	1260	154	98	1900	1969	1221	461	287
80 1696	1291	209	196	1910	2192	1100	587	505
1890 1755	1245	305	205					

Table 123 Sweden, 1870–1913: Estimated occupied population in industry including handicrafts.

	'000s		'000s		'000s		'000s		'000s
1870	154	1880	209	1890	305	1900	461	1910	587
1	167	1	224	1	324	1	449	11	599
2	184	2	232	2	322	2	453	12	623
3	203	3	237	3	324	3	481	1913	683
4	218	4	242	4	337	4	505		
5	223	5	242	5	357	5	517		
6	222	6	246	6	383	6	572		
7	217	7	247	7	408	7	596		
8	201	8	267	8	433	8	578		
1879	192	1889	293	1899	449	1909	539		

table 10, with reference to table 24A to take out those under 15. But the numbers of occupied given for 1920 in *Folkräkningen* 1920, iv, table i, are inclusive of U.F.W., who were not enumerated separately. We estimated the number of male U.F.W. in 1920 by applying to the total male labour force in agriculture in 1920 the proportion of male U.F.W. to the total male labour force, both in agriculture, in 1930, then adding the same absolute number of male U.F.W. in all other occupations as in 1930. We could not make similar use of the number of female U.F.W. reported in 1930, as this has been considered too high: instead, we extrapolated the change between 1940 and 1950 back to 1920 – the figure thereby obtained for 1930 provided a check and proved acceptable. We deducted the estimate of female U.F.W. so made for 1920 from the estimate already made, under 1861–1913, of the total of occupied F in 1920. For both M and F we assumed about the same number of U.F.W. in 1913 as in 1920. We made annual estimates over 1921–1938 by linear interpolation. (ii) In estimating the number unemployed we were guided by B. Ohlin's discussion, in his 'Economic Recovery and Labour Market Problems in Sweden' in *International Labour Review*, xxxi, April and May 1935, of the two available series – the trade union percentages, and the absolute numbers actually applying for relief. He states (p. 511) that there was little unemployment among F, and we made estimates for M only. We first applied the trade union percentages to male wage-earners. We took the percentages for 1913 from *Statistisk Årsbok 1914*, table 119; for 1920–1935 from *Statens Offentliga Utredningar*, 1936, 32, table 2; for 1936–1938 from *International Yearbook of Labour Statistics, 1942*. We took the number of male wage-earners aged 15 and over in 1930, 1940, from the censuses of those years; we made an estimate for 1920 by taking 59 per cent of the male occupied population in that year – 59 per cent is the midpoint between the percentages that would be obtained for 1920 on the assumptions that the change between 1920 and 1930 was nil, and that it was as rapid as between 1930 and 1940. Applying the trade union percentages to all male wage-earners gives a series that runs too high, because not all were trade unionists: we therefore reduced this series throughout in the ratio of an independent estimate of the actual number unemployed in 1933 to the entry for 1933 in the series. We based this independent estimate on the figure of 250,000 unemployed in March 1933, in B. Ohlin, 'Unemployment Policy', in *Social Problems in Sweden*, Annals of the American Academy of Political and Social Science, 197, May 1938: in March 1933 the trade union percentage was 28·7, and assuming the same relation between the percentage and the actual number to hold in the other months of 1933, we arrived at an average of 202,000 for 1933 as a whole. The entry for 1933 in our series was 262,000, and we reduced our series throughout in the ratio of 202 to 262. See our table 124.

(*b*) *Industry.* Census Reports: 1930, part viii, pp. 32, 43, and tables

Table 124 Sweden, 1913, 1920–1938: Estimated numbers of the gainfully occupied population, aged 15 years and over, in jobs, and of unemployed males.

	Occupied in jobs	Un-employed males		Occupied in jobs	Un-employed males		Occupied in jobs	Un-employed males
		'000s			'000s			'000s
1913	1930	30·8	1926	2291	104·1	1934	2465	156·3
			7	2328	102·9	5	2512	130·3
1920	2140	44·8	8	2374	91·2	6	2555	109·4
1	1998	221·8	9	2412	88·2	7	2592	93·9
2	2063	191·9	30	2432	103·3	1938	2612	94·7
3	2185	105·2	1	2411	145·9			
4	2240	85·4	2	2384	194·6			
1925	2267	93·4	1933	2397	202·4			

H, J, pp. 17, 21; 1940, part iii, table i. We deducted unpaid family workers, using the census figures for them in 1930 and 1940, and making our own estimate for 1920. We used linear interpolation for intercensal years, and deducted our annual estimates of all unemployed M. See our table 125.

Table 125 Sweden, 1920–1938; Estimated gainfully occupied population, aged 15 years and over, in jobs in industry including handicrafts.

	'000s		'000s		'000s		'000s
1920	743	1925	764	1930	824	1935	858
1	580	6	767	1	794	6	892
2	624	7	782	2	757	7	919
3	725	8	808	3	762	1938	931
1924	758	1929	825	1934	820		

3. *1938, 1945–1960*
(a) *Total.* We took 1938 from the preceding period. The number of *gainfully occupied* is given for 1940 in *Folkräkningen 1940*, iii; and likewise for 1945, 1950, in *Folkräkningen 1945*, ix, and *1950*, ii, save that in both years in deducting those occupied under 15 we have to guess how many of these were gainfully occupied – we have guessed one third. For 1960, in deducting those under 15 from the provisional census figures in *International Yearbook of Labour Statistics 1962*, we assumed that of the 0·2 per cent reported (equivalent to 6,500), 4,000 were M and 2,500 F. We made annual estimates by linear interpolation for M and F. We then deducted the annual numbers of unemployed given in *International Yearbook of Labour Statistics 1951–1958*, table 10, and similar tables in later volumes: in 1945–1955 these are trade union statistics, with a break in 1951, and in 1956–1960 they cover members of unemployment insurance funds. See our table 126.
(b) *Number of employees in jobs.* For 1938, we estimated the numbers of M and F by linear interpolation between the totals provided in the 1930 and 1940 census reports (named above); we then deducted the number of unemployed as estimated for 1938 in the preceding period. For later years, we used linear interpolation between the totals reported for M and F in the censuses of 1945, 1950, 1960 (reports named above); we deducted the number of unemployed obtained as above. See our table 126.

Table 126 Sweden, 1938, 1945–1960: Estimated (1) gainfully occupied population in jobs, and (2) employees in jobs, both aged 15 years and over.

	(1) Total '000s	(2) Employees '000s		(1) Total '000s	(2) Employees '000s		(1) Total '000s	(2) Employees '000s
1938	2612	1988	1949	2939	2336	1955	3103	2581
			50	2975	2372	6	3135	2629
1945	2801	2201	1	3005	2418	7	3156	2666
6	2841	2241	2	3028	2457	8	3174	2700
7	2877	2275	3	3048	2493	9	3205	2748
1948	2907	2305	1954	3076	2538	1960	3239	2798

(*c*) *In industry*, viz. mining, manufacturing and utilities. From Sveriges Officiella Statistik, Kommerskollegium or Statistiska Centralbyrån, *Industri*, annual volumes 1949–1960, table 1, we took numbers of administrative personnel and wage-earners; the numbers given for 1960 exclude utilities, which we covered on the assumption that the number occupied therein bore the same proportion to the remainder as in 1959. We added the number of proprietors from op. cit., 1953–1959, table 8; the number is small, and we assumed that it was the same in 1949–1952 as in 1953. These numbers, like the value added in D.3(*b*) above, cover only firms employing five or more persons.

United Kingdom

A. PAY

1. *1860–1913*
Content. Average annual wage-earnings in 1905, as in Appendix 1, 1.A.4, extrapolated by an index of the wage for the normal week for manual workers, the representative or average wages in the several industries being combined with variable weights corresponding to the numbers employed. The industries are agriculture (including Ireland); building; printing; shipbuilding; engineering; coal; puddling; cotton; wool and worsted; gas; furniture.

Sources and Method. G. H. Wood, *J.R.S.S.*, March 1909, 'Real Wages and the Standard of Comfort since 1850', appendix, pp. 102–103, col. 1, 'Average Money Wages'. This series is continued through 1903–1910 in Bowley, *Wages and Income in the United Kingdom since 1860*, p. 6, table I, col. 2. We extrapolated this series through 1911–1914 by splicing the index given by Bowley in col. 1 of the same table.

2. *1913, 1922–1938*
(i) *Series in Appendix 3, U.K., col. (1)*.

Content. Average annual wage-earnings in 1931, as in Appendix 1, 2.A.4, extrapolated by an index of average earnings, per normal man-year of employment, of manual workers in the main industries other than agriculture, and in some services, at constant weights proportional to employment in 1930. Earnings include payments in kind, and employers' contributions to private pension schemes but not to compulsory insurance. Cash payments are taken before deduction of direct taxes and workers' contributions to insurance. A normal man-year of employment, after allowance for periods of sickness and unpaid holidays, is taken as 49 weeks. Manual workers include foremen but not shop assistants and hairdressers, Armed Forces, or family workers other than farmers' children classed as 'operatives' in the Census.

Sources and Method. A. L. Chapman, *Wages and Salaries in the United Kingdom 1920–1938*, at table 1 gives numbers of wage- and salary-earners employed (in full man-years as units) by industries; at table 4, total wages and total salaries by industries; all annually. We divided the total wages in the following industries by the corresponding total numbers of wage-earners: mining and quarrying, manufacturing, building and contracting, transport and communications, utilities, local government, and some other services. – To link the series of this period with 1913 we needed a link that excluded agriculture. A. L. Bowley, *Wages and Income in the U.K.*, table iv, gives the increase in average weekly earnings of M, 1914–1924, as 68 per cent in agriculture and 90·6 per cent in all industries. Taking the weight for agriculture as 5·7 per cent (A. L. Bowley, *A New Index Number of Wages*, London & Cambridge Economic Service, Special Memorandum No. 28), we calculated the rise for all industries except agriculture as 92 per cent. Following Bowley, op. cit., table I, we took 1913 to be 1 per cent below 1914.

(ii) *For wage/income ratio in manufacturing* (series Appendix 3, U.K. col. 2). Chapman, op. cit., tables 1, 4.

3. *1938, 1946–1960*

(i) *Annual wage-earnings. Content.* Average annual wage-earnings in 1953, as in Appendix 1, 3, A.4, extrapolated by an index with the following coverage: (*a*) Average earnings in a week of April and October annually of all manual workers in 132 or 133 *industries* – mainly manufacturing, but with mining and quarrying (except coal); construction; gas, electricity and water; transport and communications (except railways, London Transport, British Road Services and sea transport); certain miscellaneous services; and public administration. (*b*) Average cash earnings and value of allowances in kind of all M workers in *coal mining*, in a week of April and of October annually. (*c*) Average earnings of adult M workers in the conciliation and workshop grades of *railways*, other than London Transport, in a week of April annually. (*d*) Average earnings of all registered *dockers* on daily or half-daily engagements, in a week of April and of October annually. *Sources and Method.* We took average annual wage-earnings in 1953, estimated as in Appendix 1, 3, A.4, and extrapolated in proportion to the movements of an annual series of wage-earnings, formed as follows. We made an average of the series for (*a*)–(*d*) above, drawn from the *Ministry of Labour Gazette*, and weighted by the numbers of employees (not wage-earners only) in the respective industries, drawn from: *Annual Abstract of Statistics*, total number of insured employees; *Ministry of Labour Gazette*, for adult males, all categories exclusive of officers, in railways; National Dock Labour Board's *Annual Report* from 1947, total of live and suspense registers plus the dormant register, daily workers only. For 1947 we used the same numbers as in 1948, since the insurance scheme of later years was not in force in 1947; and for 1960 we used the same numbers as in 1959, since the 1960 numbers are not available in the Standard Industrial Classification of 1948 that we followed through 1959. From *National Income and Expenditure 1962*, table 2, we took the ratio that total employers' contributions to social insurance bore to total wages and salaries annually, and raised our series of earnings by these ratios; the ratio applicable to wages alone would differ from this overall ratio, but here as in other countries we did not try to disaggregate. For 1938, the Ministry of Labour gave us the average weekly earnings of M and F, all ages, in Oct. 1938: these were 62·08s. and 28·92s. We weighted these by the numbers of M and F insured against unemployment, within the scope of the Ministry's survey of earnings in Oct. 1938, after deduction of the unemployed, from *Ministry of Labour Gazette*, Nov. 1939. We carried out a corresponding calculation for 1953, using *Annual Abstract of Statistics 1954*. The average weekly earnings thus obtained we multiplied by 49 in 1938 and 50 in 1953 to get annual earnings, and we raised each of these figures by the ratio of total employers' contributions to total pay in its year. We then applied the ratio of 1938 to 1953, in the annual figures thus estimated, to the entry for 1953 in our index of wage-earnings in Period Three.

(ii) *Average earnings of all employees.* Total pay as in D.3(*a*) below, divided by sum of (*a*) civil employees and (*b*) armed forces, less (*c*) the unemployed, and armed forces on release leave. (*a*) *Annual Abstract of Statistics (A.A.S.), 1962*, table 134, and similar tables in earlier volumes. For 1938, 1946, 1947, these give only the insured employees, but *A.A.S. 1959*, table 131, gives for 1948 both all employees and those insured, and we have applied the ratio (20·8 to 16·1) to raise the number of insured in the three earlier years. (*b*) *A.A.S. 1938–1950*, table 127, and similar tables in later volumes. (*c*) As in E.3(*a*) below.

B. COST OF LIVING

1. *1860–1913*
Content. From 1880 onwards, series for retail prices of food, clothing, fuel and sundries, with rents of small houses, combined with the weights of the Ministry of Labour's Cost of Living index, 1914–1947; before 1880, movements of cost of living index as a whole extrapolated by use of regression of that index on Sauerbeck's series for wholesale prices of food and of materials over 1880–1914.
Source. A. L. Bowley, *Wages and Income in the United Kingdom since 1860* (1937), pp. 118–126.

2. *1922–1938*
Content. As for 1880–1913; see *The Cost of Living Index Number, Method of Compilation* (Ministry of Labour, 1937). Weights proportionate to outlays in sample of wage-earning households' budgets in 1903–1904,

adjusted to prices of 1914. The basis of the index used here was narrow, and during the inter-war years it was becoming increasingly unrepresentative: but A. L. Bowley, 'Earnings and Prices, 1904, 1914, 1937–1938', *Review of Economic Studies*, 8, 3, June 1941, gives reason to believe that the outcome was in practice closely the same as would have been yielded by up-to-date coverage and weighting.
Source. Abstract of Labour Statistics and *Statistical Abstracts.*

3. *1938, 1946–1960*
Content. Retail prices and rents, weighted in accordance with patterns of a nationwide sample of household budgets, not wage-earners' only: see *Report on Revision of the Index of Retail Prices* (Cmnd 1657, March 1962), and *Report on Proposals for a New Index of Retail Prices* (Cmd 9710, March 1956). We carried the index back from 1947 in accordance with estimates made with contemporary weights by R. G. D. Allen, 'Index Numbers of Retail Prices, 1938–1951,' *Applied Statistics*, 1, 1952. *Source. London & Cambridge Economic Bulletin*, March 1963, p. xxii, Retail Prices, Total; or *The British Economy: Key Statistics 1900–1964* (London & Cambridge Economic Service, 1965), table c.

C. G.N.P. DEFLATOR
Content. With weights in brackets: indexes of (*a*) money wages, or pay of all employees (1·5); (*b*) cost of living (7); (*c*) industrial wholesale prices (1·5).
Sources. (*a*) A.1, A.2, A.3 (ii) above. (*b*) B.1, B.2, B.3 above. (*c*) *1860–1913:* P. Rousseaux's index, principal industrial products, here taken from B. R. Mitchell with P. Deane, *Abstract of British Historical Statistics* (1962), ch. xvi, table 3. *1913, 1922–1938:* Sauerbeck-Statist index of raw material prices, here taken from Mitchell & Deane, loc. cit., table 4. *1949–1960: Statistics on Incomes, Prices, Employment and Production*, F-1, all manufactured products, home market sales. No link with 1938 is available.

D. INCOME

1. *1860–1914*
(*a*) *National Income.* C. H. Feinstein, 'Income and Investment in the U.K., 1856–1914' in *Economic Journal* 71, June 1961, table iv, net domestic income of the U.K. at factor cost.

(*b*) *Sector income, G.B. only.* From P. Deane and W. A. Cole, *British Economic Growth 1688–1959*, tables 37 and 40, we took the products (gross of depreciation) at census years 1861–1901, and at the Census of Production in 1907, in (i) agriculture, forestry, fishing; (ii) manufacture (incl. utilities), mining, building; (iii) residual: trade and transport; domestic and personal; housing; government, professional and all other.

Table 127 Great Britain, 1871–1913 : Estimated income generated in mining, manufacturing, utilities and building, at current prices.

	£m.		£m.		£m.		£m.		£m.
1871	317	1880	323	1889	456	1898	561	1907	671
2	386	1	360	90	468	9	605	8	597
3	463	2	374	1	450	1900	628	9	607
4	426	3	365	2	422	1	601	10	643
5	394	4	337	3	422	2	597	1	676
6	357	5	324	4	470	3	577	2	721
7	347	6	330	5	481	4	564	1913	753
8	303	7	356	6	493	5	589		
1879	284	1888	401	1897	519	1906	632		

(*c*) *Income generated in industry, G.B. only.* (i) *Value product.* We took (ii) in (*b*) above, and reduced it by one-eleventh throughout to remove depreciation, this being approximately the proportion of depreciation in the industrial product at 1907 according to A. L. Bowley, *The Division of the Product of Industry*, p. 32. We interpolated for intercensal years according to the year to year movements within each interval of the sum of wages and profits outside agriculture, in C. H. Feinstein as in (*a*) above, after removal from this series of the wages of domestic servants. Estimates of these (incl. the value of payments in kind) for 1870–1901 were supplied to us by Dr Feinstein; we spliced to these at 1900–1901 the series in A. R. Prest with A. A. Adams, *Consumer Expenditure 1900–1919* (1954), p. 117. See our table 127. (ii) *Real Product.* We deflated (i) by an index which we formed from the following, with weights (*a*), 1; (*b*) and (*c*) each 4·5: (*a*) Building costs – K. Maywald, 'An index of building costs in the U.K.', *Econ. Hist. Rev.*, 7 Dec. 1954, here taken from B. R. Mitchell with P. Deane, *Abstract of British Historical Statistics* (1962), ch. ix, table 5. (*b*) Fixed capital assets – derived from estimates supplied by Dr Feinstein of value of fixed assets other than dwellings at 1900 prices and at current prices. (c) Merchandise exports – A. H. Imlah, *Economic Elements in the Pax Britannica* (1958), here taken from Mitchell with Deane, op. cit., ch. xi, table 15. See our table 128.

Table 128 U.K. 1870–1913: Index of industrial prices.

1890–99 =100		1890–99 =100		1890–99 =100		1890–99 =100		1890–99 =100	
1870	126	1880	117	1890	107	1900	115	1910	108
1	127	1	113	1	105	1	110	11	111
2	140	2	115	2	102	2	105	12	114
3	148	3	112	3	100	3	104	1913	120
4	142	4	108	4	97	4	104		
5	133	5	105	5	95	5	103		
6	127	6	101	6	96	6	107		
7	123	7	100	7	97	7	111		
8	118	8	99	8	99	8	108		
1879	113	1889	102	1899	104	1909	106		

2. *1913, 1922–1938*
(a) *National income. 1913:* Feinstein, as in 1 above, reduced by 3·6 per cent to provide comparability with the estimates for 1922–1938 which exclude Southern Ireland; the 3·6 per cent is derived from Bowley and Stamp, *The National Income, 1924*, p. 47. *1922–1938:* C. H. Feinstein, 'National Income and Expenditure, 1870–1963' in *London & Cambridge Economic Bulletin*, June 1964, table I, p. xi, national income less income from abroad.
(b) *Income generated in manufacturing.* I. Aristidou, 'Trends in capital, employment and output in the British manufacturing industry 1900–1962' (London Ph.D. thesis, 1965), table B.4. To express this in real terms we used the index of prices of manufactures in Aristidou, op. cit., table B.3. See our table 129.

3. *1938, 1946–1960*
(a) *National income. 1938 and 1948–1960: National Income & Expenditure 1962*, table 1. *1946, 1947: National Income & Expenditure 1957*, table 1, less income from abroad.
(b) *Income generated in industry. Annual Abstract of Statistics 1960*, table 283, and *1962*, table 293: gross domestic product at factor cost in

Table 129 A. U.K., 1924–1938: Estimates by I. Aristidou of net value added in manufacturing industry, at current prices.

	£m.		£m.		£m.		£m.
1924	1158·9	1928	1207·8	1932	980·2	1936	1423·5
5	1192·1	9	1244·9	3	1028·1	7	1590·2
6	1129·7	30	1140·7	4	1141·6	1938	1577·4
1927	1221·7	1931	1001·2	1935	1265·2		

B. U.K., 1924–1938 : I. Aristidou's index of prices of manufactures.

	1948=100		1948=100		1948=100		1948=100
1924	59·1	1928	56·0	1932	49·3	1936	50·6
5	58·9	9	55·5	3	48·4	7	53·3
6	57·8	30	53·4	4	48·6	1938	54·7
1927	56·4	1931	50·6	1935	49·3		

mining and quarrying, manufacturing, construction, utilities, transport and communications. To deduct depreciation we relied on the following figures, taken from *Statistisches Jahrbuch 1961* and *1962*, ch. xxiii, table 4, for depreciation as a percentage of gross value added in German industry in five years within 1954–1960: mining and energy, 17·8, manufacturing, 7·6; construction, 4·3; transport and communications, 15·0.

(c) *Industrial productivity*. *Key Statistics*, table B, index of output per man-year in mining, manufacturing, construction and utilities.

E. OCCUPIED POPULATION

1. *1860–1914*

(a) *Total*. All classified as occupied in the Census of Population, in Great Britain and all Ireland. *1860–1880*: We took the total population aged 15–65 inclusive reported in the Censuses of 1851, 1861, 1871. For 1851, 1861 we estimated the number aged 65 by taking one quarter of those reported in the age group 65–69. We applied to the total population aged 15–65 the ratio of 70·4 per cent which Bowley's estimate of the occupied population in 1881 (see below) bore to the corresponding population of that year. We obtained annual figures by linear interpolation. *1881–1914:* A. L. Bowley, *Wages and Income in the U.K.*, p. 91. We obtained annual figures by linear inter- and extrapolation. See our table 130.

Table 130 U.K., census years 1861–1911; Estimated total occupied population aged 15–65 years.

	'000s		'000s		'000s
1861	12,349	1881	14,450	1901	17,740
1871	13,064	1891	16,020	1911	19,700

(*b*) *By sector, G.B. only.* From B. R. Mitchell with P. Deane, *Abstract of British Historical Statistics (A.B.H.S.)*, ch. ii, i, we took (i) total occupied, and (ii) numbers occupied in agriculture. We estimated (iii) numbers occupied in industry as in (*c*) below. (iv) Numbers occupied in the residual sector – trade and transport, public service, and professional, domestic and personal services – were given by the excess of (i) over (ii) and (iii). See our table 131.

Table 131 Great Britain, census years 1871 to 1901, with 1907 by interpolation: Estimated occupied population by sectors.

	Total	Agriculture	Industry excluding transport	Residual
	'000s	'000s	'000s	'000s
1871	11870	1769	5019	5082
1881	12739	1633	5423	5683
1891	14499	1502	6227	6770
1901	16299	1425	6933	7941
1907	17524	1502	7316	8706

(*c*) *In industry, G.B. only.* (i) From *A.B.H.S.* (as in (*b*) above) we took the numbers occupied in mining, 9 manufacturing industries or groups of industries, building, and utilities, at census years, 1861–1911. These numbers include dealers in the products concerned. (ii) The same table includes 'all others occupied'. To estimate how many of these were in industry we consulted the Census of England and Wales, 1911, vol. x, part i (Cd 7018 of 1914), table 26, xxii, 'Other, General & Undefined Workers and Dealers', and for the census years 1881–1911 took the numbers in xxii, sec. 3, 1–5 and sec. 5, 2–5, as being clearly industrial. Sec. 5, 1 contains General Labourers. These were far fewer in 1911, when the occupational classification was closer, than in previous Censuses: we assumed that the 295,000 remaining in this class in 1911 were casual labourers not assignable to industry, but that the excess over 295,000 of the number in this class in each earlier Census would have been assigned to industry if the procedure of 1911 had been followed then, and we included these excesses in our totals under the present head. In each Census year we expressed the total so obtained as a percentage of the total in xxii as a whole; we assumed that the percentage in 1871 was the same as that in 1881. We then applied these percentages to the totals of 'all others occupied' in all G.B. in *A.B.H.S.* as above, and added the products to the numbers under (i). (iii) The totals so reached include 'dealers' – a term that comprises retailers. To remove these, we took from the Census of England and Wales, 1911 (as in (ii)), table 26, the total of 39 groups predominantly in wholesale and retail distribution, and in each census year 1881–1911 expressed them as a percentage of the total in the same Census within the coverage of (i) above (table 27); we estimated a percentage for 1871 by inspection. We assumed that these percentages, applied to the totals reached at the end of (ii) above, would provide tolerable estimates of the number of dealers in the whole of G.B. We deducted these estimates to arrive at the totals occupied within industry proper. (iv) We made estimates for intercensal years by linear interpolation. (v) We further deducted estimates of the numbers unemployed, made by applying the trade union unemployment percentages, taken here from *A.B.H.S.*, ch. ii.3, col. A through 1889 and col. B thereafter. It seemed permissible to apply these percentages to all occupied because those less subject to unemployment than the members of the unions concerned would be roughly offset by the unskilled workers, outside those unions, among whom unemployment was higher. See our table 132.

(*d*) *For indexes of productivity by industry, 1900–1913*: see under G below.

Table 132 Great Britain, 1871 to 1913: Estimated occupied population in jobs in mining, manufacturing, utilities and building.

	'000s		'000s		'000s		'000s		'000s
1871	4939	1880	5087	1889	5939	1898	6533	1907	7045
2	5013	1	5228	1890	6018	9	6656	8	6804
3	5039	2	5376	1	6009	1900	6690	9	6871
4	5053	3	5439	2	5901	1	6704	10	7155
5	5057	4	5205	3	5890	2	6717	11	7345
6	5028	5	5211	4	5995	3	6729	12	7392
7	5014	6	5231	5	6131	4	6698	1913	7538
8	4941	7	5456	6	6363	5	6830		
1879	4733	1888	5711	1897	6432	1906	6992		

2. *1913, 1922–1938*

(a) *Total.* All gainfully occupied persons in jobs (excluding unpaid family workers and the unemployed) in Great Britain and Northern Ireland. (i) *Population.* A. L. Bowley, *Studies in the National Income 1924–1938*, pp. 54–5, table I, gives the ratios of occupied persons to all persons, by age- and sex-group, in the census years 1911, 1921, 1931. We estimated the corresponding ratios for 1913, 1922, 1923, and applied these ratios to the population in each age- and sex-group as given by *Statistical Abstract 1936* for G.B. only; we raised the products by 1·0288 (see Bowley loc. cit.) to include Northern Ireland. For 1924–1938 we followed Bowley, op. cit., p. 56, table ii. (ii) *Unpaid family workers.* Particulars are given, but only for agriculture in G.B., in the Census reports for 1911, 1921, 1931. In England and Wales we took all those reported less those under 14 in 1931 and under 15 in 1931. In Scotland, those reported on farms were 14·0 per cent of the farmers in 1921 but 33·8 per cent in 1931: we applied the latter ratio to 1921 too. In both Census years we took the actual number reported on crofts. In both parts of G.B. we made annual estimates through 1922–1938 by linear inter- and extrapolation; we took 1913 to be the same as 1911. In N. Ireland we took the percentage of unpaid family workers in the total rural population as reported in the Census of 1951, and applied it to the rural populations reported for 1911 in the Census, and for 1926 and 1937 in the *Annual Abstract of Statistics 1935–1946*, table 12: the outcome was near 20,000 in both 1926 and 1937, and we took this figure as constant throughout 1922–1938. (iii) *The unemployed.* For 1913 we calculated absolute

Table 133 U.K., 1913, 1922–1938 : Estimated gainfully occupied population in jobs, and estimated unemployed.

	Occupied in jobs m.	Un- employed m.		Occupied in jobs m.	Un- employed m.		Occupied in jobs m.	Un- employed m.
1913	17·79	0·08	1927	19·61	1·18	1934	19·54	2·17
			8	19·63	1·29	5	19·94	2·03
1922	17·31	1·64	9	19·84	1·26	6	20·46	1·75
3	17·80	1·34	30	19·26	1·99	7	20·86	1·50
4	19·06	1·21	1	18·78	2·72	1938	20·71	1·84
5	19·10	1·34	2	18·85	2·83			
1926	19·07	1·51	1933	19·13	2·57			

numbers from the particulars of rates and coverage given for trade unions and insurance by W. H. Beveridge, *Full Employment in a Free Society*, p. 336, table 38. For 1922–1936 we took the totals aged 16 and over in *Annual Abstract of Labour Statistics, 19th Report* (Cmd 3140, P.P. xxv, 1928), pp. 46–47; and *22nd Report* (Cmd 5556, P.P. xxvi, 1936–1937), pp. 53, 55, 57. For 1937, 1938, we took the series of unemployed aged 14 and over in the *Annual Abstract of Statistics 1935–1946*, p. 113, table 136, and spliced it to the preceding series at 1935, 1936. See our table 133.

(*b*) *In manufacturing*. From the Census of England & Wales, 1931, General Report, table xlix; Census of Scotland 1931, vol. iii, table 15, we took the total number in jobs in manufacturing; for N. Ireland we based an estimate for 1931 on its own Census of 1926. From A. L. Chapman, *Wages and Salaries in the U.K.*, table 1, we took total employees in manufacturing in full-time man-years, annually 1920–1938, and we used this series as an index with which to extrapolate our figure for 1931. See our table 134.

Table 134 U.K., 1924–1938: Estimated number of occupied persons in jobs in manufacturing.

	'000s		'000s		'000s		'000s
1924	6843	1928	7168	1932	6349	1936	7569
5	6887	9	7256	3	6637	7	7975
6	6674	1930	6737	4	6962	1938	7850
1927	7168	1931	6255	1935	7149		

3. *1938, 1946–1960*

(*a*) *Total.* Defined as for 2. Armed Forces on release leave excluded. (i) *Gainfully occupied population, 1938, 1946–1947.* For G.B., *Annual Abstract of Statistics 1938–1950,* table 127, gives the 'old series' for total manpower, which in ibid. table 128 overlaps at 1948 with the 'new series', and bears to it the ratio 20·2:22·9. We raised the 'old series' in this ratio. The 'new series' is of all persons aged 15 and over who work for pay or gain, in civil employment and the Armed Forces (including those on release leave), or register themselves as available for such work; it counts part-time workers as whole units. For N. Ireland, we made an estimate for 1938 by applying to the total population of 1938, given in the Ulster Year Book 1956, pp. xxxiv, xxxv, the ratio of gainfully occupied (less Armed Forces stationed in N. Ireland) to total population, obtained for 1951; for 1946–1947 we made rough estimates from the figure obtained by difference from totals of working population given for U.K. and G.B. in 1948. *1948–1960:* For U.K., we took the series for Total Working Population in *Annual Abstract of Statistics 1959,* table 129, and *1961,* table 131. (ii) *The unemployed.* The 'registered unemployed' as reported in *Annual Abstract of Statistics 1958,* tables 136, 138; *1962,* tables 142, 143. (iii) *Armed Forces on release leave* are stated in the relevant tables of the *Annual Abstract of Statistics* cited above. We deducted (ii) and (iii) from the totals under (i).

(*b*) *In industry. Annual Abstract of Statistics 1960,* table 132. We omitted 1960, for which the numbers were affected by the change in the Standard Industrial Classification.

F. CAPITAL STOCK, CAPITAL PER OCCUPIED PERSON, CAPITAL/
   OUTPUT RATIO, AND PROFITS

1. *1870–1913*

(*a*) *Capital.* Coverage: all save agriculture and dwellings. For use with (*b*) below, as follows; for use with (*c*) and (*d*) below, the same sources and method, but taking current prices. (i) Total fixed assets excluding dwellings, at depreciated value, at prices of 1900: estimates provided by C. H. Feinstein, to be published in his *National Income, Expenditure and Output of the U.K., 1855–1965.* We converted this series to 1913 prices with the aid of the price-index

Table 135   U.K., 1874, 1892 and 1913 : Estimated capital stock in farming at prices of 1913.

	1913 £m.
1874	370
1892	334
1913	313

implicit in estimates of capital stock at first cost in current and constant prices, also supplied by C. H. Feinstein. (ii) To add a component for stock-in-trade and working capital, we raised the series in (i) by 14 per cent, the prevailing ratio of stocks to the depreciated value of fixed assets in 1920–1938 in C. H. Feinstein, *Domestic Capital Formation in the U.K. 1920–1938*, table 3.50. (iii) Capital and stocks in agriculture at current prices: *Royal Commission on Agriculture*. Minutes of Evidence, vol. iv, 1896, Appendix A, xx, p. 541, estimates by R. E. Turnbull for June 1874 and June 1892, less the wages fund. 'Farmers' capital' in 1914: J. C. Stamp, *British*

Table 136   U.K. 1871–1911 : Estimated occupied population excluding agriculture, the armed forces and domestic and personal services, in census years.

1871 '000s	1881 '000s	1891 '000s	1901 '000s	1911 '000s
9197	9911	11470	13233	14859

Incomes & Property (1920), p. 404: we assumed that this included the wages fund, which we took to be about the same as in 1892, and deducted; we took Stamp's figure to hold for 1913. See our table 135. (iv) Applying Rousseaux' price indexes for agricultural products and principal industrial products (B. R. Mitchell with P. Deane, *Abstract of British Historical Statistics*, ch. xvi, 3) to reduce the corresponding elements in (iii) to 1913 prices gave us changes over 1874–1892 and 1892–1913 inconsistent with the known course of events, and we applied prices indexes having half the swing of the originals. (v) We assumed that the 1874 figure held through 1870–1873, and filled in the two subsequent spans by linear interpolation. (vi) We deducted the series in (v) from that yielded by (ii).

Table 137 U.K., 1870–1913, all sectors excluding agriculture: (1) Rate of profit directly calculated. (2) Inferred rate of profit. (3) Wage/income ratio used for the calculation of (2).

	(1) %	(2) %	(3) %		(1) %	(2) %	(3) %
1870	13·0	10·2	61·3	1892	11·5	12·2	64·6
1	14·6	11·9	58·3	3	11·9	12·4	65·1
2	13·2	11·6	57·9	4	14·7	15·3	61·1
3	12·2	11·6	57·2	5	14·9	15·9	60·6
4	11·9	10·7	59·8	6	14·5	16·2	60·0
5	12·0	10·6	61·1	7	14·9	16·4	59·5
6	11·3	10·1	62·0	8	15·3	17·4	57·3
7	11·2	9·9	62·7	9	15·1	17·2	56·3
8	11·0	9·2	64·2	1900	13·3	15·6	57·2
9	11·3	9·3	64·7	1	12·6	14·7	59·3
80	11·6	9·9	62·4	2	13·2	15·0	59·4
1	12·4	11·4	60·1	3	12·0	13·8	61·1
2	11·9	12·0	58·8	4	11·6	12·7	62·6
3	11·5	11·2	61·3	5	12·6	14·4	59·7
4	11·1	10·0	64·7	6	13·2	14·8	59·1
5	11·2	9·3	66·8	7	13·2	14·7	59·7
6	12·4	10·3	65·7	8	11·3	12·3	63·8
7	13·2	11·7	63·9	9	11·9	13·4	61·9
8	14·5	14·0	60·6	10	12·4	14·3	61·0
9	14·7	15·8	57·8	11	12·7	15·2	58·9
90	13·2	14·5	59·6	12	13·2	16·1	57·5
1891	12·7	13·8	61·6	1913	13·1	16·1	56·6

(*b*) *Occupied population.* Coverage: all save agriculture, the armed forces, and domestic and personal services. We interpolated or extrapolated the numbers reported for census years, for G.B. in B. R. Mitchell with P. Deane, *Abstract of British Historical Statistics*, ch. ii, 1, and for Ireland from the *Census of Ireland, General Report*, 1881, part ii (C 3365 of 1882), table 86; 1891, part ii (C 6780 of 1892), table 88; 1911 (Cd 6663 of 1913), table 70. See our Table 136.

(*c*) *Output.* C. H. Feinstein, *Econ. J.*, 71, June 1961, table iv: industrial income (wages and profits) plus incomes of the salaried and self-employed, at current prices.

(*d*) *Profits in industry.* As for (*c*). See our table 137.

(*e*) *Wage/income ratio* within the approximate coverage of (*a*), for calculation of the inferred rate of profit: (i) Wage-earnings as in

A.1, divided by income generated per occupied person obtained as the quotient of: (ii) net domestic product less rent, income from agriculture, and wages of domestic servants, from C. H. Feinstein as in (*c*), divided by (iii) occupied population as in (*b*). We were unable to deduct the pay of the armed forces from (ii). See our table 137.

2. *1924–1938*

(*a*) *Capital*. (i) *All except agriculture and dwellings*. C. H. Feinstein, *Domestic Capital Formation in the U.K. 1920–1938*, sum of depreciated value of fixed assets at current prices, 3 B (f) in the following tables: 6.10, coal mining; 6.20, other mining and quarrying; 7.0, utilities; 8.0 manufacturing; 9.0 transport and communications; 10.0, distribution and other services; 11.0, social and public services; *plus* stocks in the same sectors, op. cit., table 2.80, col. 1. (ii) *Manufacturing only*: fixed assets and stocks from table 8.0, as in (i) above.

(*b*) *Occupied population within coverage of estimates of capital*. A. L. Bowley, *Studies in National Income, 1924–1938*, table ii, total U.K., annually, less the sum of those occupied in (1) agriculture, (2) armed forces, (3) domestic service, estimated as follows. (1) Occupied in agriculture in G.B., 1921 and 1931, from B. R. Mitchell with P. Deane, *Abstract of British Historical Statistics*, ch. ii, table i.D: we interpolated in 1921–1931 and extrapolated to 1938. We estimated the number occupied in agriculture in N. Ireland, in 1926 from the 1926 Census, and in 1938 on the assumption that it had changed since 1926 in the same proportion as the whole rural population (*U.K. Annual Abstract of Statistics*). We assumed the entries for 1924 and 1925 to be the same as 1926, and interpolated between 1926 and 1938. We added the above series to obtain totals for the U.K., and checked the movements of these totals after 1931 against those of the annual numbers of employed labourers in agriculture given by Bowley (as above), table A, p. 100. (2) Armed forces, in A. L. Chapman, *Wages & Salaries in the U.K. 1920–1938*, table 1. (3) Domestic service, Chapman, op. cit., table 85.

(*c*) *Output*. (i) (1) *Net domestic product* minus sum of (2) agricultural income, (3) rent of dwellings, (4) pay of armed forces, and (5) wages of domestic servants. Sources: (1) C. H. Feinstein, 'National Income and Expenditure, 1870–1963', *London & Cambridge Economic Bulletin*, June 1964, table i. (2) A. L. Bowley, *Studies in the National Income 1924–1938*, table A, p. 100. (3) Total rent in E. H. Phelps Brown and

P. E. Hart, 'The share of wages in national income', *Economic Journal*, 62, 246, June 1952, table i, minus agricultural rent from Bowley, as in (2) above. (4) Chapman, op. cit., table 4. (5) Chapman, op. cit., table 85. (ii) *Manufacturing only*. I. Aristidou, 'Trends in capital, employment and output in the British manufacturing industry, 1900–1962' (London Ph.D. thesis, 1965), table B.4.

(*d*) *Profits*. (i) *Coverage of* (*a*) (*i*) less finance and some services. Gross profits 1920–1938, from table 1.1 of P. E. Hart, *Studies in Profit, Business Saving & Investment in the U.K., 1920–1962*, vol. 1 (1965) minus depreciation in sectors taken from Feinstein, tables as in (*a*) (i) above. (ii) *Manufacturing only*. Relevant entries as in (i).

(*e*) *Wage/income ratio* within the coverage of (*a*) for calculation of the inferred rate of profit. Total wages (excluding armed forces) less wages in agriculture and domestic service (Chapman, op. cit., tables 4, 85) divided by total number of wage-earners (excluding armed forces) less those in agriculture and domestic service (Chapman, op. cit., tables 1, 85). Income as in (*c*) above, divided by the occupied population as in (*b*) above less the unemployed. We took the total unemployed (exclusive of those in agriculture, reported only in 1937, 1938) from *Statistical Abstract of the U.K. 1936*, and *1937*, and *Ministry of Labour Gazette 1938*; in 1924–1926 the coverage was of 16 years and over, in later years only of ages 16–64, and we reduced the totals of 1924–1926 by the factor of 0·971. See our table 138.

Table 138 : U.K., 1920–1938: (1) Rate of profit in manufacturing, directly calculated. (2) Rate of profit in all sectors except agriculture, finance and some services, directly calculated. (3) Inferred rate of profit in all sectors excluding agriculture. (4) Wage/income ratio used for the calculation of (3).

	(1) %	(2) %	(3) %	(4) %		(1) %	(2) %	(3) %	(4) %
1920		3·6			1930	9·9	7·4	12·2	64·4
1		2·3			1	8·7	6·6	10·0	67·4
2		5·6			2	7·0	5·6	9·2	69·2
3		7·0			3	9·2	6·9	10·4	67·5
4	9·6	7·3	7·5	71·4	4	11·0	8·1	12·6	64·6
5	9·2	7·0	9·4	68·1	5	13·3	9·0	13·9	64·3
6	7·9	6·5	7·5	71·4	6	14·4	9·7	13·0	64·0
7	9·9	7·8	8·9	69·8	7	13·9	9·5	12·7	63·8
8	10·6	7·9	9·5	68·6	1938	13·2	8·6	13·7	62·4
1929	10·3	8·0	10·6	66·8					

(*f*) *Price index.* (i) *For fixed assets:* we combined with weights 1, 4, the indexes for buildings and for unspecified plant and machinery in table 2.70 in Feinstein, op. cit. in (*a*) above. (ii) *For stocks*, Feinstein, op. cit. in (*a*) above, table 2.80, col. 2.

(*g*) *Rates of profit, directly calculated and inferred.* See our table 138.

G. PRODUCTIVITY BY INDUSTRY

(*a*) *Series of Fig. 29:* (i) (*a*) coal, (*b*) railways, (*c*) iron ore, (*d*) ship-building, (*e*) machinery; (ii) real gross investment in manufacturing. (i) Under each of the heads (i), (*a*)–(*e*), we have estimated (1) output and (2) employment as follows.

(1) *Output.* B. R. Mitchell with P. Deane, *Abstract of British Historical Statistics* (*A.B.H.S.*): (*a*) ch. iv, table 3, U.K. output in m. tons. (*b*) Total working receipts, in £s (taken here as an index of physical activity, changes in fares and freights having been small), ch. viii, G.B. table 5, Ireland table 6. (*c*) U.K. output in '000 tons, ch. v, table 1. (*d*) The sum of ch. xiii, table 5, 'gross mercantile shipbuilding in £m.' (from C. H. Feinstein, *Economic Journal*, 71, June 1961), and the following from A. Cairncross, *Home and Foreign Investment*, 1870–1913, table 23, 'value of repair work' on merchant ships, and 'value of naval building and repairs', both in £m., deflated by the 'estimated cost of steamers in £s per registered ton' in K. Maywald, 'The construction costs and value of the British merchant fleet 1850–1938', *Scottish Journal of Pol. Econ.*, 3, 1, Feb. 1956, table 1. (*e*) Cairncross, op. cit., table 37, 'value of output of machinery', in £m., deflated by (ibid.) average value of machinery per ton. Cairncross describes the problems and methods of his estimate of output, at pp. 158–163: it is based on the throughput of steel.

(2) *Employment.* (*a*) *A.B.H.S.*, iv, table 4. (*b*) G.B., *A.B.H.S.*, ch. ii, tables 1A, 1B, plus, for Ireland, *Censuses of Ireland, 1871*, part i (C 1106 vii of 1875), table 19; *1891*, part ii General Report (C 6780 of 1892) table 88; *1911*, General Report (Cd 6663 of 1913) table 70; intercensal years by linear interpolation. (*c*) G.B. only (Ireland negligible), census years, taken here from E. H. Phelps Brown and S. J. Handfield-Jones, 'The climacteric of the 1890s' in *Oxford Economic Papers* (N.S.), 4, 3, Oct. 1952, table iii, col. 6; with linear interpolation. (*d*) Number of operatives, at census years, for G.B. from Phelps Brown and Handfield-Jones, loc. cit., table iii, col. 10,

O

and for Ireland from Censuses as in (*b*) above; with linear interpolation. (*e*) Census years, England and Wales, 1881–1911, *Census of 1911*, vol. x (Cd 7018 of 1914), table 26, all sub-order X. 3, plus ironfounders in 1901 and 1911 with estimates for 1881, 1891; Scotland, *Census of 1881*, vol. ii (C 3657 of 1883), and *Census of 1891*, vol. ii, part ii (C 7134 of 1893), table xv in both years, sub-orders 10·1, 21.8, plus ironfounders estimated by us, with 1901 and 1911 from *Census of 1911*, vol. ii (Cd 6896 of 1913), table D.1, same groups as for England and Wales; Ireland, *Census of 1881*, part ii, General Report (C 3365 of 1882) table 19, sub-orders X.1, XXI.8, with corres-

Table 139 A. U.K., 1871–1911: Estimated occupied population (including unemployed) in census years, in railways and iron ore mining (for Fig. 29).

	Railways '000s	Iron ore '000s		Railways '000s	Iron ore '000s
1871	102	30·0	1901	332	19·4
1881	165	36·6	1911	386	24·3
1891	223	21·1			

B. U.K., 1871–1913: Estimated number of operatives in jobs in shipbuilding and in manufacture of machinery (for Fig. 29).

	Ship-building '000s	Mnfr. of machinery '000s		Ship-building '000s	Mnfr. of machinery '000s		Ship-building '000s	Mnfr. of machinery '000s
1871	63·0		1885	73·6	442·3	1899	118·8	673·3
2	64·4		6	75·1	446·3	1900	121·4	688·1
3	65·2		7	79·9	469·6	1	122·7	695·7
4	65·7		8	86·4	502·9	2	123·9	690·7
5	66·0		9	91·9	529·5	3	125·3	689·9
6	66·0		90	93·8	535·8	4	126·7	683·6
7	66·3		1	94·3	533·7	5	132·6	704·2
8	65·4		2	93·4	529·1	6	139·6	730·6
9	61·9		3	92·3	522·6	7	141·9	731·8
80	69·2		4	95·1	538·6	8	133·7	680·1
1	72·5	457·3	5	101·0	572·1	9	136·1	682·9
2	75·9	472·4	6	108·2	613·0	10	149·1	738·7
3	77·8	478·3	7	110·3	625·0	11	158·0	773·1
1884	73·4	445·7	1898	114·0	646·3	12	161·2	778·9
						1913	167·0	797·8

Table 140 U.K., 1870–1913: Estimates by I. Aristidou of gross investment in manufacturing at prices of 1948.

	£m.		£m.		£m.		£m.		£m.
1870	60·53	1880	69·33	1890	61·10	1900	143·32	1910	114·48
1	75·33	1	60·20	1	58·80	1	131·41	11	121·57
2	68·17	2	60·87	2	73·85	2	131·92	12	134·55
3	65·13	3	56·19	3	75·20	3	145·39	1913	171·14
4	56·00	4	54·12	4	84·13	4	138·32		
5	72·64	5	60·06	5	87·00	5	143·23		
6	90·08	6	58·46	6	99·09	6	128·65		
7	85·58	7	45·41	7	106·81	7	103·56		
8	78·45	8	57·16	8	111·51	8	104·96		
1879	59·93	1889	60·18	1899	138·47	1909	112·95		

ponding tables and sub-orders in *Censuses 1891*, part ii, General Report (C 6780 of 1892), *1901*, part ii, General Report (Cd 1190 of 1902), *1911*, General Report (Cd 6663 of 1913); with linear interpolation between the sums of the above in census years, and adjustment for unemployment from *A.B.H.S.*, ii, table 3, percentage of unemployed trade unionists in engineering, metal and shipbuilding industries, 1871–1889 series A; 1890 mean of series A, B; 1891–1913 series B. See our table 139. (ii) *Real gross investment in manufacturing*. I. Aristidou, 'Trends in capital, employment and output in the British manufacturing industry 1900–1962' (Ph.D. thesis, London 1965), gross investment at 1948 prices in manufacturing building (table A.2) and plant and machinery (table A.4). See our table 140.

(*b*) *Series of Fig. 30*. We made estimates of the occupied population in 1901, 1911, to match as nearly as possible the coverages of the following indexes of production in K. S. Lomax, 'Production and productivity movements in the United Kingdom since 1900', *J.R.S.S.*, A 22, 2, 1959, table i: total industry (which does not include transport); total manufacturing industry; mechanical engineering; total metal manufacturing; chemicals; paper and printing; mining and quarrying; utilities; textiles; clothing; food, drink and tobacco. (We omitted shipbuilding, and building and contracting, because neither includes repairs.) In the light of comments at op. cit. p. 210 we have taken it that the regional coverage of the indexes is that of the U.K. in 1924 – that is, inclusive in Ireland only of the six counties which with the cities of Belfast and Londonderry constitute Northern Ireland. We made our estimates for the occupied population from (*a*) figures by industry, 1901 and 1911, in Great Britain, after (*b*) deduction of 'dealers', together with (*c*) similarly adjusted figures for Northern Ireland; for other years we used linear interpolation and extrapolation. (*d*) In four of these series we adjusted for unemployment. – (*a*) B. R. Mitchell with P. Deane, *Abstract of British Historical Statistics* (*A.B.H.S.*), ch. ii, tables 1[A], 1[B].

Table 141 Great Britain and Northern Ireland within the frontier of 1921 (for Fig. 30)

A. Estimated numbers occupied in seven industries, in census years 1901 and 1911.

	Mining & quarrying '000s	Chemicals '000s	Textiles '000s	Clothing '000s	Leather '000s	Food, drink & tobacco '000s	Utilities '000s
1901	906	84	1249	625	108	286	62
1911	1176	118	1373	533	113	328	86

B. Estimated numbers occupied in jobs 1900–1913 : All industries ; all manufacturing ; mechanical engineering ; metals ; paper and printing.

	All industries[1] '000s	All manufacturing '000s	Mechanical engineering '000s	Metals '000s	Paper & printing '000s
1900	6922	4543	685	109	253
1	6926	4552	684	112	258
2	6936	4555	679	115	263
3	6945	4558	679	118	270
4	6932	4552	673	120	274
1905	7043	4656	693	127	278
6	7208	4766	719	135	286
7	7261	4807	720	138	292
8	7010	4644	669	131	294
9	7076	4695	672	135	298
1910	7366	4882	727	149	306
11	7558	4990	761	159	311
12	7604	5017	767	163	317
1913	7752	5121	786	170	326

[1] excludes transport.

(b) Using the *Census of England and Wales 1911*, vol. x (Cd 7018 of 1914), part i, table 26, and *Census of Scotland 1911*, vol. ii (Cd 6896 of 1913), table D.1, we took out the numbers in: board and lodging; wigmakers and hairdressing; and all 'dealers' (who include retailers). We included general labourers in industry but not in manufacturing. For mechanical engineering we included only, in England and Wales, class v, order X. 3, with order X. 8, 168, ironfounders; with the corresponding occupations in Scotland. For metal manufacture we included only, in England and Wales, order X, 155–58, 161–65; in Scotland, 133–37. (c) *Census of Ireland 1901*, part i, vol. iii, Province of Ulster (Cd 1123 of 1902), tables xix, xix.A, xx, xx.A; with corresponding tables in *Census of Ireland 1911*, Province of Ulster (Cd 6051 of 1912/1913). We excluded the same occupations as in G.B., though our estimates for dealers were in part arbitrary, as dealers were not always distinguished from makers; but the numbers are small. We excluded the more numerous general labourers in the counties, where they were said to be mainly agricultural, but they were not so described in Belfast and Londonderry, where we included them for all industry but not for manufacturing.

(d) Using *A.B.H.S.*, ch. ii, table 3, we estimated numbers of un-employed by applying rates of unemployment to the total occupied given by linear interpolation and extrapolation, as follows: all industry, the rate for all trade unions making returns; manufacturing, the foregoing rate exclusive of building, estimated by the rate for carpenters and joiners, with weights: all industry, 7, building 1; mechanical engineering and metal manufacture, the rate in the engineering, metal and shipbuilding unions; paper and printing, the rate in printing and bookbinding unions. See our table 141.

United States of America

A. PAY

1. *1860–1914*
Content. Average annual earnings (from 1889 per full-time equivalent worker) in manufacturing.

Sources and Method. We took average annual earnings, 'adjusted manufacturing', in the census years 1860, 1870, 1880, 1890, from C. D. Long, *Wages and Earnings in the U.S. 1860–1890* (1960), table 14, and lowered them by half of one per cent throughout so as to make the entry for 1890 equal to the average annual earnings in manufacturing in 1890 in A. Rees, *Real Wages in Manufacturing 1890–1914* (1961), table 10. To get yearly estimates we interpolated between the four adjusted figures by distributing the aggregate difference in each 10-year interval in proportion to the first differences of the weighted average daily wage-rate in 13 manufacturing industries in C. D. Long, op. cit., tables A.1 and A.10. We took the annual series for 1889–1914 from A. Rees, op. cit., table 10.

2. *1914, 1919–1941*

(i) *General. Content.* Weekly earnings of manual workers in manufacturing, bituminous coalmines, and class i steam railroads.

Sources and Method. We combined the series in *Historical Statistics of the U.S.* (1960), D 628, D 635, D 638, using weights proportional to the corresponding total wages in 1925–1929 in S. Kuznets, *National Income and its Composition 1919–1938* (1941), tables M3, Q4, P6, viz. manufacturing 1030, bituminous coal 66, class i railroads 234. In some years before 1923 there are no entries for coal and for railroads: we formed an index for the remaining series, and spliced it to the complete series over 1923–1925.

(ii) *For wage/income ratio in manufacturing.* S. Kuznets, op. cit., total wages, M.3(1), divided by total number of wage-earners in equivalent full-time units (see p. 152), M.22(9).

3. *1938, 1945–1960*

Content. (i) Average annual earnings, including supplements (overtime, shift premium, sick leave and vacation pay) without deduction for tax or social security contributions, generally of production and non-supervisory employees, full- and part-time, in manufacturing; mining (bituminous coal; metals; petroleum and natural gas; nonmetallic); communications (telephone; telegraph); contract construction; class i steam railroads; local railways and bus lines; gas and electric utilities.

(ii) Average annual earnings, including supplements, of all employees.

Sources and Method. (i) Abbreviations: *Business Statistics* – *B.S.*; *Statistical Abstract of the U.S.* – *S.A.U.*; *Historical Statistics of the U.S.* – *H.S.* We drew the series mainly from *B.S.* 1959 and 1961, but supplemented these as follows – mining industries, *S.A.U.* 1960 and 1961; telegraph, *B.S.* 1957, *S.A.U.* 1959, 1960, 1961; railroads, *H.S.*, and *S.A.U.* 1960 and 1961. In contract construction, we made estimates for 1938, 1939, and 1945–1947 by splicing to the series for contract construction, 1948 onwards, in *B.S.* 1961, the series for building construction in *H.S.* In utilities, we made estimates for 1938, 1939, 1945, and 1946, by splicing to the series for gas and electric utilities in *B.S.* 1961 the series for electric light and power in *H.S.* We weighted these series by the total wages 1952–1957 in the corresponding industries or groups of industries. We estimated these totals by multiplying the average weekly earnings in each industry by the total number of manual workers (sales workers, craftsmen, foremen, operatives, service workers and labourers (except mine)) recorded by the *Census 1950* as occupied in that industry. For the particular industries making up the mining, communications and service groups the numbers of manual workers were not available, only the totals of all employees: we used these totals as weights with which to calculate for each of the three groups as a whole a figure of average weekly earnings which we could then multiply by the total number of manual workers in the group. The weights finally obtained were: manufacturing, 5185; mining, 446; communications, 76; contract construction, 1677; local railways and bus lines, 129; 1st class steam railroads, 492; gas and electric utilities, 184; total 8189. We took (a) total supplements, and (b) total wages and salaries, from *Survey of Current Business*, July 1957, *Supplement* Nov. 1958, and July 1962, with *S.A.U.* 1960; we expressed (a) as a percentage of (b) annually, and applied these percentages to the weighted average of weekly earnings. Here as elsewhere we took it that in 1945–1960 there were 50 paid weeks in the year, and in 1938, 49 weeks: we therefore reduced the 1938 figure in the ratio 49:50. (ii) We took aggregate compensation of employees from *Historical Statistics* (1960), F-50, through 1955, with revised figures for 1956–1960 from *Statistical Abstract* 1960, table 403, and *Survey of Current Business*, July 1962; and divided by annual estimates of the total number of employees, derived from S. Lebergott, *Manpower in Economic Growth: the American Record since 1800* (1964) as the sum of armed forces (incl.

those overseas), appendix table A-3; civilian employees in jobs, table A-4; and domestic servants, table A-4.

1. *1860–1914*
Content. As in our table 142.
Sources and Method. 1860–1880: Ethel D. Hoover, 'Retail prices after 1850', in *Trends in the American Economy in the 19th Century* (N.B.E.R. 1960), table 1, p. 142, and table 8, p. 162. *1880–1890:* C. D. Long, *Wages and Earnings in the U.S. 1860–1890*, p. 157, table B.2 gives a consumer price index 'prepared ... for linkage with the Hoover index'. Its coverage and construction are described at pp. 56–61. We linked it to the Hoover index at 1880, obtaining an index for 1860–1890 which we linked at 1890 to the index for 1890–1914 in A. Rees, *Real Wages in Manufacturing 1890–1914*, p. 74, table 22.

Table 142 U.S.A., 1860–1914: Weights of components of index of cost of living based on family budgets of 1875, 1890–1891, 1901.

	1860–1880	1880–1890	1890–1914
Food	57·4	42·5	44·1
Rent	17·7	13·0	22·3
Fuel and light	7·0	5·3	7·2
Clothing	15·2	14·0	17·9
Home furnishings	—	3·4	4·5
Liquor & tobacco	—	—	4·0
Miscellaneous	2·7	21·8	—
	100·0	100·0	100·0

2. & 3. *1914, 1919–1939 and 1938, 1945–1960*
Bureau of Labor Statistics, Consumer Price Index, all items. Here taken from *Historical Statistics*, 1960, E.113. A major revision was effected in 1953, and the new weights were used to recalculate the index through 1950. Latest figures from *Statistical Abstract of the United States*.

C. G.N.P. DEFLATOR

Content, with weights in brackets: indexes of (*a*) money wages, or pay of all employees (1·5); (*b*) cost of living (7); (*c*) industrial wholesale prices (1·5).

Table 143 U.S.A. 1860–1913: Index of industrial wholesale prices.

1890–99 =100		1890–99 =100		1890–99 =100		1890–99 =100		*Index*
1860	142	1871	197	1882	141	1893	99	1904	115
1	134	2	216	3	135	4	90	5	119
2	157	3	208	4	122	5	96	6	128
3	208	4	183	5	113	6	95	7	133
4	295	5	168	6	111	7	90	8	117
5	285	6	159	7	112	8	92	9	123
6	253	7	144	8	113	9	112	10	127
7	228	8	129	9	112	1900	117	11	115
8	215	9	127	90	116	1	111	12	121
9	220	80	145	1	108	2	114	1913	125
1870	193	1881	138	1892	102	1903	121		

Sources. (*a*) A.1, A.2, A.3 (ii) above. (*b*) B.1, B.2 and 3 above. (*c*) *1860–1913: Historical Statistics of the U.S.* (1960). We combined the series E.4–10, E.12, in Warren and Pearson's wholesale price indexes 1860–1890, with weights as shown in brackets, here taken from Bureau of Labor Statistics, Bulletin 473 (Jan. 1929), Appendix B: hides and leather (3·65), textiles (7·96), fuel and light (16·18), metals and metal products (13·17), building materials (5·18), and chemicals and drugs (1·76), house furnishing (1·93), misc. (6·35). We linked our index at 1890 to one similarly compiled from the B.L.S. indexes 1890–1913, E.17 to E.24. See our table 143. *1914, 1919–1941: Historical Statistics of the U.S.* (1961), E.14, wholesale prices excl. farm products. *1938, 1945–1960: Statistical Abstract of the U.S. 1962*, table 459, wholesale prices excl. farm products and food.

D. NATIONAL INCOME

1. *1889–1914*
(*a*) *National income.* J. W. Kendrick, *Productivity Trends in the United States* (1961), table A.ii.b, gives 'gross national product, commerce

concept, derivation from the Kuznets estimates 1869–1929 and re-
conciliation in 1937, '48 and '53'. (The Dept. of Commerce concept is
set out in *Survey of Current Business*, Supplement, July 1954). We took
the annual estimates of G.N.P. in col. 11 of Kendrick's table A.ii.b,
and deducted annual estimates of capital consumption, supplied us
by Kendrick, to get net national product. To get national income we
further deducted annual estimates of 'indirect business tax and non-
tax liabilities'. These estimates are provided for 1897–1914 by
R. W. Goldsmith *et al.*, *A Study of Saving in the United States*, vol. iii,
table N.5, p. 435. For 1889–1896 we made a deduction in each year
of 7·4 per cent which is the average proportion that the absolute
deductions bore to the net national product in 1897–1900. See our
table 144.

Table 144 U.S.A., 1889–1914 : Estimated national income at current prices.

	$ m.		*$ m.*		*$ m.*		*$ m.*
1889	10472	1896	11156	1903	19602	1910	28558
90	11067	7	12302	4	19498	1	29210
1	11440	8	12878	5	21535	2	32052
2	12102	9	14564	6	24831	3	33599
3	11676	1900	15729	7	26244	1914	30797
4	10528	1	17614	8	23432		
1895	11149	1902	18387	1909	27664		

(*b*) *Sector income*, for only two sectors, agriculture and 'industry',
which comprises all non-farm private enterprise. E. Budd, 'Factor
Shares 1850–1910', in *Trends in the American Economy in the Nineteenth
Century* (N.B.E.R., *Income & Wealth*, 24, 1960), at p. 365, and table
1, p. 373: we took Budd's revision of estimates by W. I. King,
Wealth & Income of the People of the U.S. (1915), for the average of two
adjoining years of which the second is a census year, 1880 through
1910.

(*c*) *Income generated in manufacturing, 1879, 1889–1913* (i) *Real product.*
Kendrick, as in (*a*), table D.2, index (1929 = 100) of (physical) output
per person in manufacturing. (ii) *Value product.* We reflated (i) by the
index of industrial prices formed as in C above (table 143). We
spliced this index at 1913 to that given to base 1926 = 100 in *Historical
Statistics of the U.S.*, E.14. Applying this index to (i) gave us an index

of output per person at current prices, and we converted this into absolute figures of dollars by mounting it on the estimate of income from manufacturing divided by employment in full-time man-years, in 1929, in S. Kuznets, *National Income and its Composition, 1919–1938,* tables M.2, M.22, M.24, M.28.

The outcome compares as follows with estimates derived from E. Budd, op. cit. in (*b*) above, table 1, p. 373, income generated in the whole private sector other than agriculture in 1879–1880, 1889–1890, 1899–1900, 1909–1910; and table A.1, p. 392, employment in the same sector in 1880, 1890, 1900 and 1910.

	Budd	*Present estimates*
1889/90	$721	$668
1899/1900	$753	$737
1909/10	$877	$898

2. *1914, 1919–1941*

(*a*) *National income. 1914, 1919–1928:* as for 1897–1914. *1929–1941:* we took the estimates of G.N.P. in *Survey of Current Business (S.C.B.)* July 1959, table 1–17, p. 8, and continued as before to deduct the estimates of capital consumption provided by Kendrick and the estimates of 'indirect business tax and non-tax liabilities' in R. W. Goldsmith *et al.,* op. cit. We did not follow *S.C.B.* and Goldsmith *et al.* in also deducting 'business transfer payments' and the statistical discrepancy, and adding 'government enterprises, subsidies less current surplus', because these corrections are available only for 1929 onwards, and we preferred to maintain continuity with the earlier years; the net amount of these corrections is in any case small. See our table 145.

Table 145 U.S.A., 1914, 1919–1941 : Estimated national income at current prices.

	$ m.		*$ m.*		*$ m.*		*$ m.*
1914	30797	1924	74485	1931	61435	1938	67552
		5	77679	2	44691	9	73253
1919	67405	6	83140	3	42374	40	81657
20	76086	7	81427	4	50099	1941	104324
1	62618	8	82572	5	57273		
2	62269	9	88201	6	66706		
1923	73456	1930	75190	1937	73364		

(*b*) *Income generated in manufacturing*, (i) *Real product* as for D.1(*c*) (i).
(ii) Value product: S. Kuznets, *National Income and its Composition
1919–1938*, M.2 (10).

3. *1938, 1945–1960*
(*a*) *National income*. We took G.N.P. through 1956 from *S.C.B.*, July
1959 (as above), and for 1957–1960 from *S.C.B.*, July 1962, p. 6,
table 3. We deducted the estimates of capital consumption supplied
us by Kendrick through 1957; in 1958–1960 we deducted the *S.C.B.*
estimates of capital consumption raised in the ratio 100:78·3, which
is the average ratio of Kendrick's to the *S.C.B.* estimates in 1950–
1957. Throughout, we deducted 'indirect business tax and non-tax
liabilities', 'business transfer payments' and 'statistical discrepancy',
and added 'government enterprises, subsidies less current surplus',
as given in *S.C.B.* See our table 146.

Table 146 U.S.A., 1938, 1945–1960: Estimated national income at current prices.

	$ m.		$ m.		$ m.		$ m.		$ m.
1938	66843	1947	190149	1951	266557	1955	290363	1959	389100
		8	213868	2	281106	6	341109	1960	403500
1945	178527	9	207756	3	293959	7	356506		
1946	174520	1950	231647	1954	296903	1958	356700		

(*b*) *Income generated in industry*. At factor cost. *Survey of Current Business*,
July 1958, table 6, for 1946–1955; July 1962, table 7, for 1956–1960.
Sum of mining; manufacturing; construction; transport, communications and utilities.
(*c*) *Real product in industry*. We deflated (*b*) above by the index of
wholesale prices excluding farm products in *Statistical Abstract of the
U.S. 1962*, table 459.

E. OCCUPIED POPULATION

1. *1860–1914*
(*a*) *Total*. Figures of the total labour force aged 14 and over are
given from 1890 onwards in Clarence D. Long, *The Labor Force under
Changing Income and Employment* (1958), p. 286, table A-2. Figures of

'gainful workers' aged 10 and over are provided by the Census for years before 1890 – *Historical Statistics* (1960) D-36: for content see J. D. Durand, 'Development of the Labor Force concept, 1930–40' at Appendix A of *Labor Force Definition and Measurement* (Social Science Research Council, Bulletin 56, 1947); and J. D. Durand, *The Labor Force in the United States: 1890–1960* (Social Science Research Council,

Table 147 U.S.A., census years 1860–1920: Estimated total occupied population aged 14 years and over.

	m.		m.		m.		m.
1860	10·2	1880	16·8	1900	28·1	1920	41·4
1870	12·5	1890	22·6	1910	35·8		

1948), p. 208. We adjusted this series so as to make it as nearly as possible continuous with Long's. In the aggregate of the Census years 1890, 1900, 1910, Long's labour force amounted to 96·37 per cent of the 'gainful workers', and we applied this ratio to the 'gainful workers' of 1860, 1870, 1880. We made annual estimates by linear interpolation. See our table 147.

(*b*) *By sector.* E. Budd, 'Factor Shares 1850–1910', in *Trends in the American Economy in the Nineteenth Century* (N.B.E.R., *Income & Wealth*, 24, 1960), table A.1, p. 392, workers of 10 years and over, including unpaid family workers, in agriculture and the non-farm private sector.

(*c*) *Within manufacturing industry, 1879, 1889–1913:* estimates of numbers occupied are not needed, as the estimates of output we draw from Kendrick (D1(*a*)) are already of output per person.

2. *1914, 1919–1941*
(*a*) *Total.* We made up the total gainfully occupied labour force from the sum of armed forces and occupied civilians in jobs, less unpaid family workers, at Appendix, Tables A-3, A-4, of S. Lebergott, *Manpower in Economic Growth: the American Record since 1800* (1964). These series are designed to be comparable with the Current Population Surveys, whereas our estimates for 1860–1914 were based on Census classification.

(*b*) *In manufacturing.* S. Kuznets, *National Income and its Composition 1919–1938* (1941), sum of M22(9), M24(11), M28(9).

3. *1938, 1945–1960*
(*a*) *Total*. As in 2 (*a*) above.
(*b*) *In industry*. Mining, S. Lebergott, *Manpower in Economic Growth* (1964): employees, table A.5; self-employed, 1938 and 1940, A.9, together with figures for 1950, 1960 in *International Yearbook of Labour Statistics* (*I.Y.L.S.*) *1960* and *1965*, table 4, with interpolations. Lebergott, op. cit.: manufacturing, A.5, A.7; construction, A.5, A.7; transport, communications and utilities, employees A.5, self-employed, 1938 and 1940, A.9, with 1950, 1960 from *I.Y.L.S. 1960* and *1965*, table 4, with interpolations.

F. CAPITAL, CAPITAL PER OCCUPIED PERSON, CAPITAL/OUT-
PUT RATIO

1. *1889–1914*
(*a*) *Capital*. J. W. Kendrick, *Productivity Trends in the U.S.*, table A-xv, col. 5, capital stock in the private domestic economy in 1929 $ *minus* sum of all farm capital (including land, inventories and stock) in ibid., col. 6; non-farm private land, obtained as the excess of op. cit. table A-xvi, col. 6, over op. cit. table B-iii, p. 367, interpolated for annual estimates; and non-farm residential buildings, op. cit., table A-xv, col. 7. We converted to 1913 $ by an index-number formed with weights shown in brackets from the price indexes for metals and metal products (4), and building materials (1), in *Historical Statistics of the U.S.*, E.7, 8, 20, 21: the figures are, 1913, 84·1; 1929, 100.
(*b*) *Occupied population within coverage of estimates of capital*. Numbers in census years in E. Budd, 'Factor shares 1850–1910' in N.B.E.R., *Income & Wealth*, 24 (*1960*), *Trends in the American Economy in the 19th Century*, table A.1, p. 392, less domestic servants from S. Lebergott, *Manpower in Economic Growth*, tables A.1, A.4; with interpolation for annual estimates.
(*c*) *Output*. Kendrick, op. cit., net national product in non-farm private sector: total net domestic product, A-iii (3), *minus* sum of net output of farming, B-1 (p. 347), which we interpolated proportionally to index at B-i; government product, A-iii (6); and non-farm rent, which we estimated by applying the proportion of non-farm in all rent, from tables 43, 44, in R. F. Martin, *National Income in the U.S.*

Table 148 U.S.A., 1889–1913: Private non-farm output less estimated rent of non-farm houses, at prices of 1929.

	$m.		$m.		$m.		$m.
1889	12179	1896	15877	1903	26863	1910	34091
90	13781	7	17937	4	25626	1	36022
1	14478	8	17887	5	28365	2	36700
2	17287	9	20721	6	32901	1913	40069
3	15841	1900	21285	7	33601		
4	14573	1	25323	8	28372		
1895	17266	1902	25413	1909	34208		

1799–1938 (1939), to annual total rent derived by us from overlapping decennial averages in table iii, 10 of S. Kuznets, *National Product since 1869* (1946); all in 1929 $. See our table 148.

(*d*) *Profits*. 1889/1890, 1899/1900, 1909/1910: E. Budd, as in (*b*) above, table 1.

(*e*) *Wage/income ratio* used in reckoning inferred rate of profit: as calculated for manufacturing from A.1 and D.1 (*c*) above.

(*f*) *Inferred rate of profit*. See our table 149.

Table 149 U.S.A., 1889–1913: Inferred rate of profit.

	%		%		%		%
1889	11·8	1896	7·1	1903	13·9	1910	13·2
1890	13·7	7	7·4	4	12·1	11	9·4
1	11·0	8	10·1	5	14·2	12	13·4
2	10·4	9	13·7	6	15·8	1913	14·8
3	7·1	1900	13·0	7	14·8		
4	6·7	1	14·1	8	9·4		
1895	10·1	1902	13·9	1909	14·3		

2. *1920–1938*

(*a*) *Capital*. As in 1 (*a*) above.

(*b*) *Occupied population within coverage of estimates of capital*. Total civilian labour force (including unemployed) less employed in farming and civil government, from S. Lebergott, *Manpower in Economic Growth*, tables A.3, A.5, and domestics, *Historical Statistics* D.459–463.

(*c*) *Output*. As in 1 (*c*) above, except that we now take non-farm rent

Table 150 U.S.A., 1921–1938, private non-farm sector: (1) Estimated profits including corporate income tax, at prices of 1929. (2) Rate of profit directly calculated from (1). (3) Inferred rate of profit. (4) Wage/income ratio used for the calculation of (3).

	(1) $ m.	(2) %	(3) %	(4) %		(1) $ m.	(2) %	(3) %	(4) %
1921	2978	2·4	8·1	72·3	1930	5365	3·3	7·5	75·1
2	9256	7·3	6·3	78·0	1	−295	−0·2	4·7	80·9
3	10964	8·3	6·9	78·8	2	−4217	−2·7	1·1	91·0
4	9840	7·2	7·4	77·6	3	1003	0·7	1·1	90·8
5	11872	8·5	7·9	76·3	4	4487	3·0	3·3	85·2
6	11554	7·9	9·2	74·4	5	6849	4·7	5·7	80·8
7	10743	7·1	8·5	75·3	6	10622	7·3	8·8	75·7
8	12701	8·2	8·5	75·5	7	10298	6·9	8·0	78·9
1929	13256	8·3	9·1	74·5	1938	7463	5·0	7·8	77·3

from H. Barger, *Outlay & Income in the U.S. 1921–1938* (1942), table 22, non-farm rent paid and imputed, in current dollars, which we converted to 1929 dollars by the G.N.P. deflator (C above).

(*d*) *Profits*. Barger (as in (*c*) above), table 38, 'residual income', which pp. 8, 9, show is given after deduction of corporation income taxes; we added these back from U.S. Treasury Dept., Bureau of Internal Revenue, *Statistics of Income 1938*, part 2, p. 48, income tax plus wartime profits tax (1921–1922) and excess profits tax (1933 onwards). We converted to 1929 dollars by the G.N.P. deflator (C above). See our table 150.

(*e*) *Rate of profit in manufacturing*, G. Stigler, *Capital and Rates of Return in Manufacturing Industries* (1963), appendix, table B.1.

(*f*) *Wage/income ratio*, for inferred rate of profit: S. Kuznets, *National Income & its Composition*, total wages divided by number of wage-earners, and total income divided by number occupied, in industry, transport, trade and personal services. See our table 150.

3 Five countries, in each period: tables of the main time-series

3 Five countries, in each period: tables of the main time-series

France, 1860–1913

(1)   Estimated average annual wage-earnings in current francs.
(1a) (1) as index, 1890–1899 = 100.
(2)   Cost of living index, Paris, 1890–1899 = 100.
(3)   Index of wages in composite units of consumables, (1a) ÷ (2), 1890–1899 = 100.
(4)   G.N.P. deflator, 1890–1899 = 100.

	(1) Current Francs	(1a) 1890–99 =100	(2) 1890–99 =100	(3) 1890–99 =100	(4) 1890–99 =100
1860	545	64	94	68	103
1	553	65	99	66	105
2	561	66	95	69	103
3	579	68	95	72	105
4	579	68	94	72	104
5	587	69	93	74	101
6	596	70	98	71	104
7	604	71	104	68	107
8	621	73	105	69	108
9	630	74	98	75	103
1870	638	75	106	71	109
1	647	76	115	66	116
2	655	77	107	72	113
3	664	78	110	71	115
4	664	78	106	74	109
5	681	80	101	79	106
6	689	81	107	76	110
7	715	84	108	78	110
8	723	85	109	78	109
9	732	86	107	80	107
1880	757	89	111	80	111
1	766	90	111	81	110
2	783	92	111	83	110

	(1) Current Francs	(1a) 1890–99 =100	(2) 1890–99 =100	(3) 1890–99 =100	(4) 1890–99 =100
1883	791	93	111	84	110
4	791	93	108	86	107
5	791	93	104	89	103
6	800	94	102	92	102
7	808	95	102	93	101
8	808	95	100	95	101
9	817	96	101	95	102
1890	825	97	102	95	103
1	842	99	103	96	103
2	842	99	105	94	104
3	842	99	98	101	98
4	842	99	100	99	99
5	842	99	99	100	98
6	851	100	97	103	97
7	859	101	98	103	97
8	876	103	100	103	100
9	893	105	97	108	100
1900	893	105	94	112	100
1	902	106	95	112	99
2	893	105	95	111	99
3	902	106	97	109	101
4	910	107	95	113	100
5	919	108	97	111	101
6	953	112	98	114	105
7	962	113	98	115	106
8	962	113	97	116	102
9	970	114	100	114	105
1910	979	115	103	112	109
11	987	116	108	107	112
12	996	117	112	104	116
1913	1013	119	111	107	116

France, 1913, 1924–1938

(1)   Average annual money wage-earnings in current francs.
(1a) (1) as index, 1925–1929 = 100.
(2)   Cost of living index, Paris, 1925–1929 = 100.
(3)   Index of wage-earnings in composite units of consumables, (1a) ÷ (2), 1925–1929 = 100.
(4)   G.N.P. deflator, 1925–1929 = 100.

	(1) Current Francs	(1a) 1925–29 =100	(2) 1925–29 =100	(3) 1925–29 =100	(4) 1925–29 =100
1913	1036	15·26	18	85	17
1924	5157	76	71	108	73
5	5565	82	76	107	79
6	6515	96	100	96	102
7	6718	99	106	94	104
8	7057	104	105	99	104
9	8143	120	114	105	112
1930	8415	124	113	110	110
1	8279	122	114	107	107
2	7464	110	104	106	97
3	7464	110	96	115	92
4	7464	110	95	116	91
5	7261	107	88	122	85
6	8211	121	92	131	91
7	9704	143	117	123	116
1938	10450	154	136	113	132

France, 1938, 1949–1960

(1) Average annual money wage-earnings including employers' contributions to social security, in current Francs.
(1a) (1) as index, 1952–1959 = 100.
(1b) Estimated amount of employers' contributions included in (1), in current Francs.
(2) Cost of living index, Paris, 1952–1959 = 100.
(3) Index of wage-earnings in composite units of consumables, (1a) ÷ (2), 1952–1959 = 100.
(4) Average annual earnings of all employees including employers' contributions to social security, in current Francs.
(4a) Estimated amount of employers' contributions included in (4), in current Francs.
(5) National income per occupied person, in current Francs.
(6) G.N.P. deflator, 1952–1959 = 100.
(7) Index of real income per occupied person, (5) as index ÷ (6), 1952–1959 = 100.
(8) Annual income generated per occupied person in industry, in current Francs.
(9) Wage/income ratio in industry, (1) ÷ (8), as percentage.
(10) Index of productivity in industry (real output per occupied person), 1952–1959 = 100.
(11) Index of unit wage costs in industry, (1a) ÷ (10), 1952–1959 = 100.

	(1) Current OF '000s	(1a) 1952–59 =100	(1b) Current OF '000s	(2) 1952–59 =100	(3) 1952–59 =100	(4) Current NF	(4a) Current NF	(5) Current NF	(6) 1952–59 =100	(7) 1952–59 =100	(8) Current OF '000s	(9) %	(10) 1952–59 =100	(11) 1952–59 =100
1938	11·79	2·31	0·74	4·0	58	1614	101	2266	4	72				
1949	230·6	45	36·0	67	67	3881	614	4775	72	76	377·7	61	71	63
1950	250·7	49	39·7	75	66	4229	678	5681	84	79	433·2	58	75	65
1	329·9	65	52·9	85	76	5013	835	6600	93	82	538·4	61	83	78
2	388·8	76	64·8	94	81	5160	874	6857	88	90	613·2	63	81	94
3	398·5	78	67·5	89	88	5543	943	7286	89	94	639·9	62	84	93
4	431·4	84	73·4	89	95	5938	1002	7836	93	98	710·7	60	90	94
5	470·4	92	79·4	93	99	6590	1126	8666	98	102	683·6	69	96	96
6	522·2	102	89·2	97	105	7217	1208	9490	102	108	766·1	68	104	99
7	569·3	111	95·3	100	111	8124	1388	10836	115	109	847·0	67	112	100
8	635·6	124	108·6	115	108	8819	1543	11601	123	109	937·7	68	113	110
9	675·1	132	118·1	122	108	9575	1662	12874	129	116	1046·8	65	119	111
1960	739·3	145	128·3	127	114						1173·8	63	134	108

Germany, 1860–1913

(1) Average annual money wage-earnings in current Marks.
(1a) (1) as index, 1890–1899 = 100.
(2) Cost of living index, 1890–1899 = 100.
(3) Index of average annual wage-earnings in composite units of consumables, (1a) ÷ (2), 1890–1899 = 100.
(4) Net domestic product per occupied person, in current Marks.
(5) G.N.P. deflator, 1890–1899 = 100.
(6) Index of real income per occupied person, (4) as index ÷ (5), 1890–1899 = 100.
(7) Annual income generated per occupied person in industry, in current Marks.
(8) Wage/income ratio in industry, (1) ÷ (7), as percentage.
(9) Index of productivity in industry (real output per occupied person), 1890–1899 = 100.
(10) Index of unit wage costs in industry, (1a) ÷ (9), 1890–1899 = 100.
(11) Capital stock in 'Gewerbe' in 1913 Marks, milliards ('000m.).
(12) Capital per occupied person in 'Gewerbe', in 1913 Marks.
(13) Capital/output ratio in 'Gewerbe'.

	(1) Current Marks	(1a) 1890–99 =100	(2) 1890–99 =100	(3) 1890–99 =100	(4) Current Marks	(5) 1890–99 =100	(6) 1890–99 =100	(7) Current Marks	(8) %	(9) 1890–99 =100	(10) 1890–99 =100	(11) 1913 Marks Mrd	(12) 1913 Marks	(13) Ratio
1860	418	60	90	67	502	83	64			50	120	8·65	1651	2·64
1	428	61	92	66	501	85	61			51	121	8·89	1666	2·63
2	428	61	93	66	517	84	64			51	121	9·22	1724	2·75
3	428	61	89	69	532	81	69			57	107	9·55	1780	2·55
4	439	63	89	71	534	79	71			59	106	9·85	1832	2·54
5	439	63	89	71	525	78	71			63	100	10·00	1856	2·45
6	460	66	92	72	550	81	72			65	102	10·20	1887	2·43
7	460	66	103	64	581	85	72			66	99	10·30	1901	2·37
8	481	69	103	67	645	90	76			69	99	10·60	1952	2·32
9	501	72	96	75	627	87	76			73	99	10·90	2002	2·26
1870	523	75	99	76	641	89	75			73	102	11·70	2144	2·44
1	547	78	105	74	654	93	73			70	111	12·50	–	2·36
2	610	87	113	77	722	98	78			80	108	13·10	2064	2·16
3	694	99	118	84	777	103	79			86	116	13·70	2117	2·09
4	674	96	120	80	803	101	83			87	110	14·20	2153	2·09
5	656	94												

Year														
9	547	78	97	81	701	93	78	906	61	81	96	15·50	2148	2·23
1880	549	79	102	77	732	98	79	914	61	78	100	16·05	2201	2·35
1	561	80	102	79	738	97	79	920	65	82	98	16·80	2293	2·37
2	596	85	101	85	736	96	80	962	61	80	106	17·40	2332	2·43
3	583	83	98	85	761	96	83	944	63	85	98	18·50	2429	2·40
4	589	84	97	87	766	95	84	883	66	85	99	19·70	2510	2·46
5	586	84	97	87	767	93	86	835	70	84	99	20·80	2600	2·56
6	585	84	96	87	768	95	84	889	71	81	103	22·20	2663	2·71
7	631	90	96	94	797	96	86	922	67	85	106	23·50	2746	2·69
8	621	89	95	93	826	97	87	1003	63	86	103	25·00	2807	2·72
9	630	90	102	89	857	100	90	1047	63	90	101	26·60	2849	2·65
1890	655	94	100	93	909	104	91	1022	65	90	105	28·30	2934	2·73
1	659	94	104	91	899	104	90	968	68	91	103	29·20	3003	2·75
2	658	94	103	92	920	102	94	961	71	93	101	29·80	3036	2·76
3	680	97	99	98	918	98	98	991	67	97	101	31·30	3193	2·79
4	664	95	98	97	910	96	99	1055	64	101	94	32·90	3321	2·80
5	671	96	98	98	917	94	102	1068	66	106	90	34·60	3408	2·74
6	705	101	98	103	948	96	103	1095	68	103	97	37·40	3522	2·88
7	744	106	100	106	1003	100	105	1135	67	105	101	40·50	3674	2·96
8	763	109	100	107	1056	103	108	1242	64	107	102	44·40	3886	3·05
9	800	114	100	114	1080	103	110	1393	57	108	105	47·50	4031	3·14
1900	790	113	104	108	1114	104	113	1259	65	112	101	49·80	4097	3·11
1	815	116	105	111	1086	104	110	1262	64	109	107	51·20	4228	3·27
2	812	116	106	110	1109	105	114	1322	62	111	104	52·00	4264	3·20
3	820	117	107	111	1141	104	117	1354	62	117	100	54·00	4294	3·15
4	835	119	110	111	1177	105	118	1375	62	118	101	57·00	4390	3·20
5	856	122	113	114	1243	110	119	1456	62	119	103	60·10	4499	3·24
6	902	129	116	115	1287	113	123	1579	60	121	107	63·40	4594	3·25
7	940	134	119	115	1355	115	124	1514	63	127	106	67·00	4744	3·21
8	955	136	121	113	1342	113	125	1522	63	128	107	69·10	4921	3·32
9	959	137	122	116	1356	114	127	1585	62	133	103	71·80	5068	3·32
1910	987	141	123	118	1406	116	128	1625	63	135	104	74·30	5096	3·29
11	1016	145	129	118	1453	119	131	1756	63	139	105	77·90	5177	3·26
12	1065	152	127	123	1530	122	136	1861	61	145	105	82·00	5318	3·21
1913	1092	156			1558	120			59	149	104	85·20	5460	3·23

Germany, 1913, 1925–1938

(1) Average annual money wage-earnings in current Marks.
(1a) (1) as Index, 1925–1929 = 100.
(2) Cost of living index, 1925–1929 = 100.
(3) Index of wage-earnings in composite units of consumables, (1a) ÷ (2), 1925–1929 = 100.
(4) Net domestic product per occupied person in current Marks.
(5) G.N.P. deflator, 1925–1929 = 100.
(6) Index of real income per occupied person, (4) as index ÷ (5), 1925–1929 = 100.
(7) Annual income generated per occupied person in industry, in current Marks.
(8) Wage/income ratio, (1) ÷ (7), as percentage.
(9) Index of productivity in industry (real output per occupied person), 1925–1929 = 100.
(10) Index of unit wage costs in industry, (1a) ÷ (9), 1925–1929 = 100.
(11) Capital stock in 'Gewerbe' in 1913 Marks, milliards ('000m.).
(12) Capital per occupied person in 'Gewerbe', in 1913 Marks.
(13) Capital/output ratio in 'Gewerbe'.

	(1) Current Marks	(1a) 1925–29 =100	(2) 1925–29 =100	(3) 1925–29 =100	(4) Current Marks	(5) 1925–29 =100	(6) 1925–29 =100	(7) Current Marks	(8) %	(9) 1925–29 =100	(10) 1925–29 =100	(11) 1913 Marks Mrd	(12) 1913 Marks	(13) Ratio
1913	1071	63	69	91	1879[1]	72	96	1861[1]	59	97	65			
1925	1521	89	96	93	2273	94	89	2633	58	94	96	76·63	4579	3·38
6	1578	93	96	96	2212	89	91	2626	60	96	98	77·63	4624	3·47
7	1678	99	100	98	2828	101	104	2835	59	103	97	81·92	4863	2·78
8	1808	106	103	103	3101	108	106	2891	63	101	102	85·40	5054	2·78
9	1925	113	104	108	3116	109	106	3087	62	106	108	86·60	5108	2·71
1930	1945	114	100	114	3111	106	108	2979	65	106	109	86·70	5098	3·02
1	1795	106	92	115	2635	95	102	2629	68	103	104	83·81	4912	3·63
2	1546	91	82	111	1797	68	97	2382	65	106	87	82·27	4807	6·91
3	1483	87	80	109	2091	75	103	2343	63	110	80	82·41	4800	4·40
4	1503	88	82	108	2265	82	102	2334	64	110	81	83·96	4827	3·30
5	1540	91	83	109	2514[2]	87	107	2485[2]	62	119	77	86·62	4862	2·74
6	1583	93	84	111	2663[2]	86	114	2562[2]	62	123	77	88·86	4917	2·58
7	1629	96	89	108	2898[2]	92	116	2748[2]	59	128	76	96·03	5249	2·29
1938	1716	101	89	113	3118[2]	94	122	2897[2]	59	131	78	103·22	5574	2·18

[1] Not adjusted for change of frontier.   [2] Including the Saar.

Germany, 1938, 1950–1960

(1) Average annual money wage-earnings including employers' contributions to social security, in current Marks.
(1a) (1) as index, 1952–1959 = 100.
(1b) Estimated amount of employers' contributions included in (1), in current Marks.
(2) Cost of living index, 1952–1959 = 100.
(3) Index of wage-earnings in composite units of consumables, (1a) ÷ (2), 1952–1959 = 100.
(4) Average annual pay of all employees including employers' contributions to social security, in current Marks.
(4a) Estimated amount of employers' contributions included in (4), in current Marks.
(5) Net domestic income per occupied person, in current Marks.
(6) G.N.P. deflator, 1952–1959 = 100.
(7) Index of real income per occupied person, (5) as index ÷ (6), 1952–1959 = 100.
(8) Annual income generated per occupied person in industry, in current Marks.
(9) Wage/income ratio in industry, (1) ÷ (8), as percentage.
(10) Index of productivity in industry (real output per occupied person), 1952–1959 = 100.
(11) Index of unit wage costs in industry, (1a) ÷ (10), 1952–1959 = 100.

	(1) Current Marks	(1a) 1952–59 =100	(1b) Current Marks	(2) 1952–59 =100	(3) 1952–59 =100	(4) Current Marks	(4a) Current Marks	(5) Current Marks	(6) 1952–59 =100	(7) 1952–59 =100	(8) Current Marks	(9) %	(10) 1952–59 =100	(11) 1952–59 =100
1938	1969	39	141	57	69	1940	139	2920	61	67				
1950	3359	66	297	89	75	3223	285	4414	82	76	4134	81	75	88
1	3822	76	332	96	79	3738	324	5167	92	78	5040	76	82	92
2	4124	82	358	97	84	4038	350	5728	95	84	5488	75	85	96
3	4337	86	387	96	90	4352	388	5972	94	89	5821	75	89	97
4	4497	89	394	96	93	4500	394	6284	95	93	6086	74	95	93
5	4808	95	429	97	98	4866	434	6911	97	100	6722	72	102	93
6	5207	103	460	100	103	5251	464	7135	101	99	7106	73	103	99
7	5526	109	534	102	107	5576	539	7843	103	107	7533	74	105	104
8	5822	115	586	105	109	5976	602	8373	106	110	7914	72	107	108
9	6123	121	612	107	113	6280	627	8885	108	115	8560	72	115	106
1960	6708	133	676	109	122	6841	689	9653	112	120	9533	70		

Sweden, 1860–1913

(1) Average annual wage-earnings, in current Kronor.
(1a) (1) as index 1890–1899 = 100.
(2) Cost of living index, 1890–1899 = 100.
(3) Index of wage-earnings in composite units of consumables, (1a) ÷ (2), 1890–1899 = 100.
(4) National Income per occupied person, in current Kronor.
(5) G.N.P. deflator, 1890–1899 = 100.
(6) Index of real income per occupied person, (4) as index ÷ (5), 1890–1899 = 100.
(7) Income generated per occupied person in industry, in current Kronor.
(8) Wage/income ratio in industry, (1) ÷ (7), as percentage.
(9) Index of productivity in industry (real output per occupied person), 1892–1897 = 100.
(10) Index of unit wage costs in industry, (1a) ÷ (9), 1892–1897 = 100.

	(1) Current Kronor	(1a) 1800–99 =100	(2) 1890–99 =100	(3) 1890–99 =100	(4) Current Kronor	(5) 1890–99 =100	(6) 1890–99 =100	(7) Current Kronor	(8) %	(9) 1892–97 =100	(10) 1892–97 =100
1860	354	52			449	101	57				
1	354	52	106	49	474	103	60				
2	374	55	109	51	455	99	60				
3	381	56	103	54	456	96	61				
4	374	55	99	56	453	96	61				
5	395	58	99	58	476	98	63				
6	383	57	102	56	479	101	61				
7	395	58	108	54	456	104	57				
8	408	60	112	53	481	99	63				
9	422	62	105	59	522	96	63				
1870	429	63	101	62	555	99	71	864	50		
1	435	64	104	61	604	109	73	934	47		
2	477	70	108	65	699	118	72	1043	46		
3	521	76	116	66	694	120	77	1015	51		
4	559	82	121	68	699	117	75	1055	53		
5	571	84	120	70	705	115	78	1108	52		

1880	531	78	110	71	665	106	81	990	54		
1	553	81	113	72	637	107	78	1027	54		
2	568	83	110	76	665	106	81	1034	55		
3	567	83	109	76	668	105	83	979	58		
4	582	86	105	81	659	102	84	967	60		
5	577	85	100	85	629	98	84	963	60		
6	566	83	95	88	606	93	85	935	61		
7	571	84	92	91	576	91	82	931	61		
8	585	86	95	90	639	94	88	899	65		
9	620	91	100	91	669	99	88	922	67		
1890	634	93	102	91	708	102	90	934	68		
1	640	94	105	89	748	103	94	926	69		
2	636	93	103	91	721	101	93	975	65	82	115
3	645	95	99	96	705	98	94	1015	64	90	107
4	655	96	94	102	694	94	96	1027	64	98	99
5	666	98	96	102	736	96	100	1070	62	103	96
6	689	101	95	106	779	96	105	1185	58	114	90
7	709	104	98	106	818	99	107	1208	59	113	93
8	752	110	103	107	883	104	111	1259	60	116	96
9	784	115	107	108	905	110	106	1325	59	120	97
1900	810	119	108	110	954	113	110	1338	61	114	105
1	798	117	108	111	895	109	106	1370	58	122	98
2	812	119	106	112	917	109	109	1393	58	127	95
3	828	122	108	113	981	111	114	1443	57	131	94
4	853	125	107	117	949	111	111	1432	60	132	96
5	851	125	109	115	1001	112	116	1460	58	134	94
6	929	136	112	122	1114	117	124	1554	60	137	101
7	981	144	117	123	1200	123	127	1674	59	138	105
8	980	144	119	121	1218	123	128	1663	60	136	107
9	891	131	118	111	1184	121	127	1685	53	143	93
1910	1052	154	118	131	1267	125	131	1823	58	153	102
11	1066	157	116	135	1265	124	132	1863	57	158	101
12	1106	162	124	131	1354	132	133	1875	59	152	108
1913	1123	165	124	133	1411	133	138	1884	60	151	111

Sweden, 1913, 1920–1938

(1) Average annual money wage-earnings, in current Kronor.
(1a) (1) as index, 1925–1929 = 100.
(2) Cost of living index, 1925–1929 = 100.
(3) Index of wage-earnings in composite units of consumables, (1a) ÷ (2), 1925–1929 = 100.
(4) National income per occupied person in current Kronor.
(5) G.N.P. deflator, 1925–1929 = 100.
(6) Index of real income per occupied person, (4) as index ÷ (5), 1925–1929 = 100.
(7) Annual income generated per occupied person in industry in current Kronor.
(8) Wage/income ratio, (1) ÷ (7), as percentage.
(9) Index of productivity in industry (real output per occupied person), 1925–1929 = 100.
(10) Index of unit wage costs in industry, (1a) ÷ (9), 1925–1929 = 100.

	(1) Current Kronor	(1a) 1925–29 =100	(2) 1925–29 =100	(3) 1925–29 =100	(4) Current Kronor	(5) 1925–29 =100	(6) 1925–29 =100	(7) Current Kronor	(8) %	(9) 1925–29 =100	(10) 1925–29 =100
1913	1077	44	57	78	1756	57	95	1884	57	70	64
1920	3239	133	140	—	3820	138	—	5720	57	58	229
1	2982	122	113	87	3275	110	85	5223	57	84	146
2	2296	94	103	83	3122	102	92	4153	55	88	107
3	2228	92	101	89	3148	101	94	3739	60	84	109
4	2321	95	102	94	3167	102	96	3738	62	86	111
5	2374	97	100	96	3213	100	95	3746	63	87	112
6	2422	99	99	99	3227	99	99	3941	62	98	101
7	2465	101	99	102	3247	99	100	4054	61	103	98
8	2421	99	98	100	3407	98	101	3974	61	100	99
9	2493	102		104	3345	95	107	4293	58	114	90
1930	2565	105	95	111	3064	91	108	4325	59	130	81
1	2469	101	92	110	2870	89	103	3932	63	131	78
2	2334	96	91	105	2853	88	99	3634	64	125	77
3	2295	94	90	105			100	3531	65	123	77
4	2384	98	90	109	3158	89	109	4122	58	134	73
5	2436	100	90	111	3302	90	112	4403	55	141	71
6	2501	103	91	113	3565	92	120	4655	54	143	72
7	2609	107	94	114	3964	97	126	5283	49	140	77
1938	2689	110	96	115	4098	98	129	5662	48	160	69

Sweden, 1938, 1946–1960

(1)   Average annual money wage-earnings including employers' contributions to social security, in current Kronor.
(1a) (1) as index, 1952–1959 = 100.
(1b) Estimated amount of employers' contributions included in (1), in current Kronor.
(2)   Index of consumer prices, 1952–1959 = 100.
(3)   Index of wage-earnings in composite units of consumables, (1a) ÷ (2), 1952–1959 = 100.
(4)   Average annual pay of all employees including employers' contributions to social security, in current Kronor.
(4a) Estimated amount of employers' contributions included in (4), in current Kronor.
(5)   National income per occupied person, in current Kronor.
(6)   G.N.P. deflator, 1952–1959 = 100.
(7)   Index of real income per occupied person, (5) as index ÷ (6), 1952–1959 = 100.
(8)   Annual income generated per occupied person in industry, in current Kronor.
(9)   Wage/income ratio in industry, (1) ÷ (8), as percentage.
(10) Index of productivity in industry (real output per occupied person), 1952–1959 = 100.
(11) Index of unit wage costs in industry, (1a) ÷ (10), 1952–1959 = 100.

	(1) Current Kronor	(1a) 1952–59 =100	(1b) Current Kronor	(2) 1952–59 =100	(3) 1952–59 =100	(4) Current Kronor	(4a) Current Kronor	(5) Current Kronor	(6) 1952–59 =100	(7) 1952–59 =100	(8) Current Kronor	(9) %	(10) 1952–59 =100	(11) 1952–59 =100
1938	2870	27	14	47	58	2913¹	14¹	4154¹	42	71				
1946	4670	44	23	66	67	5064	25	6872	62	82				
7	5305	50	26	68	73	5694	28	7343	65	83				
8	5782	55	29	71	77	6270	31	8107	69	87			75	73
9	6004	57	30	73	78	6404	32	8422	71	87	10133	59	86	67
1950	6237	59	31	73	80	6604	33	8943	85	93	11049	56	89	67
1	7402	70	37	85	82	7854	39	10801	89	93	14764	50	91	77
2	8694	82	43	87	94	9110	45	11713	92	97	14309	61	91	91
3	8980	85	45	93	91	9317	46	11735	94	93	14946	60	94	90
4	9478	90	149	94	95	9825	155	12199	97	96	15861	60	94	96
5	10420	98	164	97	102	10588	167	13011	101	99	16688	62	97	101
6	10918	103	172	101	102	11167	176	13974	105	102	18009	61	100	103
7	11585	109	182	105	104	11849	187	14871	110	104	19651	59	104	106
8	12146	115	191	111	104	12241	193	15325	110	103	20534	59	107	107
9	12485	118	197	111	106	12561	198	16052		107	21644	58	112	105
1960	13332	126	426	116	109						22956	58	117	108

¹ 1938/1939.

U.K., 1860–1913

(1) Average annual money wage-earnings, in current £s.
(1a) (1) as index, 1890–1899 =100.
(2) Cost of living index, 1890–1899 =100.
(3) Index of wage-earnings in composite units of consumables, (1a)÷(2), 1890–1899 =100.
(4) Net domestic income per occupied person, in current £s.
(5) G.N.P. deflator, 1890–1899 =100.
(6) Index of real income per occupied person, (4) as index÷(5), 1890–1899 =100.
(7) Annual income generated per occupied person in industry, G.B. only, in current £s.
(8) Wage/income ratio in industry, (1)÷(7), as percentage.
(9) Index of productivity in industry (real output per occupied person), 1890–1899 =100.
(10) Index of unit wage costs in industry, (1a)÷(9), 1890–1899 =100.
(11) Capital stock excluding dwellings and agriculture, in 1913 £m.
(12) Capital, excluding dwellings and agriculture, per occupied person excluding those in agriculture, the armed forces and domestic and personal services, in 1913 £s.
(13) Capital/output ratio.

	(1) Current £	(1a) 1890–99 =100	(2) 1890–99 =100	(3) 1890–99 =100	(4) Current £	(5) 1890–99 =100	(6) 1890–99 =100	(7) Current £	(8) %	(9) 1890–99 =100	(10) 1890–99 =100	(11) 1913 £s m.	(12) 1913 £s	(13) Ratio
1860	36·5	69	130	53	54·9	124	54							
1	36·5	69	129	54	57·3	123	57							
2	37·6	71	130	55	58·0	126	56							
3	37·6	71	133	53	59·1	129	56							
4	39·7	75	133	56	61·4	129	58							
5	40·8	77	130	60	63·2	126	61							
6	42·3	80	131	61	64·5	127	61							
7	42·3	80	131	61	63·6	126	61							
8	41·8	79	130	61	62·7	125	61							
9	41·8	79	128	62	64·6	121	65							
1870	42·9	81	127	64	69·4	122	69					2282	251	3·20
1	44·5	84	130	65	74·6	125	73	64·2	69	65	130	2295	250	3·01
2	47·1	89	138	64	77·9	135	70	77·0	61	70	127	2308	249	3·10

Year														
7	48·7	92	127	72	74·3	123	73	69·2	70	72	129	2462	256	3·16
8	47·6	90	120	75	71·5	115	76	61·3	78	66	136	2499	258	3·23
9	47·1	89	116	77	68·9	112	75	60·0	79	67	132	2522	258	3·14
1880	47·1	89	121	73	71·1	117	74	63·5	74	69	129	2547	259	3·19
1	47·1	89	119	75	73·2	115	77	68·9	68	77	116	2570	259	2·98
2	47·1	89	118	75	75·1	114	80	69·6	68	77	117	2591	257	2·93
3	48·2	91	118	77	73·8	115	78	67·1	72	76	119	2619	256	2·91
4	48·2	91	112	81	70·8	109	79	64·7	75	76	120	2645	255	2·94
5	48·2	90	105	87	69·3	104	81	62·2	78	75	121	2657	252	2·93
6	47·6	91	103	87	69·7	101	84	63·1	75	79	114	2659	249	2·75
7	48·2	91	101	90	71·8	100	87	65·2	74	83	109	2660	245	2·58
8	48·7	92	101	91	75·6	100	92	70·2	69	90	102	2664	242	2·38
9	50·3	95	103	92	80·3	103	95	76·8	66	96	99	2681	240	2·29
1890	52·4	99	103	96	81·4	103	96	77·8	67	93	107	2698	238	2·38
1	52·4	99	103	96	79·8	102	95	74·9	70	91	110	2722	237	2·35
2	52·4	99	103	95	76·6	103	90	71·5	73	89	111	2752	236	2·41
3	52·4	99	104	96	76·0	102	90	71·6	73	91	108	2772	234	2·33
4	52·4	99	103	101	80·1	97	100	78·4	67	103	96	2799	233	2·15
5	52·4	99	98	103	81·0	96	103	78·5	67	105	94	2826	232	2·10
6	52·4	99	96	103	82·2	96	104	77·5	68	102	97	2866	232	2·10
7	53·4	101	98	101	84·5	98	105	80·7	66	105	96	2918	233	2·11
8	54·0	102	101	106	88·1	101	106	85·9	62	110	92	2990	235	2·11
9	55·6	105	99	104	91·8	102	110	90·9	61	111	95	3078	239	2·19
1900	57·7	109	105	105	93·7	108	105	93·9	61	104	105	3169	243	2·36
1	57·7	109	104	104	91·4	106	105	89·6	64	104	105	3275	247	2·36
2	56·6	107	104	105	90·9	105	106	88·9	64	108	100	3386	253	2·31
3	56·6	107	105	103	88·5	106	102	85·7	66	105	102	3494	258	2·38
4	56·6	107	106	102	86·8	107	99	84·2	67	103	104	3592	262	2·47
5	56·1	106	106	101	89·2	108	100	86·2	65	106	100	3681	265	2·39
6	58·2	110	107	100	93·0	112	101	90·4	64	108	103	3758	268	2·36
7	61·4	116	110	103	96·3	115	102	95·2	65	109	106	3800	267	2·33
8	60·3	114	107	105	90·2	109	101	87·7	69	103	111	3814	265	2·46
9	59·3	112	108	106	90·6	111	99	88·3	67	106	106	3832	264	2·39
1910	60·3	114	110	104	93·0	114	99	89·9	67	106	108	3852	262	2·31
11	60·3	114	112	104	96·4	116	101	92·0	66	105	108	3870	260	2·30
12	61·9	117	115	102	100·2	119	102	97·5	64	109	108	3891	259	2·27
1913	63·0	119	118	101	102·8	123	102	99·9	63	106	113	3930	259	2·32

U.K., 1913, 1920–1938

(1) Average annual money wage-earnings, in current £s.
(1a) (1) as index, 1925–1929 = 100.
(2) Average annual money wage-earnings in manufacturing, in current £s.
(3) Cost of living index, 1925–1929 = 100.
(4) Index of wage-earnings in composite units of consumables, (1a) ÷ (3), 1925–1929 = 100.
(5) Net domestic income per occupied person, in current £s.
(6) G.N.P. deflator, 1925–1929 = 100.
(7) Index of real income per occupied person, (5) as index ÷ (6), 1925–1929 = 100.
(8) Annual income generated per occupied person in manufacturing, in current £s.
(9) Wage/income ratio in manufacturing, (2) ÷ (8), as percentage.
(10) Index of productivity in manufacturing (real output per occupied person) 1925–1929 = 100.
(11) Index of unit wage costs in manufacturing, (2) as index ÷ (10), 1925–1929 = 100.
(12) Capital stock excluding dwellings and agricultural capital in 1929 £s m.
(13) Capital excluding dwellings per occupied person excluding agriculture, the armed forces and domestic service, in 1929 £s.
(14) Capital/output ratio, excluding the output of agriculture and the pay of the armed forces and domestic servants.

	(1) Current £s.	(1a) 1925–29 =100	(2) Current £s.	(3) 1925–29 =100	(4) 1925–29 =100	(5) Current £s.	(6) 1925–29 =100	(7) 1925–29 =100	(8) Current £s.	(9) Current %	(10) 1925–29 =100	(11) 1925–29 =100	(12) 1929 £s. m.	(13) 1929 £s.	(14) Ratio
1913	62·8	52		60	87	116·1	60	102							
1920	172·3	143	170·9	159	90	—	—	—							
1	161·4	134	161·8	118	113	—	—	—							
2	129·4	107	129·3	107	100	207·5	106	102							
3	119·8	99	117·4	105	95	193·4	104	97							
4	121·7	101	118·0	107	94	185·6	107	91	169·3	70	96	103	6711	391	2·48
1925	122·5	101	119·3	104	98	195·2	105	97	173·1	69	98	102	6981	404	2·34
6	119·1	99	119·1	103	96	184·3	102	94	169·3	70	98	102	6938	398	2·47
7	121·7	101	119·5	98	103	190·3	99	100	170·4	70	101	99	6980	396	2·28
8	120·0	99	119·1	98	101	191·3	98	102	168·5	71	100	99	7095	400	2·25
9	120·4	100	120·0	97	103	196·4	97	106	171·6	70	103	97	7112	397	2·18
1930	119·9	99	118·2	93	107	204·0	91	118	169·3	70	106	94	7425	411	2·10
1	117·7	98	115·6	86	113	191·3	84	119	160·1	72	106	92	7640	417	2·26
2	115·3	95	113·7	84	114	183·8	83	116	154·4	74	105	91	7420	402	2·27
3	114·3	95	113·4	83	114	185·3	82	118	154·9	73	107	89	7158	388	2·17
4	115·6	96	115·5	83	115	194·7	82	124	164·0	70	113	86	7193	390	2·01
1935	117·5	97	117·4	86	113	198·7	85	122	177·0	66	120	82	7233	387	1·99
6	120·1	99	119·7	88	113	203·1	87	122	188·1	64	124	81	7192	381	2·00
7	123·3	102	123·5	93	110	210·4	93	118	199·4	62	125	83	7057	372	2·06
1938	127·5	106	128·1	92	115	122·4	91	127	200·9	64	123	88	7472	390	2·01

P

U.K., 1938, 1946–1960

(1) Average annual money wage-earnings including employers' contributions to social security, in current £s.
(1a) (1) as index, 1952–1959=100.
(1b) Estimated amount of employers' contributions included in (1), in current £s.
(2) Index of retail prices, 1952–1959=100.
(3) Index of wage-earnings in composite units of consumables, (1a) ÷ (2), 1952–1959=100.
(4) Average annual pay of all employees including employers' contributions to social security, in current £s.
(4a) Estimated amount of employers' contributions included in (4), in current £s.
(5) Net domestic income per occupied person, in current £s.
(6) G.N.P. deflator, 1952–1959=100.
(7) Index of real income per occupied person, (5) as index÷(6), 1952–1959=100.
(8) Annual income generated per occupied person in industry, in current £s.
(9) Wage/income ratio, (1) ÷ (8), as percentage.
(10) Index of productivity in industry (real output per occupied person), 1952–1959=100.
(11) Index of unit wage costs in industry, (1a) ÷ (10), 1952–1959=100.

	(1) Current £s.	(1a) 1952–59 =100	(1b) Current £s.	(2) 1952–59 =100	(3) 1952–59 =100	(4) Current £s.	(4a) Current £s.	(5) Current £s.	(6) 1952–59 =100	(7) 1952–59 =100	(8) Current £s.	(9) %	(10) 1952–59 =100	(11) 1952–59 =100
1938	141·4	28	6·0	40	69	160·4	6·9	224·2						
1946	279·9	55	14·0	66	84	272·1	12·2	357·6	74	92			82	69
7	308·8	61	16·9	70	86	292·0	14·6	372·6	82	90			80	73
8	323·6	64	19·5	73	88	319·9	17·5	408·3	89	91			84	73
9	338·3	67	20·9	75	89	340·6	20·5	426·3	91	95	409·7	79	88	74
1950	372·7	73	22·5	82	90	355·2	21·9	447·2	93	97	439·5	77	91	80
1	402·2	79	24·5	89	89	390·2	23·5	487·2	97	98	489·1	76	92	88
2	427·5	84	27·0	92	92	420·3	25·7	532·6	102	101	507·1	79	91	89
3	454·0	89	28·0	93	96	440·7	27·8	567·7	106	103	538·2	79	95	91
4	496·0	98	30·9	98	100	462·9	28·6	593·9	109	106	573·4	81	99	97
5	535·7	105	33·7	102	103	499·3	31·1	627·0	111	107	616·5	82	101	105
6	561·2	110	36·0	106	104	540·2	34·0	678·0	113	111	657·2	81	101	109
7	583·9	115	42·0	110	105	570·1	36·5	714·1			693·1	82	102	112
8	609·2	120	44·1	110	109	599·3	43·2	752·2			716·0	80	103	111
9						627·3	45·4	784·1			756·1		108	
1960	647·8	127	45·7	111	115	661·1	46·6	820·6					113	113

U.S.A., 1860–1914

(1) Average annual money wage-earnings in manufacturing in current $.
(1a) (1) as index, 1890–1899 = 100.
(2) Cost of living index, 1890–1899 = 100.
(3) Index of wage-earnings in composite units of consumables, (1a) ÷ (2), 1890–1899 = 100.
(4) National income per occupied person in current $.
(5) G.N.P. deflator, 1890–1899 = 100.
(6) Index of real income per occupied person : (4) as index ÷ (5), 1890–1899 = 100.
(7) Annual income generated per occupied person in manufacturing in current $.
(8) Wage/income ratio in manufacturing. (1) ÷ (7) as percentage.
(9) Index of productivity in manufacturing (real output per occupied person), 1890–1899 = 100.
(10) Index of unit wage costs in manufacturing : (1) ÷ (9), 1890–1899 = 100.
(11) Capital stock excluding dwellings, agricultural capital and non-farm land in non-farm private enterprise, in 1929 $ m.
(12) Capital per occupied person, excluding dwellings, in non-farm private enterprise, in 1929 $.
(13) Capital/output ratio in non-farm private enterprise.

	(1) Current $	(1a) 1890–99 =100	(2) 1890–99 =100	(3) 1890–99 =100	(4) Current $	(5) 1890–99 =100	(6) 1890–99 =100	(7) Current $	(8) %	(9) 1890–99 =100	(10) 1890–99 =100	(11) 1929 $m	(12) 1929 $	(13) Ratio
1860	296	73	107	68		107								
1	293	72	108	67		107								
2	302	74	121	61		119								
3	313	77	149	52		147								
4	337	83	189	44		189								
5	360	89	188	47		187								
6	371	91	179	51		177								
7	375	92	168	55		166								
8	377	93	165	56		162								
9	383	94	158	60		158								
1870	382	94	151	62		149								
1	385	95	145	65		145								
2	387	95	145	66		148								
3	392	96	143	68		146								
4	384	95	138	68		138								

Year														
9	335	82		71										
1880	343	84	116	72		113								
1	351	86	118	73		117								
2	363	89	118	76		116								
3	379	93	118	81		117								
4	391	96	116	85		115								
5	370	91	114	82		113								
6	374	92	110	85		108								
7	393	97	108	88		106								
8	401	99	109	90		108								
9	417	103	109	97	475	108								
1890	425	105	105	100	490	107	94	646	65	96	109	30420	2883	2·50
1	429	106	105	100	494	107	96	689	62	99	107	32446	2960	2·35
2	431	106	105	101	511	106	98	640	67	98	109	35493	3116	2·45
3	410	101	104	97	481	105	103	614	70	100	107	39353	3332	2·28
4	376	93	99	93	425	103	98	549	75	92	95	42933	3510	2·71
5	392	96	97	99	440	97	92	512	74	94	100	44859	3543	3·08
6	393	97	97	100	438	97	96	593	66	103	95	47344	3617	2·74
7	395	97	96	102	465	97	95	547	72	96	102	49562	3669	3·12
8	394	97	96	101	477	95	103	541	73	100	99	51001	3659	2·84
9	420	103	96	108	529	96	104	614	64	111	89	52999	3691	2·96
1900	432	106	97	110	560	100	111	733	57	108	97	55425	3750	2·67
1	446	110	98	112	610	101	117	741	58	105	103	58384	3839	2·74
2	474	117	99	117	620	102	126	747	60	111	101	61460	3870	2·43
3	481	118	102	116	645	104	126	806	59	118	106	64670	3905	2·54
4	471	116	103	113	625	107	127	822	59	113	102	68452	3973	2·55
5	487	120	102	118	674	107	123	778	61	116	103	70875	3957	2·77
6	526	129	104	125	759	107	133	849	57	118	110	73207	3938	2·58
7	538	132	109	122	784	111	144	922	57	120	116	76910	3993	2·34
8	482	119	106	112	684	116	142	924	58	116	116	81407	4083	2·42
9	512	126	105	120	790	110	131	731	66	103	107	84821	4095	2·99
1910	538	132	110	121	798	111	150	887	58	119	113	86797	4077	2·54
11	545	134	110	122	803	116	145	909	59	119	121	89773	4088	2·63
12	564	139	112	124	868	114	148	778	70	112	109	91782	4050	2·55
13	585	144	114	126	896	117	156	944	60	129	109	94090	4026	2·56
1914	574	141	116	122	810	120	158	1013	58	134		98313	4084	2·45

U.S.A., 1914, 1920–1941

(1) Average annual money wage-earnings in current $.
(1a) (1) as index, 1925–1929 = 100.
(2) Average annual money wage-earnings in manufacturing in current $.
(3) Index of consumer prices, 1925–1929 = 100.
(4) Index of wage-earnings in composite units of consumables, (1a) ÷ (3), 1925–1929 = 100.
(5) National income per occupied person in current $.
(6) G.N.P. deflator, 1925–1929 = 100.
(7) Index of real income per occupied person: (5) as index ÷ (6), 1925–1929 = 100.
(8) Annual income generated per occupied person in manufacturing, in current $.
(9) Wage/income ratio in manufacturing, (2) ÷ (8), as percentage.
(10) Index of productivity in manufacturing (real output per occupied person), 1925–1929 = 100.
(11) Index of unit wage costs in manufacturing, (2) as index ÷ (10), 1925–1929 = 100.
(12) Capital stock excluding dwellings, agricultural capital and non-farm land in non-farm private enterprise in 1929 $ m.
(13) Capital excluding dwellings per occupied person in non-farm private enterprise, excluding domestics, in 1929 $.
(14) Capital/output ratio in non-farm private enterprise.

	(1) Current $	(1a) 1925–29 =100	(2) Current $	(3) 1925–29 =100	(4) 1925–29 =100	(5) Current $	(6) 1925–29 =100	(7) 1925–29 =100	(8) Current $	(9) %	(10) 1925–29 =100	(11) 1925–29 =100	(12) 1929 $ m.	(13) 1929 $	(14) Ratio
1913	553	45	585	58	77	900	58	81	1013	58	72	64			
1914			574												
1920	1317	106	1376	115	92	2012	122	87	1985	69	70	152	122086	4502	2·80
1	1122	91	1150	103	88	1756	102	90	1630	71	74	121	125436	4538	2·69
2	1107	89	1111	96	93	1633	96	90	1537	72	86	101	127028	4545	2·36
3	1196	97	1238	98	98	1798	99	96	1741	71	85	113	131913	4594	2·35
4	1193	96	1246	98	98	1839	99	98	1728	72	87	111	136667	4656	2·37
5	1221	99	1268	101	98	1843	102	95	1814	70	94	105	140448	4676	2·25
6	1239	100	1282	102	98	1920	102	99	1906	67	97	103	145632	4803	2·32
7	1234	100	1286	100	100	1878	100	99	1838	70	99	101	150976	4858	
8	1247	101	1297												

2	882	71	880	79	91	1226	77	83	975	90	90	76	158190	4562	3·68
3	869	70	854	75	94	1163	73	84	965	89	97	68	151871	4278	3·70
4	952	77	943	77	100	1294	78	87	1129[1]	84	92	79	147827	4084	3·01
5	1042	84	1015	79	106	1431	80	94	1343	76	104	76	145397	3985	2·50
6	1123	91	1082	80	114	1573	82	101	1551	70	112	75	146221	3950	2·20
7	1223	99	1180	83	119	1649	86	101	1588	74	109	84	148990	3949	2·02
1938	1158	93	1089	81	115	1586	83	100	1491	73	99	86	150108	3901	2·27
9	1231	99		80	124	1657	83	105							
1940	1288	104		81	129	1768	85	109							
1941	1493	120		85	142	2090	91	121							

[1]Average of two series.

U.S.A., 1938, 1945–1960

(1) Average annual money wage-earnings including supplements, in current $.
(1a) (1) as index. 1952–1959=100.
(1b) Estimated amount of wage-supplements included in (1), in current $.
(2) Index of consumer prices, 1952–1959=100.
(3) Index of wage-earnings in composite units of consumables, (1a)÷(2), 1952–1959=100.
(4) Average annual earnings of all employees including supplements, in current $.
(4a) Estimated amount of supplements to pay included in (4), in current $.
(5) National income per occupied person, in current $.
(6) G.N.P. deflator, 1952–1959=100.
(7) Index of real income per occupied person, (5) as index÷(6), 1952–1959=100.
(8) Annual income generated per occupied person in industry, in current $.
(9) Wage/income ratio, (1)÷(8), as percentage.
(10) Index of productivity in industry (real output per occupied person), 1952–1959=100.
(11) Index of unit wage costs in industry, (1a)÷(10), 1952–1959=100.

	(1) Current $	(1a) 1952–59 =100	(1b) Current $	(2) 1952–59 =100	(3) 1952–59 =100	(4) Current $	(4a) Current $	(5) Current $	(6) 1952–59 =100	(7) 1952–59 =100	(8) Current $	(9) %	(10) 1952–59 =100	(11) 1952–59 =100
1938	1271	29	57	51	56	1418	64	1586	48	65				
1945	2460	55	112	65	84	2365	90	2893	63	90	3086	81	79	71
6	2500	56	124	71	79	2557	127	3091	69	88	3660	77	77	82
7	2814	63	129	81	77	2766	127	3315	78	85	4158	73	80	84
8	3043	68	124	87	78	2933	120	3649	84	86	4195	78	83	88
9	3268	73	151	86	84	2962	137	3577	83	86	4683	71	89	84
1950	3335	74	169	87	85	3124	158	3889	85	91	5153	71	89	92
1	3663	82	194	94	87	3440	182	4293	93	91	5263	74	93	93
2	3869	86	202	96	89	3645	190	4472	94	95	5449	75	95	95
3	4062	91	210	97	93	3835	198	4608	96	95	5456	75	95	96
4	4111	92	225	98	94	3901	213	4746	97	97	5961	73	102	95
5	4349	97	252	97	100	4085	236	4525	97	93	6168	75	101	102
6	4596	102	282	99	104	4298	263	5195	100	103	6395	75	102	105
7	4785	107	318	102	104	4518	300	5406	103	104	6436	76	102	107
8	4897	109	330	105	104	4622	312	5495	106	103	6995	75	109	107
9	5238	117	377	106	110	4879	351	5859	108	107	7160	75	112	107
1960	5377	120	409	107	111	5032	383	5976	109	109				

References

1935 ALLEN, R. G. D. & BOWLEY, A. L., *Family Expenditure: a study of its variation.*

1967 ALLEN, R. G. D., *Macro-Economic Theory.*

1965 ARISTIDOU, I., 'Trends in capital, employment and output in British manufacturing industry 1900–1962' (Ph.D. Thesis, University of London, Dec. 1965).

1955 ASHTON, T. S., *An Economic History of England: the 18th Century.*

1933 BAGGE, G., LUNDBERG, E. & SVENNILSON, I., *Wages in Sweden 1860–1930*, part i, part ii, 1935.

1942 BARGER, H., 'Outlay and Income in the United States, 1921–1938', N.B.E.R. *Studies in Income & Wealth*, no. 4.

1957 BARNA, T., 'The replacement cost of fixed assets in British manufacturing industry in 1955', *Journ. of Royal Statistical Society*, A, 120, Part 1, 1957.

1916 BARNETT, G. E., 'Growth of Labor Organizations in the United States 1897–1913' in *Quarterly Journal of Economics*, 30, 4, Aug. 1916.

1966 BECKERMAN, W., 'The determinants of economic growth' in *Economic Growth in Britain*, ed. P. D. Henderson.

1944 BEVERIDGE, W. H., *Full Employment in a Free Society.*

1908 BOARD OF TRADE. *Report of an Enquiry by the Board of Trade into working class rents, housing and retail prices, together with rates of wages in certain occupations in the principal industrial towns of the German empire* (Cd 4032; British Parliamentary Papers 1908, vol. 108).

1908 BOARD OF TRADE. *Report of an Enquiry by the Board of Trade into working class rents, housing and retail prices, together with standard rates of wages prevailing in certain occupations in the principal industrial towns of the United Kingdom.* (Cd 3864; British Parliamentary Papers 1908, vol. 107.)

1909   BOARD OF TRADE. *Report of an Enquiry by the Board of Trade into working class rents, housing, and retail prices, with the rates of wages in certain occupations in the principal industrial towns of France* (Cd 4512; British Parliamentary Papers 1909, vol. 91, 1).

1911   BOARD OF TRADE. *Report of an Enquiry by the Board of Trade into working class rents, housing and retail prices, together with the rates of wages in certain occupations in the principal industrial towns of the United States of America* (Cd 5609; British Parliamentary Papers, 1911, vol. 88).

1921   BOWLEY, A. L., *The Division of the Product of Industry: an analysis of national income before the war.*

1937   BOWLEY, A. L., *Wages and Income in the United Kingdom since 1860.*

1927   BOWLEY, A. L. & STAMP, Sir J., *The National Income, 1924: a comparative study of the income of the U.K. in 1911 and 1924.*

1960   BRY, G., *Wages in Germany 1871–1945.*

1955   BUCKLEY, K. D., *Trade Unionism in Aberdeen 1878 to 1900.*

1960   BUDD, E., 'Factor shares 1850–1910' in National Bureau of Economic Research, *Studies in Income and Wealth*, vol. 24. *Trends in the American Economy in the Nineteenth Century.*

1938   BUREAU OF INTERNAL REVENUE (U.S.) *Statistics of Income.*

1958   BURLEY, K. H., 'An Essex clothier of the eighteenth century' in *Economic History Review*, 11, 2, Dec. 1958.

1940   BURN, D. L., *The Economic History of Steelmaking 1867–1939.*

1962   BUTLIN, N. G., *Australian Domestic Product, Investment and Foreign Borrowing 1861–1938/39.*

1964   BUTLIN, N. G., *Investment in Australian Economic Development 1861–1900.*

1953   CAIRNCROSS, A. K., *Home and Foreign Investment 1870–1913.*

1927   CARR-SAUNDERS, A. M. & CARADOG JONES, D., *A Survey of the Social Structure of England and Wales.*

1953   CHAPMAN, A. L., *Wages and Salaries in the United Kingdom, 1920–1938.*

1909   CHAPMAN, S. J., 'Hours of Labour' in *Economic Journal*, xix, 75, Sept. 1909.

1928   CLAPHAM, J. H. (later Sir John), *The Economic Development of France and Germany, 1815–1914* (3rd edn).

1938   CLAPHAM, J. H., *An Economic History of Modern Britain*, vol. iii, *Machines and National Rivalries (1887–1914)*.

1937   CLARK, Colin, *National Income & Outlay*.

1964   CLEGG, H. A., FOX, A. & THOMPSON, A. F., *A History of British Trade Unions since 1889*, vol. i, 1889–1910, chs. 2–5.

1963   COLE, Sonia, *The Neolithic Revolution* (British Museum, 3rd edn).

1921   COMMONS, J. R. & others, *History of Labor in the United States*, vol. ii.

1956   COPPOCK, D. J., 'The climacteric of the 1890s: a critical note', *Manchester School*, 24, 1, Jan. 1956.

1941   DAVIS, H. B., 'The Theory of Union Growth' in *Quarterly Journal of Economics*, 55, Aug. 1941.

1912   DAWSON, W. H., *Industrial Germany*.

1919   DAWSON, W. H., *The Evolution of Modern Germany* (2nd edn).

1918   Departmental Committee on the Engineering Trades after the War. *Report of the Committee appointed by the Board of Trade to consider the position of the Engineering Trades after the War* (Cd 9073; British Parliamentary Papers, 1918, vol. 13).

1968   DESAI, A. V., *Real Wages in Germany 1871–1913*.

1930   DOUGLAS, P. H., *Real Wages in the United States 1890–1926*.

1946   DUVEAU, G., *La Vie ouvrière en France sous le Second Empire* (6th edn).

1936   ENSOR, R. C. K., *England 1870–1914*.

1961   FEINSTEIN, C. H., 'Income and Investment in the United Kingdom, 1856–1914' in *Economic Journal*, 71, 282, June 1961.

1964   FEINSTEIN, C. H., 'National income and expenditure, 1870–1963' in *London & Cambridge Economic Bulletin*, June 1964.

1965   FEINSTEIN, C. H., *Domestic Capital Formation in the United Kingdom 1920–1938*.

1924   FLUX, A. W., 'The Census of Production' in *Journal of the Royal Statistical Society*, 87, 3, 1924.

1963   GELLERMAN, S. W., *Motivation and Productivity* (American Management Assn).

1958   GILBERT, Milton, *Comparative National Products and Price Levels* (O.E.E.C.).

1958   GINSBURG, W. L., and BERGMANN, R., 'Workers' attitudes to shorter hours', *Monthly Labor Review*, 79, 11, Nov. 1958.

1951   GOLDSMITH, R. W., 'A Perpetual Inventory of National Wealth', in N.B.E.R., *Studies in Income & Wealth*, vol. 14, *Conference on Research in Income and Wealth.*

1956   GOLDSMITH, R. W., et al., *A Study of Saving in the United States*, vol. iii.

1962   GRAHAM, R. E., and BAUMAN, J., 'Corporate profits and national output', *Survey of Current Business*, 42, 11.

1963   GRANT, A., 'Issues in distribution theory: the measurement of labor's relative share' in *Review of Economics & Statistics*, Aug. 1963.

1963   GREGG LEWIS, H., *Unionism and Relative Wages in the United States.*

1952   HALVERSON, G. C., 'Development of Labour Relations in British railways since 1860' (Ph.D. thesis, London University).

1941   HANSEN, Alvin, *Fiscal Policy and Business Cycles.*

1962   HENLE, P., 'Recent growth of paid leisure for U.S. workers', *Monthly Labor Review*, Mar. 1962.

1964   HINES, A. G., 'Trade Unions and Wage Inflation in the U.K. 1893–1961' in *Review of Economic Studies*, 31(4), 88, Oct. 1964.

1960   HOBSBAWM, E. J., 'Custom, wages and work load in nineteenth century industry' in *Essays in Labour History*, eds. A. Briggs & J. Saville.

1965   HOFFMANN, W. G. with GRUMBACH, F. & HESSE, H., *Das Wachstum der deutschen Wirtschaft seit der Mitte des 19 Jahrhunderts.*

1958   INTERNATIONAL LABOUR CONFERENCE, Report VIII, *Hours of Work.*

1932   INTERNATIONAL LABOUR OFFICE. *A contribution to the study of international comparisons of costs of living* (Studies & Reports, N.17, 2nd revised edn, 1932).

1968   JECK, A., 'The Trends of Income Distribution in West Germany' in J. Marchal & B. Ducros (eds.), *The Distribution of National Income.*

1963 JONES, E. B., 'New estimate of hours of work per week and hourly earnings, 1900–1957' in *Review of Economics & Statistics*, Nov. 1963.

1933 JONES, G. T., *Increasing Return: a study of the relation between the size and efficiency of industries, with special reference to the history of selected British and American industries 1850–1910*, edited by Colin Clark.

1966 JUNGENFELT, K. G., *Löneandelen och ekonomisk utvecklingen*.

1938 KALECKI, M., 'The lesson of the Blum experiment' in *Economic Journal*, 48, 189, March 1938.

1961 KENDRICK, J. W., *Productivity trends in the United States* (National Bureau of Economic Research. Princeton U.P.).

1956 KERR, Clark, 'Hours of work and economic growth' in *American Economic Review*, May, 1956.

1958 KERR, Clark, 'The prospect of wages and hours in 1975' in *U.S. Industrial Relations in the next Twenty Years*, ed. J. Stieber.

1926 KEYNES, J. M. (ed.), *Official Papers by Alfred Marshall*.

1964 KINDLEBERGER, C. P., *Economic Growth in France and Britain 1851–1950*.

1951 KNOWLES, K. G. J. C. and ROBERTSON, D. J., 'Differences between the Wages of Skilled and Unskilled Workers, 1880–1950' in *Bulletin of the Oxford University Institute of Statistics*, April 1951.

1962 KRAVIS, I. B., *The Structure of Income*.

1945 KUCZYNSKI, J., *A Short History of Labour Conditions under Industrial Capitalism*, vol. iii, part i, *Germany 1800 to the Present Day*.

1946 KUCZYNSKI, J., *A Short History of Labour Conditions under Industrial Capitalism*, vol. iv, *France*.

1930 KUZNETS, S. S., *Secular movements in production and prices*.

1963 LANDERS, D. S., 'Technological Change and Development in Western Europe, 1750–1914', ch. v of *The Cambridge Economic History of Europe*, ed. H. J. Habakkuk & M. Postan, vol. vi, part i.

c. 1914 LAYTON, W. T. (later Sir Walter), *Capital and Labour*.

1964 LEBERGOTT, S., *Manpower in Economic Growth: The American record since 1800*.

1968 LECAILLON, J., *Changes in the Distribution of Income in the*

French economy, in J. Marchal & B. Ducros (eds.), *The Distribution of National Income*.

1889   LEVASSEUR, E., *La Population Française* (vol. i, 1889; ii, 1891, iii, 1892).

1914   LEVINE, L., *Syndicalism in France*.

1951   LEVINSON, H. M., *Unionism, Wage Trends and Income Distribution, 1914–1947* (Michigan Business Studies, x. 4).

1938   LINDBLOM, T., *Den Svenska Fackföreningsrörelsens Uppkomst*.

1959   LOMAX, K. S., 'Production and productivity movements in the United Kingdom since 1900' in *Journal of the Royal Statistical Society*, A 22, 2, 1959.

1958   LONG, C. D., *The Labor Force under Changing Income and Employment*.

1960   LONG, C. D., *Wages and Earnings in the United States 1860–1890*.

1959   McCORMICK, B., 'Hours of work in British industry' in *Industrial & Labor Relations Review*, 12, 3, April 1959.

1921   MACKENZIE, W. A., 'Changes in the standard of living in the United Kingdom, 1860–1914' in *Economica*, 1, 3, Oct. 1921.

1938   MARJOLIN, R., 'Reflections on the Blum experiment' in *Economica*, 5 (NS), 18, May 1938.

1892   MARSHALL, A., *Elements of Economics of Industry*.

1903   MARSHALL, A., *Memorandum on Fiscal Policy of International Trade*. House of Commons, no. 321 of 1908. Reprinted in *Official Papers by Alfred Marshall* (1926), ed. J. M. Keynes.

1961   MEADE, J. E., *A Neo-Classical Theory of Economic Growth*.

1947   MINISTRY OF FOOD. *Food Consumption Levels in the United Kingdom* (Cmd 7203).

1962   *Ministry of Labour Gazette* (U.K.), 70, 2, Feb. 1962, 'Labour overseas: annual and public holidays allowable in major European countries'; 70, 3, March 1962, 'Labour overseas: annual and public holidays in Australia, Canada, New Zealand and United States.'

1965   *Ministry of Labour Gazette* (U.K.), 73,3, March 1965, 'Notes on Regional Labour Statistics, No. 3. Activity Rates'.

1962   MITCHELL, B. R. & DEANE, P., *Abstract of British Historical Statistics*.

1939   MONTGOMERY, G. A., *The rise of modern industry in Sweden*.

1922   MOSSES, W., *The History of the United Pattern Makers' Associa-tion 1872–1922.*

1950   NORTHRUP, H. R. & BRINBERG, H. R., *The Economics of the Work Week* (NICB, Studies in Business Economics No. 24).

1948   OBER, H., 'Occupational Wage Differentials 1907–1947' in *Monthly Labor Review*, April, June and August, 1948.

1962   OZANNE, R., 'A century of occupational differentials in manufacturing' in *Review of Economics & Statistics*, 44, 3, August 1962.

1959   PAIGE, D. & BOMBACH, G., *A Comparison of National Output & Productivity of the United Kingdom & the United States (O.E.E.C.).*

1959   PHELPS BROWN, E. H., *The Growth of British Industrial Relations: a study from the standpoint of 1906–1914.*

1962   PHELPS BROWN, E. H. & BROWNE, M. H. 'Earnings in industries of the U.K., 1948–1959' in *Economic Journal*, 72, September 1962.

1952   PHELPS BROWN, E. H. & HANDFIELD-JONES, S. J., 'The Climacteric of the 1890s: a study in the expanding economy', *Oxford Economic Papers*, Oct. 1952.

1952   PHELPS BROWN, E. H. & HART, P. E., 'The share of wages in the national income' in *Economic Journal*, 62, 246, June 1952.

1950   PHELPS BROWN, E. H. & HOPKINS, S. V., 'The Course of Wage-rates in five Countries, 1860–1939', *Oxford Economic Papers*, ii, 2, June 1950.

1955   PHELPS BROWN, E. H. & HOPKINS, S. V., 'Seven Centuries of Building Wages' in *Economica*, 22, 87, August 1955.

1956   PHELPS BROWN, E. H. & HOPKINS, S. V., 'Seven Centuries of the Prices of Consumables, compared with Builders' Wage-rates' in *Economica*, 23, 92, Nov. 1956.

1955   PHELPS BROWN, E. H. & OZGA, S. A., 'Economic Growth & the Price Level' in *Economic Journal*, 65, March 1955.

1958   PHILLIPS, A. W., 'The relation between unemployment and the rate of change of money wage rates in the United Kingdom, 1861–1957' in *Economica*, 25, 100, Nov. 1958.

1894   RAE, J., *Eight Hours for Work.*

1941–42   RAMSBOTTOM, E. C., 'Changes in labour conditions

during the past forty years', *Transactions of the Manchester Statistical Society.*

1955 REDFERN, P., 'Net investment in fixed assets in the United Kingdom 1938–1953', *Jour. of Royal Statistical Society* (A), 118, pt. 2, 1955.

1961 REES, A., *Real Wages in Manufacturing 1890–1914.*

1965 RICHARDSON, H. W., 'Retardation in Britain's industrial growth, 1870–1913' in *Scottish Journal of Political Economy,* June 1965.

1897 RIST, C., 'La durée du travail dans l'industrie française, 1820–1870' in *Revue d'Economie Politique,* 11, 4.

1967 ROSENBERG, N., 'Anglo-American wage differences in the 1820's' in *Journal of Economic History,* 27, 2, June 1967.

1948 ROSTAS, L., *Comparative Productivity in British and American Industry.*

1965 ROUTH, G., *Occupation and Pay in Great Britain 1906–1960.*

1902 ROWNTREE, SEEBOHM, *Poverty, a study of town life* (2nd edn).

1886 Royal Commission on the Depression of Trade, *Final Report,* C 4893.

1961 RUGGLES, R. & N., *Concepts of Real Capital Stocks & Services,* in National Bureau of Economic Research, *Studies in Income & Wealth,* vol. 25, Output, Input and Productivity Measurement.

1924 SARGANT FLORENCE, P. 'The 48-hour week and industrial efficiency' in *International Labour Review,* Nov. 1924.

1950 SAYERS, R. S., 'The springs of technical progress in Britain, 1914–1939' in *Economic Journal,* 60, 238, June 1950.

1953 SCHULLER, G. T., 'The secular trend in income distribution by type' in *Review of Economics & Statistics,* 35, 4, Nov. 1953.

1951 SÉE, H., *Histoire économique de la France,* vol. 2, *Les Temps modernes 1789–1914.*

1960 STATISTISCHES BUNDESAMT of the Federal German Republic. Preise, Löhne, Wirtschaftsrechnungen, Reihe 10, *Internationaler Vergleich der Preise für die Lebenshaltung.*

1963 STIGLER, G. J., *Capital and Rates of Return in Manufacturing Industries.*

1924 TAUSSIG, F. W., 'Labor costs in the United States compared with costs elsewhere' in *Quarterly Journal of Economics,* 39, 1.

1961–62   TAYLOR, A. J., 'Labour productivity and technological innovation in the British coal industry 1850–1914', *Economic History Review* (2nd series), 14, 1, 48.

1954   THOMAS, Brinley, *Migration and Economic Growth.*

1926   THORP, W. L., *Business Annals.*

1961   ULMAN, Lloyd, ch. 13, 'The Development of Trades & Labor Unions' in *American Economic History*, ed. S. E. Harris.

1965   ULMAN, Lloyd, 'Labor mobility and the industrial wage structure in the postwar United States' in *Quarterly Journal of Economics*, 79, 1, Feb. 1965.

1943   VERNON, H. M., *Hours of Work and their Influence on Health and Efficiency* (British Association for Labour Legislation).

1933   VITELES, M. S., *Industrial Psychology.*

1919   WEBB, S. & B., *Industrial Democracy* (1919 edn).

1920   WEBB, S. & B., *The History of Trade Unionism* (revised edn).

1967   WORSWICK, G. D. N. & TIPPING, D. G., *Profits in the British Economy 1909–1938.*

1949   WRIGHT, C. W., *Economic History of the United States.*

1958   ZEISEL, J. S., 'The work week in American industry 1850–1956', *Monthly Labor Review*, 81, 1, Jan. 1958.

1962   ZEISEL, J. S., 'Comparison of British and U.S. unemployment rates', *Monthly Labor Review*, 85, 5, May, 1962.

Index

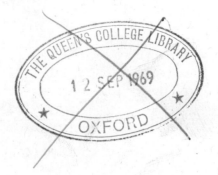